HEARSAY EVIDE]
CRIMINAL PROCE

The Criminal Justice Act 2003 re-wrote the hear: of criminal proceedings, enacting the recommer together with some proposals from the Auld R came into force a body of case-law has interpreted them and, in particular, given guidance as to how the new 'inclusionary discretion' should be exercised. Following the style of his earlier book about the new law on bad character evidence, the central part of Professor Spencer's book on hearsay evidence consists of section-by-section commentary on the relevant provisions of the Act. The commentary is preceded by chapters on the history of the hearsay rule, and the requirements of Article 6(3)(d) of the European Convention on Human Rights. It is followed by an appendix containing the text of the statutory provisions and a selection of the leading cases.

Volume 5 in the Criminal Law Library series

Criminal Law Library

Volume 1: Self-Defence in Criminal Law
Boaz Sangero

Volume 2: Evidence of Bad Character
JR Spencer

Hearsay Evidence in Criminal Proceedings

JR SPENCER

·HART·
PUBLISHING

OXFORD AND PORTLAND, OREGON
2008

Published in North America (US and Canada) by
Hart Publishing
c/o International Specialized Book Services
920 NE 58th Avenue, Suite 300
Portland, OR 97213-3786
USA
Tel: +1 503 287 3093 or toll-free: (1) 800 944 6190
Fax: +1 503 280 8832
E-mail: orders@isbs.com
Website: http://www.isbs.com

Hart Publishing, 16C Worcester Place, Oxford, OX1 2JW
Telephone: +44 (0)1865 517530 Fax: +44(0)1865 510710
E-mail: mail@hartpub.co.uk
Website: http://www.hartpub.co.uk

British Library Cataloguing in Publication Data
Data Available

ISBN: 978-1-84113-812-1

Typeset by Hope Services Ltd, Abingdon, Oxon
Printed and bound in Great Britain by
TJ International Ltd, Padstow, Cornwall

PREFACE

In 1994, the Law Commission were kind enough to engage me as a consultant on their project on the hearsay rule in criminal proceedings, and a year later I saw my input reflected in the sections of the resulting Consultation Paper where the rule was examined, the justifications for it were analysed together with the problems that it causes, the Strasbourg case law was analysed, and where readers were shown how the underlying issues are handled by the courts in France and Germany. We did not see eye to eye about the way in which the law ought to be reformed, however, and at that point we parted company. For the rest of the project, which culminated in the publication of a Report in 1997, the role of academic consultant was taken by my friend and respected colleague Professor Di Birch, of the Law Faculty at Nottingham.

The government announced that it accepted the recommendations contained in the Law Commission's hearsay Report, but then failed to implement them. In 2000, I was invited by Lord Justice Auld to be one of his consultants on the project which led to his Review of the Criminal Courts the following year. In this capacity I helped him to formulate a number of his proposals, including those for reforming the hearsay rule. On this his ideas were much more radical than those of the Law Commission four years before, favouring the abolition of the existing hearsay rule and its system of exceptions in favour of a broader 'best evidence' approach.

In his Review Auld LJ argued for a revision of the hearsay rule in the context of a long-term overhaul of the whole law of criminal evidence. The Government, however, opted instead for an instant revision of parts of it: namely evidence of bad character, and the hearsay rule, major changes to both of which were made by Part 11 of the Criminal Justice Act 2003. The reforms to the hearsay rule were, in essence, the proposals of the Law Commission, but with some adaptations to incorporate some, but not all, of the proposals formulated by Auld LJ: a solution Professor Birch, in her commentary in the *Criminal Law Review*, described as 'dishing up the Law Commission's very traditional repast with a dollop of Auld's best evidence on top'.

To cope with this new Act, the Judicial Studies Board organised a period of intense training for the judges, which took place during the first three months of 2005. Together with a number of academic colleagues, I was recruited to help with this. My part was to prepare a commentary on the new rules relating to evidence of bad character. For the reforms of hearsay evidence, this task was undertaken by two academic colleagues, Professor Di Birch and Professor David Ormerod.

It was on the crest of a wave of enthusiasm generated by this training programme that I wrote a commentary on the new law on bad character evidence, which Hart Publishing produced in the spring of 2006. It was generally well received, and that encouraged me to write this companion volume on the new law on hearsay as well. As with the earlier book, much is owed to a group of friends and colleagues with whom I have discussed this area of the law, and from whose thoughts I have greatly profited. A particular word of thanks is owed to HH Judge David Radford and his brethren at Snaresbrook Crown Court, who invited me there to talk with them, and to HH Judge John Phillips, who was kind enough to read the last chapter in draft and offer many helpful comments.

The book on bad character evidence ended with an Appendix in which the leading cases interpreting the new law were reproduced. Though castigated by one academic reviewer as a waste of paper, reviewers who were practitioners said this feature made the book more useful, and so in this new book I have therefore done the same. As readers will see, the collection begins with the decision in *Sellick*. This was decided under the earlier law, but the statements of principle that it contains are highly relevant to the new law too, and for this reason (as well as the quality of the reasoning) I believe it deserves to stand at the head of the collection.

On the face of it, the new law on hearsay that results from Part 11 of the Criminal Justice Act 2003 is very conservative. Eight years earlier, the Civil Evidence Act 1995 completely abolished the hearsay rule for the purpose of civil proceedings. But the Criminal Justice Act 2003, by contrast, retains the rule excluding hearsay, together with its half-brother, the 'rule against narrative', and to each a list of detailed exceptions is prescribed. The Law Commission's reason for adopting this conservative approach rather than the sort of simple and radical reform later proposed by Auld LJ was, in part, 'the change of attitude that this option would require on the part of practitioners and judges'. However, the new scheme includes a general 'inclusionary discretion', which a court can invoke to admit any piece of hearsay evidence which falls outside the list of prescribed exceptions, if it is satisfied that the interests of justice so require. This discretionary power was envisaged by the Law Commission for use as a last resort: a 'safety-valve', as they described it. However, the emerging case law suggests that the courts are only too glad to use it; and in consequence the new law on hearsay is much more radical in practice than the narrow drafting of the main provisions might suggest. Paradoxically, it looks as if the main effect of the reform has been to produce the change of attitude which, 10 years ago, the Law Commission believed to be impossible.

JR SPENCER
Cambridge, November 2007

CONTENTS

ABBREVIATIONS

ACPO	Association of Chief Police Officers
CEA 1968	Civil Evidence Act 1968
CEA 1995	Civil Evidence Act 1995
CJA 1988	Criminal Justice Act 1988
CJA 2003	Criminal Justice Act 2003
CLRC	Criminal Law Revision Committee
CPIA 1996	Criminal Procedure and Investigations Act 1996
ECHR	Convention for the Protection of Human Rights and Fundamental Freedoms (or European Convention on Human Rights)
PACE 1984	Police and Criminal Evidence Act 1984
PCMH	Plea and case management hearing
PNC	Police National Computer
StPO	Strafprozeßordunung (German Criminal Procedure Code)
YJCEA 1999	Youth Justice and Criminal Evidence Act 1999

TABLE OF CASES

*References in **bold** are to the page numbers of the Appendices. Otherwise references are to paragraph numbers in the commentary.*

TABLE OF LEGISLATION

*References in **bold** are to the page numbers of the Appendices. Otherwise references are to paragraph numbers in the commentary. Legislation is subdivided by country (in alphabetical order). For international legal instruments, please see the separate Table of Treaties.*

Germany

Primary Legislation

Criminal Procedure Code (Strafprozeßordunung) 1.58
  Art 244(2) 1.60
  Art 250 .... 1.59–1.60

Italy

Primary Legislation

Criminal Procedure Code
  Art 392 .... 2.52

Jamaica

Constitution
  s 13 .... **320–321**
  s 20(6)(d) **320**

Primary Legislation

Evidence Act
  s 31D **320**

New Zealand

Primary Legislation

Evidence Act 2006 .... 1.99
  s 18(2) 1.99

United Kingdom

Primary Legislation

Banker's Books Evidence Act 1879 .... 1.14

United States

Constitution

Secondary Legislation

TABLE OF TREATIES

*References in **bold** are to the page numbers of the Appendices. Otherwise references are to paragraph numbers in the commentary.*

1

INTRODUCTION

1.1 The 'rule against hearsay' is, traditionally, a prominent feature of the law of evidence as it has developed in the English-speaking world. In essence, it provides that a fact may not be established by calling A, who did not see or hear it, to tell the court that he heard B, who did, describe it; either B must be called to describe it to the court, or the incident must be proved by some other means. The classic definition comes from Sir Rupert Cross: 'an assertion other than one made by a person while giving oral evidence in the proceedings is inadmissible as evidence of any fact asserted'.[1]

1.2 This book is about the rule as it currently applies in criminal proceedings in England and Wales, and in Northern Ireland. At one time, the rule also applied in civil proceedings but, as is explained below, in civil proceedings it has now been abolished.[2] The move to abolish the rule in civil proceedings ran in parallel with a movement also to abolish it in criminal proceedings. But after a prolonged public debate, and a Report from the Law Commission in 1997, the decision was taken to retain it in criminal proceedings, albeit with some changes—in particular, a wider range of exceptions. The hearsay rule in its new form, together with the exceptions to it, are set out in Chapter 2 of Part 11 of Criminal Justice Act (CJA) 2003, on which most of the remaining chapters of this book are a commentary. In these new provisions, the hearsay rule has acquired a statutory definition.[3] Although less crisp than Cross's definition quoted in the previous paragraph, its meaning is essentially the same.

1.3 This introductory chapter will describe the evolution of the hearsay rule, the purposes that it was meant to serve, the difficulties that it caused, the movement to abolish or reform it, the steps that led up to the CJA 2003, and the broad lines of the new law that has emerged from it.

[1] Rupert Cross, *Evidence* (1st edn, London, Butterworths, 1958) 3; approved by Lord Havers LC in *Sharp* [1988] 1 WLR 7, 11.

[2] Civil Evidence Act 1995; for Northern Ireland, see the Civil Evidence (Northern Ireland) Order 1997, SI 1997/2983. The hearsay rule has also been abolished in civil proceedings in Scotland: Civil Evidence (Scotland) Act 1988.

[3] CJA 2003, ss 114(1) and 115; see Chapter 3 below.

Hearsay rule and the rise and fall of the exclusionary rules of evidence

1.4 The hearsay rule was (and still is) an *exclusionary rule.* In other words, it is a rule that does not merely require a certain form of evidence to be treated with official caution, but actually requires the tribunal of fact to be kept in ignorance of it.

1.5 Although its ultimate origins are probably older, the rule in its modern form grew up in the criminal courts together with a package of other exclusionary rules during the second half of the eighteenth and the first years of the nineteenth century. The history is that the judges, increasingly aware of the risks of innocent people being convicted,[4] began to create safeguards. One was a willingness to suppress evidence on which they thought it was inappropriate to convict. Another was to bend the rules which in theory denied counsel to defendants in felony cases: and over the years, these two developments worked together. At the trial, which was the point where counsel were first involved in the case, the means open to them to defend their clients were necessarily limited, but one was to persuade the judge to exclude pieces of evidence to which they could invent a plausible objection. The objections counsel made, when upheld, gave rise to the exclusionary rules of evidence.[5]

1.6 Of these exclusionary rules, a number were directed against the evidence of certain categories of witness, who were declared to be 'incompetent'. Another was the rule against evidence of bad character. And yet another was the rule against hearsay, which is the topic of this book.

1.7 These exclusionary rules grew up against the background of a criminal justice system that was quite radically different from what we have today. One supposed difference sometimes mentioned nowadays is the quality of jurors, who are said to have been more ignorant and prejudiced in those days than they are today[6] (although since in those days jury service was restricted to a narrow section of society, whereas today it is open to everyone, on balance it seems more likely that the opposite is true).[7] However, about the following matters there is certainly no doubt:

[4] See in particular the *Macdaniel* affair, where a number of innocent persons were sentenced to death and one executed. The story is told by Sir Leon Radzinowicz in his *History of English Criminal Law* (1956), vol 2, 326–32. See further Langbein, n 5 below, 152. And see *Macdaniel* (1756) 1 Leach 44.

[5] The story is told by John Langbein in *The Origins of Adversary Criminal Trial* (Oxford, Clarendon Press, 2003) ch 4.

[6] See Lord Griffiths in *R v H* [1995] 2 AC 596.

[7] In Blackstone's day, jury service was not universal as it is today, but was limited to those who were relatively well off, and part of his famous eulogy of juries was based on the fact that they were composed 'from among those of the middle rank', so that justice was not 'placed at random in the hands of the multitude', whose decisions 'would be wild and capricious': *Commentaries* (1768), Bk III, ch 23 (at page 379).

(1) There was no professional police force, or professional public prosecutor, and hence no regulated system for the collection, analysis, storage and presentation of evidence.
(2) In the absence of a public prosecutor, prosecutions were normally brought by private citizens, often encouraged to prosecute by a system of official rewards—a system which led (unsurprisingly) to unscrupulous persons bringing false accusations in the hope of making money.[8]
(3) There was no real concept, as there is today, that the prosecutor must act 'fairly' or as 'a minister of justice'; prosecutors were allowed—and expected—to fight rough and with the aim of winning.[9]
(4) As part of this, the prosecution was under no duty to disclose to the defence even the evidence it intended to call,[10] let alone any 'unused material' that might show the defendant to be innocent.
(5) Under the rules then governing the grant of bail, those accused of even relatively minor offences could expect to spend the time between arrest and trial in gaol, where they would have no opportunity to prepare their defence.[11]
(6) The defendant, if accused of felony, was not (at least in theory) allowed a lawyer to defend him.[12]
(7) Nor was he in any type of case allowed to testify in his defence.[13]
(8) Trials, even in serious cases, were by modern standards astonishingly short, rarely lasting longer than 30 minutes.[14]

[8] See n 4 above.

[9] The legal historian David JA Cairns describes the prosecutor's 'duty of restraint' as evolving in the early nineteenth century: *Advocacy and the Making of the Adversarial Criminal Trial 1800–1865* (Oxford, Clarendon Press, 1998) 4. So far as I am aware, the earliest reported case in which it was mentioned with approval by the judge was *Puddick* (1865) 4 F and F 497, 167 ER 662, where Crompton J castigated prosecuting counsel in a rape case for telling the jury, in his closing speech, that to acquit the defendant would be to accuse the complainant of committing perjury.

[10] Sir JF Stephen, *History of the Criminal Law of England* (London, Macmillan, 1883) vol 1. 227.

[11] Until 1826, the power of the justices of the peace to grant bail depended on the nature of the offence. Not only were the justices forbidden to bail those accused of grave offences, like murder and rape, but they had no power to bail a person accused (inter alia) of forgery, embezzlement, burglary, housebreaking, theft of horses, sheep or cattle, theft of negotiable instruments, theft from shops, or larceny of any object worth more than 12 pence. For the details, see C Petersdorff, *A Practical Treatise on the Law of Bail in Civil and Criminal Proceedings* (London, Butterworth, 1824). For the change to what is in essence the modern system, which took place in 1826, see JF Stephen, *History of the Criminal Law of England* (1883) vol 1, 239.

[12] This restriction lasted until the Prisoners' Counsel Act 1836; by the time it was enacted, the ban had been relaxed to the extent of allowing defendants' counsel to argue points of law on their behalf, and also to examine and cross-examine witnesses; but until 1836 defence counsel were not allowed to address the jury.

[13] In most cases this disadvantage was cancelled out by the previous one, because the defendant, having no lawyer, would end up telling the court his side of the story in the course of attempting to conduct his own defence; but if he did have counsel to defend him it was a serious disadvantage.

[14] JH Baker, *Introduction to Legal History* (4th edn, London, Butterworths, 2002) 510.

(9) The defendant, once convicted, had no right of appeal.[15]
(10) Mandatory capital punishment existed, at least in theory, as the penalty for some 200 different criminal offences.[16]

Viewed in this historical context, the exclusionary rules look rather like a sticking plaster hastily attached to a system that really needed not first aid but major surgery. And when evaluating arguments about whether the hearsay rule (or any other exclusionary rule) should be retained, we should remember the background against which it was created, and how radically the whole system has changed since this took place.

1.8 The basic premise of the traditional exclusionary rules was that certain types of evidence are weak, and hence liable to mislead the court, and for that reason ought to be suppressed.

1.9 In the early nineteenth century, however, Jeremy Bentham (1748–1832) wrote a famous[17] attack upon this line of reasoning.[18] His argument was that the rules of judicial evidence should conform as far as possible to those the intelligent head of a family would use in resolving some dispute within the household. To this end, the tribunal of fact should hear not only the best evidence, but all the evidence which is logically relevant, and, in principle, the more evidence the better. Rules excluding logically relevant evidence can never be justified as helping the court to perform its main task of getting to the truth, because a true conclusion can only be reached by considering everything that is logically relevant. Exclusionary rules may be justified sometimes where they serve secondary purposes, like the avoidance of delay, expense and 'vexation'—serious difficulties for the witness who would otherwise have to provide it. But even here they are a necessary evil, not to be tolerated if they impede the court in establishing the facts. English law, in Bentham's view, had got the matter back to front.

> Exclusion insofar as it is applied to prevent erroneous judgments, that is, to remove evidence which it is thought would mislead, has been admitted with remarkable prodigality. Exclusion, insofar as it is applied to prevent delay, expense and vexations, has been admitted very sparingly, and almost never with this view. Thus, in cases where this medicine would certainly be efficacious, it is seldom used; and in cases where its effects are only more or less dangerous, it is frequently used.[19]

[15] This was not introduced until the Criminal Appeal Act 1907. For the background, see R Pattenden, *English Criminal Appeals 1844–1994* (Oxford, Clarendon Press, 1996) ch 1.

[16] Radzinowicz, *A History of English Criminal Law* (London, Stevens, 1948) vol 1, 1–2.

[17] '[S]uch an attack on the system of the existing law [of evidence] as was hardly ever written on any existing system whatever': JF Stephen, *A General View of the Criminal Law* (2nd edn, London, Macmillan, 1890) 206.

[18] Put forward in his *Treatise upon Judicial Evidence* (1825) and his *Rationale of Judicial Evidence* (1827).

[19] *Treatise*, previous note, ch 4, § 6.7.

Bentham recognised that hearsay evidence was sometimes weak evidence, and expressed a strong preference for oral evidence from witnesses who can be interrogated in person at the trial. But none of this, in his view, could justify evidence being excluded. Its exclusion was only proper, he said, where 'the original narrator . . . can be produced and examined'.[20]

1.10 In the 175 years since he put them forward, Bentham's arguments about exclusionary rules of evidence have essentially prevailed. Some of the exclusionary rules (in particular, those relating to the competency of witnesses) have been abolished completely. Others, like the rule about bad character evidence, have been cut down to size.[21] When new restrictive rules about evidence have been created, they usually operate by limiting the use that can be made of a certain type of evidence, rather than preventing the court hearing it at all;[22] or if designed to exclude the evidence altogether, their rationale has been to serve some other purpose (in the spirit of Bentham's need to avoid 'vexation') rather than the desire to prevent the court from being misled.[23] Of the exclusionary rules that were invented with the supposed aim in mind of preventing the court from being misled, it is only the hearsay rule that still survives; and that only for the purpose of criminal proceedings.

Scope and evolution of the hearsay rule

1.11 In concrete terms, the rule we compendiously call 'the rule against hearsay' consists of what are really four distinct elements, only one of which bears any resemblance to the meaning of the word 'hearsay' in ordinary speech:

(a) a written (or filmed or tape-recorded) statement from a witness is not acceptable as a substitute for his live evidence delivered orally in court;
(b) a witness giving oral evidence to the court is not allowed to tell the court about a fact of which he or she heard from someone else;
(c) the evidence of a witness who gives oral evidence may not be supplemented or supported by reference to what he said on an earlier occasion (the 'rule against narrative', alias the 'rule against self-corroboration');
(d) a disputed fact may not be proved by producing a written record.

[20] *Ibid* 203.
[21] By the CJA 2003; see JR Spencer, *Evidence of Bad Character* (Oxford, Hart, 2006).
[22] See in particular the rules on evidence of eye-witness identification: *Turnbull* [1977] QB 224.
[23] Eg, the rule excluding evidence of telephone intercepts: Regulation of Investigatory Powers Act 2000, s 17.

The story of how the exclusionary rule grew to include each of these four elements is a complicated one, the finer details of which are beyond the scope of this book, although something will be said about them in later chapters, as a prelude to a discussion of certain aspects of the law as it now stands in the light of the CJA 2003.

1.12 On the positive side, this group of rules has some desirable effects. They shut out a certain amount of evidence that is likely to be weak because the maker was not on oath and is not available for cross-examination; they ensure that the defendant in a criminal trial has the chance to question his accusers; and they also help to maintain the oral character of the English trial. But on the negative side, the hearsay rule as so defined is obviously much too restrictive, and exceptions must be recognised to prevent miscarriages of justice resulting from important and cogent pieces of evidence being excluded. In consequence of this, a great many exceptions were made to it: to the extent, in fact, that by the time of the reform in 2003, nobody was entirely sure exactly how many there were.[24]

1.13 Many of these exceptions were invented by the courts themselves. A particularly important common law exception, which seems to have grown up in parallel with the rule itself, concerns 'admissions and confessions', the rules of which were codified in the Police and Criminal Evidence Act (PACE) 1984. Other well-known common law exceptions were 'public records', *res gestae* statements (known as 'excited utterances' in the USA), and—the lurid one that even the most forgetful law student could usually remember—'dying declarations'.

1.14 To the long list created by the judges, Parliament added many others. At first it intervened in a small way, with limited exceptions covering depositions and documentary records, of which one of the best known is the Banker's Books Evidence Act 1879, which made entries in bank ledgers admissible as evidence of the transactions they record. Then, in the later part of the twentieth century, Parliament created some further exceptions that were bigger and more general. Section 9 of the CJA 1967 made the written statements of absent witnesses ('section 9 statements') admissible in criminal proceedings where both prosecution and defence were prepared to agree to this. And 21 years later, the 'documentary evidence' provisions of CJA 1988 created a set of new exceptions for the written statements of witnesses who were now unavailable, and a general exception in respect of 'records'.[25]

[24] In its Report No 245 the Law Commission discussed 16 common law exceptions plus four important statutory exceptions—a list of 20 well-known exceptions—and it also mentioned a number of minor statutory exceptions, of which it did not provide an exhaustive list.

[25] The third in a line of ever-wider provisions: see § 7.3 below.

1.15 However, while Parliament was passing legislation to relax the hearsay rule, two important decisions from the House of Lords did much to tighten the rule up. Taking them in reverse chronological order, *Kearley*, decided in the 1990s, extended the scope of the rule, and *Myers*, decided in the 1960s, held that it was not open to the courts to create any new exceptions to it, however desirable or necessary they might be.

1.16 The point at issue in *Kearley*[26] was whether the hearsay rule applied not only to evidence of a person's words or gestures which were meant to assert a fact ('Mary told me that Tom always smells of sweat'), but also to words or gestures which are not meant to assert a fact, but which nevertheless imply one ('I saw Mary walking out of Tom's office holding her nose'). Resolving a point which had previously been uncertain, the House of Lords decided that the hearsay rule prohibits evidence of 'implied assertions' as well as of express ones. At Kearley's trial for possessing drugs with intent to supply, police witnesses had been allowed to testify that, while they were searching his premises, seven people had called at the door asking if they could buy drugs, and 11 more had telephoned to ask if he had drugs for sale. This evidence was given, of course, with a view to establishing that Kearley was in the business of supplying drugs. By a majority of three to two, the House of Lords held that this evidence had been wrongly admitted, just as it would have been if, instead of trying to buy drugs from Kearley, each caller had allegedly said 'Hello? Is that the police? I wish to report that Kearley deals in drugs'.

1.17 This decision was open to criticism for a number of connected grounds. One of the main reasons for the hearsay rule is always said to be the risk that the person whose statement is reported by another person may have been lying, and if the original speaker is not before the court, his sincerity cannot be tested in cross-examination. As it is usually easier to tell a lie than to act one, with 'implied assertions' the risk of fabrication is obviously smaller. To quote an example from an American writer: if the passengers in an allegedly underheated carriage did not complain, or were even seen to be sitting in their shirt-sleeves, this is unlikely to be because 'all the other passengers were Eskimos or stockholders of the company or masochists'.[27] Thus, the extension of the hearsay rule to cover implied assertions had the practical effect of rendering debatable a great deal of material which was likely to be reliable, and which prior to the decision in *Kearley*, everyone would have assumed to be admissible as circumstantial evidence. (For example, to support P's evidence that D uttered a threat to shoot him, it would no longer be possible, apparently, to prove that the other drinkers in the bar had immediately fled.)

[26] [1992] 2 AC 228; comment [1993] CLJ 40.
[27] JB Weinstein, 'The Probative Force of Hearsay' (1961) 46 *Iowa Law Review* 331, 343.

1.18 In *Myers*,[28] D had been convicted of a series of offences arising from what the prosecution alleged had been a 'car-ringing' enterprise. The prosecution case was that he had been buying cars that had been wrecked in accidents, and attaching their identity to stolen cars, which he then passed off as legitimately obtained. To prove the case against him, the Crown wanted to establish which engine had originally gone with which chassis and, in order to do so, it produced the cards on which the workers in the car factory had recorded this information as the cars were being assembled. By a majority of three to two, the House of Lords held that this evidence was wrongly admitted. The notes on the cards were, in law, statements of fact made by the workers, who did not give oral evidence at the trial, and hence fell within the scope of the hearsay rule. Although there was no reason to doubt that the information on the cards was true, no existing exception to the hearsay rule applied to them. It was also held that the courts today, irrespective of what their predecessors might have done a century before, could not create a new exception to the rule to enable the reception of such evidence, however reliable it might be, and however foolish it might seem to reject it.[29]

1.19 The immediate effect of *Myers* was quickly negatived by a statute which made trade or business records admissible in evidence.[30] But the wider impact of the decision remained. As regards the hearsay rule more generally, *Myers* had made two points all too clear. The first was that the hearsay rule, though originally invented to exclude evidence that was inherently weak, had now definitively parted company from its underlying purpose and turned into a technical rule, which had to be obeyed, just because rules have to be obeyed. The hearsay rule, as first created, was an expression of a judicial preference for evidence that was reliable over evidence that was inherently weak. But as applied in *Myers*, the rule required the court to reject the stronger form of evidence in favour of the weaker. To prove the information about the serial numbers on the chassis and the cylinder-blocks, the Crown, in theory, was supposed to find the workers who had put the cars together months or even years before, and then to bring them to court to testify, from memory, which cylinder-block they had inserted into which chassis, and could not replace this impossible charade by using the records they had made, which no one doubted were reliable. The second point was that the courts, though previously willing to prevent the hearsay rule causing grave injustices by recognising new exceptions to it when obviously necessary, had now officially given up and were no longer prepared to do this.

[28] [1965] AC 1001.

[29] But despite this, the House of Lords affirmed the conviction because it thought the rest of the evidence was overwhelming.

[30] CEA 1965; which was replaced by PACE 1984, s 68; which was replaced by CJA 1988, s 24; and which has now been replaced by CJA 2003, s 117 (see Chapter 7 below).

Hearsay rule in criminal law as it stood before the 2003 reform: justifications for the rule

1.20 As part of the process that eventually led to the reform in 2003, the Law Commission published a Consultation Paper[31] and then a Report,[32] in which it listed and analysed the traditional justifications for the hearsay rule as follows.

1.21 *Not the best evidence* The first justification for the hearsay rule is that 'hearsay is not the best evidence', because it is inherently inferior to oral testimony delivered to the court on oath, which common lawyers traditionally regard as superior to every other sort.[33] The answer to this, as the facts of *Myers* show us, is that some hearsay evidence is much more reliable than oral testimony would be, if there were any, and in such cases the supposed justification does not apply; and even where oral evidence would be better, in many cases (for example, where the original speaker is now dead) hearsay may be the best that is available; and where this is so, it is perverse to exclude it for this reason.

1.22 *Hearsay evidence is dangerous* The second (and very usual) justification for the hearsay rule is that hearsay evidence is inherently dangerous, because it falls outside the reach of all the mechanisms which a court normally applies to ensure so far as possible that evidence on which it is invited to act is truthful and accurate. These mechanisms are three: the oath, cross-examination and the fact that the court can observe the demeanour of the witness. Where a witness testifies orally in court about a matter of which he or she has first-hand knowledge, all three of these mechanisms operate. However, if witness A is reporting what non-witness B has told him, there is no guarantee as to whether what B said to A is true. B did not speak to A on oath; the court is unable to observe B's demeanour; B cannot be cross-examined about what he said, if we try to cross-examine A about it, every probing question will usually be met by the answer 'I'm sorry, I don't know—I can only repeat to you what he told me'.

1.23 In addition, with hearsay evidence, unlike direct evidence, there are risks of errors in transmission: A may have misheard or misunderstood what B said.

[31] Law Commission, *Evidence in Criminal Proceedings and Related Matters* (Consultation Paper No 138, 1995) (hereafter 'LC Consultation Paper').

[32] Law Commission, *Evidence in Criminal Proceedings: Hearsay and Related Topics* (Report No 245, Cm 3670, June 1997) (hereafter 'LC Report').

[33] I think this preference is largely cultural. Some years ago, I explained, to their mounting puzzlement, the 'rule against narrative' to an audience of French judges and prosecutors. When they had finally grasped it, one said: '*Mais cela vous expose à la fragilité du témoignage oral*' ('But that exposes you to the weakness of oral testimony').

This author once heard from a colleague about a case in which the written witness statement that the police had taken from a motorist involved in a collision recorded his words thus: 'I was driving to Cambridge on the wrong side of the road. Coming round the corner was X's car and I was unable to avoid a collision'. In fact the motorist had dictated: 'I was driving to Cambridge. On the wrong side of the road, coming round the corner, was X's car and I was unable to avoid a collision'. On top of that, there is also the risk of bad faith by A, who (like Iago in Shakespeare's *Othello*) may have invented B's words, or deliberately distorted them. Evidence of this sort is particularly easy to invent, and A may have distorted B's words intentionally, or even concocted the whole conversation.

1.24 All this adds up to a formidable case for treating hearsay evidence with caution. However, it certainly does not justify a total ban on 'hearsay' as English law defines it, and it is questionable whether it even justifies a general ban subject to exceptions. First, by no means everything that English law traditionally classifies as 'hearsay' suffers from all these inherent risks and defects. A letter written by the absent witness is not subject to the risk of transmission error, for example, nor a fortiori is a tape-recorded interview. If the interview is video-recorded, furthermore, then one of the traditional safeguards is present, because the court can observe the demeanour of the speaker. And if the lawyer for the opposing side was present at the interview, and able to ask questions of the witness, not one but two of the traditional safeguards would be in place.

1.25 Secondly, in this whole area a sense of proportion is required. Though of some help, the traditional mechanisms on which the law relies to ensure accuracy and truthfulness (the oath, cross-examination and the ability to observe the demeanour of the witness) are not infallible, whether taken singly or even in combination. A great deal of direct evidence which is legally admissible because it can be subjected to these three tests is potentially every bit as unreliable as some of the indirect evidence that is legally inadmissible because it cannot: for example, oral evidence of 'fleeting glance' identifications, or of events that took place in the distant past, or of incidents observed by a witness who was heavily under the influence of alcohol. In the end, the objection that hearsay evidence is 'inherently dangerous', like the objections often made to certain types of direct evidence, comes down to this: that it is potentially of little weight. That may justify a rule requiring most of it to be treated with caution, and may possibly justify the exclusion of certain forms of it (for example, 'multiple hearsay'—where A, instead of repeating B's eye-witness account, regurgitates the tale that B tells him he has previously heard from C). But it certainly does not justify a total ban. And in the view of many commentators (including the author of this book) it does not justify a general ban, even when subject to a list of specified exceptions.

1.26 *Hearsay evidence is likely to mislead a lay tribunal* The third justification sometimes given for the hearsay rule, which is closely related to the second, is its supposed tendency to 'mislead a lay tribunal'. Professional judges, who understand these matters, may be able to grasp the fact that hearsay evidence is likely to be weak, but not jurors or lay magistrates, who are likely to be over-persuaded by it. This justification was examined by the Law Commission at considerable length before they finally pronounced it wanting;[34] but it is so obviously unconvincing that, in retrospect, one wonders why it has been taken so seriously in the past. Some 25 years earlier, the Criminal Law Revision Committee dismissed it as follows:

> Anybody with common sense will understand that evidence which cannot be tested by cross-examination may well be less reliable than evidence which can. In any event judges will be in a position to remind juries that the former is the case with hearsay evidence, and sometimes the judge may think it advisable to mention this to the jury at the time when the statement is admitted. On the other hand there is some hearsay evidence which would rightly convince anybody. Moreover, juries may have to consider evidence which is admissible under the present law, and there are kinds of evidence which they may find more difficult to evaluate that hearsay evidence—for example, evidence of other misconduct.[35]

1.27 With this assessment it is difficult to argue. There are good reasons to be sceptical of the ability of inexperienced lay people (and in particular, of jurors drawn from the community at random) to evaluate evidence. But there is no intelligible reason to suppose that they are likely to make a more incompetent job of evaluating hearsay evidence than of any other sort. With inexperienced fact-finders the real problem, surely, is with types of evidence where the danger is one which lay people may not understand, for example, eye-witness identification. And paradoxically, one form of evidence which psychological research suggests inexperienced lay people may be particularly prone to misevaluating is oral testimony. Ordinary people, and indeed the law, commonly work on the assumption that it is possible to make a reliable assessment of a speaker's sincerity and accuracy from his 'demeanour'. But psychological research suggests that this assumption is mistaken. The signs that lay people interpret as indicators of lying are really signs of stress, and a witness may be stressed because it is uncomfortable to tell a lie, or because it is uncomfortable to tell the truth.[36] And the sign that lay people commonly interpret as indicating accuracy is the speaker's apparent confidence, which in reality tells us little about whether his observation is accurate.[37]

[34] LC Consultation Paper, n 31 above, §§ 6.63–6.80.

[35] Criminal Law Revision Committee, *Eleventh Report (Evidence) General* (Cmnd 4991, London, HMSO, 1972) (hereafter 'CLRC Evidence Report') § 247.

[36] LC Consultation Paper, n 31 above, 80, referring to J Spencer and R Flin, *The Evidence of Children, the Law and Psychology* (2nd edn, London, Blackstone Press, 1993)) 280–1.

[37] *Ibid.*

1.28 *Excluding hearsay protects the right to confrontation* A fourth justification put forward for the hearsay rule is the need to protect the defendant's 'right to confrontation'. An essential element in a fair system of criminal justice, it is said, is the right of the defendant to confront his accusers, and if hearsay evidence is admitted he is robbed of this essential right.

1.29 The issue of confrontation is a complex one, and is further explored in the second chapter of this book. For now, it will be taken as a given that defendants in criminal cases ought, in principle, to have the right to put questions to their accusers. The main reason for this is to protect the defendant against the risk of conviction on evidence that is false or inaccurate: by challenging his accuser, the defendant has the chance to expose his testimony as false. But some people also believe that the defendant's right to confrontation has an important symbolic value. Aside from its practical or symbolic value, the defendant's right of confrontation in proceedings is guaranteed (at least to some extent) by two international instruments to which the United Kingdom has subscribed: the European Convention on Human Rights, and the UN Covenant on Civil and Political Rights, both of which provide that a person charged with a criminal offence has the right '*to examine or have examined witnesses against him* and to obtain the attendance and examination of witnesses on his behalf on the same conditions as witnesses against him' (emphasis added).[38]

1.30 However, if the defendant's right of confrontation is important, no one seriously claims that it is absolute. In order to do its basic job of catching and punishing offenders, every legal system is obliged to make at least certain minimal exceptions to it. The point was graphically made in a cartoon by Plantu in *Le Monde*, inspired by a proposal to try Saddam Hussein before an international tribunal for genocide:[39] from inside the courtroom the judge calls 'Bring in the witnesses' and outside the door there is a pile of corpses. Thus, even if there is a hearsay rule, there must be some exceptions to it—and with them, to the defendant's right to confrontation. The question, once again, is whether this particular justification requires a general exclusionary rule subject to exceptions, as English criminal procedure has known for the last 175 years, or whether a less rigid structure would be sufficient.

1.31 *The need to protect the defendant* A fifth justification for the hearsay rule is that it is necessary to make sure that the defendant gets a fair trial. Without it, it is said, the prosecution could use evidence against him which is of dubious value, for all the theoretical reasons which have already been discussed. This justification is

[38] ECHR, Art 6(3)(d); ICCPR, Art 14(3).
[39] Reproduced in Plantu, *Le petit juge illustré* (Seuil, Paris, 1999) 145.

an amalgam of the two justifications previously mentioned, and there is no need to discuss it further. However, as a justification for the hearsay rule in its traditional English form it is not at all convincing, because although the rule is often justified as necessary to ensure that defendants get a fair trial, the exclusionary rule operates against defendants as well as for them; and one of the strongest criticisms of the hearsay rule in the past has been that it occasionally prevents defendants putting cogent evidence of their innocence before the court.

1.32 *The hearsay rule saves judicial time* A sixth justification sometimes given for the hearsay rule is that it is necessary to prevent the time of the courts being wasted with hearing evidence of little weight.[40] However, as the Law Commission said:

> It would be nearer the truth, perhaps, to say the opposite: that the existence of the hearsay rule consumes some court time (and public money) by making courts hear oral evidence which could be more easily, quickly and cheaply presented in written form. The complexities of the rule can also be responsible for using up court time, since the courts have to spend time in hearing argument about whether evidence is legally admissible. Indeed, the driving force behind a whole series of inroads on the hearsay rule has been the desire to avoid the waste of time and money.[41]

And as the Law Commission pointed out, neither the English nor the Scottish civil courts have found themselves overwhelmed with poor-quality evidence since the hearsay rule was abandoned in civil proceedings.[42]

1.33 The 'waste of time' justification has often been put forward with particular reference to the variety of the hearsay rule known as the 'rule against narrative' or the 'rule against self-corroboration': the rule that where a witness gives oral testimony, evidence of his previous statements on the subject are inadmissible, except for the purpose of undermining the credibility of what he said in court. Thus, when the Criminal Law Revision Committee proposed the abolition of this part of the rule in its 1972 Report,[43] the General Council of the Bar in its response described the proposal as 'unnecessary': because a witness's earlier statement would either be the same as what he said at trial, when it would be redundant, or else it would be different, in which case the two statements would cancel each other out.[44] But this seems to miss the point, which is that where a witness is honest, the previous

[40] R May and S Powles, *Criminal Evidence* (5th edn, London, Sweet & Maxwell, 2004) § 8-01. Sir Richard May spent the last years of his life as a judge at the International Criminal Tribunal for the Former Yugoslavia. In this tribunal the hearsay rule did not apply; and in a conversation with me in Cambridge in 2003, he expressed the view to me that, in the absence of the rule, the Tribunal had to waste much valuable time examining evidence of little weight.

[41] LC Consultation Paper, n 31 above, § 6.97.

[42] *Ibid* § 9.96.

[43] CLRC Evidence Report, n 35 above.

[44] General Council of the Bar, *Evidence in Criminal Cases: Memorandum on the Eleventh Report of the Criminal Law Revision Committee* (London, 1973).

statement will usually neither duplicate nor contradict his courtroom testimony, but be a fuller and more complete version of it, because it was given nearer to the event in question, and memories are inclined to fade with time.

Criticisms of the hearsay rule

1.34 *Irrationality of the hearsay rule* The most obvious criticism of the rule was its fundamental irrationality. In every scientific discipline, and in every area in which human beings have to ascertain the facts as the basis for decision, it is taken for granted that the only sensible way to proceed is by considering all the evidence that is logically relevant. Relevant evidence may have little weight, but if so, that is usually only a reason for taking less notice of it than of other information that is weightier: no one suggests that it is a valid reason for refusing to consider it. Where time and resources are limited, some information may not be gathered because it does not seem to justify the cost of collecting it. Other relevant information may be out of bounds to protect some other interest, like privacy of individuals or national security. But nowhere except in a court of law would anyone think of refusing to consider information which is both relevant and available for fear that it might mislead him if he had it: and even in a law court, no one would think of this outside the common law world. This was, in essence, Bentham's argument about exclusionary rules of evidence: that they could be justified by the need to avoid delay, expense or 'vexation', but not by the fear that the information would mislead. It is the gradual acceptance of this idea that has led, over the years, to a great erosion of the exclusionary rules—including, in civil proceedings, the rule against hearsay.

1.35 Furthermore, if the main part of the rule against hearsay can be justified as shutting out evidence which is presumptively unreliable because it is not subject to the traditional safeguards of truthfulness, this does not justify the 'rule against narrative' (see § 1.11 above), which suppresses the previous statements of those who do come to court to give live evidence, who can be cross-examined, under oath, about their previous statements, while the eyes of the court are fixed upon them. If there are two scientific facts about the psychology of human memory which are clear beyond any doubt, one is that memory for an event fades gradually with time, and the other is that stress beyond a certain level can impair the power of recall. Thus, the rule against narrative stands the scientific knowledge on this question on its head, requiring us to accept the two following propositions: first, that memory improves with the passage of time and secondly, that stress improves the process of recall.[45]

[45] Spencer and Flin, n 36 above; quoted by Michael Wills, MP, when the Criminal Justice Bill was before the House of Commons: Hansard, Standing Committee B, 2003, col 643 (28 January 2003).

1.36 This point was taken by the Criminal Law Revision Committee as long ago as in 1972, when it said:

> assuming, as one must, that a person called as a witness in criminal proceedings is more likely than not to intend to try to tell the truth, it follows that what he said soon after the events in question is likely to be at least as reliable as his evidence given at the trial and will probably be more so[46]

and on this basis recommended that the rule against narrative be abolished, as indeed it already had been for the purpose of civil proceedings.[47]

1.37 *Lack of underlying principle to the traditional exceptions* The list of exceptions to the hearsay rule, though long, appeared to lack any underlying unifying principle. Some seemed to be based on the general idea that hearsay is acceptable where there is something about it that makes up for the fact that hearsay tends to be unreliable. This was the case with *res gestae* (excited utterances), for example, and also dying declarations. In the USA, this notion led the draftsman of the Federal Rules of Evidence to crown his list of specific exceptions with a general 'residual exception' covering any hearsay statement which has 'equivalent circumstantial guarantees of trustworthiness'.[48] But that is not a route down which, in England, either Parliament or the courts had been prepared to go.

1.38 Then other exceptions to the hearsay rule seemed to be based on the general idea that, although direct evidence is preferable to hearsay, it is stupid to reject hearsay when the original maker of the statement can no longer be produced: for example, CJA 1988, section 23, which made hearsay evidence admissible where the original maker was unable to testify because he was dead, or unavailable for certain other reasons. But if necessity is a good reason for having any specific exception to the hearsay rule, it would equally seem to justify a further general exception, making admissible the hearsay statement of any witness who can no longer be produced—as is to be found, once again, in the US Federal Rules of Evidence.[49]

[46] CLRC Evidence Report, n 35 above, § 239.

[47] CEA 1968, s 2.

[48] Federal Rules of Evidence, Rule 807: 'A statement not specifically covered by Rule 803 or 804 but having equivalent circumstantial guarantees of trustworthiness, is not excluded by the hearsay rule, if the court determines that (A) the statement is offered as evidence of a material fact; (B) the statement is more probative on the point for which it is offered than any other evidence which the proponent can procure through reasonable efforts; and (C) the general purposes of these rules and the interests of justice will best be served by admission of the statement into evidence. However, a statement may not be admitted under this exception unless the proponent of it makes known to the adverse party sufficiently in advance of the trial or hearing to provide the adverse party with a fair opportunity to prepare to meet it, the proponent's intention to offer the statement and the particulars of it, including the name and address of the declarant'.

[49] Federal Rules of Evidence, Rule 804 (5).

1.39 *Other objections* In its Consultation Paper, the Law Commission, surprisingly, played these two basic objections down. But it listed seven other strong objections to the hearsay rule (and its attendant body of exceptions) as the law then stood: it was overcomplicated; this led, in consequence, to a needless waste of time; it was truth-defeating, because it sometimes caused cogent evidence to be excluded; it was also truth-defeating in another way, because it sometimes made it harder for witnesses to give their evidence; it was arbitrary, too often leaving the decision as to whether a key piece of evidence would be admitted to the discretion of the court; it was undiscriminating, in that, once hearsay evidence was admissible by way of an exception to the rule, the law officially accorded it the same weight as a piece of direct evidence, even if it was manifestly weak; and that in various ways it was (at least arguably) incompatible with the European Convention on Human Rights. Taking each of these in turn:

1.40 *Excessive complication* As already explained, this area of law consisted of an exclusionary rule, to which there were some 20 well-known exceptions, plus an uncertain number of other more obscure ones.[50] In terms of bulk alone, this body of law was very daunting. At the time of the Law Commission's Report, large sections of the textbooks, and of practitioners' books, were devoted to explaining the outlines and finer points of it; and with each edition these sections were getting longer.[51] This large chunk of legal learning was (and still is) something which the criminal justice systems of our continental neighbours seemed to manage fairly well without;[52] and in the United Kingdom, the civil justice systems too, since the hearsay rule was abolished with respect to them.

1.41 Yet despite its size, the law relating to the hearsay rule was remarkably obscure. Fundamental doubts existed both as to the reach of the basic rule and the scope (and even the existence) of a number of the exceptions.[53] Even the highest courts found this area of the law difficult to apply, as witness the fact that, in two of the leading cases (*Myers* and *Kearley*) the House of Lords divided three to two.

[50] See n 24 above. Fifty years ago, Rupert Cross estimated that there were about 20: 'The Scope of the Rule Against Hearsay' (1956) 72 LQR 91.

[51] In the third edition of *Cross on Evidence*, which appeared in 1967, the hearsay rule took up 164 pages; in the seventh edition, which appeared in 1990, it took 228. At the time the Consultation Paper came out it also took up 115 pages of the current edition of *Blackstone's Criminal Practice* (LC Consultation Paper, n 31 above, 101).

[52] The current (fifth) edition of GJM Corstens, *Het Nederlandse strafprocesrecht*, the standard 900-page Dutch text on criminal procedure, deals with this area of law in 15 pages. The French equivalent, R Merle and A Vitu, *Traité de droit criminal. Procédure pénale* (4th edn, 1989) devotes five pages to the subject out of 991.

[53] 'The rule against hearsay is one of the oldest, most complex and most confusing of the exclusionary rules of evidence . . . One of the reasons is that its definition and the ambit of exceptions to it are both unclear': the opening words of ch XIII of the seventh edition of *Cross and Tapper on Evidence*, quoted by the Law Commission at LC Report, n 32 above, 45.

In the lower courts, of course, it gave rise to daily difficulties in the form of arguments about whether a given piece of evidence fell within the rule, and if so whether it was saved by one of the exceptions, all of which consumed valuable and expensive time.[54] And (as with evidence of bad character) the obscurity of the rules had a 'chilling effect', sometimes causing prosecutors and defendants to avoid producing evidence that was both relevant and admissible because of a misguided belief that it was inadmissible as hearsay.[55]

1.42 *Exclusion of cogent evidence* A major objection to the hearsay rule as it stood when the Law Commission examined it was that, by excluding valuable evidence, it posed an obstacle to accurate fact-finding by the courts. Despite the existence of a long list of exceptions, the rule still caused cogent pieces of evidence to be excluded. The most obvious example was the telephone calls from the would-be drug purchasers in *Kearley*. As one of the dissentients in that case, Lord Griffiths, put it:

> It is hardly surprising that the jury convicted the appellant for as a matter of common sense it is difficult to think of much more convincing evidence of his activity as a drug dealer than customers constantly ringing his house to buy drugs and a stream of customers beating a path to his door for the same purpose . . .
>
> I believe that most laymen if told that the criminal law of evidence forbade them even to consider such evidence as we are debating in this appeal would reply 'Then the law is an ass'.

That the rule should prevent the court from hearing cogent evidence of guilt was worrying enough. But even more worryingly, it also sometimes prevented the court hearing cogent evidence of innocence. In one well-known case it prevented a white man who was accused of assaulting a little girl of three, who was not called as a witness, from leading evidence that she had initially described her attacker as black.[56] Similarly, it also prevented a defendant from showing that another person had confessed to the crime for which he was on trial, or had said things indicating that he might have been done it.[57]

1.43 In some cases where cogent defence evidence had been excluded at the trial on account of the hearsay rule, the Court of Appeal had come to the rescue afterwards by looking at the evidence, despite the fact that it was strictly speaking inadmissible, and deciding that its existence cast enough doubt on the conviction for it to be quashed;[58] but in other cases it had refused to do this.[59] This state of affairs, as JUSTICE pointed out, was deeply unsatisfactory:

[54] LC Consultation Paper, n 31 above, 109.
[55] Roderick Munday, *Evidence* (4th edn, Oxford, OUP, 2007) § 9.8.
[56] *Sparks v R* [1964] AC 964.
[57] *Blastland* [1986] AC 41.
[58] Notably in *Cooper* [1969] 1 QB 267.
[59] Eg *Wallace and Short* (1978) 67 Cr App R 291.

We think that it is a powerful argument against a strict exclusionary rule that miscarriages of justice can be avoided only if the appellant is lucky enough to find a court prepared to decide his case otherwise than according to law.[60]

1.44 As is explained below, the Law Commission's recipe for dealing with this problem was to retain the hearsay rule, but to restrict its definition, and to expand the range of exceptions to it, so that in future cogent evidence of the types described in the previous three paragraphs would become legally admissible; and the hearsay provisions of the CJA 2003 were designed to implement the Law Commission's recommendations.

1.45 *Confusion of witnesses* The hearsay rule was also criticised as truth-defeating in another way, because of its tendency to inhibit witnesses when giving evidence. As Professor RM Jackson explained:

A man is giving evidence as to why he remembered the time when he started to drive home. He says: 'I had to be home by ten, and it was getting foggy, so at nine I rang Muriel, and I says, 'Muriel, what's the fog like your end' and she says . . .'. At this point he is stopped. What Muriel says is hearsay, and not admissible. The poor man is confused and bewildered, because his natural way of speaking is apparently taboo: the proper course is to go in for circumlocution whereby he makes it clear that in consequence of information received he decided to leave earlier than he otherwise would have done.[61]

1.46 *Arbitrariness* When making new exceptions to the hearsay rule, Parliament in recent years had usually adopted a formula under which the new exception operated, or not, subject to the discretion of the court. This was so, for example, with the important range of new exceptions created by the CJA 1988, and it was also the case when videotapes of interviews with children were made admissible in certain types of cases in 1991. The fact that important parts of the hearsay rule operated subject to the discretion of the court opened it to a further criticism: that it was arbitrary. On the face of it this was not so, because the statutory provisions set out at length the factors which the court was required to consider in making its decision. However, in reality many of these factors pulled against each other, so leaving the court more or less free to follow its own inclination. This arbitrariness the Law Commission criticised as a reproach to the existing law.[62]

1.47 *Lack of discrimination* As the Law Commission explained:

A large and complicated body of law has been created on the premise that hearsay evidence is weaker than direct oral testimony, and must therefore be kept out. But once a piece of hearsay passes through one of the exceptions to the rule, the law apparently loses

[60] JUSTICE, *Miscarriages of Justice* (1989) § 3.41; quoted in LC Report, n 32 above, § 4.13.
[61] *Jackson's Machinery of Justice* (8th edn, JR Spencer (ed), Cambridge, CUP, 1989) 266.
[62] LC Report, n 32 above, § 4.31.

sight of this basic premise, and treats the hearsay as something which is capable of bearing the same weight as any other piece of evidence, irrespective of the reason, theoretical or real, for the exception.[63]

Thus, in one case, for example, the Privy Council upheld a murder conviction (and consequent death sentence) where the only piece of evidence against the defendant was a 'dying declaration'.[64] And, contrary to the position in a number of other jurisdictions, an English court could (and in theory still can) convict where the only item of evidence is the accused person's extra-judicial confession.[65]

1.48 In the hope of dealing with this problem, the Law Commission proposed a rule requiring the judge in a jury trial to stop a case which is based wholly or partly on insubstantial hearsay; a recommendation which, as we shall see, was implemented by the CJA 2003.[66]

1.49 *Incompatibility with the European Convention on Human Rights* The Law Commission identified three ways in which the existing law on hearsay might be incompatible with the European Convention on Human Rights. First, his inability to call cogent evidence of his innocence (see § 1.42 above) might infringe the defendant's general right to a fair trial under Article 6(1). Secondly, the possibility of the defendant's being convicted solely on hearsay statements originating from people whom he had had no chance to question at any stage in the proceedings might infringe his specific right under Article 6(3)(d) to 'examine or have examined witnesses against him'. And thirdly, 'if the system works to prevent certain crimes from being prosecuted because the victim is unable to give oral evidence, and there is no other way in which that essential evidence can be received, it is possible that there could be a contravention of Article 8(1)'. This is the Article which guarantees a person's right to 'respect for his private and family life, his home and his correspondence' and in one case, the European Court of Human Rights had condemned the Netherlands for breach of this Article, because a series of complications of Dutch criminal procedure had combined to make it impossible to prosecute a person who had committed a sexual assault upon a person who suffered from a mental handicap.[67]

63 LC Consultation Paper, n 31 above, § 7.80.

64 *Nembhard v The Queen* [1981] 1 WLR 1515.

65 Although in practice, the Court of Appeal seems to be uneasy about convictions where this was all the evidence there was: for an example, see *R v Greenwood* [2004] EWCA Crim 1388, [2005] 1 Cr App R 7 (99).

66 CJA 2003, s 125; see further, Chapter 15 below.

67 *X v The Netherlands* (1985) Series A No 91, (1985) 8 EHRR 235.

Hearsay rule as seen by legal writers

1.50 Those who have written about hearsay evidence since Bentham can be divided into three camps according to how they have reacted to his central argument about the fundamental illogicality of rules designed to exclude evidence that might tend to mislead.

1.51 In the first camp there are those who have never heard of Bentham's views, or have chosen to ignore them. This is true of many practitioners' texts, which either continue to justify the rule on the ground that hearsay is inherently unreliable, or just state the rule without any justification at all.[68]

1.52 In the second camp are those who have faced Bentham's arguments, and concluded that despite them some sort of rule excluding hearsay is necessary, whilst admitting (with various degrees of enthusiasm) that the present rules need to be rationalised, or clarified, or simplified. In this camp belong the classic English writer Sir James Fitzjames Stephen (1829–94)[69] and, in the USA, JH Wigmore (1863–1943).[70] More recently, this also seems to have been the position of Sir Rupert Cross (1912–80),[71] and is the position adopted by Colin Tapper, the current editor of Cross's classic text on evidence.[72]

1.53 In the third camp are those who would go the whole way with Bentham, and argue that the rule excluding hearsay should be discarded, either completely, or in favour of some other more flexible rule designed to guard against the worst of the risks against which the hearsay rule was originally created. Among the classic writers who took this position was the American, JF Thayer (1831–1902), who proposed replacing the rigid exclusionary rule with a set of flexible guiding principles, the first of which should be that 'the jury must, so far as possible, personally see

[68] The 37th edition of Archbold, which appeared in 1969, reprinted at § 1070 the passage justifying the rule that John Frederick Archbold himself wrote for the first edition in 1822, which appeared before Bentham's works were published; the current edition of Archbold, *Criminal Pleading, Evidence and Practice* (2007) (hereafter 'Archbold') makes no attempt to justify the rule.

[69] Set out in his book *The Indian Evidence Act, with an Introduction to the Principles of Judicial Evidence* (1863), and his *General View of the Criminal Law* (2nd edn, 1890) ch 16.

[70] Wigmore, *A Treatise on the System of Evidence in Trials at Common Law* (3rd edn, Boston, Little Brown and Co,1940).

[71] Although he allegedly once said 'I am working for the day when my subject is abolished' (William Twining, *Rethinking Evidence* (Oxford, Blackwell, 1990) 1) he wrote in favour of rationalising the hearsay rule and its exceptions rather than abolishing it, and later publicly defended the proposals of the Criminal Law Revision Committee, which were along those lines: see [1973] *Criminal Law Review* 329, 340.

[72] Now called *Cross and Tapper on Evidence* (11th edn, Oxford, OUP, 2007); see Tapper's article 'Hearsay in Criminal Cases: an Overview of Law Commission Report No. 245' [1997] *Criminal Law Review* 771.

and hear those whose statements of fact, oral or written, they are asked to believe'.[73] Similar views were expressed by his compatriots Edmund M Morgan (1878–1966)[74] and Charles T McCormick (1889–1963), the last of whom once wrote:

> the values of hearsay declarations and writings, and the need for them, in particular situations cannot be thus minutely ticketed in advance . . . Too much worthless evidence will fit the categories, too much that is vitally needed will be left out.[75]

1.54 In England, Glanville Williams (1911–97) also championed Bentham's views:

> the present rigid law should be confined to cases where the witness is available to be called; where he is not available his evidence should be available at second hand, subject to a judicial discretion to exclude it if its probative value is outweighed by the risks of undue prejudice, undue surprise or confusion of issues which its reception would carry.[76]

1.55 Contemporary English writers who are in the Bentham camp include Professor John Jackson, who summed up a lengthy analysis of the reform debate by saying 'It may be concluded that there are no functional reasons why the hearsay rule is needed in criminal proceedings any more than in civil proceedings'.[77] They include Adrian Zuckerman, who proposed scrapping the present rules in favour of a general inclusionary discretion: the judge should have power to admit hearsay whenever it is of sufficient probative value. In his view, this is something that should be determined at a pre-trial review.[78] And they also include Andrew Choo,[79] who has adopted a similar but distinct approach. He argued that the hearsay rule and its exceptions should be abolished, and that the admissibility of out-of-court statements should be decided on a case-by-case basis. Where the prosecution wish to use them, they should be admissible provided (i) the original maker of the statement is unavailable, and (ii) the judge is satisfied that the statement is reliable, in the sense of being free from the most obvious dangers that can affect a piece of hearsay evidence. Where the defence seek to adduce them, they should be admissible provided condition (ii) is satisfied, but without any need to satisfy condition (i).

73 'The Present and Future of the Law of Evidence' (1898) 12 *Harvard Law Review* 71, 93.
74 In the American Law Institute Model Code of Evidence.
75 'Tomorrow's Law of Evidence' (1938) 24 *American Bar Association Journal* 507, 512.
76 G Williams, *The Proof of Guilt* (3rd edn, London, Stevens, 1963) 204.
77 'Hearsay, the Sacred Cow that Refuses to be Slaughtered' (1998) 2 *International Journal of Evidence and Proof* 166, 187.
78 Zuckerman, *The Principles of Criminal Evidence* (Oxford, Clarendon Press, 1989) 216; 'The Futility of Hearsay' [1996] *Criminal Law Review* 4, commenting critically on the Law Commission's Consultation Paper.
79 *Hearsay and Confrontation in Criminal Trials* (Oxford, Clarendon Press 1996).

1.56 To sum up, the legal writers who had examined this area of law all agreed that it was a blot on the legal landscape about which something needed to be done. But there was a dispute between the conservatives, who believed the structure served a useful purpose and thought the way forward was to refurbish it, and the radicals who thought that it was useless and should be demolished. This division of opinion has left its marks on the hearsay provisions of the CJA 2003, as we shall see later.

The 'directness principle' or 'best evidence' approach[80]

1.57 In Germany, as elsewhere in continental Europe, criminal procedure was traditionally a process where the fact-finders decided upon guilt or innocence on the basis of a file of written statements collected by an examining judge in the course of interrogations carried out in private. During the nineteenth century this system came under heavy criticism from reformers, including Anselm von Feuerbach[81] (1775–1833) and Carl Mittermaier (1789–1867),[82] who argued that it was incompatible with two qualities that are essential for a system that works fairly and commands public confidence: openness and orality. They pointed to the common law system of criminal procedure as preferable to the existing continental systems in this respect. Their arguments in favour of openness and orality won the day, and when in 1877 a new criminal procedure code was drawn up for the newly united Germany, provisions to ensure these qualities were included.[83]

1.58 These provisions, however, did not incorporate the English hearsay rule. In the course of the public debate preceding the reform the hearsay rule was examined, but the idea of an exclusionary rule was discarded as incompatible with another influential notion, this time drawn from French legal thinking: 'the free evaluation of evidence'.[84] This was the notion that, contrary to the traditional position in continental criminal procedure, which contained rigid rules about the

[80] An account in English (which I wrote) is printed at the end of LC Consultation Paper, n 31 above, 268–72. For another comparative account, see H Reiter, 'Hearsay Evidence and the Criminal Process in Germany and Australia' (1984) 10 *Monash Law Review* 51. And see also the chapter on evidence in M Delmas-Marty and J Spencer (eds), *European Criminal Procedures* (Cambridge, CUP, 2002).

[81] AR von Feuerbach, *Betrachtungen über die Oeffentlichkeit und Mündlichkeit der Gerechtigkeitspflege* (Giessen, 1821 and 1825).

[82] CJA Mittermaier, *Die Mündlichkeit, das Anklageprinzip, die Oeffentlichkeit and das Geschworenengericht*, (Stuttgart and Tübigen, 1845). On von Feuerbach's and Mittermaier's contribution to German criminal law in general, see Eberhard Schmidt, *Einfuhrung in die Geschichte der deutschen Strafrechtspflege* 3d edn, (1964), (reprinted by Vandenhoeck & Ruprecht, Göttingen, 1995) §§ 248–65.

[83] Klaus Geppert, *Der Grundsatz der Unmittelbarkeit im deutschen Strafverfahren* (Berlin/New York, Walter de Gruyter, 1979) Pt I.

weight to be attached to different types of evidence,[85] all relevant evidence should be admissible and the tribunal of fact should be given a free hand to evaluate it. Instead of the hearsay rule, the Germans formulated something called the 'directness principle' (*Grundsatz der Unmittelbarkeit*), which is put into legislative form by the German Criminal Procedure Code (Strafprozeßordunung, or StPO).

1.59 Article 250 of the StPO provides that:

> Principle of personal examination [*Grundsatz der persönlichen Vernehmung*]
>
> If the evidence of a fact is based upon a person's observation, this person shall be examined at the trial. The examination may not be replaced by reading the record of an earlier examination, or by reading a written statement.

StPO article 251 then sets out a number of exceptions to this principle, covering cases where the witness who made a previous declaration is unable to appear for oral examination at the trial.

1.60 At first sight, this 'directness principle' looks similar to the hearsay rule. However, this apparent similarity is deceptive, because unlike the hearsay rule the directness principle is an inclusionary rule, not exclusionary. The directness principle does not prevent the court from hearing hearsay evidence. What it does is to oblige the court to hear evidence from the original source of the information if that person is still available. If an accused wishes to complain that the court has disregarded the directness principle, his complaint is not that the court received inadmissible evidence, but that it failed to carry out its obligation to summon the witness who could have given the court a direct account, an obligation imposed on it by StPO article 244(2), under which:

> In order to search out the truth the court shall on its own motion extend the taking of evidence to all facts and means of proof that are important for the decision.

1.61 Thus in Germany, unlike England, hearsay is not in principle inadmissible as evidence. And so in Germany, for example, there would be no legal objection to the mother of the child whom the defendant is accused of assaulting repeating to the court in evidence what the child allegedly said to her, something which the English hearsay rule in principle forbids. This is not to say, however, that German courts, unlike English courts, fail to recognise that hearsay can be dangerously misleading. But rather than declare it inadmissible, as English law has done, the German courts have created a duty to handle it with caution. According to German case law, hearsay evidence is normally insufficient on its own to found a conviction, and must be corroborated by other evidence of a more reliable type.

[85] A body of rules known to French lawyers as *la preuve légale*; for a brief account, see A Esmein, *History of Continental Criminal Procedure, with special reference to France* (Boston, 1913) 251 and Appendix B.

1.62 The impact of German legal thought has been felt far beyond the limits of the German-speaking world, and as part of this, the 'directness principle'—unlike the English hearsay rule—has been widely adopted in other European countries.[86] During the build-up to the 2003 reform in England, there was a move to adopt it as the solution to the problem here as well. But as explained below, it did not succeed.

Abolition of the hearsay rule in civil proceedings

1.63 In 1938, Parliament passed an Evidence Act[87] which loosened the grip of the hearsay rule in civil proceedings, albeit to a minimal degree. Under this legislation, a hearsay statement could be used in civil proceedings in place of oral evidence from the maker if three conditions were met: (a) it was contained in a document; (b) the maker either had personal knowledge of the matter in question, or else the document formed part of a 'continuous record'; and (c) the maker was now 'dead, or unfit by reason of his bodily or mental condition to attend as a witness, or if he is beyond the seas and it is not reasonably practicable to secure his attendance, or if all reasonable efforts to find him have been made without success'.[88]

1.64 Thirty years later, following the proposals of the Law Reform Committee,[89] Parliament went a stage further with the Civil Evidence Act (CEA) 1968.[90] This created a new system under which, for the purpose of civil proceedings, (i) the previous statement of a witness who gave oral evidence became generally admissible, and (ii) hearsay statements by non-witnesses became admissible where (as under the Evidence Act 1938) the original maker was unavailable, or if he was available, where the court gave leave. Although more radical than the Evidence Act 1938, the new scheme was also rather limited. One restriction was that, except for statements contained in documents, it only applied to 'first-hand hearsay'. Another limitation was that it did not apply to the full range of civil proceedings, civil

[86] In Poland, for example: see Polish Criminal Code, art 174.

[87] The Evidence Act 1938 implemented the recommendations of a committee of judges, and the Bill that gave rise to it was introduced in the House of Lords by Lord Maugham, shortly before he became Lord Chancellor: see RFV Heuston, *Lives of the Lord Chancellors 1885–1940* (Oxford, Clarendon Press, 1964) 556. For Maugham's own account of the matter, see (1939) 17 *Canadian Bar Review* 469.

[88] Phraseology which was then recycled at intervals afterwards: see CEA 1968, s8(2)(b) and CJA 1988, s 23.

[89] Law Reform Committee, *Thirteenth Report, Hearsay Evidence in Civil Proceedings* (Cmnd 2964, 1966). A part-time body, the Law Reform Committee was one of the ancestor's of the Law Commission. See *Jackson's Machinery of Justice* (8th edn, Cambridge, CUP, 1989) 500.

[90] For a fuller account, see *Cross on Evidence* (6th edn, 1985) ch XVI.

proceedings in the magistrates' courts being excluded from it.[91] A third practical limitation was that a party wishing to call hearsay evidence was required to serve a notice on the other side, so giving him the opportunity to issue a counter-notice requiring him to produce the original maker of the statement, unless the court were prepared to rule otherwise. A further criticism of the CEA 1968 was its drafting, which was convoluted and opaque.

1.65 In 1986, the Scottish Law Commission recommended that the hearsay rule be abolished for civil proceedings north of the Border, though subject, as in England, to a system of 'notice and counter-notice', so giving the court the discretionary power to require the production of the original maker of the statement, if available.[92] The government law officers liked the proposal but not the limitation, and promoted legislation that simply abolished the hearsay rule. The result was the Civil Evidence (Scotland) Act 1988, under which hearsay (including 'second-hand hearsay') became freely admissible in civil proceedings in Scotland. The fact that the evidence is hearsay thenceforth went only to its weight, and the incentive to parties to call oral evidence if it was available was the knowledge that the court was more likely to believe it.

1.66 Encouraged by this, as well as by the public reaction when the idea was floated in a Consultation Paper,[93] the English Law Commission put forward a similar proposal on hearsay in civil proceedings in a Report in 1993.[94] This was accepted by the government, and became the basis of the CEA 1995, which completely abolished the hearsay rule for civil proceedings in England too. Two years later, the reform was extended to Northern Ireland.[95]

1.67 By section 2 of the CEA 1995, as elaborated by Rule 33.2 of the Civil Procedure Rules, a party intending to call hearsay evidence is required to give notice to the other side, with an explanation of why the original maker of the statement will not be called. Failure to comply with this rule does not make the hearsay evidence inadmissible, however, but it may be taken into account by the court in 'exercising its discretionary powers, particularly in relation to costs; and as

[91] This was not obvious from the face of the Act. But CEA 1968, s 20 gave the Lord Chancellor the power to bring the Act into force in respect of some courts but not others, and this power was used to exclude the magistrates' courts, where the law continued to be governed by the Evidence Act 1938.

[92] Scottish Law Commission, *Evidence: Report on Corroboration, Hearsay and Related Matters in Civil Procedure* (Report No 100, 1986).

[93] Law Commission, *The Hearsay Rule in Civil Proceedings* (Consultation Paper No 117, 1991). According to § 3.44 of the Report (see n 94 below) the proposal was welcomed by judges, magistrates, academics, solicitors and certain sections of the Bar, but the Reform Committee of the Bar Council was opposed to it.

[94] Law Commission, *The Hearsay Rule in Civil Proceedings* (Law Com No 216, Cm 2321, 1993).

[95] Civil Evidence (Northern Ireland) Order 1997, SI 1997/2983.

adversely affecting the weight of the evidence'.[96] The party receiving a hearsay notice may apply to the court for permission to call the original maker of the statement for cross-examination, a request which may be granted or refused.[97]

1.68 The use (or otherwise) of hearsay evidence in civil proceedings has also been affected by the new 'case management' powers conferred upon the courts by the reformed Civil Procedure Rules[98] that came into force in April 1999. Foremost among these is Rule 32.1, which is as follows:

> Power of court to control evidence
>
> (1) The court may control the evidence by giving directions as to—
>   (a) the issues on which it requires evidence;
>   (b) the nature of the evidence which it requires to decide those issues; and
>   (c) the way in which the evidence is to be placed before the court.
>
> (2) The court may use its power under this rule to exclude evidence that would otherwise be admissible.
>
> (3) The court may limit cross-examination.

By virtue of this power, the court may require either or both of the parties to produce oral evidence; or conversely, in the interests of speed and economy, it may order them to dispense with oral evidence and produce written statements in their place.

1.69 Thus, in civil proceedings in all parts of the United Kingdom, the demolition of the exclusionary rule against hearsay is now complete.

Background to the 2003 reform: Criminal Law Revision Committee, Fraud Trials Committee, Law Commission and Auld Review

1.70 After the decision in *Myers* (see § 1.18 above) the Home Secretary referred the whole of the law of criminal evidence to the Criminal Law Revision Committee (CLRC), which after nearly eight years' work produced a wide-ranging Report in 1972.[99] As regards hearsay, the CLRC proposed the complete abolition of the 'rule against narrative',[100] plus automatic admissibility for statements made by non-witnesses who could not be produced to give oral evidence for any of a range of

96 CEA 1995, s 2(4).
97 CEA 1995, s 3 and CPR, Rule 33.4.
98 Civil Procedure Rules 1998, SI 1998/3132.
99 CLRC Evidence Report, n 35 above.
100 *Ibid* § 1.10, and see Chapter 12 below.

solid reasons.[101] It also recommended a new and wider exception for records, and special provision for statements produced by computers. This Report also contained radical proposals to curtail the right of silence, as a result of which it foundered; these attracted such hostility that successive governments thought it prudent to leave the whole Report to gather dust upon the shelf. Strangely, it was these very provisions on the right of silence which, 22 years later, a Conservative government (by then committed to an aggressive 'law and order' policy) decided to push through Parliament, despite the inevitable outcry this provoked.[102] But meanwhile, the CLRC's equally central but far less controversial proposals in relation to hearsay evidence had been allowed to languish, though certain ancillary parts of them did find their way into PACE in 1984.[103]

1.71 In 1986, the Fraud Trials Committee[104] recommended a change in the hearsay rule to make it easier to admit company records, letters and other documents as evidence in fraud trials. Seizing the opportunity, the Home Office inserted in a Bill a set of clauses under the heading 'documentary evidence' which went far beyond this, and which would have made admissible in evidence the statements which a wide range of witnesses absent from the trial had earlier given to the police: a matter which raised very different policy considerations. These clauses passed the House of Commons without difficulty, but ran into trouble in the House of Lords, which forced the government to redesign its reform on less ambitious lines.[105] The result was the hearsay provisions of the CJA1988,[106] which made 'records' more widely admissible in evidence, and—more significantly—also made the written statements of witnesses who were 'unavailable' for a number of stated reasons admissible, subject to various complex and overlapping requirements about judicial leave.[107]

[101] Death; unfitness to testify, on medical grounds; 'that he is beyond the seas and it is not reasonably practicable to secure his attendance'; that being a compellable witness he refuses to be sworn, being a competent witness he declines to testify; that 'all reasonable steps have been taken to identify him, but he cannot be identified'; and that 'his identity being known, all reasonable steps have been taken to find him but that he cannot be found'. (From the Draft Bill annexed to the CLRC Evidence Report, n 35 above, 190).

[102] Criminal Justice and Public Order Act 1994, ss 34–39.

[103] Wider admissibility of 'records' (PACE 1984, s 68, replaced by CJA 1988, s 25, which was itself replaced by CJA 2003, s 117; see Chapter 7 below); computer evidence (PACE 1984, s 69, subsequently repealed by the Youth Justice and Criminal Evidence Act 1999); and provisions concerning evidence of previous convictions (PACE 1984, ss 73–75, which are still in force).

[104] Roskill Committee, *Fraud Trials Committee Report* (London, HMSO, 1986).

[105] D Wolchover, 'Criminal Trials: Proof by Missing Witnesses—an Election Issue' (1987) 137 *New Law* Journal 525, 805, 833; 'Proof by Missing Witnesses: a Safeguard Restored' (1988) 138 *New Law Journal* 202, 242, 261, 461.

[106] CJA 1988, ss 23–28. For an exposition, see *Cross on Evidence* (9th edn, 1999) ch XV.

[107] To add to the confusion, in 1996 Parliament (already entering its current state of permanent overdrive as regards criminal justice legislation) enacted the Criminal Procedure and Investigations Act 1996, s 68, which apparently made any document contained in the file on the basis of which the defendant had been committed by the magistrates to the Crown Court admissible in evidence if this was 'in the interests of justice'. This draconian result was probably an unintended side-effect of the provisions, and in practice prosecutors seem not to have relied on it. On this draconian provision, see further § 6.7 below.

1.72 In 1994, at the suggestion of the Royal Commission on Criminal Procedure (the Runciman Commission), the government referred hearsay evidence (and for good measure, the rules about bad character evidence) to the Law Commission, thereby starting the train of events which eventually led to the major reforms of criminal evidence in Part 11 of the CJA 2003.

1.73 In the following year, the Law Commission produced its Consultation Paper on hearsay in criminal proceedings.[108] This concluded (unsurprisingly) that the current law was unsatisfactory, and then set out a list of options for reforming it. These ranged from the total abolition of the hearsay rule, through its replacement by a version of the 'directness principle', to various more traditional schemes under which the exclusionary rule would be retained, subject to a new and reordered list of statutory exceptions. Of these three broad possibilities, the Commission (more conservative than it had been when dealing with hearsay in civil proceedings)[109] expressed its provisional preference for the third. And, more conservatively than the CLRC 25 years earlier, it also favoured retaining the 'rule against narrative'.

1.74 Its Report,[110] which appeared two years later, followed the lines already laid down in the Consultation Paper. In essence, the Law Commission's scheme contained nine elements:

(a) retention of the exclusionary rule, but redefined so as to limit it to statements by non-witnesses which were intended to be assertive (the reversal, in other words, of *Kearley* (see § 1.16 above));
(b) an exception to cover cases where the original speaker was 'unavailable'; to be modelled on CJA 1988, section 23, but unlike that provision, hearsay covered by this exception would in future be admissible automatically, rather than at the discretion of the court;
(c) a exception to cover 'records', to be modelled on CJA 1988, section 24, but (as with the new 'unavailable witness' exception) evidence falling within the exception would be admissible automatically;
(d) a further list of eight existing exceptions to the hearsay rule would be expressly confirmed, and the rest formally abolished;
(e) a new exception, permitting the court to admit hearsay evidence not otherwise admissible where the interests of justice compellingly require it; (to make the point that they meant it to be rarely used, the Law Commission called this 'the safety-valve');

[108] See n 31 above.
[109] Between the two Reports there had been a major change in the personnel at the Law Commission.
[110] See n 32 above.

(f) a new power in the court to refuse to admit hearsay evidence of little weight, the hearing of which would waste the time of the court;
(g) retention of the 'rule against narrative', but with the existing exceptions recast in an improved statutory form;
(h) the previous statement of a witness, where admissible under an exception to the 'rule against narrative', would henceforth count as evidence of the matters contained in it, and no longer have the inferior status which the common law attached to it;
(i) in a jury trial, a new duty would be imposed on the judge to stop a case which depends 'wholly or partly' on hearsay evidence which is 'unconvincing'.

1.75 This package was hardly revolutionary. Of the nine main elements it contained, most involved readjustments of the existing rules, and only two ((e) and (h) in the list above) involved any really substantial change. To those who could not conceive of a legal world without the hearsay rule, this conservatism was reassuring. But for those who were hoping for something more radical, the mountain, after prolonged and painful labour, had given birth to a mouse.

1.76 Naturally, the main disappointment for the radicals was the basic decision to retain a system composed of an exclusionary rule, subject to a long list of detailed exceptions. But for them, the scheme was open to particular criticism on three other more specific grounds.

1.77 One was the Law Commission's summary dismissal of the 'directness principle' as a possible alternative. In the Report this was discussed at length, and rejected, inter alia, because the overwhelming majority of those who had responded to the Consultation Paper were opposed to it. But as the earlier Consultation Paper had earlier written it off in a few brief lines as a German invention, appropriate to 'the inquisitorial system' but incompatible with 'the accusatorial system', a negative response was hardly surprising.

1.78 The second ground was the refusal of the Law Commission to accept the need for a system for taking the evidence of witnesses who are likely to die, forget or disappear ahead of trial. Under the Law Commission's scheme, the only mechanism for this purpose was the eventual use, at trial, of the statement that the witness originally gave to the police, which, unlike a deposition taken formally before a judge or magistrate, is not on oath, is not subject to cross-examination and (if recorded in writing) is subject to the risk of transmission errors. (This point is taken up in Chapter 2.)

1.79 The third ground was the decision to retain the 'rule against narrative'. The only justification for the rule against narrative is that it is essential in order to protect the court against a torrent of repetitive evidence that is superfluous—an argument which the Law Commission, having rejected it when looking at justifications for the hearsay rule proper,[111] then surprisingly resurrected as a good reason for retaining the rule against narrative.

1.80 The government, having announced that it accepted the Law Commission's scheme, then took no steps to implement it, and it began to look as if the Law Commission's Report would suffer the same fate as that of the CLRC a quarter of a century earlier. Meanwhile, the government had commissioned Lord Justice Auld to review the whole of criminal procedure, and in October 2001 his Review of the Criminal Courts was published.[112]

1.81 Auld LJ was critical of the Law Commission's scheme:

> The Law Commission's proposals for relaxation of the rule against hearsay, looked at individually, represent useful improvements on the present law. They relax some of the rigidity of the present rule through a widening of the exceptions and the introduction of the limited inclusionary discretion. However, their implementation would not significantly change the present landscape nor, I believe, remove much of the scope for dispute that disfigures and interrupts our present trial process.[113]

1.82 The 'rule against narrative', he said, should clearly be abolished. In his view:

> Where a witness has made a prior statement, in written or recorded form, it should be admissible as evidence of any matter stated in it of which his direct oral evidence in the proceedings would be admissible provided he authenticates it as his statement; an integral part of the new rule should be that a defendant's previous statement should in principle be admissible whether it supports or damages his case[114] and the fact that it may appear to be self-serving should go only to weight; and the witness should be permitted, where appropriate, to adopt the statement in the witness box as his evidence in chief.[115]

[111] See § 1.32 above. And compare the views of the Law Reform Committee on this, expressed 40 years earlier (see n 89 above) § 10: 'As respects the danger of the prolongation of evidence, we think that this can easily be exaggerated. The Evidence Act of 1938 itself presented such a possibility, but it has not happened. Litigation is conducted by lawyers, and with the object of winning. It is each party's intent to adduce that evidence which has the highest probative value of any disputed fact in issue which he desires to establish and, where direct oral evidence of such a fact is available, he will, we think, continue to call it. Safeguards against his seeking to buttress this unreasonably by superfluous hearsay can be devised'.

[112] *Review of the Criminal Courts of England and Wales: Report* (London, The Stationery Office, October 2001).

[113] *Ibid* ch 11, § 102 (page 559).

[114] Which, as Auld LJ pointed out, had been the position at common law until the nineteenth century, and had been incorporated by Stephen into the Indian Evidence Act as late as 1872: *ibid* ch 11, § 91 (pages 553–4).

[115] *Ibid* ch 11, § 92 (pages 554–5).

1.83 As regards the hearsay rule itself, the way forward, he suggested, was to abandon the traditional approach of an exclusionary rule plus a list of exceptions, and to replace it by a rule that made hearsay admissible where it was the best evidence available—along the lines of the 'directness principle', which the Law Commission had rejected.

1.84 The Law Commission's objections to the 'directness principle' (also called the 'best evidence principle') Auld LJ found unconvincing. A 'best evidence' rule, the Law Commission had said, would be difficult for the courts to police; but, said Auld, 'if our courts are expected to police an exclusionary system hedged with exceptions, they could surely do the same with a system based on the availability of the witness'.[116] The Law Commission predicted that, if the hearsay rule and the rule against narrative were abolished, the courts would be swamped by evidence of poor quality; but in this, said Auld, they had underestimated the ability of the criminal courts 'to restrict where appropriate the use of unhelpful or simply repetitious hearsay by the mechanism of judicial permission'.[117] The Law Commission's view that such a rule was unworkable in 'the accusatorial system' failed to take account of the fact that 'the boundaries between the adversarial and inquisitorial systems of trial are blurring', and that 'judges and magistrates are assuming an increasingly active role in the preparation of cases for trial and becoming more interventionist in the course of it than has been traditional'.[118] Nor was he impressed with the Law Commission's clinching argument against a reform along these lines, which was 'the change of attitude that this option would require on the part of practitioners and judges':[119]

> Whilst respect should be given to the views of judges and practitioners trained in and with long experience of the present system, their resistance to a particular form of change should not hold sway if there is otherwise a compelling case for it.[120]

1.85 Still more radically, Auld LJ thought that there was a strong case for introducing a system under which, when serious crimes are being investigated, police interviews with witnesses are routinely audio- or video-recorded, and the recording is then admitted in evidence at the trial, either to supplement the witness's oral evidence-in-chief or, where appropriate, to replace it.

[116] *Ibid* ch 11, § 104 (page 560).
[117] *Ibid* ch 11, § 89 (page 552); § 104 (page 560).
[118] *Ibid* ch 11, § 104 (page 560).
[119] LC Report, n 32 above, § 6.32.
[120] Auld Review, n 112 above, ch 11, § 104 (page 560).

Reform: Criminal Justice Act 2003, Part 11, Chapter 2

1.86 Confronted with two contradictory proposals for reform, the government might have been expected to select one or other. But instead of doing this, it looked for a 'third way'. The clauses relating to hearsay in the Criminal Justice Bill that was introduced into the House of Commons in November 2002 were a compromise, in which the Law Commission's scheme and Auld LJ's proposals had been stitched together: a scheme one commentator pithily described as 'dishing up the Law Commission's very traditional repast with a dollop of Auld's best evidence on top'.[121]

1.87 In essence, the reform proposed in the Criminal Justice Bill was the Law Commission's scheme, as drafted in the Draft Bill annexed to its Report, complete with a reworked version of the exclusionary rule, retention of the 'rule against narrative' and the other elements listed in § 1.74 above. But there were three significant deviations.

1.88 The first was in the way in which the ban on hearsay was presented. In the Law Commission's Draft Bill, this was set out in the opening sentence of the first clause in uncompromising terms: 'In criminal proceedings, a statement not made in oral evidence in the proceedings is *not* admissible as evidence of any matter stated *unless* . . .' In the Criminal Justice Bill, the tone had become slightly more positive: 'In criminal proceedings a statement not made in oral evidence *is* admissible as evidence of any matter stated *if*, and only if . . .'. It was in this subtly more permissive form that it eventually become law in CJA 2003, section 114(1).[122]

1.89 The second deviation concerned the new 'inclusionary discretion'. This the Law Commission had called the 'safety-valve' and had tucked away discreetly after the clauses in its Draft Bill containing the specific exceptions to the rule. But the government brought it out of its hiding-place and resited it in a prominent spot, next to the restatement of the exclusionary rule itself. Thus, the first clause that dealt with hearsay (now the first section of this chapter of the CJA 2003)[123] set out the exclusionary rule, and then listed (in outline) four exceptions, the fourth of which was the 'inclusionary discretion'. In its new and prominent position, the Law Commission's designation no longer seemed to fit: instead of being a 'safety-valve', for use in emergency when all else fails, it now looked more like an alternative tap, which a court could open whenever it felt appropriate.

[121] Di Birch, 'Hearsay: Same Old Story, Same Old Song?' [2004] Crim LR 556, 569.
[122] Emphasis added.
[123] CJA 2003, s 114.

1.90 The third modification was the addition, under the bland heading 'Miscellaneous and Supplemental', of Auld LJ's radical proposal about the use in evidence at trial of audio- and video-recordings of police interviews with witnesses, which in due course became CJA 2003, sections 137 and 138.

1.91 In the House of Commons the hearsay provisions had a relatively easy passage,[124] but then ran into choppy water in the House of Lords. There the scheme came under simultaneous attack from two opposite directions. A group of Liberal Democrat peers led by Lord Thomas of Gresford, QC, opposed the scheme because it went too far: to give the court a general inclusionary discretion, they said, was to introduce an 'unsafe and uncertain principle', which might lead to miscarriages of justice. And approaching the matter from the other end, a group of legal peers led by Lord Cooke of Thorndon[125] complained that the scheme did not go far enough. In taking this position, Lord Cooke quoted from a memorandum on the Bill prepared by the Lord Chief Justice and the other senior judges on the criminal side.

1.92 In this memorandum the judges had said:

> We question whether the complexity of the [hearsay] provisions is necessary. What has happened is that the complex common law rules are being replaced by complex statutory rules, some of which are a repetition of the common law rules.
>
> What happens now in civil proceedings is that a judge has a general discretion to determine how matters are to be proved. The judge has to exercise the discretion in the interests of justice. He is assisted in doing this, because the probative value of the evidence depends upon its nature and source. If it is not first-hand evidence, then it has the disadvantage that it has not been tested by cross-examination. Whether this matters depends on the circumstances. If we have got to the stage where it is considered that it is safe to allow juries to hear evidence, then we must be accepting that they can be trusted to use that evidence in accordance with the directions of the judge. Instead of the detailed and complex provisions which are contained in Chapter 2 [of the Bill], what is needed is a simple rule putting the judge in charge of what evidence is admissible and giving him the responsibility of ensuring that the jury use the evidence in an appropriate manner.[126]

Under this two-pronged attack, the key clause, containing the restatement of the exclusionary rule and an outline list of the exceptions, on which the rest of the hearsay provisions depend, was solemnly deleted from the Bill.[127] After some

[124] Where they were the subject of a focussed but good-tempered scrutiny before Standing Committee B, on 28 January 2003: Hansard, Session 2002–3, Standing Committee B, cols 595–686.

[125] Vigorously supported by Lord Ackner, who as one of the majority judges in *Kearley* had helped to bring about the problems which the reform was designed to correct—who had evidently taken a walk along the Damascus Road in the interval!

[126] The key parts of the Memorandum were published in Michael Zander, 'Lord Woolf's Criticisms of Mr Blunkett's Criminal Justice Bill' (2003) 153 *New Law Journal* 1228 and 1264.

[127] Hansard, HL vol 652, col 1124 (18 September 2003).

urgent last-minute consultation, the government eventually found a slightly different formula which both the House of Commons and the two groups of attackers in the Lords were prepared to accept, and in this doctored form the vital clause was restored to the Bill the day before it received the Royal Assent.[128] (Details of the drafting changes are set out in § 5.5 below).

1.93 The Criminal Justice Bill received the Royal Assent on 20 November 2003, and most of the hearsay provisions were brought into force on 4 April 2005.[129] A notable exception, however, are sections 137 and 138, which carry out Auld LJ's proposal in relation to audio- and video-recordings (see § 1.85 above), which at the time of writing are still not in force, and no commencement date has yet been announced.

1.94 The provisions were extended to Northern Ireland by the Criminal Justice (Evidence) (Northern Ireland) Order 2004,[130] the relevant parts of which came into force on 18 April 2005.[131] There, as in England and Wales, the articles relating to recorded evidence are not yet in force.

Conclusion: provisional assessment of the reform

1.95 How far has the 2003 reform cured the problems with the hearsay rule which existed previously?

1.96 As we have seen (§§ 1.39–1.49 above), the Law Commission listed a number difficulties with the existing law: it was excessively complicated, and in consequence time-wasting; it caused cogent evidence to be excluded, and so led to miscarriages of justice; it made it harder for witnesses to give their evidence; it was arbitrary, leaving key decisions on vital pieces of evidence to the discretion of the court; it was undiscriminating; and it was dubiously compatible with the European Convention on Human Rights.

[128] Hansard, HL vol 654, col 2005 (19 November 2003).

[129] CJA 2003, ss 114–131 and 133–136: Criminal Justice Act 2003 (Commencement No .8 and Transitional and Saving Provisions) Order 2005, SI 2005/950; ss 139–141: Criminal Justice Act 2003 (Commencement No .3 and Transitional and Saving Provisions) Order 2004, SI 2004/829. Section 132, which confers a power to make Criminal Procedure Rules, came into force on 20 January 2004: Criminal Justice Act 2003 (Commencement No. 2 and Saving Provisions) Order 2004, SI 2004/81.

[130] SI 2004/1501 (NI 10).

[131] Criminal Justice (Evidence) (Northern Ireland) Order 2004 (Commencement No 2) Order 2005, SI 2004/242.

1.97 Some of these problems have been addressed by the reform, but it responds less adequately to others.

1.98 By cutting back the scope of the exclusionary rule, extending the exceptions and creating a new 'inclusionary discretion' enabling the court to admit cogent hearsay that still manages to fall outside the revised exceptions, the CJA 2003 has (one hopes) eliminated the risk of miscarriages of justice caused by the exclusion of evidence that is cogent and reliable. In practical terms this was the most serious criticism of the earlier law, and that it has been answered is altogether to the good. The reform also deals with the problem that the previous law was undiscriminating, in that once hearsay was admitted, however weak it was, the law placed no limit on the use that could be made of it. This is met (at least as regards trials on indictment) by section 125 of the Act, which requires the judge in a jury trial to stop a case where the only prosecution evidence is hearsay that is insubstantial. By relaxing the exclusionary rule to let more hearsay evidence in, whilst also putting a restriction on the use that can then be made of it if it is weak, the CJA 2003 also seems to meet the criticism that the previous law was incompatible with the European Convention.[132]

1.99 The reform scores less well on the issue of complexity. To some extent, the law resulting from the reform is less complex than it was. The slaughter of all the common law exceptions to the hearsay rule other than those explicitly preserved by section 118, for example, is a simplification, and this simplification is reflected in the books: *Cross on Evidence*, which before the reform needed 228 pages to explain the hearsay rule, is now able to cover it in 122; and *Blackstone's Criminal Practice*, which used to need 115, now does the job in 90. But if easier than it was, the law is still far from simple, and it is questionable whether it needs to be as complicated as it is. The hearsay provisions of the CJA 2003 employ nearly 6,500 words, and some of its sections are dense and complex. By contrast, in New Zealand, the Evidence Act 2006 has managed to rewrite the law on hearsay (for civil and well as criminal proceedings) in just over 1,250 words. And the provisions of that Act, by contrast, are simple, and easy to understand.[133]

1.100 There are also two problems in the Law Commission's list which the reform does not address at all. The first is the criticism that the law is arbitrary because it leaves too much to the discretion of the court. The second is the criticism that the exclusionary rule makes it harder than it need be for witnesses to give their evidence.

[132] See § 1.49 above.

[133] The central provision is NZ Evidence Act, s 18(2), which is as follows: '(1) A hearsay statement is admissible in any proceedings if (a) the circumstances relating to the statement provide reasonable assurance that the statement is reliable; and (b) either (i) the maker of the statement is unavailable as a witness; or (b) the Judge considers that undue expense or delay would be caused if the maker of the statement were required to be a witness'.

1.101 Excessive judicial discretion was something that the Law Commission identified as a problem, and with that in mind, drafted the new 'unavailability' and 'records' exceptions to ensure that any evidence that fell within them would be 'automatically admissible'. However, what the reform gives with one hand it takes away with the other, because the hearsay provisions of the CJA 2003 are packed with new discretionary elements. In section 116, which in principle makes the hearsay admissible automatically where the maker is 'unavailable', a judicial discretion to exclude is provided for the case where the maker is 'unavailable' through fear. Another judicial discretion to exclude is built into section 121, which deals with multiple hearsay. Section 126 gives the court a general discretion to exclude hearsay evidence that is otherwise admissible, where it is satisfied that admitting it would be a waste of time; and for good measure, also provides that nothing in this part of the Act prejudices either PACE 1984, section 78 or any other power of the court to exclude evidence in its discretion. As well as all these different discretionary powers to exclude, CJA 2003, section 114(1)(d), as we have seen, gives the court a correspondingly wide 'inclusionary discretion'.

1.102 The problem that the hearsay rule confuses witnesses when giving evidence was minimised by the Law Commission in its Report, saying that today 'any sensible judge' would allow a witness to continue his story uninterrupted, 'provided naturally that the recounted hearsay does not provide apparent evidence of some material fact'.[134] However, this does not really answer the objection. Not all judges, or magistrates, are sensible—and much less all advocates, some of whom may raise objections, and so interrupt a witness, even if the court then allows him to carry on. As a matter of principle, it does not give a legal rule a clean bill of health if sensible judges are obliged to bend it to ensure that justice is done. It is possible, however, that the other changes in the 2003 reform will introduce a 'culture change' towards hearsay evidence, as a result of which objections of this sort are taken less often than they were.

1.103 The most significant defect of the reform, however, is that it fails to deal with the more basic criticisms of the earlier law: that the rule against hearsay in general, and the rule against narrative in particular, are fundamentally illogical; and that the list of exceptions to them that the law provides lack any underlying unifying principle.

1.104 Although the new law on hearsay that emerges from the CJA 2003 is better than the old, the reform (like the Law Commission's Report on which it is mainly based) is backward-looking in spirit, and displays little sense of where English criminal procedure has come from, or the direction in which it is currently evolving.

[134] LC Report, n 32 above, § 4.56.

1.105 The impetus for the creation of the hearsay rule, as we saw at the beginning of this chapter, was the desire to improve the position of the defendant in a system of criminal procedure where the cards were stacked against him to a degree which, by modern standards, seems barely credible. If fundamentally irrational, in the context of criminal procedure as it then was, the hearsay rule was a corrective in which there was some basic sense.

1.106 As various writers have pointed out,[135] at the time the hearsay rule arose, English criminal procedure was dominated by the following three features:

—the fact-finders were usually a jury of lay people, who gave no reason for their decision; and so there was no effective means of making sure that they did not give excessive weight to weak evidence, once they had heard it;

—the process of fact-finding was concentrated at a brief trial, for which there was little preparation, and no possibility of adjournment, and hence if a hearsay statement was admitted, there was no practical possibility of tracking down the original maker of a statement to check whether what he had said was true;

—the procedure was adversarial, in the sense that the court system left the parties to decide what evidence should be produced and took no official responsibility for the discovery of the truth.

1.107 Since those days, all three features have been heavily eroded. First, there is a clear move towards fact-finders giving reasons for decisions. In practice, most contested trials now take place in the magistrates' courts, which are now expected to explain what evidence they accepted and acted on, and within limits, why;[136] and although juries still give unreasoned verdicts, it must be questionable how long this can remain.[137] Secondly, the criminal courts, unlike their predecessors even 50 years ago, are now in permanent session, and trials (insofar as they still happen) no longer occur 'out of the blue', but as the culmination of a pre-trial phase, part of the purpose of which is to control the quality and quantity of the evidence that is eventually produced at the final stage. Thirdly, it is now part of the official philosophy that the primary purpose of criminal procedure is to deal with cases justly, which means first and foremost acquitting the innocent and convicting the guilty, and the courts have a duty to act positively to secure this end.[138]

1.108 Against this background, the reform of hearsay in the CJA 2003 looks anachronistic. In its defence, however, it may be that it achieved as much as was

[135] M Damaska, *Evidence Law Adrift* (New Haven, Yale University Press, 1997); Jackson, n 77 above.

[136] *R (McGowan) v Brent Justices* [2001] EWHC Admin 814, (2002) 166 JP 29, [2002] Crim LR 413.

[137] See Auld Review, n 112 above, ch 5, § 88–§ 98 (pp 168–73).

[138] Criminal Procedure Rules 2005, Rule 1.1 ('the overriding objective').

politically acceptable at the time; and there can be no doubt that the resulting law is, at any rate, a good deal better than it was.[139]

Date of entry into force

1.109 As previously mentioned, most of the hearsay provisions in the CJA 2003 were brought into force on 4 April 2005.[140] Section 141 of the CJA 2003 provides that 'No provision of this Part' has effect in relation to criminal proceedings begun before the commencement of that provision'; and in *Singh*[141] the Court of Appeal held that, when properly construed, 'criminal proceedings' means 'trials', with the result that the new law applies in any trial that began after the commencement date, irrespective of when the prosecution was commenced.

1.110 If the trial begins after the commencement date, the fact that the alleged offence took place at some earlier date is, of course, irrelevant. Thus, in one 'historic abuse' case, the new law on hearsay was applied to evidence in relation to incidents that had allegedly occurred between1962 and 1979.[142]

139 See IH Dennis, *The Law of Evidence* (3rd edn, London, Sweet & Maxwell, 2007) 696–7.

140 See n 128 above.

141 [2006] EWCA Crim 660, [2006] 1 WLR 1564 [**page 298 below**], applying the same reasoning as it had earlier adopted in relation to the bad character evidence provisions in *Bradley* [2005] 1 Cr App R 24 (397); see JR Spencer, *Evidence of Bad Character* (Oxford, Hart, 2006) §§ 1.67–1.71.

142 *Ely* [2005] EWCA Crim 3248.

2

HEARSAY AND THE EUROPEAN CONVENTION ON HUMAN RIGHTS

The confrontation principle

2.1 It is generally accepted that an essential requirement for a fair trial is an opportunity for the defendant to challenge his accusers. This is often called the 'right to confrontation'.[1]

2.2 The 'right to confrontation' is related to the hearsay rule, but it is distinct from it. The hearsay rule is a rule to the effect that disputed facts may not be proved except by oral evidence, and as such, restricts the means of proof available to both prosecution and defence. The 'right to confrontation', by contrast, is something that belongs to the defendant only: it is purely one-sided. However, as was explained in Chapter 1, one of the traditional justifications for the hearsay rule has always been that it protects the defendant's right to confrontation; although as a tool for this purpose, it is something of a sledge-hammer to crack a legal egg.

2.3 In the common law world, the importance of the right to confrontation, and the self-evident injustice of refusing it, is traditionally illustrated by the trial of Sir Walter Raleigh in 1603.[2] Raleigh was accused of treason, having allegedly involved himself in a plot to put Arabella Stuart on the throne in place of James I. The prosecution evidence consisted almost entirely of a written 'confession' obtained from Lord Cobham, a supposed co-conspirator, who in the course of his examination by the Council had named Raleigh as involved. Raleigh sought to have Cobham called to court to testify on oath. His request was refused, on the ground that if Cobham were required to give oral evidence he might then retract

[1] See generally S Maffei, *The European Right to Confrontation in Criminal Proceedings* (Groningen, Europa Law Publishing, 2006) ch 1. Ben Emmerson and Andrew Ashworth, *Human Rights and Criminal Justice* (2nd edn, London, Sweet & Maxwell, 2007) §§ 15–121 to 15–149; Andrew Choo, *Hearsay and Confrontation in Criminal Trials* (Oxford, Clarendon Press 1996).

[2] *Howell's State Trials*, vol II, col 1, at col 18.

his earlier statement (!) Warburton J said 'My Lord Cobham hath perhaps been laboured [pressured] in that, and to save you, his old friend, it may be that he will deny all that he hath said'. On the strength of Cobham's statement to the Council, Raleigh was duly convicted of treason and, 15 years later, executed.

2.4 In the USA, the 'right to confrontation' is expressly protected by the Sixth Amendment to the Constitution which, among other guarantees, provides that:

> In all criminal prosecutions, the accused shall enjoy the right . . . to be confronted with the witnesses against him.

In the USA, this right has been interpreted in the most literal sense of requiring prosecution witnesses to give their evidence in the physical presence of the accused, on the theory that 'It is always more difficult to tell a lie about a person "to his face" than behind his back'.[3]

2.5 But this reasoning is deeply suspect. It is harder to tell lies about other people in their presence than behind their back, but it is also harder to tell the truth, particularly if it is unpleasant; and the physical presence of the person spoken of, though it may make it uncomfortable for the speaker, does not make it any more likely that his words are true.[4] Asking the speaker awkward questions about his evidence at the instance of the defendant does indeed enable the truth of his story to be tested. But for this, it is not necessary for the witness and the defendant to be physically together, much less for them to be in eye-contact.

2.6 In the United Kingdom, as in the USA, the right to confrontation is thought to be important. But here it has never been thought essential for the defendant to be physically present. In practice it is the usual arrangement: but it is one that can be departed from if the defendant's presence inhibits the witness from testifying freely. The judges, many years ago, took the initiative in this respect,[5] and the possibilities they created were later extended by Parliament.[6] In *R (D) v Camberwell Green Youth Court*[7] the House of Lords held that special measures of this sort are compatible both with the English law tradition and Article 6 of the European Convention on Human Rights (ECHR).

[3] Per Scalia J in *Coy v Iowa* 108 S Ct 2798 (1988).

[4] For a fuller discussion see JR Spencer and R Flin, *The Evidence of Children, the Law and the Psychology* (2nd edn, London, Blackstone Press, 1993) 277–9.

[5] *Smellie* (1919) 14 Cr App R 128; *X, Y and Z* (1990) 91 Cr App R 36.

[6] Youth Justice and Criminal Evidence Act 1999, Pt II ('special measures').

[7] [2005] UKHL 4, [2005] 1 WLR 393.

ECHR, Article 6(3)(d)

2.7 It was in this more muted English form that the defendant's 'right to confrontation' found its way into the European Convention on Human Rights in 1951. So far as relevant, Article 6 of the Convention is as follows (emphasis added):

1. In the determination of his civil rights and obligations or of any criminal charge against him, everyone is entitled to *a fair and public hearing* within a reasonable time by an independent and impartial tribunal established by law . . .
2. Everyone charged with a criminal offence shall be presumed innocent until proved guilty according to law.
3. *Everyone charged with a criminal offence has the following minimum rights: . . .*

d. *to examine or have examined witnesses against him* and to obtain the attendance and examination of witnesses on his behalf under the same conditions as witnesses against him.

2.8 The scope and implications of Article 6(3)(d) were first considered by the European Court of Human Rights (Strasbourg Court) in *Unterpertinger v Austria*[8] in 1986. In this case the applicant, Unterpertinger, was accused of beating his wife and step-daughter. Although both women had given statements to the police, both refused to give evidence at trial, making use of a privilege in Austrian law to refuse to testify against close relatives, whereupon the court accepted their witness statements as evidence and convicted him on those. At no stage in the proceedings had Unterpertinger been able to put questions to his accusers, and the Strasbourg Court held that the resulting conviction infringed his rights under Article 6(3)(d). Since then, the provision has been considered on many occasions, creating a body of case law of which only the outline can be given here.[9]

2.9 At first, those concerned with English criminal law tended to overlook the Convention. Thus, in 1993 the Runciman Commission made no mention of the ECHR from end to end, and the Commission recommended, in the interests of efficiency and saving trouble for witnesses, the wider use in evidence of police witness statements.[10] But with the advent of the Human Rights Act in 1998 this

[8] (1986) Series A no 110; reported in (1991) 13 EHRR 175.

[9] *Barbera, Messegue and Jabardo v Spain* (1989) 11 EHRR 360; *Bricmont v Belgium* (1990) 12 EHRR 217; *Kostovski v The Netherlands* (1990) 12 EHRR 434; *Windisch v Austria* (1990) 13 EHRR 281; *Isgro v Italy* (1990) Series A/194; *Artner v Austria* (1992) Series A/242a; *Delta v France* (1993) 16 EHRR 574; *Asch v Austria* (1993) 15 EHRR 597; *Ludi v Switzerland* (1993) 15 EHRR 173; *Saidi v France* (1994) 17 EHRR 251; *Doorson v The Netherlands* (1996) 22 EHRR 330; *Trivedi v United Kingdom*, Application no 31700/96; *AM v Italy* [1999-IX] RJD 45; *Lucà v Italy* (2003) 36 EHRR 46; *Ferrantelli and Santangelo v Italy* (1997) 23 EHRR 288; *Van Mechelen v The Netherlands* (1998) 25 EHRR 647; *Birutis and others v Lithuania*, Application nos 47698/99 and 48115/99, 28 March 2002; *PS v Germany* (2003) 36 EHRR 61; *Papageorgiou v Greece* (2003) 38 EHRR 30; *SN v Sweden* (2004) 39 EHRR 13; *Rachdad v France*, Application no 71846/01, 13 November 2003; *Gunes v Turkey* (2006) 43 EHRR 15; *Eskelinen v Finland* (2007) 45 EHRR 1.

[10] Report of the Royal Commission on Criminal Justice (Chairman: Viscount Runciman of Doxford) (Cm 2263, 1993) § 44.

quickly changed. By section 3 of that Act, the courts must, so far as possible, interpret primary legislation 'in a way which is compatible with Convention rights'; and by section 6, public authorities (including courts) are forbidden to act 'in a way which is incompatible with a Convention right'. In consequence, Article 6(3)(d) of the ECHR and its attendant case law are now treated as highly relevant to the decisions of the English courts.

2.10 In the context of Article 6 of the Convention, the Strasbourg Court does not lay down detailed rules. On many occasions it has made it clear that the Contracting States are free, within broad limits, to build their laws of evidence as they wish:

> While Article 6 guarantees the right to a fair hearing, it does not lay down any rules on the admissibility of evidence as such, which is therefore primarily a matter for regulation under national law.[11]

2.11 Furthermore, the Strasbourg Court does not look at Article 6(3)(d) in isolation, but treats compliance with it as just one element in the broader question of whether the defendant has received 'a fair trial'. And in consequence:

> no clear distinction has been drawn between the 'overall' concept of a fair trial and the specific provisions concerning the taking and assessment of testimonial evidence. This is why it is so difficult to ascertain whether the [Strasbourg Court] rulings are specifically grounded upon evidential arguments or upon a rather nebulous assessment of judicial fairness.[12]

2.12 Nor, when examined minutely, is all the Strasbourg Court case law entirely consistent in terms of outcome. The result in the *Unterpertinger* decision, for example, is difficult to square with the later case of *Asch v Austria*,[13] another domestic violence case where, on facts very similar to those in *Unterpertinger*, the Strasbourg Court (by a majority) rejected the complaint, observing, inter alia, that in this sort of case the defendant's right under Article 6(3)(d) 'cannot be allowed to block the prosecution'.[14]

2.13 That said, however, some broad guidelines from the Strasbourg Court case law do emerge. In the next sections of the chapter the case law will be examined in order to discover the answer to the following three questions: (i) Who constitutes a 'witness' for the purposes of Article 6(3)(d)? (ii) What is meant by 'a right to examine or have examined' a witness as so defined? and (iii) To what extent, if any, is it ever possible to base a conviction on the evidence of a witness or witnesses

[11] Eg *Khan v United Kingdom* (2001) 31 EHRR 45 at [34].

[12] Maffei, n 1 above, 68.

[13] (1993) 15 EHRR 597.

[14] The wording of the French text is 'ne saurait auboutir à paralyser des poursuites', which sounds even more dramatic.

whom the defendant was unable 'to examine or have examined' without infringing his rights under Article 6(3)(d)?

Who is a 'witness' for the purposes of ECHR, Article 6(3)(d)?

2.14 In a narrow sense, a 'witness' is a person who comes to court to give evidence, and this, indeed, is the meaning which the American courts until recently gave the term in the context of the 'right to confrontation' in the Sixth Amendment. According to the case law over many years, the defendant's right to confrontation only extended to those who were called to testify against him at the trial, and if the out-of-court statement of an absent witness was admitted in evidence against him under an exception to the hearsay rule, he was unable to complain of an infringement of his Sixth Amendment rights. In 2004, however, the US Supreme Court changed direction, and took the position that the defendant's right to confrontation could in principle be infringed by the admission of hearsay evidence.[15]

2.15 The Strasbourg Court, by contrast, has always interpreted the word 'witness' as including anyone who has made a formal statement to the authorities which the prosecution then put in evidence at trial. This point was implicit in the *Unterperinger* decision, and then made explicitly in a number of the cases that followed it.[16] In that case, and many others like it, the person who made the statement was the alleged victim of the offence; but the same principle applies where the source of the information is a co-defendant, who 'grasses up' his colleague during the investigation. He too counts as a 'witness'.[17]

2.16 However, all of those whom the Strasbourg Court has so far categorised as 'witnesses' have been persons who fed information, consciously and voluntarily, into a criminal justice system, the ears of which were officially open to them. In English terms, the cases are about depositions to magistrates, or witness statements made to the police.[18] It does not follow from this that the Strasbourg Court would treat it as a statement from a 'witness' (and therefore trigger the defendant's right to question the person concerned) if another witness, giving oral evidence, casually repeated a remark that a third party had made to him; as where a policeman giving evidence says 'The landlord of the Red Lion told me that Smith had gone to the church with a ladder, so I went there, and found him on the roof stripping the

[15] *Crawford v Washington* 124 S Ct 1354 (2004).

[16] *Kostovski v The Netherlands* at [40]; *Delta v France* at [34]; *Artner v Austria* at [19]; *Windisch v Austria* at [23] (all at n 9 above).

[17] *Lucà v Italy* (2003) 36 EHRR 46 at [41].

[18] A point made by the Court of Appeal in *Owen* [2001] EWCA Crim 1018: see § 2.38 below.

lead'.[19] A remark like this would, of course, fall foul of the hearsay rule in England. But it would be considered unobjectionable in courts in continental Europe, and it seems unlikely that the Strasbourg Court would say that by admitting it the trial court had automatically infringed the defendant's rights under Article 6(3)(d). However, if what the absent person had allegedly said was crucially important, and the court then blocked the attempt to have him called as a witness, this might be treated as a denial of the defendant's general right to a 'fair trial'.[20]

2.17 Much less is it likely that the Strasbourg Court would consider that Article 6(3)(d) was automatically infringed by the use in evidence of documents, other than depositions or police witness statements: for example, trade or business records which reveal transactions which are part of the ingredients of the offence charged. In fact, in the context of Article 6(3)(d), the Strasbourg Court case law seems to equate 'documents' with 'witnesses': the prosecution are free to use such documents as evidence, but must allow the defence a proper chance to examine them. In *Papageorgiou v Greece*,[21] the applicant was convicted of fraud, key pieces of prosecution evidence being cheques he had allegedly misused, and print-outs from the central computer of a bank. However, the prosecution insisted on producing photocopies of the disputed cheques rather than the originals, and written affidavits from the bank's computer staff about the operation of the computer, rather than the staff themselves as witnesses and the Greek courts upheld this stance. At Strasbourg this was held to infringe the defendant's rights under Article 6(3)(d).

2.18 Unlike English law, many foreign legal systems treat expert witnesses (as we would call them) as a special category, 'experts', and in some cases they are called not by the parties but by the court. In *Eskelinen v Finland*,[22] in which a national prosecuting authority had put in evidence as part of its case a written opinion on the meaning of the relevant law from a legal expert whom the defendant did not have a chance to question at the trial, the Strasbourg Court expressed the view that although Article 6(3)(d) gives the defendant the right to examine 'witnesses', it does not give him an automatic right to examine 'experts' too; although the Court also said that if the defence is not allowed a chance to contest the opinion of an expert, the result may be to undermine his general right to a fair trial under ECHR, Article 6(1).

[19] Law Commission, *Evidence in Criminal Proceedings and Related Matters* (Consultation Paper No 138, 1995) (hereafter 'LC Consultation Paper') § 5.9.

[20] See *Vidal v Belgium*, Application no 12351/86, 22 April 1992, (1992) Series A/235b.

[21] See n 9 above.

[22] (2007) 45 EHRR 1.

What is meant by 'a right to examine or have examined witnesses against him'?

2.19 *Examination by the defendant, his lawyer or the court?* Article 6(3)(d) refers to the defendant's right 'to *examine* or *have examined* the witnesses against him' (emphasis added). To an English lawyer this suggests two possibilities: the unrepresented defendant, who must be allowed to question the witness himself, and the defendant who is legally represented, whose lawyer must be allowed to put questions to the witness on his behalf. However, the phrase 'to have examined the witnesses against him' was in fact included with a different possibility in mind. In many of the Contracting States, witnesses are not examined by the parties but by the presiding judge, and the phrase was included to make it plain that in those systems the defendant's right is respected if he can have his questions put to the witness by the judge.[23]

2.20 Thus if, as has sometimes been proposed, the duty of examining certain types of vulnerable witness were to be given to the judge, this would not infringe the defendant's rights under the Article.[24] In *SN v Sweden*, a conviction for child abuse had been returned on the basis of tape-recorded police interviews with the complainant, before one of which the suspect's lawyer had agreed with the police officer which aspects of the case he wished to be explored. The Strasbourg Court dismissed the defendant's application, saying:

> Having regard to the special features of criminal proceedings concerning sexual offences . . ., [Article 6(3)(d)] cannot be interpreted as requiring in all cases that the questions be put directly by the accused or his or her defence counsel, through cross-examination or other means.[25]

2.21 However, if the special procedures adopted in the interests of vulnerable witnesses deprive the defendant of any chance to confront the witness with his side of the story, Article 6(3)(d) is likely to have been infringed. A contrasting case is *PS v Germany*.[26] There, the child's account of what had happened was relayed to the court via her mother and a police officer, and the court convicted the applicant on this evidence, supplemented by a report from a child psychologist who had examined the child and expressed the view that her statements were credible. At no

[23] Maffei, n 1 above, 17.

[24] As was proposed by the Pigot Committee in the case of very young or seriously traumatised children: *Report of the Advisory Committee on Video Evidence* (Home Office, 1989).

[25] See n 9 above; and cf *Magnusson v Sweden*, Application no 53972/90, [2004] Crim LR 847. For an account in English of the methods used in a range of foreign countries to deal with the evidence of children see JR Spencer, G Nicholson, R Flin and R Bull (eds), *Children's Evidence in Legal Proceedings: an International Perspective* (Cambridge Law Faculty, 1990); the text is also available on the Law Faculty website at www.law.cam.ac.uk/docs/view.php?doc=3503.

[26] See n 9 above.

point did the defence have any input into her questioning. Here the Strasbourg Court upheld the applicant's complaint.

2.22 *Waiver of the right to examine* The defendant's right to examine prosecution witnesses can of course be waived. In *SN v Sweden* the police had in fact offered the applicant's lawyer the chance to be present at the second interview, but he chosen not to do so; and, furthermore, if he was unhappy with the interview it was open to him to ask for another one, but this he had not done. In the light of this, the Strasbourg Court held that the defendant was in no position to complain that his rights under Article 6(3)(d) had been infringed.

2.23 *Examination at the trial, or at earlier hearing?* From time to time, the Strasbourg Court has made statements suggesting that, as a general rule, witnesses should give their evidence, and be subjected to examination, at the defendant's trial. In the *Barbera* case, for example, it said 'All evidence must in principle be produced in the presence of the accused at a public hearing with a view to adversarial argument'.[27]

2.24 However, the Strasbourg Court has repeatedly qualified these remarks by saying that the defendant's rights are not infringed if the court hears or reads the statements of an absent witness, provided the defence had an opportunity to put their questions at an earlier stage. In *Kostovski v The Netherlands* it said this:

> In principle, all the evidence must be produced in the presence of the accused at a public hearing with a view to adversarial argument . . . This does not mean, however, that in order to be used as evidence statements of witnesses should always be made at a public hearing in court: to use as evidence such statements obtained at a pre-trial stage is not in itself inconsistent with paragraphs 3(d) and 1 of Article 6, provided the rights of the defence have been respected.
>
> As a rule, these rights require that an accused should be given an adequate and proper opportunity to challenge and question a witness against him, either at the time the witness was making his statement or at some later stage in the proceedings.[28]

2.25 These remarks have been repeated in many later cases, to the point of becoming, it seems, a piece 'boiler-plate text' to be incorporated in every decision in which Article 6(3)(d) is discussed.[29]

2.26 Thus, if the statement was taken at a preliminary hearing at which the defence did have a chance to put questions, the Strasbourg Court does not see its

[27] *Barbera, Messegue and Jabardo v Spain*, n 9 above, [78].

[28] *Kostovski v The Netherlands*, n 9 above, [41].

[29] *Delta v France* at [36]; *Asch v Austria* at [27]; *Saidi v France* at [43]; *Windisch v Austria* at [28–31]; *Ludi v Switzerland* at [43]; *Van Mechelen v The Netherlands* at [69]; *SN v Sweden* at [44]; *Lucà v Italy* at [40] (all at n 9 above).

later use at trial as contravening the defendant's right under Article 6(3)(d). In *Isgro v Italy*,[30] for example, a key witness to a kidnapping and murder was examined by a judge at a pre-trial hearing at which Isgro, the defendant, was permitted to question him. By the time of the trial the witness had gone missing, and the trial court convicted the defendant on the basis of the absent witness's earlier statements. The Strasbourg Court rejected Isgro's complaint that Article 6(3)(d) had been infringed.[31]

2.27 *The right to examine the witness, and the legal status of his previous statements* It sometimes happens that a witness makes a statement to the police incriminating a defendant in his absence, which he then retracts when he is examined in the presence of the defendant at the trial. If the court receives evidence of the earlier statement, and acts on it, does this mean that the defendant's rights under Article 6(3)(d) have been infringed? This is an important question in England, given that one of the significant changes wrought by the CJA 2003 is in the legal status of a witness's previous inconsistent statements. Previously, they were admissible only for the purpose of undermining the credibility of the witness's oral evidence at trial, but now they are admissible as evidence of the matters of fact contained in them.[32]

2.28 This issue was one of many discussed by the Strasbourg Court in *Doorson v The Netherlands*.[33] Part of the evidence on which the Dutch courts had convicted was the statement which a witness, N, had made to the police but then retracted at the trial. Dismissing Doorson's complaint about this, the Strasbourg Court said that it:

> cannot hold in the abstract that evidence given by a witness in open court and on oath should always be relied on in preference to other statements made by the same witness in the course of criminal proceedings, even when the two are in conflict.

2.29 This remark was later applied by the Court in *Camilleri v Malta*.[34] The applicant had been convicted of drug offences committed while he was in prison, on the basis of statements which a fellow prisoner had made out of court, but then retracted at the trial. The trial court took the view that the original statements were true, and the retraction false and the result of pressure from other prisoners. Finding the application inadmissible, the Strasbourg Court said:

[30] See n 9 above.

[31] cf *Verdam v The Netherlands*, Application no 35253/97, where the ECtHR ruled inadmissible the complaint of a man who had been convicted of the rape of three prostitutes, none of whom had testified at trial, but two of whom had been questioned by the police in the presence of a defence counsel.

[32] CJA 2003, s 119. See further, Chapter 12 below.

[33] See n 9 above.

[34] Application no 51760/99, 16 March 2000. A earlier decision to similar effect is *X v Federal Republic of Germany*, Application no 8414/78, 4 July 1979, which is discussed in § 5.26 of the LC Consultation Paper, n 19 above.

> the applicant was able to call [the witness] at his trial before the court of magistrates and to cross-examine him as to the reasons which led him to make the incriminating statement. In the Court's opinion the opportunity allowed to the applicant to undermine the probative value of that statement more than compensated for any alleged disadvantage which may have resulted from the fact that the statement was made in circumstances in which he was unable to challenge its veracity. It cannot be maintained therefore that the rights of the defence were not secured at trial.

Does a conviction based on evidence from witnesses whom the defendant was unable to examine invariably infringe his rights under ECHR, Article 6(3)(d)?

2.30 A literal reading of Article 6(3)(d) suggests that the answer to this question is 'yes'. Article 6(1) guarantees the defendant a trial that is in broad terms fair, and Article 6(3) lays down certain minimum rights without which it cannot be so: of which one is the right of the defendant to 'examine or have examined the witnesses against him'. And the first cases decided by the Strasbourg Court appear to take this fundamentalist line. Thus, in the *Unterpertinger* case, the facts of which are given in § 2.8 above, the defendant's conviction on the basis of statements earlier made against him by his wife and step-daughter, who then refused to testify at trial, was unanimously held to infringe his rights even though the court had before it other evidence in the shape of medical reports, his criminal record for similar behaviour, and the fact that he had given the authorities conflicting explanations of what had happened. A case similar in spirit is *Windisch v Austria*,[35] where the defendant had been convicted of burglary on the basis of statements from two anonymous women informants, plus other evidence, including the fact that he had been seen 'casing the joint'. Upholding the applicant's complaint, the Strasbourg Court said (at [30]):

> The collaboration of the public is undoubtedly of great importance to the police in their struggle against crime. In this connection the Court notes that the Convention does not preclude reliance, at the investigation stage, on sources such as anonymous informants. However, the subsequent use of their statements by the trial court to found a conviction is another matter . . . The right to a fair administration of justice holds so prominent a place in a democratic society that it cannot be sacrificed.

2.31 Later cases, however, take a less fundamentalist approach, and tend to treat the defendant's right to examine the accusing witnesses as just one ingredient in his right to a 'fair trial', the absence of which can be made good by corroborating evidence. In *Asch v Austria*,[36] the facts of which are very similar to those in *Unterpertinger*, the Strasbourg Court, this time by a majority, held that the defend-

[35] See n 9 above.
[36] See n 9 above.

ant's Article 6(3)(d) rights had not been contravened, distinguishing the earlier case on the ground that here there was corroboration, though the items identified as such were virtually identical to the supporting evidence in *Unterpertinger*. To similar effect is *Artner v Austria*.[37] Here the applicant had been convicted of defrauding a woman, Miss L, who had vanished by the time of trial, at which her previous statements were used in substitution for her oral evidence. The Strasbourg Court rejected Artner's complaint because 'Miss L's contested statements were not the only evidence on which [the Austrian court] based its ruling'. In addition to her statements, the trial court had had before it incriminating documents, Artner's criminal record, and 'similar fact evidence' for a related offence for which he was tried and convicted in the same proceedings. In *Ferentelli and Santangelo v Italy*,[38] a murder case in which crucial evidence implicating the defendants was a statement given before his death by V, an accomplice who had committed suicide, the Strasbourg Court dismissed the complaint based Article 6(3)(d), because of other incriminating evidence, including 'the fact that all the accused had made statements implicating each other, the fact that the applicants had helped V to buy and transport the two gas bottles used in the attack . . . and the lack of a convincing alibi for either of the accused' (at [52]). And in *Trivedi v United Kingdom*,[39] where a Grimsby doctor had been convicted of defrauding the NHS by charging for non-existent visits, a key piece of evidence being a witness statement taken from an elderly patient who was too ill to testify at trial, the Commission dismissed the defendant's application because the disputed statement was corroborated by other evidence: prescription forms that appeared to be fraudulent, and for which the doctor could provide no intelligible explanation.

2.32 A factor which clearly influences the attitude of the Strasbourg Court is the reason why the defendant was unable to put his questions to the witness and, in particular, whether the authorities were at fault in the matter. The case law suggests that, if the authorities could have provided the defendant with a chance to question the witness if they had tried a little harder, then the resulting conviction will infringe Article 6(3)(d), even if the decision of the court was based in part on corroborating evidence.[40]

2.33 The case law also suggests that, in deciding whether the defendant's rights have been infringed, it is proper to consider the Convention rights of other people. In *Doorson v The Netherlands*,[41] a case primarily concerned with the related issue of witnesses who testify anonymously, the Strasbourg Court said (at [70]):

[37] See n 9 above.
[38] See n 9 above.
[39] See n 9 above.
[40] As in *Bricmont v Belgium*, n 9 above; see ECtHR judgment at [83]–[85]; cf *Barbera, Messegue and Jabardo v Spain*, n 149 above, [86] and *Gunes v Turkey*, n 9 above, [83]–[93].
[41] See n 9 above.

> It is true that Article 6 does not explicitly require the interests of witnesses in general, and those of victims called upon to testify in particular, to be taken into consideration. However, their life, liberty or security of person may be at stake, as may interests coming generally within the ambit of Article 8 of the Convention. Such interests of witnesses and victims are in principle protected by other, substantive provisions of the Convention, which imply that Contracting States should organise their criminal proceedings in such a way that those interests are not unjustifiably imperilled. Against this background, principles of fair trial also require that in appropriate cases the interests of the defence are balanced against those of witnesses or victims called upon to testify.

So if providing the defendant with a right to confront the witness would have put the witness or his family in danger, a conviction based on the witness's out-of-court statement is unlikely to infringe the defendant's Convention rights, provided it is supported by corroboration.

2.34 But how much corroboration? The Strasbourg Court sees the task of evaluating evidence as strictly for the national courts, and with that in mind, has made little attempt to specify how much, or what types of supporting evidence are sufficient to compensate for the defendant's inability to put questions in a given case. However, in *Rachdad v France*,[42] where the national court had convicted the applicant of drug offences on the basis of the witness statements of no less than six absent witnesses, the Strasbourg Court did rule that his rights under Article 6(3)(d) had been infringed, notwithstanding the fact that the statements were consistent, and the makers were independent of one another (though in this case, it should be stressed, there was no suggestion that the missing witnesses had been intimidated).

2.35 *Absent witnesses who are also anonymous*[43] The defendant's ability to challenge the credibility of a prosecution witness is obviously undermined if he does not know who he is. However, the Strasbourg Court (like the English courts)[44] are prepared to accept that the use of anonymous witnesses, within limits, does not necessarily undermine the defendant's right to a fair trial. Such use is compatible with a fair trial if anonymity for the witness is necessary to protect their Convention rights,[45] the conviction is not based solely or mainly on such evidence and the legal system has taken steps to minimise the disadvantages for the defendant. The problems posed for the defendant by anonymous witnesses are worse, of course, if they are not only anonymous but absent: if their evidence is delivered to the court as statements given to the authorities pre-trial, when the defence had no opportunity to challenge or question them. In a number cases where this was

[42] See n 9 above.
[43] Maffei, n1 above, 87–8.
[44] *Davis, Ellis and others* [2006] EWCA Crim 1155, [2006] 1 WLR 3130.
[45] See *Doorson v The Netherlands* at § 2.33 above.

the position, the Strasbourg Court has dealt with the matter in basically the same way as it does with convictions based on statements from 'unchallenged' witnesses who were merely absent: the defendant's rights under Article 6(3)(d) are infringed if the conviction is based solely or mainly on this sort of evidence, but not if it is corroborated by evidence of another type.

2.36 However, in *Birutis and others v Lithuania*[46] a stricter line was taken. Here three people had been convicted for taking part in a prison riot. The conviction of the first was based almost exclusively on statements taken from other prisoners during the investigation, who were anonymous, and whom the defendants had had no opportunity to challenge, and this, unsurprisingly, was held to infringe the applicant's Article 6(3)(d) rights. The two others were convicted on a combination of such statements and a body of other evidence. But the Strasbourg Court held that their convictions had infringed Article 6(3)(d) as well, because the national courts had failed to take a number of obvious steps to counteract the disadvantages to the defence stemming from the fact that the statements were anonymous: on the facts, they could have arranged for defence questions to be put to the witnesses, and it was open to the courts to 'examine, of their own motion, the manner and circumstances in which the anonymous statements had been obtained' (at [34]).

The English case law on ECHR, Article 6(3)(d)

2.37 The English courts are now well aware of the need to take account of Article 6 of the Convention and there is now a large a body of case law discussing Article 6(3)(d). Most of the cases were decided under the law on hearsay as it was before the 2003 reform, but the principles enunciated in them are equally applicable to the law as it now is under the CJA 2003. As might be expected, the same broad lines emerge from the English cases as emerge from cases decided in Strasbourg.

2.38 First, the courts have recognised that the scope of Article 6(3)(d) is limited. In *Owen*,[47] the defendant was accused of a conspiracy to smuggle drugs into a prison, a central piece of evidence being intercepted telephone conversations between his alleged co-conspirators in which his part in the plot had been discussed. On appeal, he claimed that the admission of this evidence infringed his rights under Article 6(3)(d); to comply with the Article, the prosecution should have called his co-conspirators as witnesses and so given him the chance to cross-examine them. Dismissing his appeal, the Court of Appeal said that the Strasbourg Court case law concerned the use of statements, given after the crime, to the

[46] See n 9 above.
[47] [2001] EWCA Crim 1018.

authorities, and Article 6(3)(d) was not engaged by the use of evidence of the type that was in issue here. Similarly, in *Xhabri*[48] the Court of Appeal said that Article 6(3)(d) was not engaged by the use in evidence of the previous statements of a prosecution witness who then gave evidence at trial. Article 6(3)(d), they said, was aimed at the use of statements made by witnesses whom the defendant was unable to cross-examine, and where as here the witness was in court to give evidence, she could be cross-examined at trial about what she had said earlier.

2.39 Secondly, an important factor in deciding whether it is proper to admit a statement from a person whom the defendant had no chance to examine is whether the prosecution made proper efforts either to secure his attendance as a witness at the trial or (insofar as this is possible) to arrange for his evidence to be taken out of court at a session where the defence were able to put questions to him. Thus in *Radak*,[49] the Court of Appeal ruled that it was not proper to admit a police witness statement taken from a witness overseas, when the prosecution, had it been more organised, could have issued letters rogatory arranging for him to make a formal deposition before a foreign judge at a hearing at which the defence would have been represented. And in *McEwan v DPP*[50] the Divisional Court held that if the prosecution, by its incompetence, had failed to secure the attendance of a key witness, the court should not 'save its bacon' by invoking its new 'inclusionary discretion'[51] to allow them to substitute the written witness statement earlier given to the police. In this situation, the proper course is for the trial to be adjourned.[52]

2.40 Thirdly, where the statement does come from a witness whom the prosecution have been genuinely unable to produce for adversarial examination, an important factor in the eyes of the English courts (as well as the Strasbourg Court) is whether the hearsay statement is merely part of a bigger evidential jigsaw implicating the defendant in the crime, or stands as the central piece of evidence against him. This point emerges from *Gokal*,[53] the first case in which the Court of Appeal considered Article 6(3)(d), although the court did not make the point explicitly. The defendant, accused of a major fraud,[54] brought an interlocutory appeal to

[48] [2005] EWCA Crim 3135, [2006] 1 Cr App R 26 [**page 283 below**].

[49] [1999] 1 Cr App R 187.

[50] [2007] EWHC 740 (Admin), 171 JP 308. In *Adams* [2007] EWCA Crim 3025, however, the Court of Appeal held (without reference to *McEwan*) that, even where the prosecution has been negligent, it was proper to admit the written statement of an absent prosecution witness whose evidence was not central to the case; and in *Sak v Crown Prosecution Service* [2007] EWHC 2886 (Admin) the Divisional Court declined to extend *McEwan* to the situation where the prosecution were not to blame for the witness's absence.

[51] Under CJA 2003, s 114(1)(d).

[52] *R (CPS) v Uxbridge Magistrates' Court* [2007] EWHC 205 (Admin), 171 JP 279.

[53] [1997] 2 Cr App R 266.

[54] The celebrated BCCI fraud, in which Gokal was the central player, a role which finally cost him a 14-year prison sentence and an order to pay £2.9 million in compensation: *Gokal* [1999] EWCA Crim 669.

challenge the judge's decision to admit in evidence a statement from one of his associates, now living abroad and unwilling to come to England to give evidence. The defendant argued that admitting this evidence would infringe his rights under Article 6(3)(d), but the Court of Appeal rejected this, saying that this question could not be decided in advance, because it was part of a broader question, namely whether his trial was fair; and deciding that question meant looking at a bigger picture which would only emerge at the trial.

2.41 To similar effect is *D*.[55] The defendant was accused of a sexual offence against an elderly woman who suffered from Alzheimer's disease, and at a preliminary hearing the judge ruled that her account of the incident could be put before the court in the form of a video-interview. The Court of Appeal, having mentioned that there was other evidence implicating him in the form of seminal stains on the victim's clothing, and a blood-stain on her pillow that corresponded to a cut on the defendant's lip,[56] upheld the ruling and rejected D's complaint that receiving the video-interview in evidence infringed his Convention rights.[57] A case similar on the facts is *Al-Khawaja*,[58] where the complainant in an indecent assault case had died before the trial, and at trial her written statement to the police was read, and the Court of Appeal held that this was compatible with the defendant's rights under Article 6(3)(d). Although this point was not stressed in the judgment, there was supporting evidence against the defendant in the form of three independent complaints of similar behaviour from three other witnesses.

2.42 Another case similar in principle is *Arnold*.[59] Here, the defendant appealed against his conviction for wounding, the prosecution case being that, when fighting drunk, he had for no apparent reason slashed a man's face with a knife. The victim was unable to identify his attacker, but a bystander gave the police a statement that implicated the defendant. Before the trial the bystander was threatened and refused to come to court, in response to which the prosecution was allowed to use his witness statement as evidence. This was not the only evidence against Arnold, however, because in the course of the same drinking-bout he had made an identical attack on someone else, who was able to identify him. So, though uttering a general warning about the undesirability of using police witness statements when their makers can be produced to give evidence at the trial, the Court of Appeal upheld Arnold's conviction, rejecting his complaint that the use of the bystander's witness statement had infringed his rights under Article 6(3)(d).

[55] [2002] EWCA Crim 990, [2002] 2 Cr App R 36 (601).
[56] *Ibid* at [11].
[57] *D* was followed in the very similar case of *Sed* [2004] EWCA Crim 1294, [2004] 1 WLR 3218.
[58] [2005] EWCA Crim 2697, [2007] 1 WLR 1079.
[59] [2004] EWCA Crim 1293.

2.43 By contrast, in *M*,[60] where the statement of the absent witness was the only evidence that implicated the defendant in a stabbing (and where, furthermore, the maker of the statement was a person whom the police had initially suspected of committing the offence himself), the Court of Appeal held that the decision to admit the evidence had infringed M's rights under Article 6.

2.44 What is the position where there is corroborating evidence, but it comes from the statement of another absent witness whom the defendant is unable to confront at trial? The Strasbourg Court case law, as we have seen, suggests that a conviction in this case would infringe the defendant's Convention rights.[61] But in the recent case of *Cole* the Court of Appeal upheld the defendant's conviction for wounding his girlfriend (who subsequently committed suicide) where the bulk of the prosecution evidence consisted of hearsay statements, some of it accounts from live witnesses of what the girlfriend (now deceased) had told them about his violence towards her, and some of it a statement from a person who claimed to have witnessed acts of violence, but who was unable to attend the trial because she was giving birth.[62]

2.45 *The problem of witness intimidation* In *Sellick and Sellick*[63] the Court of Appeal was confronted with a murder case in which where there was a considerable body of evidence against the defendants, but crucial parts of it had been delivered to the court in the form of witness statements, because four witnesses were not prepared to come to court to testify orally. The background was a 'turf war' between two violent gangs competing for the market in illegal drugs, and the four witnesses had 'gone to ground' after making statements to the police as a result, the judge found, of intimidation by the defendants and their associates.[64] The defendants argued that, although it may be compatible with Article 6(3)(d) to convict on the basis of a hearsay statement which is corroborated by evidence of a different type, it is not so where the only corroborating evidence consists of other hearsay statements from other absent witnesses. After carefully examining the Strasbourg Court case law, the Court of Appeal accepted that it seemed to suggest this. However, the Court of Appeal nevertheless rejected the defendants' arguments and dismissed their appeals. In doing so it faced the issue squarely (at [51]–[53]):

> Certainly at first sight paragraph 40 of [*Lucà v Italy*] seems to suggest that in whatever circumstances and whatever counterbalancing factors are present his statements are read

[60] [2003] EWCA Crim 357, [2003] 2 Cr App R 21 (322). The decision is not easy to reconcile with *Tahery*, § 2.46 below.

[61] See *Rachdad v France*, 2.34 above.

[62] [2007] EWCA Crim 1924, [2007] 1 WLR 2716 [**page 315 below**]. There was also a certain amount of circumstantial evidence.

[63] [2005] EWCA Crim 651, [2005] 1 WLR 3257 [**page 257 below**].

[64] The judge said he was 'sure' the defendants were responsible in one case and found it 'highly probable' in another: see [61] and [62].

there will be a breach of Article 6, if the statements are the sole or decisive evidence. Furthermore there is some support for that position in the previous authorities. But neither Lucà nor any of the other authorities were concerned with a case where a witness, whose identity was well known to a defendant, was being kept away by fear, although we must accept that the reference to Mafia-type organisations and the trials thereof in paragraph 40 shows that the court had extreme circumstances in mind.

The question we have posed to ourselves is as follows. If the [Strasbourg Court] were faced with the case of an identified witness, well known to a defendant, who was the sole witness of a murder, where a national court could be sure that the witness had been kept away by the defendant, or by persons acting for him, is it conceivable that it would hold that there were no 'counterbalancing measures' the court could take which would allow that statement to be read. If care had been taken to see that the quality of the evidence was compelling, if firm steps were taken to draw the jury's attention to aspects of that witness's credibility and if a clear direction was given to the jury to exercise caution, we cannot think that the European Court would nevertheless hold that the defendant's Article 6 rights had been infringed. In such a case, as it seems to us, it is the defendant himself who has denied himself the opportunity of examining the witnesses, so that he could not complain of an infringement of Article 6(3)(d), and the precautions would ensure compliance and fairness in compliance with Article 6(1). We for our part see no difficulty in a clear case.

More difficulty arises in cases where it is not quite so clear cut, but the court believes, to a high degree of probability, that identified witnesses are being intimidated for and on behalf of the defence . . . In our view, having regard to the rights of the victims, their families, the safety of the public in general, it still cannot be right for there to be some absolute rule that, where compelling evidence is the sole or decisive evidence, an admission in evidence of a statement must then automatically lead to defendant's rights being infringed. That would lead to a situation in which the more successful the intimidation of the witnesses, the stronger the argument becomes that the statements cannot be read. If the decisive witness can be 'got at' the case must collapse. The more subtle and less easily established intimidation provides defendants with the opportunity of excluding the most material evidence against them. Such an absolute right cannot have been intended by the European Court in Strasbourg.

2.46 The decision was applied soon afterwards in *Campbell*,[65] where the facts were similar, except that here almost the entire evidence against the defendant consisted of the hearsay statement of one single witness who had apparently been intimidated. And it was applied again in *Tahery*,[66] where (as in *Campbell*) the hearsay statement was from the one key witness whose evidence clearly pointed to the defendant, and where (as in *Campbell*) the court was satisfied that he had been intimidated, but where, this time, the court below had made no finding as to whether it believed the defendant or his associates were or might have been responsible.

65 [2005] EWCA Crim 2078.
66 [2006] EWCA Crim 529.

2.47 The problem of intimidated witnesses has also arisen in the context of domestic violence. In *R (Robinson) v Sutton Coldfield Justices*[67] the defendant was accused of assault occasioning actual bodily harm upon a woman with whom he had been briefly living, and who refused to give evidence at trial because she feared that, if she did, the defendant and his associates would be able to trace her. The Divisional Court, having considered the case law, held that the justices had acted properly in admitting in evidence her statement to the police. A similar result was reached on similar facts in *Boulton*,[68] where, at a preliminary hearing, the unwilling complainant had told the judge 'I am not averse to duty, your Honour, I am just averse to martyrdom'. In both of these cases there was some independent evidence of the complainant's injuries, and also plenty of evidence that the defendant was of bad character. These factors appear to have been absent in *Crown Prosecution Service (Durham) v E*.[69] There the defendant was accused of raping the woman with whom he had been cohabiting at the time, and who was unwilling to give evidence through fear.[70] The defence was consent, the case was her word against the defendant's, and the only evidence the prosecution had of either the offence or the complainant's fear was a videotape of her interview with the police. The trial judge refused to allow the tape to be used in evidence and, observing that such decisions are necessarily 'evaluative and fact sensitive', the Court of Appeal rejected the prosecutor's appeal.

2.48 Where the defendant has intimidated the key witness there is no unfairness, in principle, in allow him to be convicted where the prosecution case consists largely or entirely of statements from that witness, the truth of which the defendant is unable to challenge by cross-examination at the trial. His disadvantage is one that he has then brought upon himself, and by doing so he can be said to have waived the right that Article 6(3)(d) and the attendant Strasbourg Court case law gives him. Similar reasoning can be applied to other situations; as in *Keet*,[71] for example, where the defendant's trial was delayed for three and half years because he had absconded and the complainant, an elderly woman, had become mentally incompetent in the interval. But where it is not the defendant's behaviour that has caused the key witness or witnesses to be unavailable it is harder to argue that a conviction based entirely on statements from absent witnesses is compatible with Article 6(3)(d). In *Cole* (see § 2.44 above) the Court of Appeal was prepared to accept that a conviction in such circumstances could, in principle, be fair:[72] although in that case there was a certain amount of further evidence.

[67] [2006] EWHC Crim 307, [2006] 2 Cr App R 13 (208).
[68] [2007] EWCA Crim 942.
[69] [2006] EWCA Crim 1410.
[70] She also had mental health and alcohol problems.
[71] Reported together with *Cole* [2007] EWCA Crim 1924, [2007] 1 WLR 2798 [**page 315 below**].
[72] See *Cole*, n 62 above, [14]–[22]; on this, see comments by James Richardson in (2007) 31 *Current Law Week* no 6.

2.49 *Did the inability to cross-examine the missing witness seriously impede the conduct of the defence?* A final factor that has influenced the courts is the extent to which the inability to cross-examine the absent witness has, in reality, deprived him of the chance to dent the credibility of the evidence. In *Archer*[73] the defendant had been convicted of conspiracy to import cocaine. The prosecution case was that Archer and his co-conspirators had collected a consignment of drugs in Switzerland. Unknown to them, their activities had been monitored by Swiss policemen, whose superiors would not allow them to come to England to testify: in consequence of which the trial judge admitted their evidence in the form of written statements. The Court of Appeal held that this had not infringed the defendant's rights under Article 6(3)(d), inter alia because the defence were unable to explain how cross-examining the Swiss police officers would have been likely to advance their case (at [15]):

> The reason why inability to cross-examine may in some cases render the trial unfair is because a defendant has no proper opportunity either to establish that the evidence is untrue or to establish from the witness some proposition which may help him. Unless the possibility of one or other of those advantages accruing to him is demonstrated to the judge, the judge is entitled to conclude, as this judge did, that the trial is perfectly fair.

2.50 *The English case law on ECHR, Article 6(3)(d): conclusion* The intimidation of witnesses, particularly in the context of gang crime and armed criminals, is a very grave problem, as the Court of Appeal has recognised, first when dealing with hearsay evidence in *Sellick*,[74] and then more recently in *Davis, Ellis and others*,[75] when dealing with the related issue of when witnesses should be allowed to testify at trial anonymously. It is also a delicate problem because, as the Strasbourg Court recognises in both these situations, most of the measures that can be devised to cope with the problem create the possibility of a collision with Article 6 of the Convention, and in particular, Article 6(3)(d).

2.51 In the leading cases, the Court of Appeal has faced the conflict with intellectual honesty, and has done the best it can to resolve it with the legal tools that are available in English law. Regrettably, however, the tools that English law currently makes available are inadequate, because English law does not provide the means by which the evidence of a witness who might become unavailable can be recorded with due formality before a judge, at a session where the defence are represented and able to put their questions. Instead, as we have seen, the current solution to the problem is to bend the hearsay rule to make admissible at trial the statement the witness originally gave to the police.

73 [2007] EWCA Crim 930.
74 See § 2.45 above and [**page 257 below**].
75 [2006] EWCA Crim 1155, [2006] 1 WLR 3130.

2.52 In other jurisdictions, the law usually provides a mechanism for certain types of witnesses to be judicially examined ahead of trial. A classic example of the genre is the institution in Italian criminal procedure called an *incidente probatorio*. Under article 392 of the Criminal Procedure Code, either prosecution or defence may, in certain stated circumstances, request the formal examination of a witness before a judge. The witness is adversarially examined, and the resulting statements are then admissible in evidence at the eventual trial.[76] Another example is to be found nearer to home: in Scots law there is a general provision for the taking of evidence in criminal cases by commission.[77]

2.53 At one time, furthermore, procedures of this sort were available under English law as well. Before 1967, criminal proceedings for serious offences invariably included committal proceedings, at which the key prosecution witnesses were examined on oath, in the presence of the defence, which had the opportunity to ask questions. The deposition so given was taken down in writing, and could be used at trial in substitution for the witness's live testimony where nobody wished to dispute his evidence, or where the witness 'is proved by the oath of a credible witness to be dead or insane, or so ill as not to be able to travel, or to be kept out of the way by means of the procurement of the accused or on his behalf'.[78] This general provision was supplemented by other statutory provisions under which formal depositions could be taken for use at trial from merchant seamen,[79] witnesses to offences committed on aircraft,[80] young children,[81] and persons who were dangerously ill.[82]

2.54 For the last 20 years, however, the government—apparently either unaware of Article 6(3)(d) or else unwilling to face up to it—has pursued a policy of eliminating procedures for the taking of formal depositions before magistrates, and trying to fill the place they formerly occupied in the legal system with witness statements taken from witnesses by the police in the course of their investigation. Thus, by a series of labyrinthine changes, police witness statements eventually came to replace oral depositions at committal proceedings.[83] In similar vein, the provi-

[76] See Mario Chiavario, *Diritto processuale penale* (Turin, Utet, 2005) 325–30; Paolo Tonini, *Manuale di procedura penale* (7th edn, Giuffrè, Milan, 2006) 442–9; for brief accounts in English, see Maffei, n 1 above, 148–9; and Antoinette Perrodet in M Delmas-Marty and J Spencer (eds), *European Criminal Procedures* (Cambridge, CUP, 2002) 380–1.

[77] Criminal Procedure (Scotland) Act 1995, s 272.

[78] Criminal Justice Act 1925, s 13. This provision codified a rule that had evolved over many years at common law.

[79] Merchant Shipping Act 1995, s 286, a provision dating from 1854.

[80] Civil Aviation Act 1982, s 95.

[81] Children and Young Persons Act 1933, ss 42 and 43 (provisions which date from 1894).

[82] Magistrates' Courts Act 1980, s 105: a provision which dated from 1867, and which was repealed by the Criminal Procedure and Investigations Act 1996, s 47, Sch 1. But the equivalent provision for Northern Ireland, Magistrates' Courts (Northern Ireland) Order 1981, SI 1981/1675 (NI 26), art 41, is still in force.

[83] The hearing of oral evidence at committal proceedings was made optional in 1967, and then completely abolished by Criminal Procedure and Investigations Act 1996, s 47, Sch 1. Committal proceedings themselves are abolished by CJA 2003, s 41, Sch 3.

sions about taking depositions from witnesses who are sick have been quietly repealed (except in Northern Ireland). The provisions relating to deposition evidence from children are rarely used, inter alia because the evidence must be taken down in writing; and when in 1988 and 1991 moves were made to make these more serviceable by enabling the deposition of a child to be recorded on tape instead the Home Office opposed the change.[84] Meanwhile, as we saw in Chapter 1, from 1988 onwards the Home Office has promoted legislation the effect of which is to make admissible in evidence, in substitution for the oral evidence of witnesses who are unavailable, the statements which they gave to the police.[85]

2.55 Police witness statements, unlike formal depositions taken before magistrates, are liable to suffer from all the traditional defects of hearsay evidence in response to which the exclusionary rule was originally invented. Unlike police interviews with suspects, there are no formal rules[86] as to how interviews with witnesses are to be conducted, or how the speaker's words are to be recorded. The police may have recorded what the witness told them spontaneously, or what he said in response to heavy prompting. Unless they record the interview on tape, which they are not obliged to do, there is no way of telling whether the witness was prompted, and aside from the prompting issue there are risks of 'transmission errors'. Even if the interview is tape-recorded, those who are interviewed by the police do not speak on oath, and at police interviews neither the defendant nor his lawyer are present, either to observe or put their questions. In consequence, even where the police witness statement is made formally admissible by statute, admitting it in evidence may infringe the defendant's rights under Article 6(3)(d).

2.56 From this, it might be thought that the need in England for a formal system of taking evidence in advance from certain types of witness is both obvious and pressing. Yet in its Consultation Paper, the Law Commission did not think so. After a brief discussion, it concluded—overlooking the recent history of the matter—that:

> the introduction of a system for taking evidence on commission would constitute a radical change to English criminal procedure, and should perhaps be considered in the context of a separate enquiry into the evidence of vulnerable witnesses.

2.57 In its Report, the Law Commission said (no less surprisingly) that the problem would be adequately met by its proposal to make more readily admissible in

[84] JR Spencer, 'Reformers Despair' (1991) *New Law Journal* 787. See Standing Committee H, 22 March 1988; Hansard, HC vol 186, col 754 (25 February 1991).

[85] See 1.71 above.

[86] But there is an official Code of Practice for taking evidence from children and other vulnerable witnesses: *Achieving Best Evidence in Criminal Proceedings: Guidance for Vulnerable or Intimidated Witnesses, including Children* (see § 15.3 below). For a fuller discussion of the rules that apply when the police question witnesses, see §§ 15.1 to 15.7 below.

evidence at trial the statements that absent witnesses had made to the police. Needless to say, no provisions on the subject were included in the CJA 2003.

2.58 A move towards the pre-trial examination of witnesses (though only a small one) was made in the Youth Justice and Criminal Evidence Act 1999. Part II of this Act creates a scheme of 'special measures' designed to make it easier for vulnerable witnesses to give their evidence, and by section 28, one of these is for the whole of the vulnerable witness's evidence, including cross-examination, to be video-recorded ahead of trial, with a view to the video-tape replacing the witness's live evidence. However, this provision has not been brought into force, and it now seems to be accepted that it never will be.[87]

2.59 What was envisaged in this section was not the taking of a preliminary deposition, with the defendant or his representative present, which might then be used as a substitute for the witness's live evidence if necessary, but (in effect) the holding of a section of the eventual trial in advance. In the view of most practitioners and judges, this was not practicable—and that was why the scheme was never brought into force.

2.60 A mechanism for taking the evidence of such a witness 'on commission' would not, of course, solve all the problems. The witness might still be intimidated or become otherwise unavailable before the formal deposition could be taken. However, it would help to solve the problem of the witness who is unavailable in some cases,[88] and insofar as it did so, would remove some of the potential unfairness to the defendant which the present law involves.

2.61 As we saw earlier, one of the factors that the Strasbourg Court takes into account in deciding whether the statement of an absent witness infringes the defendant's rights under ECHR, Article 6(3)(d) is the extent (if any) to which the authorities were at fault in creating the situation in which the defendant was denied the chance to question his accuser. In England, the defendant's inability to put questions in a case where a witness is unavailable and a police witness statement is read at trial is not the fault of the prosecution. But in a broader sense it is the fault of 'the authorities', because the absence of any means of taking the evidence of a witness in a criminal case on commission is the result of a policy decision taken by the government. In the light of this, it is questionable whether the current arrangements in England would be found acceptable at Strasbourg.

[87] See Office for Criminal Justice Reform, *Improving the Criminal Trial Process for Young Witnesses: a Consultation Paper* (June 2007).

[88] Eg in a case like *Dragic* [1996] 2 Cr App R 232, where the suspect was identified by a witness immediately after the offence, and the witness, after giving his statement to the police, contracted cancer and was too ill to give evidence by the time of the trial six months later.

3

THE SCOPE OF THE REFORM, THE SHAPE OF THE NEW EXCLUSIONARY RULE AND THE NEW SCHEME OF EXCEPTIONS

Abolition of the common law exclusionary rule: the demise of *Kearley*

3.1 As was explained earlier,[1] the scheme for reforming hearsay which the Law Commission devised, and the government accepted, consisted of three main elements: (a) the abolition of the exclusionary rule as it was at common law; (b) its replacement with a narrower exclusionary rule; and (c) the creation of a rationalised list of exceptions.

3.2 In the Draft Bill annexed to the Law Commission's Report, the abolition of the exclusionary rule at common law was given a prominent place, making its appearance in clause 1. According to clause 1(2):

> The common law rules governing the admissibility of hearsay evidence in criminal proceedings are abolished (except for the rules preserved by section 6).

The 'section 6' referred to was the later clause which was intended to preserve a list of common law exceptions to the rule, and which in due course became section 118 of the CJA 2003.

3.3 In the Bill the government eventually introduced in Parliament, however, this abolition clause was detached from the beginning of the hearsay sections and attached to the end of what is now section 118. The first part of section 118 sets out a list of six pre-existing exceptions to the hearsay rule which are preserved, and after this there comes subsection (2), which says:

[1] See § 1.71 *et seq* above.

> With the exception of the rules preserved by this section, the common law rules governing the admissibility of hearsay evidence in criminal proceedings are abolished.

3.4 This relocation was a bad move (in a double sense). It meant that casual readers overlooked it, and of those who did notice it, many reasonably assumed from its position that it was simply meant to abolish the remaining common law exceptions to the hearsay rule, and not the rule itself.

3.5 This led, briefly, to the growth of a theory that the common law exclusionary rule against hearsay continued to exist alongside the new statutory rule enacted by CJA 2003, sections 114(1) and 115. As the common law exclusionary rule, thanks to the House of Lords decision in *Kearley*,[2] extended to cover 'implied assertions', the result was that 'implied assertions' (like the telephone calls received at the alleged drug-dealer's premises while the police raid was in progress) were, as previously, inadmissible in evidence.[3]

3.6 As one of the main aims of the reform had been to reverse *Kearley* and put implied assertions outside the scope of the hearsay rule, this result would have been extremely inconvenient, and unsurprisingly, the Court of Appeal took the first opportunity to explode the theory, and to make it plain that this reading of the CJA 2003 was incorrect.

3.7 This opportunity arose in *Singh*,[4] a case in which the defendant had been convicted of conspiracy to carry out a kidnapping (and sentenced to eight years' imprisonment), partly on the basis of evidence from the memories of mobile phones belonging to the other persons involved showing that they had made a large number of calls to Singh's mobile phone at the time the kidnapping was taking place. On appeal, Singh sought to argue that the phone calls were 'implied assertions' by the other kidnappers that he was a member of their gang, and that in the light of *Kearley*, which had survived the CJA 2003, the evidence had been admitted wrongly. This argument was rejected. The effect of section 118(2), the court said, was not merely to abolish the remaining common law exceptions to the hearsay rule, but also the common law exclusionary rule itself. In consequence (at [14]):

> What was said by the callers in *Kearley* would now be admissible as direct evidence of the fact that there was a ready market for the supply of drugs from the premises, from which could be inferred an intention by an occupier to supply drugs. The view of the majority in *Kearley*, in relation to hearsay, has been set aside by the Act.

[2] [1992] 2 AC 228; see § 1.16 above.
[3] It was put forward by Prof Stephen Uglow in [2005] 5 *Archbold News* 6.
[4] [2006] EWCA Crim 660, [2006] 1 WLR 1564 **[page 298 below]**.

Singh sought to appeal further, and the Court of Appeal certified the survival or otherwise of *Kearley* as a point of law of public importance, but the House of Lords refused leave to appeal.[5]

3.8 With the abolition of the common law exclusionary rule, and its replacement with a new exclusionary rule that is limited to statements clearly intended to be assertive, it is now possible to forget not only about *Kearley*, but also the forensic acrobatics that were occasionally displayed in later cases in order to avoid applying it.[6] For the future, words or conduct not intended to be assertive are admissible or inadmissible depending on whether they are or are not logically relevant to a disputed issue in the case—and that is that.

The new exclusionary rule: CJA 2003, Sections 114(1) and 115

3.9 The new exclusionary rule is contained in CJA 2003, section 114(1), as elaborated by section 115. Section 114(1), so far as relevant, is as follows:

> In criminal proceedings a statement not made in oral evidence in the proceedings is admissible as evidence of any matter stated in it if, but only if—
>
> [one of the exceptions numbered (a) to (d) applies to it].

In the next section, the terms 'statement' and 'matter stated' are then restrictively defined. Section 115 provides that:

> (1) In this Chapter references to a statement or to a matter stated are to be read as follows.
> (2) A statement is any representation of fact or opinion made by a person by whatever means; and it includes a representation made in a sketch, photofit or other pictorial form.
> (3) A matter stated is one to which this Chapter applies if (and only if) the purpose, or one of the purposes, of the person making the statement appears to the court to have been—

[5] [2006] 1 WLR 2206. The Court of Appeal also pointed out that even if the defence arguments about implied hearsay had been otherwise correct the phone calls would still have been admissible as 'statements made by a party to a common enterprise', a common law exception preserved by CJA 2003, s 118.

[6] Notably in *Warner and Jones* (1993) 96 Cr App R 324, where the Court of Appeal held that, although *Kearley* prohibited the use in evidence of telephone-calls to D's house from people trying to buy drugs, the prosecution could use the fact that, during a period of police observation, a string of people were seen to pay brief visits to D's house, of whom no less than eight had previous convictions for possessing or supplying heroin. For a further display of now-redundant judicial ingenuity, see *Lawal* [1994] Crim LR 746.

(a) to cause another person to believe the matter;
(b) to cause another person to act or a machine to operate on the basis that the matter is as stated.

3.10 Insofar as they define the new exclusionary rule, these sections are the Law Commission's handiwork. The opening words of section 114(1) match those of the opening words of clause 1(1) of its Draft Bill, which were 'In any criminal proceedings a statement not made in oral evidence in the proceedings is not admissible as evidence of any matter stated unless . . .'; and section 115 exactly reproduces the Law Commission's clause 2. In the following paragraphs the key elements of the new exclusionary rule that emerged from these two sections will be examined.

3.11 . . . *'a statement not made in oral evidence in the proceedings . . .'* The new exclusionary rule, like the old one, is directed against all statements other than those made by witnesses in the course of giving evidence orally in court. What is banned, it should be noted, is 'a statement not made in oral evidence in the proceedings', and not 'a statement made by a person who does not give oral evidence in the proceedings'. So the new exclusionary rule covers not only the statements of non-witnesses, but also the previous statements of witnesses who do come to court in order to give oral evidence. Thus, for better or for worse,[7] the new rule preserves not only the central element of the old hearsay rule, but also the 'rule against narrative'.

3.12 . . . *'is admissible as evidence of any matter stated in it if but only if . . .'* The new rule, like the old exclusionary rule which it replaces, is directed only against the use of an out-of-court statement *as evidence of any matter stated in it.* Under the new law, as under the old, the fact that a person made a statement can be put in evidence without having to confront the rule against hearsay if the purpose of proving it was made is to convince the court of something other than the truth of the matters it contained.

3.13 The most obvious example is where the making of the factual statement is part of the actus reus of a criminal offence for which the maker is on trial, such as fraud or incitement to racial hatred. The fraudulent salesman's statement that 'this car has only done 10,000 miles' is admissible because it is proved, not to establish the mileage of the car, but to show that he told a lie about it; and the racist's statement that 'all Tobleronians are paedophiles' is admissible because it is not being used to establish what their sexual morals are, but to show that the defendant has been inciting his fellow-citizens to hate them.

[7] See § 1.33 above.

3.14 A less obvious example is where the making of the statement is proved not in order to establish the matters contained in it, but to show, where this is relevant, what was in a person's mind at a given time. That John was heard to say to Mary 'Fred is dead' is not admissible to prove the death of Fred; but it is admissible to prove, if these facts are material, that John believed Fred to be dead, or that news of Fred's death had reached the ears of Mary. Similarly, a menacing statement that a non-witness has made can be proved, without reference to the hearsay rule, in order to establish that the person to whom it was made was in a state of fear (and hence acting under duress).[8]

3.15 The distinction described in the last four paragraphs can be a subtle one, and was traditionally much appreciated by those who task it was to set examination papers in the law of evidence, who will no doubt be pleased to learn that this part of their old world remains the same.

3.16 *The meaning of 'a statement'* Section 114 sets out a general prohibition on the use of out-of-court 'statements', a term which section 115 then defines. The nub of the definition is contained in the first sentence of section 115(2), which is as follows: 'a statement is any representation of fact or opinion made by a person by whatever means'.

3.17 The first point to note about this definition is that it is limited to statements 'made by a person'. The new exclusionary rule (like the old one) has no application to statements made by machines that make observations automatically: for example, the reading from a fuel-gauge or a thermometer, or the print-out from a computer which automatically logs telephone calls, or the use of swipe-cards to operate the doors on a building. Much less does it apply to the products of machines, like CCTV cameras, that take pictures or record the sounds of events actually happening. Statements made by machines are admissible as 'real evidence', on the basis of their relevance, and without reference to the hearsay rule. This was, of course, the position reached under the earlier law as well, though not without a rearguard struggle from those who unsuccessfully tried at various times to persuade the courts that statements from machines as well as persons fell within the hearsay rule (on the basis, presumably, that fairness to the defendant required the machine to come to court for cross-examination).[9]

3.18 Under the old law the position was different, of course, with regard to statements from machines that did not record events automatically, but merely stored

[8] As in *Subramanian v Public Prosecutor* [1956] 1 WLR 956.

[9] *The Statute of Liberty* [1968] 1 WLR 739 (the records of an automatic radar system); *Dodson and Williams* [1984] 1 WLR 971 (photographs from security cameras); cf *Taylor v Chief Constable of Cheshire* [1986] 1 WLR 1479 (video from a security camera).

information entered by those who were in charge of them. Here, the courts, sensibly enough, took the view that the 'statements' such machines regurgitated were, in law, only as admissible as the information that had been fed into them,[10] and this state of affairs the Law Commission was anxious to preserve. With that in mind, it drafted the clause which has now become CJA 2003, section 129:

> Representations other than by a person
>
> (1) Where a representation of any fact—
>
> (a) is made otherwise than by a person, but
>
> (b) depends for its accuracy on information supplied (directly or indirectly) by a person,
>
> the representation is not admissible in criminal proceedings as evidence of the fact unless it is proved that the information is accurate.
>
> (2) Subsection (1) does not affect the operation of the presumption that a mechanical device has been properly set or calibrated.

3.19 We know from the Report of the Law Commission that this was simply meant to ensure that a hearsay statement made by a non-witness did not become admissible in evidence just because it had been typed into a machine, and then printed out again.[11] But if read literally it goes further, and renders potentially inadmissible in evidence *any* statement that has been stored in a machine and then printed out from it 'unless it is proved that the information is accurate'. If this is so, the fact that information has been stored in a computer and printed out again does not merely fail to enhance its admissibility in evidence, it actually reduces it. The courts, presumably, will construe the section in the light of what it was meant to do, and treat it as subordinate to the exceptions to the hearsay rule set out in sections 116, 117 and 118, rather than displacing them.

3.20 Though a 'statement' for the purposes of the new definition does not include a statement produced *by* a machine, it does potentially cover a statement that is made *to* one. This is clear from section 115(3)(b), which in setting out the characteristics which a statement must display in order to be within the new exclusionary rule requires it to be made either for the purpose of causing someone to believe it, or of causing 'another person to act *or a machine* to operate on the basis that the matter is as stated'. So if in the course of buying (say) a ticket from an automatic machine X was asked to give his date of birth and typed it in, this inputting of information would count as making a statement; and if in later criminal proceedings either prosecution or defence sought to establish X's date of birth by reference

[10] *R v Coventry Justices, ex p Bullard* (1992) 95 Cr App R 175.

[11] Law Commission, *Evidence in Criminal Proceedings: Hearsay and Related Topics* (Report No 245, Cm 3670, June 1997) (hereafter 'LC Report') §§ 7.46–7.50.

to the 'statement' he so made to the machine, this statement would be hearsay, and so be admissible only if it fell within one of the exceptions to the rule.[12]

3.21 The second point to note is that for the purposes of the new exclusionary rule, the statement must constitute *a representation of fact or opinion*. In other words, it must be an assertion that something is so, or an assertion of something that the speaker believes. Thus, the definition does not cover (for example) a promise or a threat: as where X says 'If you give me that watch, I will give you £100', or Y says 'If you do that, I will shoot you'. Both of these statements, if relevant to an issue in later criminal proceedings, would be admissible as real evidence, and without the need to find an exception to the hearsay rule.

3.22 But if the statement does constitute a representation of fact or opinion, *it matters not how it was made*. By section 115(2), as we have seen, a statement 'is any representation of fact or opinion made by a person by whatever means; and it includes a representation made in a sketch, photofit or other pictorial form'.

3.23 The last part of this phrase was included to reverse the decision in *Cook*,[13] in which it was held that where the victim of an assault later put together with the help of the police a photofit picture of her attacker which resembled the defendant, this did not constitute a statement for the purpose of the old hearsay rule, and hence was admissible in evidence against him on the same basis as a photograph taken of him as he committed the offence. Though welcomed as a blow for common sense by some, the decision was criticised by others who pointed out (correctly) that constructing a photofit picture of a suspect is logically the same as giving a verbal description of him, which would certainly constitute a 'statement'; and heeding the critics, the Law Commission were anxious to reverse it. The result is that, if the facts of *Cook* were to recur today, the victim's construction of the photofit would now constitute a statement and hence be prima facie inadmissible as hearsay; but if the witness gave evidence, it would be admissible under one of the exceptions mentioned in CJA 2003, section 120.[14]

3.24 The third (and more important) point to note is that, in order to fall within the new exclusionary rule, *the statement must have been meant as an assertion*. If it was not so meant, it is now admissible without restriction, provided it is relevant. And so it is that, as Rose LJ said in *Singh*, the telephone calls to Kearley's flat from would-be customers would now be admissible to prove his house is a market-place

[12] In fact it would almost certainly be admissible by virtue of the common law exception preserved by CJA 2003, s 118(1) no 1; see § 9.10 below.

[13] [1987] QB 417.

[14] See § 12.21 below.

for drugs. And so too with other 'statements' which were not intended as assertions, though they incidentally tell us something about the maker's knowledge or belief; such as the letters written to a person alleged to be mentally incompetent, which from their tone and content suggest that the writers believed him to be sane, which were held to be hearsay under the old law in *Wright v Tatham*;[15] or the decision of a sea-captain to sail on a vessel with all his family, thereby suggesting that he believed it to be seaworthy, which in that case was treated as an example of hearsay too.[16]

3.25 This requirement that, to count as hearsay, the statement must be intended as an assertion is imposed by section 115(3), which, to remind us, is as follows:

> A matter stated is one to which this Chapter applies if (and only if) the purpose, or one of the purposes, of the person making the statement appears to the court to have been—
> (a) to cause another person to believe the matter, or
> (b) to cause another person to act or a machine to operate on the basis that the matter is as stated.

3.26 At first sight this provision seems to take a complicated route to make a simple point, and it is not immediately clear why so many words have been used. It is obvious that, to be 'assertive', a statement must be made with the intention of causing another person to believe it; but what is usefully added by the second limb 'or to cause another person or a machine to operate on the basis that the matter is as stated'? This limb was included because the Law Commission thought that the word 'believe' was inappropriate to internal processes of a machine, however 'intelligent'; and also inappropriate for the situation where A makes a statement to B, whom he knows will act on it without thinking about whether it is true, as where the accountant in a large (and slack) organisation pays out expenses claims without questioning them.[17] Thus, thanks to section 115(3)(b), it is still prima facie impossible to establish the fact that A travelled to Manchester on X date by proving that on the following day he filed an expenses claim with B for the reimbursement of his train-fare, because his claim was an 'assertive statement', and hence hearsay.[18]

3.27 *Two old problems resolved: 'negative hearsay' and 'identifying documents'* The Law Commission thought that limiting the exclusionary rule to statements meant to be assertive would remove from the scope of the rule two types of case that

[15] 1834–38; the final stage of the case is reported in 5 Cl and Fin 670, 7 ER 559.
[16] By Baron Parke, in the early stages of the case; 7 Ad and El 383, 388; 112 ER 488, 516.
[17] See LC Report, n 11 above, § 7.17 onwards.
[18] But if the claim was processed, the record would probably be admissible under the exception for 'business and other documents' in CJA 2003, s 117: see Chapter 7 below.

caused theoretical problems under the earlier law (although in practice the courts had managed to find their way around them).

3.28 The first was 'the dog that did not bark': the situation where, if something had happened, some person would have been expected to make a note of it, and so the absence of a note or record suggests that it did not. In practice, the courts treated the absence of a record as 'real evidence', and hence admissible without reference to the rule against hearsay.[19] But some theorists thought this reasoning was suspect, and condemned it as what one called a 'hearsay fiddle'.[20] However, as the hearsay rule is now limited to statements intended to be assertive, 'negative hearsay' of this sort now clearly falls outside the rule. If a person fails to record an incident he is not, by his inaction, seeking to assert that it did not happen, although from his inaction, others may infer that it did not. (Of course, if a person makes an entry in a record that something he was expecting to happen did not happen, that is another matter.)

3.29 The second old problem now solved is the case where some document or object is found which happens to have a person's name on it, from which the court is asked to infer that the person in question was (or may have been) at a given place at a given time. The classic example is *Rice*,[21] in which the prosecution was allowed to adduce a used air ticket with Rice's name on in order to show that he had travelled to Manchester on a particular flight. Another example is *Lydon*,[22] where the prosecution were allowed to adduce as evidence against Sean Lydon the fact that, near the scene of a robbery, was found a discarded gun, plus two screwed-up pieces of paper, on one of which was written 'Sean rules' and on the other 'Sean rules 1985'. In both *Rice* and *Lydon* the Court of Appeal later held the evidence was rightly admitted, though some commentators thought the reasoning was questionable. Under the new law, however, neither document would even arguably fall within the hearsay rule, since neither contained a statement that was meant to be assertive.

3.30 *And a new difficult case: private diaries* In *N*[23] the defendant had been convicted of having sexual intercourse with his 13-year-old niece. The matter had come to light when her mother had read an entry in the girl's diary in which she

[19] As in *Shone* (1983) 76 Cr App R 72, where the fact that shop-workers would have noted the fact on record cards if certain items had been lawfully disposed of was held to be direct evidence of the fact that they had been stolen; cf *Muir* (1983) 79 Cr App R 153 and *Patel* (1981) 73 Cr App R 117.

[20] DJ Birch, 'Hearsay-logic and Hearsay-fiddles: *Blastland* Revisited' in Peter Smith (ed), *Essays in Honour of J.C. Smith* (London, Butterworths, 1987) 24. (Professor Birch did not quarrel with the result; her criticism was directed at the narrowness of the hearsay rule, which required 'fiddles' of this sort to prevent the legal system seizing up because of it.)

[21] [1963] 1 QB 857.

[22] (1987) 85 Cr App R 221.

[23] [2006] EWCA Crim 3309, 171 JP 158.

mentioned what had happened (and how unhappy it had made her). The Court of Appeal concluded that, as the diary was a private one and intended for the eyes of no one but the maker, the purpose of making the statements contained in it was not 'to cause another person to believe the matter'. In the light of that, it did not constitute a 'statement' for the purposes of section 115, and hence fell outside the hearsay rule, with the consequence that it was admissible as a piece of evidence relevant to the central issue in the case (at [21]):

> It is real or direct evidence outside the hearsay rule. The statutory restrictions upon the admissibility of hearsay have no occasion to apply to an action by the complainant which never had as its purpose, principal or supplementary, that any other person should believe or act upon it. It is simply a fact from which the jury is entitled, but not bound, to infer that [the complaint's] uncle had had intercourse with her. It is a fact from which that may, but not necessarily will, be inferred, in exactly the same way as if she has been observed by other people kissing him, for example, passionately—or making a booking of a hotel room for an afternoon in his name.

The new definition of hearsay: conclusion

3.31 The new definition of hearsay is obviously an improvement on its predecessor, to the extent that it reduces the amount of cogent evidence that falls within the scope of it, and hence is excluded by the rule. But whether the new line it draws is either rational or clear is more debatable.

3.32 The idea behind drawing a line between statements that were and were not meant to be assertive is that the statements of the first type are more prone to fabrication than the second, and hence presumptively less reliable. But from what has been said in the preceding paragraphs it will already be clear that, if generally true, it is not always so. Assertive statements are often as credible and cogent as non-assertive statements; and some non-assertive statements are of very questionable weight.

3.33 An example of a cogent statement that falls on the wrong side of the new line is A's hypothetical expenses claim in respect of his journey to Manchester. Unless we accept the proposition that most expenses claims are fraudulent (or believe that A is in the habit of fiddling his) this is cogent evidence that A went there. Yet as an 'assertive statement' this is hearsay and hence only admissible if an exception to the rule applies to it, and there is no obvious one,[24] apart from the 'inclusionary

[24] If A's employer notes the claim in his records, though still hearsay, it will then be admissible under the 'records' exception in CJA 2003, s 117, though it is difficult to see why the fact that B logged A's statement makes it any more likely to be true.

discretion' (which is the subject of Chapter 4 below). And yet if a railway ticket has been issued with A's name on it, this by contrast is 'real evidence' and is admissible to prove his presence in Manchester without reference to the hearsay rule, although the issue of a ticket in A's name does not conclusively prove he made the journey, any more than the fact that he later claimed expenses for having done so.

3.34 In similar vein, let us imagine that someone had found, on the floor of a cafe in Manchester where the owner had apparently dropped it, a book, on the cover of which was written 'this book belongs to A'. This too is evidence of A's presence there that is worth taking notice of, albeit not conclusive. Yet the phrase 'this book belongs to A' appears to be an 'assertive statement' and hence it counts as hearsay, and would only be admissible under an exception to the exclusionary rule.[25] However, if the cover had merely been defaced with a graffito that said 'A rules' or a shopping-list in what appeared to be A's hand-writing, these would not be assertive statements and would be admissible as 'real evidence'.

3.35 Meanwhile, as we have seen, the reflections of a teenage girl about her sexual experiences written in her private diary do not constitute 'assertive statements', and hence are automatically admissible without reference to the hearsay rule, although what she writes there is no more likely to true, and just as likely to be fantasy, as her confidences on the subject to her friends, which as 'assertive statements' are excluded by the hearsay rule. Distinctions of this sort, it might be thought, do little credit to the law, particularly one which was promoted as replacing the old law 'with a modern, comprehensive and intelligible legislative scheme'.[26]

3.36 Furthermore, in practice it will often not be clear whether or not a given statement was intended by its maker to be assertive. An example is the old case of *Teper v R*.[27] The issue here was whether it was Teper who had set fire to a shop belonging to his wife, and as part of the evidence to prove it was, the prosecution called a police officer to say that, as a car drove away, he heard an unidentified woman bystander shouting 'Your place burning and you going away from the fire!' Here, as the Law Commission solemnly informed us,[28] the status of the statement under the new law would depend on whether she was shouting abuse *at* Teper, when her statement would not have been assertive, because she would not

[25] Although in *Lilley* [2003] EWCA Crim 1789, which was decided under the earlier law, the Court of Appeal contrived to hold that the words 'Sharon's book' *were* admissible in evidence to show the book was hers; the reasoning is criticised by Di Birch in 'Hearsay: Same Old Story, Same Old Song?' [2004] Crim LR 556, 561.

[26] Hansard, HL vol 653 (10 Sept 2003), col 1121; and see DCO's (David Ormerod's) comments on *Singh* at [2006] Crim LR 647, 651.

[27] [1952] AC 480.

[28] See LC Report, n 11 above, § 7.28.

have been trying to convince him of the truth of anything; or shouting abuse to the crowd *about* him, in which case it would be. And what her intention was, of course, is impossible to determine.

3.37 This difficulty arose under the new law in *Isichei.*[29] The point at issue here was whether the defendant was one of two men who had attacked and robbed two girls in the street as they were on their way home from a night out 'clubbing'. Their attackers, they said, were two men who, earlier in the evening, had been present in the last night-club that they had visited. There had been difficulty in first locating this club and then in gaining entry to it, and in order to overcome these difficulties an unknown man with whom the girls were by then wandering around (having fallen in with him earlier in the evening) was twice heard by them to make a phone call to someone, apparently inside the club, to whom he referred as 'Marvin'. At trial the prosecution put this in evidence as suggesting that a man called Marvin had been present in the club; and as Isichei's first name was also Marvin, and the girls said they seen their attackers earlier in the club, this went some way to show that they had correctly identified Isichei as one of them. On appeal, the defence sought to argue that the unidentified man's remarks that he was 'calling Marvin' were 'assertive statements' and thus hearsay, and hence inadmissible.

3.38 Upholding the conviction, the Court of Appeal said that the assignment of these remarks to one class or the other was no easy matter, and that in treating them as 'non-assertive' the trial judge might have got it wrong. But if he had erred, however, this did not matter, because if the remarks did count in law as hearsay then it was proper to admit them under the 'inclusionary discretion', ie the 'safety-valve'. Auld LJ said (at [41]):

> Whatever the position, it seems to us that the evidence was clearly admissible in the interests of justice under section 114(1)(d) as part of the story of a common sense series of events, the one leading from the other.

3.39 So to sum up, the new definition of hearsay, if better than the old one, is neither sound as a discriminator between statements that are reliable and unreliable, nor easy to apply; but neither difficulty matters, because the courts can disregard the result it gives if they think it is contrary to the interests of justice—a state of affairs which leaves the sceptical reader wondering why the law requires the courts to go through the exercise of applying it in the first place.

3.40 If it was really necessary to draw a line between out-of-court statements which are prima facie excluded and only exceptionally admitted and those that are admitted automatically, the proper distinction to have drawn, I believe, would

[29] [2006] EWCA Crim 1815, 170 JP 753, [2007] Crim LR 484.

have been between statements made to the authorities in the course of their investigations, and everything else. People do not usually lie to strangers outside night clubs about the names of men they are calling on their mobile phones, in the hope of framing them for offences yet to be committed. But once a crime has been committed, and the police are investigating it, risks of invention and distortion start to become important, and from that point on, it is right and proper for the law to expect the maker of the statement to come to court to give his evidence again orally, so that the defendant can dispute it. And that, of course, is the logic that underlies Article 6(3)(d) of the ECHR and its attendant case law, which was examined in Chapter 2.

Scheme of exceptions

3.41 In the Law Commission's Draft Bill, the exceptions to the redefined hearsay rule were arranged according to a scheme which had an evident logic to it. Clause 1 restated the rule, which applied unless:

(a) a statutory exception applied;
(b) a common law exception preserved by the Act applied;
(c) all parties were agreed that the hearsay evidence should be admitted.

3.42 In the CJA 2003, however, the exceptions to the rule are arranged according to a scheme the logic of which is not immediately apparent. Section 114(1), which is the first of the set of provisions in the Act which deals with hearsay, is as follows:

> Admissibility of hearsay evidence
>
> (1) In criminal proceedings a statement not made in oral evidence in the proceedings is admissible as evidence of any matter stated if, but only if—
>
> (a) any provision of this Chapter or any other statutory provision makes it admissible,
> (b) any rule of law preserved by section 118 makes it admissible,
> (c) all parties to the proceedings agree to it being admissible, or
> (d) the court is satisfied that it is in the interests of justice for it to be admissible.

3.43 What has happened here is that the government took one of the Law Commission's new 'statutory exceptions' (the new 'inclusionary discretion', alias the 'safety-valve') and singled it out for special mention, with the deliberate aim (as Chapter 5 explains) of raising its status and importance. Yet if that was the idea of giving it a special mention, it is odd that when it did so it assigned to it the bottom place in the list, after (c), which covers hearsay admitted by agreement.

3.44 In the the next six chapters of this book, the main exceptions to the hearsay rule 'proper' which are treated in the CJA 2003 will be discussed in what I believe to be a descending order of importance, which is as follows:

(a) agreement of the parties (Chapter 4);
(b) the 'inclusionary discretion' (Chapter 5);
(c) statutory exceptions:
    (i) unavailable witnesses: section 116 (Chapter 6);
    (ii) records: section 117 (Chapter 7)
    (iii) other statutory exceptions (Chapter 8);
(d) common law exceptions: section 118 (Chapter 9).

3.45 The remaining chapters of the book will discuss confessions (Chapter 10), multiple hearsay (Chapter 11), the 'rule against narrative' (Chapter 12), video-taped evidence (Chapter 13), provisions in the CJA 2003 relating to expert evidence and the proof of documents (Chapter 14), and, finally, various practical issues (Chapter 15).

4

HEARSAY ADMITTED BY AGREEMENT

4.1 CJA 2003, section 114(1)(c) provides that a statement is not excluded by the hearsay rule where 'all the parties are in agreement to it being admissible'. This continues a process that was initiated 40 years earlier, in the Criminal Justice Act 1967.

4.2 Before 1967, the basic rule was that, in a contested case, every material fact, whether disputed or not, had to be established by evidence that was legally admissible, and 'legally admissible evidence' usually meant oral testimony. This meant much time was wasted by busy people giving oral evidence pointlessly, and to solve this problem the Criminal Law Revision Committee in 1966 proposed two important changes: first, that the defendant should be allowed to make a formal admission of any part of the prosecution case, and secondly, that the evidence of witnesses which neither side wishes to dispute should be delivered to the court by means of a written statement instead of oral evidence.[1]

4.3 These two changes were enacted by CJA 1967, sections 9 and 10, both of which remain in force. For the purpose of the hearsay provisions in CJA 2003, CJA 1967, section 9, which deals with proof by written statements, counts as one of the 'other statutory provisions' mentioned in CJA 2003, section 114(1)(a), which provides that hearsay evidence may be admitted, inter alia, where '(a) any provision of this Chapter *or any other statutory provision* makes it admissible'.

4.4 In its current form, CJA 1967, section 9 is as follows:

Proof by written statement

(1) In any criminal proceedings, other than committal proceedings, a written statement by any person shall, if such of the conditions mentioned in the next following subsection as are applicable are satisfied, be admissible as evidence to the like extent as oral evidence to the like effect by that person.

[1] Criminal Law Revision Committee, *Ninth Report: Evidence (Written Statements, Formal Admissions and Notices of Alibi)* (Cmnd 3145, 1966). For a contemporary reaction see RN Gooderson, 'Previous Consistent Statements' (1968) 26 *Cambridge Law Journal* 64.

(2) The said conditions are—

(a) the statement purports to be signed by the person who made it;
(b) the statement contains a declaration by that person to the effect that it is true to the best of his knowledge and belief and that he made the statement knowing that, if it were tendered in evidence, he would be liable to prosecution if he wilfully stated in it anything which he knew to be false or did not believe to be true;
(c) before the hearing at which the statement is tendered in evidence, a copy of the statement is served, by or on behalf of the party proposing to tender it, on each of the other parties to the proceedings; and
(d) none of the other parties or their solicitors, within seven days from the service of the copy of the statement, serves a notice on the party so proposing objecting to the statement being tendered in evidence under this section:

Provided that the conditions mentioned in paragraphs (c) and (d) of this subsection shall not apply if the parties agree before or during the hearing that the statement shall be so tendered.

(3) The following provisions shall also have effect in relation to any written statement tendered in evidence under this section, that is to say—

(a) if the statement is made by a person under the age of eighteen, it shall give his age;
(b) if it is made by a person who cannot read it, it shall be read to him before he signs it and shall be accompanied by a declaration by the person who so read the statement to the effect that it was so read; and
(c) if it refers to any other document as an exhibit, the copy served on any other party to the proceedings under paragraph (c) of the last foregoing subsection shall be accompanied by a copy of that document or by such information as may be necessary in order to enable the party on whom it is served to inspect that document or a copy thereof.

(4) Notwithstanding that a written statement made by any person may be admissible as evidence by virtue of this section—

(a) the party by whom or on whose behalf a copy of the statement was served may call that person to give evidence; and
(b) the court may, of its own motion or on the application of any party to the proceedings, require that person to attend before the court and give evidence.

(5) An application under paragraph (b) of the last foregoing subsection to a court other than a magistrates' court may be made before the hearing and on any such application the powers of the court shall be exercisable by a puisne judge of the High Court, a Circuit judge or Recorder sitting alone.

(6) So much of any statement as is admitted in evidence by virtue of this section shall, unless the court otherwise directs, be read aloud at the hearing and where the court so directs an account shall be given orally of so much of any statement as is not read aloud.

(7) Any document or object referred to as an exhibit and identified in a written statement tendered in evidence under this section shall be treated as if it had been produced as an exhibit and identified in court by the maker of the statement.

(8) A document required by this section to be served on any person may be served—
  (a) by delivering it to him or to his solicitor; or
  (b) by addressing it to him and leaving it at his usual or last known place of abode or place of business or by addressing it to his solicitor and leaving it at his office; or
  (c) by sending it in a registered letter or by the recorded delivery service or by first class post addressed to him at his usual or last known place of abode or place of business or addressed to his solicitor at his office; or
  (d) in the case of a body corporate, by delivering it to the secretary or clerk of the body at its registered or principal office or sending it in a registered letter or by the recorded delivery service or by first class post addressed to the secretary or clerk of that body at that office; and in paragraph (d) of this subsection references to the secretary, in relation to a limited liability partnership, are to any designated member of the limited liability partnership.

4.5 To give false information in written statement provided under section 9 is, by CJA 1967, section 89, a criminal offence punishable with up to two years' imprisonment.

4.6 'Section 9 statements' (as they are invariably called) are enormously important in practice, but despite this, the provision has generated little case law. The section, though very long, is clearly drafted and the procedure it creates usually works smoothly. A difficulty that sometimes arises, particularly in the magistrates' courts, is that the prosecution duly serves a section 9 statement on the defence, and the defence, having failed to object in advance, then seeks to dispute the truth of the statement at the trial. In *Lister v Quaife*[2] the Divisional Court held that the party on whom a section 9 statement has been served is entitled to do this, but if he does, the other side may then ask the court for an adjournment in order to call the witness, or the court, unasked, may order one on its own initiative.[3]

4.7 Section 9 is mirrored by a number of other more specific statutory provisions which, in the context of particular offences, allow the prosecution to use a written statement or certificate to prove something, provided that it gives advance notice to the defence and the defence does not object. Of these, one that is constantly used in the magistrates' courts is Road Traffic Offenders Act 1988, section 11, which allows the prosecution to prove ownership of a motor vehicle by means of a certificate.[4] Another is section 16 of that Act, which in drink-driving cases allows the prosecution to prove the defendant's blood-alcohol level by producing a written certificate from the analyst, instead of calling the analyst to give oral evidence.[5]

[2] [1983] 1 WLR 56.

[3] For such further case law as there is on CJA 1967, s 9, see *Blackstone's Criminal Practice* (2008) (hereafter '*Blackstone*') § D21.24 and Archbold, *Criminal Pleading, Evidence and Practice* (2008) § 10.51.

Yet another provision of this sort is Theft Act 1968, section 27(4), which in a prosecution for theft of goods in transit makes admissible a written declaration by the sender to prove that the goods were despatched, provided notice is given to the defence and they do not object.

4.8 To these possibilities, CJA 2003, section 114(1)(c)—following the recommendation of the Law Commission[6]—now adds a more general rule that hearsay evidence is admissible where 'all parties to the proceedings agree to it being admissible'.

4.9 To some extent this new provision duplicates CJA 1967, section 9 and its fellows, because among the types of hearsay which could be admitted under it are written statements provided by a living witness whom the parties do not wish to call. But it is much wider, because it renders admissible hearsay evidence of any type. For example, it could be used to admit evidence of a record which fell outside the narrow requirements of the 'records' exception in CJA 2003, section 117. It could also be used to admit evidence of an oral witness's previous statements. And it could also be used to admit hearsay statements embedded in the evidence of a witness who testifies orally; for example, the witness's account of who said what to whom in the family row she overheard in *GJ*,[7] or the comment in the victim's oral evidence in *Isichei*[8] that the person with a mobile phone outside the night-club said that he was 'ringing Marvin'.

4.10 Taken with the 'inclusionary discretion' in section 114(1)(d), this new provision has had a powerful effect. Where a piece of hearsay evidence is cogent, the parties now often foresee that, if its admissibility is disputed, the court is likely to admit it: and to save time, trouble and expense, they are likely to admit it by agreement. The result, in practice, is a 'culture change' towards the admissibility of hearsay evidence.

4.11 The CJA 2003 prescribes no formalities for agreeing to admit hearsay evidence, and in principle it is open to prosecution and defence to do so informally.[9] However, Part 34 of the Criminal Procedure Rules[10] requires a party who intends to call hearsay evidence to give notice, and also provides that the party who receives such a notice may issue a counter-notice if he objects. Part 34 was made under a rule-making power conferred by CJA 2003, section 132(4), which states

4 See *Blackstone*, n 3 above, § C2.5.

5 *Ibid* § C5.22.

6 Law Commission, *Evidence in Criminal Proceedings: Hearsay and Related Topics* (Report No 245, Cm 3670, June 1997) § 8.150.

7 [2006] EWCA Crim 1939; see § 5.36 below.

8 [2006] EWCA Crim 1815; see § 3.37 above.

9 Where they do so, they are expected to inform the court: see CPR, Rule 34.8.

10 See Appendix II, below.

that rules made by the Criminal Procedure Rule Committee in the exercise of this power may provide that, where the party on whom a hearsay notice is served fails to issue a counter-notice, the hearsay 'is to be treated as admissible by agreement'. However, the Rules currently in force do not go as far as this; and as the law stands, a party who received a hearsay notice and then failed to serve a counter-notice is not deemed to have agreed and is still entitled to object. However, a party who objects having failed to serve a counter-notice in due time cannot expect the court to be pleased with him. Under section 114(1)(d), the court has a general power to admit hearsay evidence where 'it is satisfied that it is in the interests of justice for it to be admissible', and the court could properly take into account the last-minute nature of the objection when deciding where the interests of justice lie.[11]

[11] See § 5.12 below.

5

THE 'INCLUSIONARY DISCRETION' AND THE GENERAL DISCRETION TO EXCLUDE

Discretionary inclusion under CJA 2003, section 114(1)(d): 'safety-valve' or alternative tap?

5.1 The basic rules now governing the admissibility of hearsay evidence are set out in CJA 2003, section 114, which is as follows:

Admissibility of hearsay evidence

(1) In criminal proceedings a statement not made in oral evidence in the proceedings is admissible as evidence of any matter stated if, but only if—

(a) any provision of this Chapter or any other statutory provision makes it admissible,

(b) any rule of law preserved by section 118 makes it admissible,

(c) all parties to the proceedings agree to it being admissible, or

(d) the court is satisfied that it is in the interests of justice for it to be admissible.

(2) In deciding whether a statement not made in oral evidence should be admitted under subsection (1)(d), the court must have regard to the following factors (and to any others it considers relevant)—

(a) how much probative value the statement has (assuming it to be true) in relation to a matter in issue in the proceedings, or how valuable it is for the understanding of other evidence in the case;

(b) what other evidence has been, or can be, given on the matter or evidence mentioned in paragraph (a);

(c) how important the matter or evidence mentioned in paragraph (a) is in the context of the case as a whole;

(d) the circumstances in which the statement was made;

(e) how reliable the maker of the statement appears to be;

(f) how reliable the evidence of the making of the statement appears to be;

(g) whether oral evidence of the matter stated can be given and, if not, why it cannot;

(h) the amount of difficulty involved in challenging the statement;
(i) the extent to which that difficulty would be likely to prejudice the party facing it.

(3) Nothing in this Chapter affects the exclusion of evidence of a statement on grounds other than the fact that it is a statement not made in oral evidence in the proceedings.

5.2 The first part of this section outlines the new exclusionary rule, and then proceeds to list as (a) to (d) four 'exceptions', of which (a) and (b) are really references to groups of exceptions, (c) is a general exception for hearsay which prosecution and defence agree shall be admissible, and (d) is the 'inclusionary discretion': a general exception for hearsay which, though otherwise inadmissible, the court believes should be heard 'in the interests of justice'. Then in respect of this last and general exception (though not the others), section 114 sets out the matters that are relevant to its application.

5.3 This position gives the 'inclusionary discretion' a degree of prominence which in the Draft Bill attached to the Law Commission's final Report it did not have. The Law Commission referred to it as 'the safety-valve' and envisaged it as something which the courts would regard 'as an exception to be used in very limited circumstances'.[1] With that in mind, in its Bill it was placed discreetly out of sight, in a brief clause tucked away at the back of the long, elaborate and detailed clauses in which the specific exceptions were set out. As explained above (see §§ 1.87–1.92), the government relocated the 'inclusionary discretion' as part of its plan to produce a 'third way' between the Law Commission's highly conservative approach to reforming the hearsay rule and the much more radical ideas in the Auld Review. As the junior Home Office minister explained, 'we are about introducing a more inclusionary approach'.[2] Plainly, the government's idea was that the inclusionary discretion now contained in section 114(1)(d) was something the courts were intended to use regularly, and not just as a last resort.

5.4 But what in reality the 'intention of Parliament' was in respect of section 114(1)(d) was it is impossible to say, because the form of words eventually adopted were a compromise, agreed at the last minute, to satisfy both those who were afraid that the government's formula went too far, and those who thought it did not go

[1] Law Commission, *Evidence in Criminal Proceedings: Hearsay and Related Topics* (Report No 245, Cm 3670, June 1997) (hereafter 'LC Report'), § 8.143.

[2] Michael Wills, House of Commons Standing Committee B, 28 January 2003, col 600. Compare Baroness Scotland's remarks in the House of Lords: 'the Government have since reconsidered what form the primary rule should take in the light of Sir Robin Auld's recommendation that hearsay should be generally admissible, subject to the principle of best evidence. We have concluded that there are advantages in expressing the hearsay rule in a positive way, whereby all relevant hearsay is potentially admissible unless there are good grounds for excluding it'. Hansard, HL vol 410, col 1123.

far enough.[3] In the government's original Bill, the 'inclusionary discretion' exception would have allowed the court to admit hearsay evidence where 'the court is satisfied that, despite the difficulties there may be in challenging the statement, it would not be contrary to the interests of justice for it to be admissible', rather than 'the court is satisfied that it is in the interests of justice for it to be admissible', which are the words of section 114(1)(d) are they are now. From what was said in the course of the parliamentary debates it is clear that some people voted for the provision believing they were implanting in the CJA 2003 a safety-valve, and others a primary tap; and close textual analysis does not really enable us to resolve the doubt as to which it really was.

5.5 On the one hand, the wording of section 114(1)(d) is extremely broad and there is no other express wording in the CJA 2003 either to limit it, or to say that it is in any way subordinate to the other exceptions.[4] As against this, it might be said that its position at the end of the list suggests this.[5] But then, as against that it could also be said, with equal justice, that the list of matters the court is required to consider in applying the 'inclusionary discretion' are, unlike similar matters relevant to the other exceptions, set out in section 114(2), at the head of the hearsay provisions, in a prominent position, suggesting that this exception is meant to be more significant than the others.

5.6 In consequence, the courts were left free to decide whether section 114(1)(d) should be treated as an exception to the hearsay rule for routine use, or for emergency use only. Given that the senior judiciary had made it known that they thought the hearsay rule needed major surgery rather than minor rearrangement,[6] it is not surprising that the emerging case law[7] suggests that the 'inclusionary discretion' can be used liberally, and not just in 'very limited circumstances', as the Law Commission had proposed.

[3] See § 1.92 above.

[4] See DCO's (David Ormerod's) comment on *Taylor* [2006] Crim LR 639, 640.

[5] Roderick Munday, 'The Judicial Discretion to Admit Hearsay Evidence' (2007) 171 *Justice of the Peace Newspaper* 276. In *Y* [2008] EWCA Crim 10 the Court of Appeal said 'There is no basis on which section 114(1) can be read so as to subordinate subparagraph (d) to (b)'; see further § 10.35 below.

[6] See § 1.92 above.

[7] The bulk of which is already large. To date, the main cases are *Xhabri* [2005] EWCA Crim 3135, [2006] 1 CrAppR 26 (413) [**page 283 below**]; *Maher v DPP* [2006] EWHC 1271 (Admin) [**page 302 below**]; *Taylor* [2006] EWCA Crim 260, [2006] 2 CrAppR 14 [**page 292 below**]; *Singh* [2006] EWCA Crim 660, [2006] 1 WLR 1564 [**page 298 below**]; *Isichei* [2006] EWCA Crim 1815; *GJ* [2006] EWCA Crim 1939; *Lamb* [2006] EWCA Crim 3347; *S* [2006] EWCA Crim 2272; *Lynch* [2007] EWCA Crim 3035; *O'Hare* [2006] EWCA Crim 2512; *Kavallieratos* [2006] EWCA Crim 2819; *Musone* [2007] EWCA Crim 1237, [2007] 1 WLR 2467; *Finch* [2007] EWCA Crim 36, [2007] 1 WLR 1645 [**page 308 below**]; *McEwan v DPP* [2007] EWCA 740 (Admin); *Richards* [2007] EWCA Crim 709; *McLean and others* [2007] EWCA Crim 219, [2008] 1 CrAppR 11 (155); *DPP v R* [2007] EWHC 1842 (Admin) *S* [2007] EWCA Crim 335, [2007] All ER (D) 119; *Walker* [2007] EWCA Crim 1698; *Sajjad and Iqbal* [2007] EWCA Crim 1059; *Williams* [2007] EWCA Crim 211; *Meade* [2007] EWCA Crim 1116 *Y* [2008] EWCA Crim 10.

5.7 Where the hearsay evidence is cogent, the courts are more than willing to use section 114(1)(d) to get around the limitations imposed by the overtight drafting of a specific exception which common sense suggests should really cover it. An example is *Maher v DPP*.[8] V's car, parked in a supermarket car-park, was dented by a carelessly driven car of another shopper while V was inside the shop; W, who saw the collision, wrote the registration number of the offending car on a slip of paper and stuck it under V's windscreen-wiper. V found the slip and phoned the details to the police, who entered them in their records, but V then lost the slip. Maher, the owner of the offending car, admitted that she had been in the car-park at the relevant time, but denied the collision. Having analysed the 'records' exception to the hearsay rule set out in CJA 2003, section 117, the Divisional Court found that—surprisingly—it did not apply. Although it would have applied if W had given the number of V's car to the car-park attendant, had there been one, it did not apply where, as here, W had given it to the owner of the damaged car (!) Remarking that 'the sweeping-up provisions with regard to the admissibility of hearsay should be applied with a measure of common sense and realism', the Divisional Court (in a judgment delivered by Lord Woolf CJ) held that the contents of the note should be admitted 'in the interests of justice' under section 114(1)(d).

5.8 More radically, where there is doubt about the admissibility of a statement which the courts see as a piece of cogent evidence, they sometimes use section 114(1)(d) to 'cut the cackle' and avoid the need for a minute analysis of the other provisions of the CJA 2003, as was done in *Isichei*, which was examined in Chapter 3.[9]

5.9 In similar vein, the courts, when presented with a piece of cogent hearsay evidence which they are fairly certain falls within the scope of one of the more specific exceptions, often use section 114(1)(d) as a 'belt and braces'. They say, in effect, 'We believe this piece of evidence was admissible under section X or Y or Z; but if we are wrong about this, the interests of justice required it to be admitted, and it was therefore admissible under section 114(1)(d)'. The leading example of this is *Xhabri*, where the prosecution alleged that the defendant had held a young woman captive and forced her to work against her will as a prostitute, and an issue arose about the admissibility in evidence of urgent messages she had sent from captivity to friends and relatives explaining her predicament and begging for help. The defence argued that these statements were inadmissible by reason of the 'rule against narrative'[10] and so should have been excluded. The Court of Appeal thought that they were admissible under CJA 2003, section 120; but failing that, it said, they were admissible under section 114(1)(d), because there was 'no basis on

[8] See n 7 above.
[9] See §§ 3.37–3.38 above.
[10] See § 1.11 above and Chapter 12 below.

upon which it could be suggested that the admission of this evidence was not in the interests of justice' (at [36]).[11]

5.10 The Law Commission, though it did not expressly say so, seems to have envisaged its 'safety-valve' as intended primarily for the defence;[12] of the three examples it gave to justify the need for it, all were cases where the exclusion of the evidence would have created the risk of a wrongful conviction. But the case law, as we have seen, shows that the courts are more than content to use it to secure the admission of cogent evidence at the instance of the prosecution; at any rate, provided (as in *Xhabri*) admitting the evidence would not infringe the defendant's right of confrontation under Article 6(3)(d) of the ECHR.[13]

5.11 Finally, a decision which clearly shows the willingness of the appeal courts to encourage the use of the 'inclusionary discretion' is *Taylor*, where, as is further explained below, the Court of Appeal ruled that although the court is obliged by section 114(2) to 'consider' a list of factors in deciding whether to admit the evidence, it is not obliged, in respect of each and every one of them, to reach and announce a finding, let alone to hear evidence in relation to each of them. This decision obviously 'confers considerable freedom on judges to admit otherwise inadmissible hearsay via section 114(1)(d)'.[14]

What are 'the interests of justice'?

5.12 Section 114(1)(d) gives the court a general discretion to admit hearsay evidence 'when it is satisfied that it is in the interests of justice for it to be admissible'. A thumbnail sketch of what is meant by 'the interests of justice' in criminal procedure is set out in the 'overriding objective' which forms the opening section of the Criminal Procedure Rules, which is as follows:

> 1.1 The overriding objective
>
> (1) The overriding objective of this new code is that criminal cases be dealt with justly.
>
> (2) Dealing with a criminal case justly includes—
>
> (a) acquitting the innocent and convicting the guilty;
> (b) dealing with the prosecution and the defence fairly;
> (c) recognising the rights of a defendant, particularly those under Article 6 of the European Convention on Human Rights;
> (d) respecting the interests of witnesses, victims and jurors and keeping them informed of the progress of the case;

[11] [2005] EWCA Crim 3135, [**page 283 below**]. For another example, see *Singh*, n 7 above, [15].
[12] Munday, n 5 above.
[13] See generally Chapter 2 above.
[14] Munday, n 5 above, 283.

(e) dealing with the case efficiently and expeditiously;
(f) ensuring that appropriate information is available to the court when bail and sentence are considered; and
(g) dealing with the case in ways that take into account—
  (i) the gravity of the offence alleged,
  (ii) the complexity of what is in issue,
  (iii) the severity of the consequences for the defendant and others affected, and
  (iv) the needs of other cases.

5.13 From this, it is clear that the 'interests of justice' are first and foremost the need to secure a result that is factually accurate; and hence the first consideration should be whether or not the evidence in question appears to the court to be cogent. But as against this, the court must also protect the defendant's Convention rights; and so hearsay evidence must not be admitted (whether under section 114(1)(d) or any other exception) if this would infringe his right of confrontation under ECHR, Article 6(3)(d) and its attendant case law.[15] Subject to these two considerations, the 'interests of justice' also extend to wider matters. 'Dealing with the prosecution and the defence fairly' must include preventing each side playing fast and loose with the Criminal Procedure Rules, and in particular Part 34 about giving notice of the intention to produce hearsay evidence; so in principle, a proper matter to take into account in relation to an application to admit hearsay under section 114(1)(d) would be the fact that the applicant had given notice of his intention to use it, and the other side had failed to enter an objection. In this situation, the need 'to deal with the case efficiently and expeditiously' would point towards admitting the evidence. But where the offence in question is a grave one, and the defendant if convicted faces heavy punishment, item (g) in the list makes it clear that administrative considerations of this sort should not outweigh the need for an accurate result.

5.14 In addition to these general considerations, section 114(2), as we have seen (§ 5.1 above), sets out a list of no less than nine different factors to which 'the court must have regard' when deciding whether hearsay evidence should be admitted under section 114(1)(d); and for good measure, it also requires the court to have regard to 'any other facts it considers relevant'. How much 'consideration' is it required to give?

5.15 *No need to reach a conclusion on all the stated factors* In *Taylor*,[15a] two of the witnesses to an ugly incident of violence were juveniles, with whom the police had conducted 'video-interviews', which the prosecution wished to put in evidence as a substitute for their live evidence-in-chief, as the law permits in the case of a

[15] See Chapter 2 above.
[15a] [2006] EWCA Crim 260, [2006] 2 CrAppR 14 (222), [**page 292 below**].

vulnerable witness, provided he or she is available for cross-examination at the trial.[16] The defence objected to certain passages in these video-interviews, because they incidentally contained statements which were hearsay: remarks to the effect that 'Later on, we were told that the name of the person we saw carrying out the attack was Taylor'. This objection the trial judge overruled, applying section 114(1)(d). In doing so, however, he explicitly mentioned that he had been unable to form a clear view on some of the factors set out in section 114(2), including 'the circumstances in which the hearsay statement had been made' and 'the reliability of the informant'; in other words, what the person who had given the information repeated in the interview was like, and how he had come to communicate it to the witness.

5.16 On appeal, the defence argued that, on account of this omission to make findings on these matters, the judge's ruling was wrong. This argument was rejected. Observing that if the defence argument was correct

> . . . and those words denote an obligation on a trial judge to embark on an investigation, resulting in some cases in the hearing of evidence, in order that he may reach a conclusion established by reference to each of the nine factors, it is apparent that trials are likely to be considerably elongated,

the Court of Appeal held that the judge is required to 'give consideration' to all of the factors mentioned in section 114(2), but (at [39]):

> [t]here is nothing in the wording of the statute to require him to reach a specific conclusion in relation to each or any of them. He must give consideration to those identified facts and any others which he considers relevant (as expressed in s 114(2) before the nine factors are listed). It is then his task to assess the significance of those factors, both in relation to each other and having regard to such weight as, in his judgment, they bear individually and in relation to each other. Having approached the matter in that way, he will be able, as it seems to us, in accordance with the words of the statute, to reach a proper conclusion as to whether or not the oral evidence should be admitted.

5.17 *Appeal courts are reluctant to 'second-guess'* If the court has made its decision after 'considering' the factors that subsection (2) requires it to consider, the appeal courts (as in other situations of this sort) 'will only interfere with such an exercise of judgment if it is satisfied that the judge's conclusion was plainly wrong';[17] or as the Court of Appeal explained in another case at slightly greater length:

> This was a situation calling for the exercise of the judgment of the trial judge. This court will interfere if, but only if, he has exercised it on wrong principles or reached a conclusion which was outside the band of legitimate decision available to him.[18]

[16] Youth Justice and Criminal Evidence Act 1999, s 27. CJA 2003, ss 137 and 138, which are not yet in force, create a wider power to do this: see Chapter 11.

[17] *Richards*, n 7 above, [25].

[18] *Finch*, n 7 above, [23].

5.18 However, it will interfere if the court below has misunderstood any of the factors. Thus, in one case, the trial judge had dismissed factors (e) and (f) (which refer to the reliability of the maker and of the statement made) by saying (in effect) 'all that is a matter for the jury'. This, said the Court of Appeal, was wrong: the judge, at a jury trial, is obliged to consider the issue of reliability when deciding whether or not the hearsay statement should be put before them.[19] In another case, the trial judge, confronted with a request by one of three joint defendants in a murder case to admit via section 114(1)(d) a hearsay statement made by the second of the three co-defendants placing the blame for the victim's death on the shoulders of the third, had refused the application on the ground that granting it would go against the well-known rule that what one co-defendant said against another out of court is inadmissible in evidence. This, said the Court of Appeal, was wrong, because the effect of section 114(1)(d) was to reverse the well-known rule. Accordingly it quashed the conviction, and ordered a new trial.[20]

5.19 In addition to the nine factors mentioned in section 114(2), the courts are likely to take into account the need to avoid unnecessary delay and expense. In this spirit, the Court of Appeal has allowed section 114(1)(d) to be used to put before the court a short summary, prepared by the prosecution, of the main evidence in a previous fraud trial at the end of which the defendant had been convicted, in order to show in simple terms that his previous offence was very similar to the present one, and that he was therefore in the habit of committing this particular type of crime.[21] Conversely, the courts would be unlikely to permit the adduction of otherwise inadmissible hearsay evidence under section 114(1)(d) if it would be of little value and protract the trial to no good purpose: as in *Recica*,[22] where two brothers jointly tried for immigration offences blamed each other, a 'satellite issue' arose between them, bearing upon the credibility of the evidence of one of them, as to whether he had at one point lied or told the truth about the death of their father, and the judge refused to admit in evidence a written statement from an official of the British Council in Kosovo stating that a person had recently visited him and claimed to be their father—a refusal the Court of Appeal said was justified, as the evidence 'went only to the collateral issue of credibility'.[23]

5.20 Another factor which judges and magistrates will be expected to consider where the application comes from the prosecution is the defendant's right 'to examine or

[19] *Musone*, n 7 above, [25]–[26]. Having said this, the Court of Appeal held that in the circumstances the decision to admit the disputed hearsay statement was correct.

[20] *McLean and others* [2007] EWCA Crim 219 [2008] 1 CrAppR 11 (155).

[21] [2007] EWCA Crim 335.

[22] [2007] EWCA Crim 2471.

[23] In fact s 114(1)(d) was not mentioned in the judgment, which dealt with the matter on the basis that, if admissible at all, the statement was multiple hearsay, to which CJA 2003, s 121 applied; on which see Chapter 11.

have examined witnesses against him', as protected by ECHR, Article 6(3)(d).[24] If admitting the prosecution evidence under section 114(1)(d) would contravene the defendant's right under this provision, as interpreted by the case law from both the Strasbourg and the English courts, then it must not be admitted: as was held by the Divisional Court in *McEwan v DPP*,[25] a case that was discussed in at § 2.39 above. Where the application comes from the prosecution, it is also relevant, at least in theory, to consider PACE 1984, section 78, although in practice it is hard to imagine how a court could first decide that it was 'in the interests of justice' to admit a hearsay statement and then go on to decide that 'the admission of the evidence would have such an adverse effect on the fairness of the proceedings that the court ought not to admit it'.

5.21 *A factor significant in practice: signs of fabrication* When the idea of an 'inclusionary discretion' was first floated, the Crown Prosecution Service told the Law Commission that it would lead to 'a large number of unmeritorious applications'.[26] The case law suggests that this fear was justified, in that some defendants do now indeed try to persuade courts to admit, via section 114(1)(d), out-of-court statements non-witnesses are implausibly alleged to have made, either confessing to the offence themselves or claiming that they saw someone else commit it. But it also suggests that the courts will reject this type of evidence as presumptively unreliable where they can smell fabrication. In *O'Hare*[27] the Court of Appeal declined to admit an alleged confession by a third party as 'fresh evidence', inter alia because it 'was made at a meeting which was set up for the purpose of discussing ways of to get [the defendant] out of prison'. In *Richards*[28] the Court of Appeal endorsed the trial judge's refusal to allow the defence to call X to swear that Y had told him he had seen someone other than the defendant commit the crime, first because X was closely associated with the defendant, and secondly because Y had been traced and at trial had given live evidence that said the opposite.[29]

Particular applications of CJA 2003, section 114(1)(d)

5.22 *To circumvent the limitations of section 116 ('unavailable witnesses')* CJA 2003, section 116, creates a general exception to the hearsay rule in respect of the

[24] See generally, Chapter 2 above.
[25] [2007] EWHC 740 (Admin), (2007) 171 JP 308.
[26] LC Report, n 1 above, § 8.143.
[27] *O'Hare* [2006] EWCA Crim 2512 at [30].
[28] [2007] EWCA Crim 709.
[29] And compare *Sajjad and Iqbal* [2007] EWCA Crim 1059, where the Court of Appeal endorsed a trial judge's refusal to admit, via s 114(1)(d), evidence of 'cell non-confession': evidence from a person who had at one point been in the cells with the defendants, and who claimed that he had heard one or other of the Sajjad's co-defendants tell him that 'he should not worry, that it was nothing to do with him, that he was innocent and that he should get bail' (at [29]).

evidence of absent witnesses who are 'unavailable'. It deals with the issue in considerable detail and most of the situations where 'the interests of justice' (in a broad sense) might seem to require the court to hear the evidence of an absent witness are expressly covered. In the light of this, the courts are (unsurprisingly) reluctant to allow section 114(1)(d) to be used in order to admit the out-of-court statement of an absent witness who is not covered by section 116. As Scott-Baker LJ said in *O'Hare*, 'We think it important to point out that, as a matter of generality, section 114 cannot and should not be applied so as to render section 116 nugatory'.[30]

5.23 In reality, most cases where advocates invoke the 'inclusionary discretion' in an attempt to persuade the court to admit the hearsay statement of an absent witness to which section 116 does not apply are made when the 'missing' witness was in fact available to testify, or might have been, if greater efforts had been made to secure his attendance; and in such cases the courts are unsympathetic. Where the defence wish to use the hearsay statement of a witness who is absent but unavailable, the court usually suspects that the defence are afraid the witness would tell a different story if he got into the witness-box, and so would rather use the hearsay.[31] And where the prosecution wish to do this, it is usually because they have been too disorganised to secure the witness's attendance: as in *McEwan v DPP* (discussed above),[32] or as in *Williams*,[33] where the sole independent witness to a wounding was an 11-year-old boy whose parents were reluctant to allow him to give evidence, and (in the Court of Appeal's view) the police and the CPS had not really tried to change their minds. Furthermore, where the absent prosecution witness is central to the prosecution case, the courts are doubly unwilling to admit his evidence as hearsay because this might contravene the defendant's rights under ECHR, Article 6(3)(d).[34]

5.24 In *Musone*,[35] however, the Court of Appeal did endorse the decision of a trial judge who had used the 'inclusionary discretion' to admit, as prosecution evidence, the hearsay statement of a witness who was not technically 'unavailable'. Reid, a prisoner, had been murdered in his cell at Ryehill prison. A number of pieces of evidence pointed to Musone as the culprit, including the fact that, just before he died, Reid allegedly told a fellow prisoner, Patterson, that it was Musone who had stabbed him. Patterson gave this information to the police but then refused to testify at trial. This being so, the judge applied section 114(1)(d) to admit in evidence his statement to the police.

[30] [2006] EWCA Crim 2512 at [30].
[31] As in *O'Hare*, n 27 above; and see *Finch*, 5.28 below.
[32] See § 5.20 above.
[33] [2007] EWCA Crim 211.
[34] See generally Chapter 2 above.
[35] [2007] EWCA Crim 1237, [2007] 1 WLR 2467.

5.25 At first sight, this decision might seem difficult to square with cases like *McEwen v DPP* and *Williams*, but there are two important differences. First, there was other strong evidence against Musone and it was not on Patterson's evidence that the case against him stood or fell. Secondly, Patterson, unlike the witnesses in the cases discussed in the previous two paragraphs, was in reality 'unavailable', even though in his case the formal requirements of section 116 were not met. As is explained below,[36] a witness only counts as 'unavailable' for the purposes of section 116 if he cannot be produced for one of the five reasons listed in that section, and these do not include the case of the witness who, despite the threat of punishment for contempt of court, simply refuses point-blank to go into the witness-box or, having done so, will not utter. This omission seems distinctly odd; under the equivalent legislation in Scotland, for example, a witness such as Patterson would certainly count as 'unavailable', so enabling his previous statement to be used.[37] By allowing section 114(1)(d) to be used in this case, in other words, the English courts are not using it to make good the negligence of the prosecution, but rather the deficient drafting of the CJA 2003.

5.26 This suggests another situation in which the courts would probably be prepared to use section 114(1)(d) to admit the hearsay statement of a witness who is in reality unavailable, although not 'unavailable' as defined by section 116. This is the witness who, at the time of making the statement, was demented. By CJA 2003, section 123, section 116 cannot be used to admit the statement 'if it was made by a person who did not have the required capability at the time when he made the statement'. So if, for example, a person suffering from dementia to the point where she would be incompetent to give evidence as a witness makes a statement which, when put together with other pieces of evidence, indicates that she has been abused by the defendant, this statement cannot be put in evidence under section 116. CJA 1988, section 23, which CJA 2003, section 116, has now replaced, was not subject to this restriction; and under the earlier provision, the courts saw no injustice in admitting statements from demented persons in this type of case.[38] It seems likely that, where this situation arises now, they will invoke section 114(1)(d).[39]

5.27 *To admit statements by co-defendants and accomplices* Not infrequently, D1 wishes to use in evidence a statement that his alleged accomplice, D2, made out of court to the police (or other authorities) and which is favourable to D1's case. D2 may have confessed, for instance, in terms which relieve D1 of blame or, though

[36] See Chapter 6 below.

[37] Criminal Procedure (Scotland) Act 1995, s 259(2)(e).

[38] *D* [2002] EWCA Crim 990, [2002] 2 Cr App R 36 (601); *Sed* [2004] EWCA Crim 1294, [2004] 1 WLR 3218; see § 2.41 above.

[39] See *DPP v R* [2007] EWHC 1842 (Admin). This possibility was recognised by the Law Commission, LC Report, n 1 above, § 8.143, where they said that for the inclusionary discretion to apply '[t]he declarant need not have been competent as a witness'.

not amounting to a confession, D2's statement may contain matters which support D1's defence. If D1 and D2 are both prosecuted, and as co-defendants appear in the dock together, D1 cannot in law require D2 to testify as a witness for him.[40] However, if in this situation D2 is not prepared to testify in favour of D1 voluntarily, PACE 1984, section 76A (examined in Chapter 10) sometimes enables him to put in evidence D2's statement to the police, where this amounts in law to a 'confession', and is helpful to D1's case. Where D1 cannot make use of section 76A of PACE, then the courts are now prepared (in principle at least) to consider admitting it under the 'inclusionary discretion' in section 114(1)(d).[41]

5.28 The law described in the previous paragraph only applies where the two accomplices are, in law, co-defendants. Accomplices are not co-defendants, obviously, if one or other of them is not prosecuted. Less obviously, accomplices do not count in law as 'co-defendants' where both were prosecuted together initially, but by the time of trial one of them has dropped out, as where he pled guilty, for example, or where separate trials were ordered, or the proceedings against one of them is dropped. Where they are not co-defendants, it is then open to each one of them to call the other as a witness; and according to the Court of Appeal in *Finch*,[42] that is the proper course for D1 to take if he then wishes to make use of D2's evidence in his defence. In this situation, D1 cannot put D2's confession in evidence by virtue of section 76A of PACE because this only applies where D1 and D2 are co-defendants.[43] Because D1 is able to call D2 as a witness at his trial, it is not in the interests of justice to allow D1 to put D2's hearsay account before the court by invoking the 'inclusionary discretion' in section 114(1)(d).

5.29 In this case, Finch and Richer were stopped by the police when driving together in Richer's car, in which the police discovered a gun, packed in a bag which had Finch's fingerprints on it. When interviewed by the police, Richer took the blame and assured them (rather implausibly, in the light of the fingerprint evidence) that Finch did not know the gun was in the car. Both were charged with illegal possession of the gun, and when Richer pled guilty and Finch denied the offence, the proceedings continued against Finch alone. At his trial, Finch sought to put Richer's exculpatory statement before the court as part of his defence, but the judge refused to let it in, for the reasons mentioned in the previous paragraph. Upholding the decision of the trial judge, the Court of Appeal said:

> Whatever might be the situation if an erstwhile co-accused were to be unavailable or had demonstrably good reason not to give evidence, it will, as it seems to us, often not be in the interests of justice for evidence which the giver is not prepared to have tested, to

[40] Criminal Evidence Act 1898, s 1(1).

[41] See *McLean and others*, discussed at § 5.18 above.

[42] [2007] EWCA Crim 36, [2007] 1 Cr App R 33 (439), [2007] 1 WLR 1645 **[page 308 below]**.

[43] *Finch*, n 7 above, [11]–[19]. The Court of Appeal certified a point of public importance, but refused leave to appeal.

be put untested before the jury. It is not, in short, the law that every reluctant witness's evidence automatically can be put before the jury under section 114 of the 2003 Act.[44]

By implication, the courts might be prepared to admit the accomplice's statement under section 114(1)(d) where the accomplice was not merely reluctant but actually refused to testify, either because he was able to shelter behind the privilege against self-incrimination or because he was prepared to defy the law.

5.30 In principle, section 114(1)(d) could not only be used by a defendant to put the exculpatory statement of his co-accused before the court, but also by the prosecution to put before the court an out-of-court statement by one co-accused which incriminates the other. But in so holding in the recent case of *Y*[44a], the Court of Appeal made it clear that, before allowing an application under section 114(1)(d) that was directed to this end, the court should be very careful to consider all the factors listed in section 114(2), and also whether 'overall it is genuinely in the interests of justice'. Admitting evidence against a defendant his co-accused's statement in this way could potentially run into conflict with the incriminated defendant's rights under ECHR, Article 6(3)(d), at any rate, if it was the key piece of evidence against him.[45]

5.31 *To circumvent the limitations of section 117 ('business and other documents')* If the courts are understandably cautious about using the 'inclusionary discretion' to circumvent the limits of CJA 2003, section 116, which deals explicitly with the evidence of witnesses who are 'unavailable', they have no such inhibitions about using section 114(1)(d) to let in cogent evidence contained in a 'record' which falls foul of the drafting technicalities in section 117, which in principle creates an exception to the hearsay rule for statements contained in 'business and other records'. This clearly emerges from *Maher v DPP*, discussed at § 5.7 above (but as is explained in § 5.39 below, they are likely to take a stricter line where the 'record' is known to be inaccurate).

5.32 *To admit the previous statement of a witness in circumvention of the 'rule against narrative'* Similarly, the courts have few inhibitions about allowing section 114(1)(d) to be used to circumvent the 'rule against narrative', which the CJA 2003 lovingly preserves, together with a crop of complicated and technical exceptions.[46] This is clear from *Xhabri*, the facts of which were given at § 5.9 above. As the witness is before the court, the Court of Appeal said, she could be cross-examined not only on the evidence she gave orally at trial but also as to the truth of the previous statements,

[44] At [24]. But it should perhaps be noted that in the slightly earlier case of *Lamb* [2006] EWCA Crim 3347, which was not referred to in *Finch*, the trial judge had permitted a defendant to put the statement of an 'erstwhile co-defendant' before the court by using s. 114(1)(d): and the Court of Appeal let this pass without adverse comment.

[44a] [2008] EWCA Crim 10; the issue of principle is further discussed at § 10.35 below.

[45] *Lucà v Italy*; see § 2.15 above.

[46] See generally Chapter 12 below.

and in the light of that, to admit evidence of her previous statements was neither unfair to the defendant nor in conflict with his rights under ECHR, Article 6(3)(d).[46a]

5.33 *To admit the previous statement of the defendant* Traditionally, the defendant's previous statements, if adverse to his case, were admissible against him as 'confessions', and if partly adverse and partly favourable, admissible as evidence both for him and against him as 'mixed statements'. But if the defendant denied the offence, however convincingly, the law branded his denial as a 'self-serving statement' and not admissible in evidence for the defence. When 'self-serving statements' were made to the police, the courts would frequently get to hear about them, but in theory they had no evidential status. In *S*[47] the defendant, who was accused with others of a robbery, unsuccessfully tried to persuade the trial judge to admit in evidence on his behalf the 'self-serving' statement he had made to his solicitor in which he minimised his part in the events, invoking the 'inclusionary discretion'. Dismissing his appeal, the Court of Appeal pointed out that his statement, far from helping him, was inconsistent with the account of the events he later gave, and if admitted would have hindered his defence rather than assisted it. But the judgment seems to accept that, where the defendant's 'self-serving' statement was actually helpful to his defence, it might have been admitted under section 114(1)(d).

5.34 *To help the witness tell a coherent story* One of the long-standing criticisms of the hearsay rule is that, if rigorously applied, it makes it harder for a witness to give his evidence in a coherent manner: in order to avoid repeating anything that he heard from someone else, he is forced to jump over parts of his narrative or rephrase parts of it with awkward circumlocutions.[48] It seems that the courts are prepared, where necessary, to invoke section 114(1)(d) to make this unnecessary. This was essentially the case in *Taylor*.[49] The evidence-in-chief of the young witnesses consisted, in that case, of the video-interviews that the police had earlier conducted with them, in the course of which they described the attack and the attacker, at some point in the story mentioning 'and someone later told us he was called Taylor'. Given that they had said in their evidence that they recognised him by sight at the time of the attack, the fact that someone later told them the name of the person whom they recognised was not particularly detrimental to the defendant's case and there was really no point in breaking the flow of their narratives to cut this piece of information out.

[46a] In *Lynch* [2007] EWCA Crim 3035, the Court of Appeal approved the use of section 114(1)(d) to admit the words that a witness said at an identification parade, describing what the person she identified was doing—and said that this was the sort of situation the provision was designed to cover.

[47] [2006] EWCA Crim 2272.

[48] See § 1.45 above.

[49] See § 5.15 above [**page 292 below**].

5.35 Similar in spirit is *Walker*.[50] Here the defendant was accused of murder, and part of the evidence against him was that immediately after the killing he had taken steps to dispose of the gun. In his evidence, Walker's cousin Bogle described how, shortly after, one of Walker's associates, Campbell, had given him the gun to look after, saying 'Your cousin said hold this and he'll collect it in the morning'. The Court of Appeal said that the judge had acted properly in invoking section 114(1)(d) to allow Bogle to repeat what Campbell had said, inter alia, because the fact that Walker's gun had been deposited with his cousin Bogle was in itself quite damning and Campbell's alleged statement did not really add much of significance.

5.36 The desirability of allowing witnesses to give their evidence freely is also reflected in *GJ*.[51] Here the defendant was accused of sexually abusing his step-daughter over a period of time. The defence case was that the whole story was a recent invention by the complainant. A prosecution witness was a close friend of the family, who described how on a number of occasions she was present when the defendant's improper behaviour towards his step-daughter was the subject of a family row, and in the course of her evidence, she was allowed to tell the court who had said what to whom. The Court of Appeal held this evidence was properly admitted for a number of legal reasons, including section 114(1)(d).[52]

5.37 To similar effect again is *Meade*.[53] The prosecution case against Meade was that he was selling drugs, and his defence was that, when the police raided, he just happened to be at the local 'crack-house' buying drugs for his own use. When the police raided the premises, they asked a woman whom they found there what she was doing and she told them 'I've come to the local crack-house to buy drugs'; and the woman then went on to describe the two people who were running it, the physical appearance of one of whom matched that of Meade. The defence insisted that the prosecution call the woman police officer to whom the woman had spoken, so that they could get her to repeat the female drug-addict's statement that the premises were a crack-house; and the judge, having allowed the police officer to repeat this part of the addict's statement, allowed her to repeat the other part of it, in which the addict described one of the people who ran it as matching the physical description of Meade.

5.38 In *Isichei*,[54] the facts of which were set out in Chapter 3, Auld LJ justified the decision to allow the girls to repeat in evidence their companion's remark that he

[50] [2007] EWCA Crim 1698.

[51] [2006] EWCA Crim 1939

[52] Parts of it were also admissible under CJA 2003, s 116 because one of the participants in the row (the complainant's mother) was now dead; and also because the defence had agreed that it should be admitted.

[53] [2007] EWCA Crim 1116.

[54] [2006] EWCA Crim 1815.

was 'calling Marvin' because it was 'part of the story of a common sense series of events, the one leading to the other'.

5.39 *To establish the details of a previous criminal offence* The 'bad character evidence' provisions of the CJA 2003 now make it possible for the prosecution, in a wide range of cases, to make use of the defendant's previous convictions. Where the defendant disputes the fact of the conviction, the courts have said that this must in principle be established by producing a certificate of conviction from the court of trial; and this is not to be circumvented by producing a print-out from the Police National Computer (PNC), because information held it in does not satisfy the requirements of the 'record' exception in CJA 2003, section 117.[55] As the PNC is often inaccurate,[56] and the courts are aware of this, the courts are unwilling allow the prosecution to avoid the trouble of obtaining a formal certificate of conviction by admitting the print-out from the PNC under section 114(1)(d).[57] However, it is sometimes necessary for the prosecution to establish not just the fact that the defendant has a previous conviction, but also details of the crime which the official certificate of conviction does not reveal. In this situation, the courts encourage the prosecution and defence to agree the facts. But if this is not possible, then in such a case the prosecution must in principle establish the disputed facts using legally admissible evidence; and if the courts were strict about this, this could mean forcing the prosecution to produce the witnesses to the original trial to give evidence again. In *S*,[58] the defendant was accused of an advance fee fraud, and the prosecution wished to use in evidence the fact that he had previously been convicted of another fraud which was virtually identical. The prosecution were unable to reach agreement with the defence as to what the details of the previous fraud were, so the prosecution sought to establish them by means of a document which contained a distillation of the defendant's evidence in the earlier case, supplemented by what he had said to the police in interviews leading up to it. This the judge decided to admit, by applying section 114(1)(d). Upholding the judge's decision, the Court of Appeal said 'It was clearly in the interests of justice that the document went before the jury. There was no reason why the jury should be encumbered with any more of the material in the evidence than was necessary for them to have a sensible understanding of how the prosecution was putting its case'.

[55] *Humphris* [2005] EWCA Crim 2030; see further Chapter 6; and JR Spencer, *Evidence of Bad Character* (Oxford, Hart, 2006) § 5.17.

[56] *Ibid* § 5.4.

[57] *Kavallieratos* [2006] EWCA Crim 2819.

[58] [2007] EWCA Crim 335, [2007] All ER (D) 119.

Discretionary exclusion: CJA 2003, section 126

5.40 The general discretion conferred on the court by section 114(1)(d) to override the hearsay rule in favour of admitting evidence that would otherwise be inadmissible is matched by another provision which gives the court a general discretion to exclude hearsay evidence which is in principle admissible as a result of one of the exceptions to the rule. This is section 126, which is as follows:

> Court's general discretion to exclude evidence
>
> (1) In criminal proceedings the court may refuse to admit a statement as evidence of a matter stated if—
>
> (a) the statement was made otherwise than in oral evidence in the proceedings, and
>
> (b) the court is satisfied that the case for excluding the statement, taking account of the danger that to admit it would result in undue waste of time, substantially outweighs the case for admitting it, taking account of the value of the evidence.
>
> (2) Nothing in this Chapter prejudices—
>
> (a) any power of a court to exclude evidence under section 78 of the Police and Criminal Evidence Act 1984 (c. 60) (exclusion of unfair evidence), or
>
> (b) any other power of a court to exclude evidence at its discretion (whether by preventing questions from being put or otherwise).

5.41 This section derives from clause 15 of the Law Commission's Draft Bill. In proposing it, the Law Commission pointed out that similar statutory provisions have been enacted in a number of other parts of the common law world.[59] (In England, too, it was foreshadowed by CJA 1988, sections 25 and 26, which gave the court wide powers to exclude hearsay evidence which the preceding sections of that Act had made admissible.) The aim, of course, is to answer one of the classic objections to reforming the law so as to make hearsay evidence more readily admissible: that to do so would result in court time being wasted in hearing evidence of tangential relevance and little weight.[60]

5.42 There is a large overlap between section 126 and other sections of the CJA 2003, which give the courts a measure of discretion when confronted with evidence that is hearsay: section 114(1)(d), discussed earlier in this chapter; section 116(2)(d) and (4), which make admissible the hearsay statement of a witness who

[59] Law Commission, *Evidence in Criminal Proceedings and Related Matters* (Consultation Paper No 138, 1995) § 11.35; LC Report, n 1 above, § 11.16. Provisions of this sort are also found in the Criminal Procedure Codes in some parts of continental Europe: see eg art 309 of the French Code de procédure pénale: 'The presiding judge maintains order in court and conducts the proceedings. He dismisses anything which might tend to compromise their dignity or protract them without expectation of any greater degree of certainty in the outcome of the hearing'.

[60] See § 1.32 above.

does not give evidence through fear, but only where the court gives leave;[61] section 117(7), which requires the court to reject documentary hearsay otherwise admissible under that provision if it is satisfied that it is unreliable;[62] and section 121, which requires the court to reject 'multiple hearsay' unless it is satisfied as to its value and reliability.[63] Furthermore, where the evidence in question is tendered by the prosecution, there is also an important overlap between section 126 and PACE 1984, section 78.

5.43 Where section 126 overlaps with these other provisions, the overlap is not complete. Some of them (notably PACE 1984, section 78) are wider, and also require the court to exclude otherwise admissible evidence for reasons other than its potential unreliability.[64] Some of them are narrower, notably section 116(2)(d) and (4), which is mainly concerned with ensuring that efforts have been made to enable the fearful witness to give live evidence, and avoiding embarrassment to the other side arising from their inability to test his evidence in cross-examination.[65] But although the overlap is not complete, it still seems big enough to ensure that the number of cases in which section 126 is invoked, and then becomes crucially important, are relatively few.

5.44 Section 126 is most likely to be applied, presumably, in cases where the evidence in question is of peripheral relevance: for example, where it bears upon the credibility of a witness, rather than the central issue in the case.[66] However, it is drafted in general terms, which appear quite wide enough to enable the court, if it thought it appropriate, to exclude weak evidence which was directly relevant.[67]

5.45 But although the marginal note describes the section as creating a 'general discretion' to exclude hearsay evidence, the wording of the provision itself suggests that the power it confers is intended to enable the courts to exclude hearsay evidence which, by reason of its poor quality or low relevance, is likely to generate more heat than light, and not on more general grounds of 'fairness', as is the case with PACE, section 78.[68]

[61] See § 6.25 below.

[62] See § 7.23 below.

[63] See Chapter 11 below.

[64] See § 15.27 below.

[65] See *Gyima* [2007] EWCA Crim 429 at [29].

[66] As in *Recica* § 5.19 above.

[67] Thus, in *Gyima* n 65 above, the Court of Appeal thought that it potentially enabled the court to exclude the statement of one of the eye-witnesses to a street robbery.

[68] On this, see David Ormerod's comment on [2006] EWCA Crim 197, at [2006] Crim LR 637; and the comment by James Richardson at [2006] 25 *Current Law Week* 8.

6

STATEMENTS OF WITNESSES WHO ARE UNAVAILABLE (CJA 2003, SECTION 116)

6.1 Section 116 of the CJA 2003 creates an exception to the hearsay rule for statements made by witnesses who are 'unavailable'. It applies where the witness is unavailable for any one of five listed reasons: death, physical or mental illness, absence abroad, disappearance, and fear.

6.2 This list of possible cases covers most of the usual reasons why a witness might be unavailable to give evidence, but not all of them. It fails, in particular, to deal with the case where a witness refuses to give evidence: as he may do legally, where he is non-compellable or able to claim a privilege, or illegally, by simply refusing. (This issue is discussed at § 6.36 to § 6.37 below.)

6.3 Although not limited to this type of case, CJA 2003, section 116 was drawn up with the case in mind of the witness who, when the crime was being investigated, gave a formal statement about it to the police or to the defence lawyers, and then for some reason became unavailable, and this is the usual situation in which it is invoked. For that reason, it is interesting to place it in the context of earlier legislative attempts to make such formal statements admissible at trial.

History: earlier provisions

6.4 *CJA 1925, section 13(3)* Formerly, cases prosecuted on indictment invariably reached the Crown Court[1] via 'committal proceedings', a preliminary hearing before magistrates at which the key prosecution witnesses gave evidence orally, on oath, and were subject to cross-examination by the defence. The evidence so given

[1] Or, before the Courts Act 1971, Assizes or Quarter Sessions.

was taken down in writing and signed by the justice, and the resulting document was called a *deposition*. The depositions were included in an official file, on the strength of which, if the magistrates thought the evidence was strong enough, the accused was formally *committed for trial*. By CJA 1925, section 13(3), it was provided that the deposition could be used in place of the maker's live evidence at trial where he had became unavailable for any of three reasons: death, illness (physical or mental), or where he was 'kept out of the way by means of the procurement of the accused or on his behalf'.[2]

6.5 The CJA 1967 provided for a new 'short form' of committal proceedings under which, where the accused agreed, he was committed without the justices hearing oral evidence and on the basis of a file containing the written statements taken from the prosecution witnesses by the police; and it also provided that, where this was done, the police witness statements counted as 'depositions' for the purpose of CJA 1925, section 13.[3]

6.6 *CJA 1988, section 23*[4] In 1988 Parliament, at the instance of the Home Office, which in turn was reacting to the recommendations of the Roskill Committee on Fraud Trials,[5] included in the CJA 1988 some sections which created new exceptions to the hearsay rule. Of these, section 23 dealt with the problem of witnesses who were 'unavailable'.[6] Under this new provision, hearsay evidence could be given where the witness had become unavailable for any of a list of five reasons, two more than in CJA 1925, section 13. The new list was death, physical or mental illness, absence abroad, disappearance, and fear: the same as the list that now appears in CJA 2003, section 116. However, the 1988 provision was significantly narrower than the new provision. In the first place, unlike the new provision, it was limited to *written* statements. Secondly, unlike the new provision it did not operate automatically: in some situations the court had a discretion to exclude the statement, and in others, judicial leave was needed before it could be admitted. But even with these restrictions, CJA 1998, section 23 made an important change. In practice it was widely used, and a sizeable body of case law grew up around it.[7] It overlapped, of course, with CJA 1925, section 13, which remained in force alongside it.

6.7 In 1996, Parliament, in the course of changing yet again the rules relating to committal proceedings, repealed CJA 1925, section 13(3) and replaced it with a

[2] Criminal Justice Act 1925, s 13, which in this respect codified the rules which had earlier evolved at common law.
[3] CJA 1967, s 2(7), later re-enacted as Magistrates' Courts Act 1980, s 102(7).
[4] The text in its form as originally enacted is reproduced as an Annex to this chapter.
[5] Fraud Trials Committee (Roskill Committee), *Report* (London, HMSO, 1986).
[6] For the discussions surrounding its enactment, see 1.73 above.
[7] See Archbold, *Criminal Pleading, Evidence and Practice* (2002) para 9.26 *et seq.*

new provision[8] which, on the face of it, provided that any statement which was part of the written file on the basis of which the magistrates committed a person for trial in the Crown Court could be used as evidence, whether the maker was available to give oral evidence at trial or not, unless the trial judge, 'in the interests of justice', ruled otherwise. On the face of it, this astonishing provision made CJA 2003, section 23 largely redundant. The clause that did this emanated from the Home Office, without prior public consultation, and was slipped through Parliament in an obscure part of a Bill most of which was concerned with something else, circumstances which led to public accusations of sharp practice.[9] Notwithstanding the attractive new possibilities that it apparently offered prosecutors, this provision seems in practice to have been little used; and in its Report on hearsay in 1997 the Law Commission condemned it and recommended that it be repealed.[10] A provision buried in one of the Schedules to the CJA 2003[11] has, in theory, done this; but at the time of writing, this repealing provision has not been brought into force, and so the death sentence pronounced upon the provision four years ago is still suspended.[12]

The new provision: CJA 2003, section 116

6.8 CJA 2003, section 116 is as follows:

> Cases where a witness is unavailable
>
> (1) In criminal proceedings a statement not made in oral evidence in the proceedings is admissible as evidence of any matter stated if—
>
> (a) oral evidence given in the proceedings by the person who made the statement would be admissible as evidence of that matter,
>
> (b) the person who made the statement (the relevant person) is identified to the court's satisfaction, and
>
> (c) any of the five conditions mentioned in subsection (2) is satisfied.
>
> (2) The conditions are—
>
> (a) that the relevant person is dead;
>
> (b) that the relevant person is unfit to be a witness because of his bodily or mental condition;

[8] Criminal Procedure and Investigations Act 1996, Sch 2, para 1.

[9] Roderick Munday, 'The Drafting Smokescreen' (1997) 147 NLJ 972, 860.

[10] Law Commission, *Evidence in Criminal Proceedings: Hearsay and Related Topics* (Report No 245, Cm 3670, June 1997) 197, Recommendation 21.

[11] CJA 2003, Sch 3, Pt 2, para 66(8).

[12] So as a companion to the long-standing problem of 'virtual law', there now exists a new one: 'virtual repeals'.

(c) that the relevant person is outside the United Kingdom and it is not reasonably practicable to secure his attendance;

(d) that the relevant person cannot be found although such steps as it is reasonably practicable to take to find him have been taken;

(e) that through fear the relevant person does not give (or does not continue to give) oral evidence in the proceedings, either at all or in connection with the subject matter of the statement, and the court gives leave for the statement to be given in evidence.

(3) For the purposes of subsection (2)(e) 'fear' is to be widely construed and (for example) includes fear of the death or injury of another person or of financial loss.

(4) Leave may be given under subsection (2)(e) only if the court considers that the statement ought to be admitted in the interests of justice, having regard—

(a) to the statement's contents,

(b) to any risk that its admission or exclusion will result in unfairness to any party to the proceedings (and in particular to how difficult it will be to challenge the statement if the relevant person does not give oral evidence),

(c) in appropriate cases, to the fact that a direction under section 19 of the Youth Justice and Criminal Evidence Act 1999 (c. 23) (special measures for the giving of evidence by fearful witnesses etc) could be made in relation to the relevant person, and

(d) to any other relevant circumstances.

(5) A condition set out in any paragraph of subsection (2) which is in fact satisfied is to be treated as not satisfied if it is shown that the circumstances described in that paragraph are caused—

(a) by the person in support of whose case it is sought to give the statement in evidence, or

(b) by a person acting on his behalf,

in order to prevent the relevant person giving oral evidence in the proceedings (whether at all or in connection with the subject matter of the statement).

Section 116 replaces CJA 1988, section 23, which has been repealed.[13]

6.9 This new provision adopts the wording proposed in the Law Commission's Draft Bill;[14] and that in turn was modelled to a large extent on CJA 1988, section 23, which it replaces. In particular, as already mentioned, the new section uses the same list of five conditions as its predecessor. In one important respect it is wider than the provision it replaces, however, because whereas under section 23 of the CJA 1988 the statement of a witness 'unavailable' for one of these reasons was admissible only subject to the discretion of the court, under CJA 2003, section 116, the statement is now automatically admissible (at least in principle)[15] if the wit-

[13] CJA 2003, s 332, Sch 37, Pt 6 repeals all of Part II of the CJA 1988.

[14] Clauses 3 and 5.

[15] Even in these cases, the court has power to exclude the statement under CJA 2003, s 126 (see § 6.23 below), and if it is prosecution evidence, under PACE 1984, s 78.

ness is unavailable through death, physical or mental illness, absence abroad, or disappearance; and it is only where fear is the reason for the witness's absence that the leave of the court is needed before the statement may be adduced.[16]

6.10 However, in two significant respects section 116 is narrower than CJA 1988, section 23, which it replaces. First, unlike section 23, it only operates where the absent witness can be identified; and secondly, unlike section 23 (as interpreted by the courts) it does not operate if the witness was mentally incompetent. These two limitations emerge from subsection (1), which sets out two preconditions, both of which must be present before the rest of the section can operate.

6.11 *The two preconditions: section 116(1)* Taking them in reverse order, section 116(1)(b) poses a precondition that 'the person who made the statement (the relevant person) is identified to the court's satisfaction'. Thus, section 116 could not be used to admit the statement from the unidentified bystander in *Teper v R*,[17] for example. The theory behind this, of course, is that unless the maker is identified, there is no possibility of investigating whether he is credible. Section 116(1)(a) poses a precondition that 'oral evidence given in the proceedings by the person who made the statement would be admissible as evidence of that matter'. This second precondition means in reality two different things. First, the statement must consist of matters which are legally admissible. The evidence must, of course, be relevant; and even if relevant, it must not consist of material which some other exclusionary rule makes it impossible to use in evidence. So, for example, as evidence obtained under torture is not admissible,[18] section 116 could not be used to admit in evidence the written statement from a guard in Guantanamo Bay, to the effect that X had given certain information under torture. And obviously, the section could not be used to admit a written statement from a person which merely repeats what he has heard from other people. Secondly, it means that the maker of the statement must have been competent as a witness at the time the statement is made. This second point is rammed home, in detail and at length, by section 123, which is as follows:

> Capability to make statement
>
> (1) Nothing in section 116, 119 or 120 makes a statement admissible as evidence if it was made by a person who did not have the required capability at the time when he made the statement.
>
> (2) Nothing in section 117 makes a statement admissible as evidence if any person who, in order for the requirements of section 117(2) to be satisfied, must at any time have supplied or received the information concerned or created or received the document or part concerned—

[16] Like its predecessor, s 116 does not affect the law relating to confessions: see CJA 2003, s 129(2).

[17] [1952] AC 480; see § 3.36 above.

[18] *A v Secretary of State for the Home Department (No 2)* [2005] UKHL 71, [2006] 2 AC 221.

(a) did not have the required capability at that time, or
(b) cannot be identified but cannot reasonably be assumed to have had the required capability at that time.

(3) For the purposes of this section a person has the required capability if he is capable of—

(a) understanding questions put to him about the matters stated, and
(b) giving answers to such questions which can be understood.

(4) Where by reason of this section there is an issue as to whether a person had the required capability when he made a statement—

(a) proceedings held for the determination of the issue must take place in the absence of the jury (if there is one);
(b) in determining the issue the court may receive expert evidence and evidence from any person to whom the statement in question was made;
(c) the burden of proof on the issue lies on the party seeking to adduce the statement, and the standard of proof is the balance of probabilities.

6.12 Provided these preconditions are met, the statement from the absent witness is admissible if he was available for one of the five reasons set out in section 116(2): death, physical or mental illness, absence abroad, disappearance, or fear. Taking each of these in turn, as follows.

6.13 *(a) that the relevant person is dead* This reason requires little explanation or discussion. Although with the other four conditions a question of degree may well arise, with death this is not so: in principle, a person is either dead or he is not. However, it is interesting to recall that, under the common law of England,[19] the fact that a witness was now dead did not of itself displace the hearsay rule, and some further condition had also to be present, for example, that the statement amounted to a 'dying declaration'. Dying declarations are not among the relics of the earlier law preserved by CJA 2003, section 118, but a dying declaration would, of course, now be admissible under section 116.[20]

6.14 *(b) that the relevant person is unfit to be a witness because of his bodily or mental condition* This was one of the reasons for admitting hearsay under CJA 1988, section 23, and the case law relating to that section is presumably still relevant. This suggested that the term 'unfitness' was not to be too narrowly construed.[21] Thus, a witness is unfit because of his bodily condition not only where he is bedridden and unable to get to court, but also where he could get there but there was

[19] It was otherwise in Scotland: WG Dickson, *A Treatise on the Law of Evidence in Scotland* (2nd edn by J Skelton, Edinburgh, Bell and Bradfute, 1864) §102; ID Macphail, *Evidence* (vol 10 of the *Stair Memorial Encyclopedia*, Edinburgh, Butterworths, 1991) §711.

[20] As in *Musone* [2007] EWCA Crim 1237 [2007] 1 WLR 2467.

[21] Roderick Munday, *Evidence* (4th edn, Oxford, OUP, 2007) § 9.30.

a high risk that it would make him ill.[22] A witness is also unfit because of his mental condition not only where he is (to put it crudely) raving mad, but also where, though sane, he is now unable to give evidence about the incident in question because of supervening amnesia.[23] However, to this generosity there are obviously limits. In one of the first decisions under the new provision, the Divisional Court held that magistrates were wrong to find that a witness was unfit on the basis of a certificate from a doctor which merely said that the patient 'has a past history of depressive illness with panic attacks', and 'I would suggest that it would be in her best interests if she was able to submit written evidence rather than having to appear in court'.[24] If the illness of a key witness is serious enough to prevent his or her attendance now, but he or she is likely to get better, the sensible solution, of course, is for the hearing to be adjourned. In *R (CPS) v Uxbridge Magistrates*,[25] the Divisional Court understandably criticised the court where, in this situation, it had both refused an adjournment and declined to admit the statement of the witness under section 116.

6.15 *(c) that the relevant person is outside the United Kingdom and it is not reasonably practicable to secure his attendance* This was another reason for admitting hearsay evidence under CJA 1988, section 23, and again the earlier case law is presumably still relevant. From this, and the emerging case law under the new provision, it is possible to sketch the main matters that the courts regard as relevant to the question whether it was 'reasonably practicable' to secure the attendance of the absent witness.

6.16 The first thing to remember here is that there is no legal mechanism by which it is possible to force a witness to travel from abroad to the United Kingdom to give evidence in person if he or she is not prepared to do so; and this is so not only in respect of distant countries like South Africa or China, but also as regards the Member States of the EU, like France or the Republic or Ireland.[26] So the question is not whether it is physically possible to transport the witness to England, but whether he can be persuaded to come voluntarily: so 'the word practicable is not the equivalent to physically possible'.[27]

[22] *Millett* [2000] EWCA Crim 50; and cf *Loveridge* [2007] EWCA Crim 1041, where the witness, the victim of a robbery, was aged 88, frail, deaf, half-blind and terrified at the prospect of going to court, and his doctor reported that 'the prospects of attending might be detrimental to his mental state'.

[23] *Setz-Dempsey* (1994) 98 Cr App R 23.

[24] *R (Meredith) v Harwich Justices* [2006] EWHC 3336 (Admin) 171 JP 249.

[25] [2007] EWHC 205, (2007) 171 JP 279.

[26] However, if an EU Member State has implemented Art 10 of the European Mutual Legal Assistance Convention of 2000, it is possible (at least in principle) to require the witness to give evidence via a video-link. See generally, JR Spencer, 'The Problems of Trans-border Evidence and European Initiatives to Resolve Them' (2007) 9 *Cambridge Yearbook of European Legal Studies* 465.

[27] Per Beldam LJ in *Malone* [1994] Crim LR 525; cited with approval in *Castillo* [1996] 1 Cr App R 437 and *Yu*, 6.18 below, [29].

6.17 In deciding whether or not it is 'reasonably practicable' to persuade the witness to come, the courts consider what efforts, if any, the party seeking to rely on the evidence made to secure the physical presence of the witness at the trial, and what other steps, if any, he could have taken. If there were other steps that were not taken, the court will ask itself whether it would have been 'reasonable' to take them; and in answering this question, the court will have to balance various competing factors. On the one hand, there are the cost and delay that would have been involved. On the other hand, there is the importance of the case: it may be reasonable to fly a witness across the world to give evidence in a murder trial, it is unlikely to be so where the charge is shoplifting or careless driving. And there is also 'the importance of the evidence that the witness can give and whether or not it was prejudicial, and how prejudicial it would be to the defence[28] that the witness did not attend'.[29] On the issue of prejudice, a relevant issue is the impact, if any, which cross-examination might have made upon the evidence of the witness in question, had it been possible. If the witness is someone who might be biased or mistaken, his evidence might be expected to look very different after cross-examination. But if he is (for example) an independent public official who has no motive to lie,[30] or where the statement is backed up by other independent evidence, such as records of bank transfers,[31] the party opposing the admission of the statement may be asked to explain what questions, if any, he would want to put to the witness if he were there.

6.18 These points are illustrated by two recent cases: *C and K*[32] and *Yu and Yu.*[33] In *C and K*, the defendants were being prosecuted for a fraud. A prosecution witness, P, was in South Africa. His evidence was central. Although the prosecution case was that he had been duped by C and K, the South African police had regarded him at one point as a suspect, and so there were obvious reasons why it was highly desirable to have his evidence tested in cross-examination. Having originally agreed to come to England to give evidence, he had then changed his mind, after which the prosecution had not made any serious attempt to find out why, or to persuade him to change it back again. On these facts, the Court of Appeal reversed the ruling of the trial judge admitting hearsay evidence of P's statements under section 116(2)(c). In *Yu and Yu* (which was decided under the CJA 1988) the defendants had been convicted of false imprisonment and blackmail. The prosecution case was that in England they had kidnapped two Chinese immigrants and forced their families in China to pay for their release. The main evidence against them was the oral testimony of the victims, but the prosecution also produced written statements that the families had given to the Chinese police, acting in

[28] Or the prosecution, of course, if it is the defence which is seeking to call the evidence.
[29] *Malone*, n 27 above.
[30] *Archer* [2007] EWCA Crim 930; see § 2.49 above.
[31] *Yu*, § 6.18 below.
[32] [2006] EWCA Crim 197, [2006] Crim LR 637 (with note by DCO (David Ormerod)).
[33] [2006] EWCA Crim 349, [2006] Crim LR 643 (with note by DCO (David Ormerod)).

collaboration with the British police, details of which were corroborated by banking documents recording the payments the families had made to the defendants. To bring the family members to England would, of course, have been expensive; and it would have been difficult, because they would have needed to obtain passports and exit visas, and it was doubtful whether these could have been obtained. The Court of Appeal held that the written statements had been rightly admitted.

6.19 In deciding whether to admit hearsay evidence under section 116(2)(c), the court considers not only whether it would have been 'reasonably practicable' to secure the witness's physical presence in the court, but also whether it would have been 'reasonably practicable' to enable him to give evidence in a way that would have secured some or all of the traditional safeguards associated with oral testimony: the oath, cross-examination and the ability of the court to observe the witness's demeanour.[34] Thus in *Yu*, the Court of Appeal noted with approval that the trial judge had considered whether it might have been possible either to get the families to give evidence from China by a video-link, or to have their statements taken with the defendant's lawyer present, though he found neither to be practicable. In *C and K*, the Court of Appeal was influenced by the fact that the prosecution said that, if they were unable to use P's written statements, they 'would co-operate in seeking to set up a procedure in South Africa under which the witness could be examined and cross-examined, or at least interviewed in the presence of both parties'.

6.20 *(d) that the relevant person cannot be found although such steps as it is reasonably practicable to take to find him have been taken* This reason is also carried over from CJA 1988, section 23. Cases from the earlier provision hold that, as a matter of principle, 'reasonably practicable' means the same in the context of efforts to trace a witness who has 'gone over the side' in the United Kingdom as it does in the context of trying to secure the attendance of a witness who is abroad. Thus here, as there, it is 'open to the judge not only to consider the importance of the witness but also to consider the resources of the police'.[35]

6.21 What is and is not reasonable in any given case will ultimately be a matter of fact. But an idea of what the courts expect can be gained from examining two cases, *Coughlan*[36] and *Henry*.[37] In the first case, Coughlan was accused of assaulting another man, Judson, in a night-club. According to Judson's evidence Coughlan was the attacker but Coughlan claimed it was someone else. Judson's account was corroborated in a statement given to the police by Judson's friend, Armitage. At trial, the judge allowed the prosecution to read Armitage's statement, the police claiming that Armitage was in South Africa. However, when asked by the defence

[34] See §§ 1.21–1.24 above.
[35] *Coughlan*, CACD 2 March 1999, [1999] 5 *Archbold News* 2.
[36] *Ibid.*
[37] [2003] EWCA Crim 1296.

what other enquires had been made, the officer in charge of the case admitted there were none: he had made no enquiries at Armitage's former place of work nor had he asked further questions of Judson, who during his evidence at trial then informed the court that Armitage had told him that he planned to go to South Africa only if he was unsuccessful in joining the army; and after the trial it then emerged that Armitage had joined the Household Cavalry, where he still was. The Court of Appeal said that the judge's decision to admit the written statement was wrong and quashed Coughlan's conviction.[37a]

6.22 In *Henry*, the defendant was convicted of a hideous sadistic murder, evidence against him including traces of the victim's blood and body tissue on his clothes and body, his blood at the scene of the crime and an admission from him that he had been in the victim's flat on the night she died. In addition, at trial a statement was read from her ex-boyfriend, X, in which he described his (X's) movements on the night in question. X was never regarded by the police as a suspect, or even a particularly important witness, but at the start of the trial, the defence advanced the theory that the murder might have been committed by him rather than by Henry. Not foreseeing this development, the police had not intervened with the immigration authorities when, some time before the trial, X was deported back to Jamaica as an illegal immigrant. This was partly because they had an address for him in Jamaica, and also because they thought they could also contact him via his aunt in England, although in fact he had now vanished. In these circumstances, the Court of Appeal endorsed the decision to admit his written statement at the trial.

6.23 *Admissibility is automatic* If any of the conditions stated in section 116(2)(a)–(d) is met, then in principle the hearsay evidence is admissible. The leave of the court is not needed and once it has decided that the condition is met, the court does not need to (and indeed, should not) then go through any kind of 'balancing act' to see whether the evidence is admissible under section 116.[38] However, though the requirements of section 116 are met, that is not the end of the story, because the court still has a discretionary power to exclude the evidence under section 126 if it thinks the evidence is of insufficient weight to justify the trouble of hearing it; and if the prosecution is seeking to adduce the evidence, it will exclude the evidence under PACE, section 78 if it believes that admitting it would make the trial 'unfair'. One of the reasons why it might so find, obviously,

[37a] In *Adams* [2007] EWCA Crim 3025 the prosecution, having in September secured the agreement of a witness to give evidence on Monday 15 January, did not contact him again until the Friday before the trial, when they left a message on his mobile phone; the Court of Appeal said that, in the circumstances, insufficient efforts had been made to justify the use of s 116(2)(d) when he failed to appear.

[38] The courts have sometimes overlooked this point. In *Cole and Keet* [2007] EWCA Crim 1924, [2007] 1 WLR 2716 [**page 315 below**], the Court of Appeal seems to have thought that it was necessary to examine, in this context, the discretionary factors set out in CJA 2003, s 114(2): see at [39] and [73]; and cf *R (CPS) v Uxbridge Magistrates* [2007] EWHC 205 (Admin) at [11].

is that to do so would infringe the defendant's right to question the prosecution witnesses, guaranteed by ECHR, Article 6(3)(d).

6.24 *(e) fear: that through fear the relevant person does not give (or does not continue to give) oral evidence in the proceedings, either at all or in connection with the subject matter of the statement, and the court gives leave for the statement to be given in evidence* That the witness was in fear was also one of the possible reasons for admitting hearsay evidence under CJA 1988, section 23, but in this case, CJA 2003, section 116 departs from the wording of the earlier provision in a number of significant respects. In particular, whereas the 'fear' provision in the CJA 1988 was drafted so that the only statements that were admissible under it were those made to the police or other official investigators, the new provision is not so limited. In section 116 the term 'fear' has been defined in a way intended to give it a wider scope than it had before. In consequence, as the Court of Appeal recognised in *Davies*,[39] this part of section 116 is intended to mark a new start.

6.25 *Requirement of judicial leave* Where the witness is absent for any of the reasons set out in section 116(1)(a) to (d), his statement is admissible 'automatically', as explained in § 6.23 above. But where fear is the reason, then as a result of the final words of subsection (1)(e) it is admissible only where 'the court gives leave for the statement to be given in evidence'. A leave requirement in this case, but not the others, looks distinctly odd. Witnesses often die, fall ill, emigrate and vanish without the direct involvement of anyone involved in the case, but those who are in fear have almost always been intimidated with a view to prevent their giving evidence; and so fear looks like a particularly strong case for admitting hearsay evidence, rather than a weak one. However, a leave requirement was imposed here at the instance of the Law Commission, which thought 'there is a very genuine risk that, if the statements of frightened witnesses were automatically admissible, prospective witnesses could give statements to the police in the knowledge that they could at a later stage falsely claim to be frightened, with the result that they could avoid having to go to court and be cross-examined'. This scenario may or may not be plausible,[40] but if it is plausible, section 116(4), in which the leave requirement is elaborated, seems ill-adapted to detecting it. It is as follows:

> (4) Leave may be given under subsection (2)(e) only if the court considers that the statement ought to be admitted in the interests of justice, having regard—
>
> (a) to the statement's contents,
>
> (b) to any risk that its admission or exclusion will result in unfairness to any party to the proceedings (and in particular to how difficult it will be to challenge the statement if the relevant person does not give oral evidence),

[39] [2006] EWCA Crim 2643 [2007] 2 All ER 1070 at [14]; see § 6.29 below.

[40] The Law Commission reported that this fear had been expressed by judges, but for a sceptical reaction, see Munday, n 21 above, § 9.35.

(c) in appropriate cases, to the fact that a direction under section 19 of the Youth Justice and Criminal Evidence Act 1999 (c. 23) (special measures for the giving of evidence by fearful witnesses etc) could be made in relation to the relevant person, and
(d) to any other relevant circumstances.

6.26 *Fear—of what?* Section 116(3), carrying out the suggestion of the Law Commission, provides that 'For the purposes of subsection (2)(e) "fear" is to be widely construed and (for example) includes fear of the death or injury of another person or of financial loss'. Thus it potentially covers not only threats of violence to the witness or his family, but also threats to damage property, or threats to put a person out of business.[41] It is, indeed, extremely wide, and as some critics have pointed out, the wording could cover some highly unmeritorious cases, for example, fear, in a witness who has told lies to the police, that they will be exposed as such at trial and that he might in consequence be prosecuted for perjury;[42] or fear of 'financial loss' in the form of lost fees through having to give up a day's work to come to court.[43] When objections of this sort were made at the time the legislation was being drafted and then enacted, the official response was that, in practice, the courts would find a way of refusing to admit as hearsay the statement of a witness who was in 'fear' in circumstances such as these; and any court that learnt that the absent witness was 'in fear' for some reason of this sort would, presumably, hold that it was not 'in the interests of justice' to admit the hearsay statement, and refuse leave.[44]

6.27 It seems unlikely, furthermore, that the courts would hold that section 116(2)(e) covers 'fear' of the general unpleasantness of having to give live evidence in court. This much appears from *Boulton*,[45] in which the appellant, who had been convicted of raping his former partner, sought to argue that the real reason for her absence from the witness-box had been 'an unwillingness on her part to submit to the trauma of giving evidence against the appellant' (at [13]), and in upholding the appeal the Court of Appeal said that that there was strong evidence in this case of threats of violence, rather than that 'unwillingness to submit to the trauma of giving evidence' would have been sufficient.

6.28 *Fear—how grave?* Where duress is raised as a defence in criminal law, it only operates where a person of reasonable firmness would have given in to the threat

[41] In *Martin* [1996] Crim LR 589, under the earlier law, where the witness had been approached by a person whom he had once seen setting fire to a shop.

[42] A Heaton-Armstrong and D Wolchover, 'Obtaining, Recording and Admissibility of Out-of-court Witness Statements' in A Heaton-Armstrong, E Shepherd, G Gudjonsson and D Wolchover (eds), *Witness Testimony* (Oxford, OUP, 2006) 171, 176.

[43] This possibility provoked a long discussion in Parliament: House of Commons, Standing Committee B, 2002–3, 625–38.

[44] Cf *Parkinson* [2004] EWCA Crim 3195, a decision under the CJA 1988.

[45] [2007] EWCA Crim 942.

which induced the defendant to act as he did. But for the purpose of deciding whether a witness was put in fear, the test is a subjective one. So much appears from *Doherty*,[46] where a witness to a wounding, who was a solicitor in Ireland,[47] refused to come to testify in England following some odd phone calls that he had received, which he interpreted as oblique threats. At trial, the judge allowed his statement to be read, expressly saying that section 116 lays down 'a subjective test'. Upholding the judge's decision, and the appellant's conviction, the Court of Appeal said (at [34]):

> As to [the witness's] fears, while some people might not have been deterred from giving evidence by the veiled threat which was made, his fear cannot, in our judgment, be characterised as irrational or sufficiently unfounded to make it unfair for the judge to rule that his evidence should be read.

6.29 *Fear—of whom?* Under of the CJA 1925, section 13, the deposition of the witness was admissible on grounds of fear only when this emanated from the defendant or his associates.[48] But CJA 2003, section 116, like CJA 1988, section 23, does not require this and if the witness is afraid, who is responsible for this does not matter. Thus it can operate where, as in *Doherty*, the witness had grounds to suspect that the odd phone calls he had received were inspired by the defendant, but it was not clear that this was so. It can also operate when no approaches have been made to the witness by anyone at all, as in one case where a 13-year-old defence witness in a wounding case saw the alleged victim's friends sitting in the public gallery, and their presence scared him into silence;[49] and as in another case, where a group of young witnesses to a stabbing incident failed to attend court because they were scared of the defendant, a woman, apparently with a drink problem, whom they knew and knew to be aggressive.[50]

6.30 However, although the source of the fear is not directly relevant to section 116, the fact that the defendant or his associates are responsible for it does have a bearing on the applicability or otherwise of ECHR, Article 6(3)(d). As explained in Chapter 2, the defendant's right under this Article will be infringed if he is convicted wholly or mainly on the basis of evidence of absent witnesses which he was unable to challenge by putting questions, whether or not they were absent for reasons that are acceptable under section 116. But the defendant is not in a position to complain of disregard of his Article 6(3)(d) rights where this situation arose because he or his associates have scared the witnesses away.

[46] [2006] EWCA Crim 2716.

[47] As there is no legal means of compelling the attendance of a witness from the Republic of Ireland, his written statement was also admissible under s 116(c).

[48] See § 6.5 above.

[49] *B* [2006] EWCA Crim 1978. At trial, the defence had asked the judge to clear the public gallery but he refused, although it is hard to see why he did this.

[50] *Davies* [2006] EWCA Crim 2643 [2007] 2 All ER 1070.

6.31 *Fear—how proved?* In *Neill v North Antrim Magistrates' Court*,[51] an appeal from Northern Ireland, the House of Lords held that the fact that a witness is in fear must be established by evidence that is legally admissible. The case concerned two boys whose statements to the police were read to the court under the Northern Ireland equivalent of CJA 1988, section 23.[52] As evidence that the boys were in fear, the magistrate accepted the evidence of a police officer, who had heard this from their mothers. The House of Lords ruled that, if the police officer had heard about the boys' fear directly from their own mouths this, though hearsay, would have been admissible under a common law exception to the rule relating to 'statements relating to a physical sensation or a mental state'; but this information received at second-hand from their mothers was inadmissible. As this common law exception is one which CJA 2003, section 118 preserves, it follows that the fact that a witness is in fear can in principle be established by the evidence of a police officer who has spoken to him. And in principle, it should be equally possible to prove the fear by producing a written statement from the witness, provided of course that it can be shown that it is really his.[53]

6.32 In *R v Belmarsh Magistrates, ex p Gilligan*,[54] however, the Divisional Court held that a written statement from the witness was not sufficient. In *H, W and M*[55] the Court of Appeal also said that, in principle, a court ought not to make a finding that a witness is in fear unless it has actually heard oral evidence as to this from the witness himself. But then in *Davies*[56] (the case of the aggressive woman with a knife, which was decided under the new provisions) the Court of Appeal declined to follow this line of authority and held that the trial judge had been entitled to found his decision that the witnesses were in fear on the basis of what they had said in the witness statements they had given to the police. Moses LJ said:

> The law previously referred to, particularly *H*, is no longer that which should guide the courts under the new regime. Indeed, the courts are ill-advised to seek to test the basis of fear by calling witnesses before them, since that may undermine the very thing that section 116 was designed to avoid.

6.33 *Reluctance of appeal courts to interfere with decisions at first instance* As in other similar cases where courts of first instance are required to make an evaluative decision, the appeal courts are unwilling to criticise or overturn a trial court's decision under section 116. In *Doherty* the Court of Appeal indicated that it would do so only

[51] [1992] 1 WLR 1221.
[52] Criminal Justice (Evidence etc) (Northern Ireland) Order 1988, SI 1988/1847 art 3(3)(b).
[53] As seems to have been the case in *Rutherford* [1998] Crim LR 490.
[54] [1998] 1 Cr App R 14.
[55] [2001] Crim LR 815.
[56] See n 39 above.

where the court below had failed to take into account the facts that it was required to consider, or reached a result that is 'obviously wrong . . . perverse or unreasonable'.[57]

6.34 *Standard of proof* Applying normal principles, the prosecution must prove the existence of a reason justifying the admission of hearsay evidence under section 116 beyond reasonable doubt;[58] but the defence need only prove it on the balance of probabilities.[59]

6.35 *Applicant responsible for the witness's absence* An all-too-common scenario is that one side (usually the defendant) procures the absence of a key witness by killing, injuring or intimidating him, and the other side (usually the prosecution) then wishes to use in evidence the statement the witness made to police before this happened. For the party who removed the witness from the scene to seek to use his out-of-court statements as evidence is in practice most unlikely, and reminds us of the Jewish joke about the definition of *chutzpah*: 'the man who kills both his parents and then begs the sentencing court to have mercy on an orphan'.[60] But the Law Commission, with the close attention to minor detail that marked its work, thought this case should be expressly provided for; and accordingly section 116(5) states (at some length) that a person who has caused the absence of the witness is disqualified from using the section.

6.36 *A case not catered for: witnesses who refuse to testify or claim privilege* In principle, a valid reason for admitting evidence of the previous statement of a witness who does not give oral evidence is that he has been asked to testify, but refuses: either in defiance of the law or lawfully because he can claim a privilege or immunity. The previous statement of such a witness is not inherently less worthy of belief than that of a witness who is dead, sick, mad, abroad, missing, or in fear. To get oral evidence out of him is equally impossible for the party that would like to call him. If it is right on policy grounds to accept hearsay evidence in the five cases listed in section 116, it seems no less right in this case too. In 1972, indeed, this was one of the exceptions to the hearsay rule which was proposed by the Criminal Law Revision Committee.[61] Following a recommendation of the Scottish Law Commission,[62] it became one of the statutory exceptions in Scotland;[63] and it is also an exception under US Federal Rules of Evidence.[64]

[57] See n 46 above at [28], citing with approval *CPS v CE* [2006] EWCA Crim 1410 at [14].

[58] *R v Acton Justices, ex p McMullen* (1990) 92 Cr App R 98.

[59] *Mattey and Queely* [1995] 2 Cr App R 409.

[60] See Richard D Friedman, 'Confrontation and the Definition of Chutzpah' (1997) 31 *Israel Law Review* 506.

[61] Criminal Law Revision Committee, *Eleventh Report (Evidence) General* (Cmnd 4991, London, HMSO, 1972) Draft Bill, clause 34(2)(b) and (c)(ii).

[62] Scottish Law Commission, *Evidence: Report on Hearsay Evidence in Criminal Proceedings* (SLC No 149, 1995).

[63] Criminal Procedure (Scotland) Act 1995, s. 259(2)(d) and (e).

[64] Rule 804(a)(1).

6.37 In England, however, the Law Commission, having proposed the exception in its Consultation Paper, rejected it in its Report, because 'some respondents thought that to admit a statement without inquiring into the reasons for the refusal made it too easy for fabricated statements to be admitted where the witness simply did not want to be cross-examined'.[65]

6.38 Even if this flabby reason is plausible as regards witnesses who refuse to testify, it is certainly not so in the case of those able to claim immunity or privilege. As suggested elsewhere,[66] it seems likely that, where the evidence of such a witness appears to be relevant and cogent, the court would admit it under the 'inclusionary discretion' in section 114(1)(d).

6.39 *CJA 2003, section 116: conclusion* In *Kordasinski*[67] the court described the hearsay provisions of the CJA 2003 as 'labyrinthine', and those who have managed to read to the end of this chapter are likely to agree. Section 116 does seem to be needlessly complicated, and there is also a troubling circularity about the procedures that it makes it necessary for the courts to follow, in that the same issues and factors keep on recurring. For example, how significant the evidence is, and whether it would be unfairly prejudicial to the other side if it were admitted in the form of hearsay, are relevant to whether sufficient efforts were made to secure the attendance of the witness under section 116(2)(c) or to find him under section 116(2)(d). The same two factors are relevant again in deciding whether leave should be given to admit the hearsay statement of a frightened witness under section 116(4). Then if the statement is in principle admissible under section 116, these factors are relevant again in deciding whether it should be excluded under PACE, section 78. And if the statement is in principle inadmissible under section 116, they come into the picture yet again in deciding whether it is possible to admit the statement under the 'inclusionary discretion' in section 114(1)(d).

6.40 In the end, all these complexities have an air of futility about them. If the hearsay statement manages to pass through all the legal hoops set out in section 116, and the court believes it is not in the interests of justice to admit it, it may still exclude it under either section 126 or section 78 of PACE; and if the statement fails to pass through all the hoops set out in section 116, and the court believes that it is in the interests of justice to admit it, it will admit it under the 'inclusionary discretion' conferred upon it by section 114(1)(d). All of which must leave judges wondering why the hoops are there at all.

[65] LC Report, n 10 above, para 8.45.
[66] See § 5.25 *et seq* above.
[67] [2006] EWCA Crim 2984, [2007] 1 Cr App R 17 (238).

6.41 As was pointed out in Chapter 2, the 'unavailable witness' exception to the hearsay rule would be of less practical importance if English criminal procedure, like that of many or most other countries, had a procedure for taking the evidence of certain types of witness on commission in advance of trial, but this idea did not appeal to the Law Commission and no provision for this was included in the CJA 2003.

Annex: Criminal Justice Act 1988, Section 23 (Now Repealed)[68]

(1) Subject—

- (a) to subsection (4) below;
- (b) paragraph 1A of Schedule 2 to the Criminal Appeal Act 1968 (evidence given orally at original trial to be given orally at retrial, and
- (c) to section 69 of the Police and Criminal Evidence Act 1984 (evidence from computer records),

a statement made by a person in a document shall be admissible in criminal proceedings as evidence of any fact of which direct oral evidence by him would be admissible if—

- (i) the requirements of one of the paragraphs of subsection (2) below are satisfied; or
- (ii) the requirements of subsection (1)(i) below are satisfied.

(2) The requirements mentioned in subsection 1(i) above are—

- (a) that the person who made the statement is dead or by reason of his bodily or mental condition unfit to attend as a witness;
- (b) that—
  - (i) the person who made the statement is outside the United Kingdom and;
  - (ii) it is not reasonably practicable to secure his attendance; or
- (c) that all reasonable steps have been taken to find the person who made the statement, but that he cannot be found.

(3) The requirements mentioned in subsection (1)(ii) above are—

- (a) that the statement was made to a police officer or some other person charged with the duty of investigating offences or charging offenders; and
- (b) that the person who made it does not give oral evidence through fear or because he is kept out of the way.

(4) Subsection (1) above does not render admissible a confession made by an accused person that would not be admissible under section 76 of the Police and Criminal Evidence Act 1984.

[68] Set out here as originally enacted, it was amended in 1996 and 1999.

7

DOCUMENTARY HEARSAY (CJA 2003, SECTION 117)

History

7.1 At first sight it is not obvious why the hearsay rule should exclude statements contained in documentary records, or at any rate, those made before it could have occurred to the maker that the transaction noted might end up in a court of law. Not surprisingly, it seems that the common law originally accepted this sort of documentary evidence freely. The restriction grew up in the early part of the seventeenth century, as a result of widespread fears that dishonest tradesmen were making false entries in their books and claiming double payment or payment for goods never requested or supplied. Important procedural changes at that time[1] had suddenly made it easier for traders to sue in the Royal courts, whereas at that time (and for long afterwards) the parties themselves were incompetent to give evidence. As the traders' books were admissible in evidence, this meant that an unscrupulous one could produce his book in evidence to support a claim, while the alleged debtor was unable to give evidence to rebut it.

7.2 To modern eyes, the obvious solution would have been to make both parties competent as witnesses. However, the response from Parliament was to make trade records inadmissible after a year from the alleged transaction;[2] and the next step was for the courts to go further, and to make statements contained in private documents inadmissible altogether.[3] The exclusionary rule did not, of course, prevent the parties producing legal instruments, like deeds, where the point at issue was the rights and duties that the instrument created; the exclusionary rule only prevented the parties from using documents to prove assertions of fact contained in them. And it was limited to *private* documents, so if the document was

[1] JH Baker, *Introduction to Legal History* (4th edn, London, Butterworths, 2002) 341–50.

[2] (1609) 7 Jac I c 12. Nearly 70 years later, similar fears led to the Statute of Frauds: Baker, *ibid.*

[3] *Wigmore on Evidence* (3rd edn, Boston, Little, Brown & Co, 1940) para 1518: 'the books of a party ceased after the 1600s to form the subject of a hearsay exception at common law in England'.

considered to be a public one, such as a parish register, it was evidence of the matters recorded in it. But even as so limited the rule was extremely inconvenient, and many piecemeal exceptions were made to it, both by the courts and by Parliament. The result, of course, was a body of law that was extremely complicated, and yet in some respects too narrow.

7.3 In civil law, the problem was eased by the Evidence Act 1938 and then removed altogether by the Civil Evidence Act 1968. In criminal cases, however, the difficulty remained, where it was dramatically shown up by the decision in *Myers v DPP*[4] in 1964. This decision led, over a period of less than 40 years, to no less than four statutory attempts to create a general exception to the hearsay rule in respect of private records. The first was the Criminal Evidence 1965; the second was PACE 1968, section 68; the third was CJA 1988, section 25; and now the fourth and latest attempt in the series is CJA 2003, section 117.

Underlying issue: 'records' of different types

7.4 One of the difficulties about creating a legislative exception to the hearsay rule to cover 'records' is that there are types of records, and different types give rise to different issues. Not only is there the distinction, long known to the common law, between 'public records' (such as parish registers) and 'private records'. In the field of private records, there is an important distinction between records that exist to hold the details of ordinary transactions, and which are occasionally relevant as shedding light on crimes, and those maintained by official bodies, like the police and other law-enforcement agencies, for the specific purpose of gathering information about crimes. Examples of the first type are the records of customers' accounts held by a bank, or the payroll records of an employer. The prime example of the second is the file that the police open on a case when a crime has been reported to them.

7.5 As regards private records that merely record ordinary everyday transactions, it is hard to think of any intelligible reason why their contents should not be routinely admissible, if they are incidentally relevant to prove the commission (or non-commission) of a crime. If D, for example, denies that his car was involved in an accident, it seems obvious that the prosecution should be able to produce as evidence from the files of his insurance company the claim-form he submitted afterwards, stating that it was, and it is absurd that, in order to do so, they must first identify the exception to the hearsay rule by reason of which it is admissible.[5]

[4] [1965] AC 1001; see § 1.18 above.

[5] As it must, even after the CJA 2003: see *Watson v DPP* [2006] EWHC 3429.

But case-files created by the police and similar agencies raise different issues. These typically contain statements made to them by witnesses accusing specific people of committing specific crimes, and elicited from them, quite often, by agents who have already formed the view that the suspect is guilty. If the contents were routinely admissible, this would short-circuit the requirement that witnesses to the basic elements of a criminal offence must give their evidence orally to the court and, potentially, the defendant's right to put questions to the prosecution witnesses which is guaranteed by ECHR, Article 6(3)(d).[6] Attempts to reform the hearsay rule with respect to 'records' have, quite rightly, taken account of this distinction, and in this respect, section 117 of the CJA 2003 follows in the footsteps of its predecessors. Although section 117 potentially applies to records of this type, they are admissible only subject to extra safeguards.[7]

7.6 Section 117 also applies, potentially, to 'public records'. These were admissible under an important exception to the hearsay rule at common law which, by way of 'belt and braces', has been explicitly preserved by section 118.[8]

CJA 2003, section 117

7.7 The text of CJA 2003, section 117 is as follows:

Business and other documents

(1) In criminal proceedings a statement contained in a document is admissible as evidence of any matter stated if—
   (a) oral evidence given in the proceedings would be admissible as evidence of that matter,
   (b) the requirements of subsection (2) are satisfied, and
   (c) the requirements of subsection (5) are satisfied, in a case where subsection (4) requires them to be.

(2) The requirements of this subsection are satisfied if—
   (a) the document or the part containing the statement was created or received by a person in the course of a trade, business, profession or other occupation, or as the holder of a paid or unpaid office,
   (b) the person who supplied the information contained in the statement (the relevant person) had or may reasonably be supposed to have had personal knowledge of the matters dealt with, and

[6] On which see generally Chapter 2 above.

[7] The first in the series, the Criminal Evidence Act 1965, was limited to records 'relating to any trade or business'. Its successors apply to records of any sort.

[8] See Chapter 9 below.

(c) each person (if any) through whom the information was supplied from the relevant person to the person mentioned in paragraph (a) received the information in the course of a trade, business, profession or other occupation, or as the holder of a paid or unpaid office.

(3) The persons mentioned in paragraphs (a) and (b) of subsection (2) may be the same person.

(4) The additional requirements of subsection (5) must be satisfied if the statement—

(a) was prepared for the purposes of pending or contemplated criminal proceedings, or for a criminal investigation, but

(b) was not obtained pursuant to a request under section 7 of the Crime (International Co-operation) Act 2003 (c. 32) or an order under paragraph 6 of Schedule 13 to the Criminal Justice Act 1988 (c. 33) (which relate to overseas evidence).

(5) The requirements of this subsection are satisfied if—

(a) any of the five conditions mentioned in section 116(2) is satisfied (absence of relevant person etc), or

(b) the relevant person cannot reasonably be expected to have any recollection of the matters dealt with in the statement (having regard to the length of time since he supplied the information and all other circumstances).

(6) A statement is not admissible under this section if the court makes a direction to that effect under subsection (7).

(7) The court may make a direction under this subsection if satisfied that the statement's reliability as evidence for the purpose for which it is tendered is doubtful in view of—

(a) its contents,

(b) the source of the information contained in it,

(c) the way in which or the circumstances in which the information was supplied or received, or

(d) the way in which or the circumstances in which the document concerned was created or received.

7.8 This provision, like section 116, is closely modelled on the equivalent provision of the CJA 1988. While not pleasurable to read it is, however, rather more intelligibly drafted than its predecessor. In terms of substance, it differs from the CJA 1988 in two respects, one more significant than the other. The first is that it removes an unfortunate 'bug' that affected the CJA 1988 as regards the admissibility of police records. CJA 1988, section 24 made a statement in a police record admissible only where 'the maker of the statement' was, for various stated reasons, unavailable to give oral evidence; and whereas common sense suggested that the 'unavailable' person should be the informant who gave the information to the police, the section appeared to make it the policeman who received it.[9] The second

[9] *Derodra* [2000] 1 Cr App R 41. See JC Smith, 'Sections 23 and 24 of the Criminal Justice Act 1988: Some Problems' [1994] Crim LR 426 and Law Commission, *Evidence in Criminal Proceedings: Hearsay and Related Topics* (Report No 245, Cm 3670, June 1997) (hereafter 'LC Report') § 4.39.

difference is that, whereas CJA 1988, section 24, made the admissibility of statements in records subject to the general discretion of the court, section 117 makes them admissible automatically—or that, at least, is the general idea. This automaticity is undermined by section 117(6) and (7), which require the court to exclude the statement if it is satisfied that it is unreliable; and, of course, by the more general exclusionary powers contained in CJA 2003, section 126[10] and, where it is prosecution evidence, section 78 of PACE 1984.

7.9 It should go without saying that, where it applies, section 117 only makes the statement contained in the record admissible in evidence. Unlike some other statutory provisions about records,[11] section 117 does not create a presumption that the information is correct, much less that the record is conclusive proof of the matters contained in it: as the Administrative Court had to remind an impertinent optician, disciplined by the General Medical Council for fraud, who tried to argue that the false statements he had manufactured, having made their way into a record to which section 117 applied, must be deemed to be true for all legal purposes(!)[12]

7.10 It also goes without saying that the decision as to whether a statement is admissible under section 117 is a decision of law, which in a jury trial means that it is decided by the judge.[13]

7.11 For section 117 to apply, there are three preliminary conditions that arise from subsection (1). The first is that the statement in question should be contained in a 'document'. This is not a requirement difficult to satisfy, however, since section 134(1) provides that 'document' means anything in which information of any description is recorded'. The second is that the information should concern some matter on which 'oral evidence given in the proceedings would be admissible as evidence of that matter'. This means, of course, that the information in question should be something that is potentially admissible in evidence. So, obviously, section 117 cannot be used to put before the court some piece of evidence which is irrelevant to the case or which, though relevant, is inadmissible by reason of some other exclusionary rule, for example, information supplied by someone interrogated under torture.[14] The third condition is that the 'the document . . . was created or received by a person in the course of a trade, business, profession or other

[10] See §§ 5.40–5.45 above.

[11] See Chapter 8 below.

[12] *Razzaq v General Medical Council* [2006] EWHC 1300 (Admin). The Administrative Court also pointed out that, even if they had been broken, the rules of criminal evidence were inapplicable to these proceedings in any event.

[13] *Lewendon (Practice Note)* [2006] 1 WLR 1278.

[14] *A v Secretary of State for the Home Department (No 2)* [2005] UKHL 71, [2006] 2 AC 221; and see § 6.11 above.

occupation, or as the holder of a paid or unpaid office'. Case law decided under the equivalent provisions of the CJA 1988 suggest that the presence of this condition can be inferred from the appearance of the documents themselves, and need not be proved by extra evidence.[15]

7.12 If these preliminary conditions are met, section 117 operates to make the statement admissible where (in essence) the information originated from someone with first-hand knowledge, and was then stored by someone (whether the original observer or someone else) for whom storing such information was a matter of routine:

> The underlying idea is that whilst it must be shown that the facts originated in someone who had or could be taken to have had personal knowledge of them, from thereon it must only be transmitted through a chain of command of parties whose callings require or entitle them to handle such information until the final document is created or filed.[16]

7.13 Though section 117 is wide enough to cover most cases in which information is routinely collected and stored in circumstances suggesting that a court would be foolish to refuse to look at it, this is not invariably the case. The section is subject to three important limitations.

7.14 The first is that the person from whom the information originated must be someone who would have been competent as a witness. This point is made—indeed, rammed home—by CJA 2003, section 123(2) and (3), which are as follows:

> (2) Nothing in section 117 makes a statement admissible as evidence if any person who, in order for the requirements of section 117(2) to be satisfied, must at any time have supplied or received the information concerned or created or received the document or part concerned—
>
> (a) did not have the required capability at that time, or
> (b) cannot be identified but cannot reasonably be assumed to have had the required capability at that time.
>
> (3) For the purposes of this section a person has the required capability if he is capable of—
>
> (a) understanding questions put to him about the matters stated, and
> (b) giving answers to such questions which can be understood.
>
> (4) Where by reason of this section there is an issue as to whether a person had the required capability when he made a statement—

[15] *Foxley* [1995] 2 Cr App R 523; *Department of the Environment etc v Atkinson* [2002] EWHC 2023 (Admin).

[16] Roderick Munday, *Evidence* (4th edn, Oxford, OUP, 2007) § 9.40.

(a) proceedings held for the determination of the issue must take place in the absence of the jury (if there is one);
(b) in determining the issue the court may receive expert evidence and evidence from any person to whom the statement in question was made;
(c) the burden of proof on the issue lies on the party seeking to adduce the statement, and the standard of proof is the balance of probabilities.

So section 117 would presumably not make admissible, for example, a record in an 'incident book' kept at a nursing-home for persons suffering from Alzheimer's disease, in which complaints by patients had been noted.

7.15 The second limitation is the double requirement that the person who initially fed the information into the system must be someone who had first-hand knowledge, and all the people through whom the information then passes on its way to its final resting-place in the file must have 'received the information in the course of a trade, business, profession or other occupation, or as the holder of a paid or unpaid office'. That this can be quite restrictive is illustrated by the following two cases involving information that had found its way into records maintained by the police.

7.16 In *Maher v DPP*, [17] W saw a car collide with V's car, which was parked in the car-park at a supermarket, and then drive off. W wrote down the registration number of the offending car on a piece of paper which she put under the windscreen-wiper of the damaged car where the owner, V, later found it. V gave the number to the police, who noted it in their records, and V then lost the original piece of paper. The Divisional Court held that the police record was not admissible under section 117, because the person who had fed the information into the record-keeping system, V, was not someone who had first-hand knowledge of it; though, as the court pointed out, section 117 would have applied if W had given the note to the car-park attendant, who then passed it on to the police, because in that case the information would have reached the police file via a chain of people, all of whom had handled it in the course of their business.[18]

7.17 In *Humphris*,[19] the prosecution sought to prove the details of D's previous offences (which they could use against him thanks to the 'bad character evidence' provisions of the CJA 2003) by means of a print-out from the Police National Computer (PNC), a national database into which the police routinely feed information about crimes, criminals and criminal convictions. This print-out, said the Court of Appeal, was not admissible under section 117, because the

[17] *Maher v DPP* [2006] EWHC 1271 (Admin); see further [**page 302 below**], § 5.7 above.

[18] The Divisonal Court held that the information was, however, admissible under the 'inclusionary discretion' in section 114(1)(d)': see § 5.7 above.

[19] [2005] EWCA Crim 2030, (2005) 169 JP 441.

information about the convictions had been fed into the system by police officers who did not themselves have first-hand information about these matters.[20] But by way of contrast, in *R (Wellington) v DPP*,[21] the Administrative Court held that section 117 did enable a print-out from the PNC to be used in evidence, on which it was stated that Mr Wellington, whom the prosecution claimed had fled from questioning by the police having first given the name of Robert Vernon, sometimes used the name of Robert Vernon as an alias. That piece of information, said Jackson J, was likely to have been input by police officers who 'had or may reasonably be supposed to have had personal knowledge' of it, unlike the details of the previous crimes for which Humphris was responsible, which were not.

7.18 The third limitation on section 117 concerns confessions. By virtue of section 128, nothing[22] in any of the 'hearsay' provisions of the CJA 2003 'makes a confession by a defendant admissible if it would not be admissible under section 76 of the Police and Criminal Evidence Act 1984'.

Extra conditions for the admissibility of police records

7.19 Section 117(4) provides that a statement cannot be admitted via section 117 unless one of the further conditions applies, if it 'was prepared for the purposes of a pending or completed criminal proceedings, or for a criminal investigation'. The paradigm case of a document that falls into this category is a statement taken from a witness by the police in the course of their enquiries. Another clear example would be the statements fed into the PNC. In this category would also fall, presumably, a police custody record.[23] A more doubtful case would be the log that is kept of emergency calls to the police.[24] It is suggested that this would not count as being 'prepared for the purposes of criminal proceedings'. When members of the public dial '999' they are seeking urgent help, not trying to institute a prosecution.

7.20 The extra conditions that must be met where the statement 'was prepared for the purposes of a pending or completed criminal proceedings, or for a criminal investigation' are set out in section 117(5). These are that the 'relevant person' (meaning the person who originally supplied the information)[25] is unavailable for

[20] As to how the prosecution can put such information before the court, see *S* [2007] EWCA Crim 335, [2007] All ER (D) 119, and the discussion at § 5.39 above.

[21] [2007] EWHC 1061 (Admin).

[22] Apart from CJA 2003, s 128(1), which adds a new s 76A to PACE 1984; see § 10.44 below.

[23] See *Hogan* [1997] Crim LR 349 and DJB's (Di Birch's) note, 351.

[24] In *Devon* [2006] EWCA Crim 388, the Court of Appeal had no doubt that such a log is, in principle, admissible under s 117, but it did not deal with the point under discussion here.

[25] See s 117(2)(b), reversing *Derodra*, n 9 above.

one of the reasons listed in section 116(2), which was examined in Chapter 6; to remind us, these conditions are that he is dead, ill, absent abroad, has vanished, or is in fear. An alternative extra reason, provided by section 117(5)(b), is that the relevant person:

> cannot reasonably be expected to have any recollection of the matters dealt with in the statement (having regard to the length of time since he supplied the information and all other circumstances).

7.21 This extra condition is worded rather narrowly, so that it applies where the original source of the information cannot be expected 'to have *any* recollection' of the matter. From this, the defendant in *R (Wellington) v DPP* tried to argue that, since the police officer who had logged into the PNC the information about Wellington's choice of alias might still have *some* recollection of the incident that provoked him make the entry, the condition did not apply. But Jackson J would not accept this:

> [counsel] urges that the relevant police officer could well have a recollection of the aliases, especially if he had only recently input such data into the system. In my judgment, this is the wrong approach to the sub-section. If pressed to its logical conclusion, this argument could lead to the exclusion of many relevant and uncontroversial details commonly found in a PNC print-out. The crucial fact is that alias names are not unusual. Police officers keep a record of alias names given by offenders as a matter of routine. Although it is possible that police officers will have a recollection of alias names given, these are not the kind of details of which police officers could reasonably be expected to retain a recollection. I am satisfied that in this case the requirements of section 117(5)(b) were met. (at [32])

7.22 By virtue of section 117(4)(b), these extra conditions do not apply to documents from police files obtained from overseas by using formal procedures for mutual legal assistance.

Discretion to exclude

7.23 Section 117(6) and (7) give the court a power to exclude documentary evidence which would otherwise be admissible under section 117. Under CJA 1988, the court also had discretionary powers to exclude otherwise admissible evidence. But the power conferred by CJA 2003, section 117(6) and (7) is more tightly focussed than the powers that existed under the earlier Act, because it is limited to the case where the court thinks that the evidence is unreliable. The conditions for its exercise are set out in section 117(7), which is as follows:

> The court may make a direction under this subsection if satisfied that the statement's reliability as evidence for the purpose for which it is tendered is doubtful in view of—
>
> (a) its contents,
> (b) the source of the information contained in it,
> (c) the way in which or the circumstances in which the information was supplied or received, or
> (d) the way in which or the circumstances in which the document concerned was created or received.

This power is in addition to the courts' other powers of exclusion. Thus, although section 117(6) and (7) do not enable the court to exclude a piece of documentary evidence that the prosecution wishes to adduce because they think that this would be unfair, they can do so under PACE 1984, section 78. And if the court believes that hearing the evidence would be a waste of time, it can exclude it under CJA 2003, section 126, whether it is evidence for the prosecution or for the defence.

7.24 Once upon a time, there was a common law rule that a party wishing to produce a document in evidence must use the original if he has it, and not a copy. After the invention of carbon paper and then the photocopier this rule lost its purpose, and CJA 2003, section 133 now provides:

> Proof of statements in documents
>
> Where a statement in a document is admissible as evidence in criminal proceedings, the statement may be proved by producing either—
>
> (a) the document, or
> (b) (whether or not the document exists) a copy of the document or of the material part of it,
>
> authenticated in whatever way the court may approve.[26]

Documentary evidence and real evidence

7.25 Section 117 creates an exception to the hearsay rule which, as explained earlier, only applies in the context of assertive statements made by human beings. Thus, documentary evidence only becomes entangled with the hearsay rule (and hence section 117 is only needed to resolve the problem) where the document in question records an observation made by a person. A documentary record that was compiled automatically (for example, a print-out from a computer that records the use of swipe-cards to open the doors of a building) is a piece of 'real

[26] CJA 2003, s 133 reproduces (with one small change) PACE 1984, Sch 3, para 13. See further §§ 14.7–14.12 below.

evidence', admissible on the basis of its relevance and without reference to the hearsay rule. This was explained in Chapter 3. Chapter 3 also contained a discussion of CJA 2003, section 129, which provides (in effect) that such a statement only counts as 'real evidence' where the whole process was automatic. So if information provided by human beings is stored in a computer from which it is later printed out, the fact that it has been processed by a computer does not elevate its legal status and displace the hearsay rule, if the rule would otherwise apply to it.[27]

CJA 2003, section 117: conclusion

7.26 Section 117, like section 116, seems to be unnecessarily complicated. For example, why does the court need an extra discretionary power to exclude evidence otherwise admissible under section 117, given the general powers of exclusion conferred by CJA 2003, section 126 and PACE 1984, section 78? As regards records that are kept as a matter of routine and with no eye to subsequent criminal proceedings, why is it not possible to have a simple rule to the effect that they are admissible wherever they are relevant, instead of what we have, a basic rule that they are inadmissible, tempered by admissibility where they pass through the series of tests set out in section 117? As with section 116, one is left with a feeling that, at the end of the day, the complications are rather futile. If the document satisfies the tests set out in section 117, the courts will still exclude it under any one of a range of statutory powers available to them if they think that it is contrary to the interests of justice to admit it. And if the document fails to satisfy the tests set out in section 117, and the courts believe the interests of justice require its admission, they will admit it under the 'inclusionary discretion' conferred on them by section 114(1)(d): as they did, as we saw, in *Maher v DPP*.[28]

[27] See § 3.18 above.
[28] See [**page 302 below**], § 7.16 above.

8

OTHER STATUTORY EXCEPTIONS

8.1 As we saw earlier, CJA 2003, section 114(1)(a) provides that hearsay evidence is admissible where it is rendered admissible by any later provision of the Act, or 'any other statutory provision makes it admissible'. Of these 'other statutory provisions' there are very many: so many, indeed, that the Law Commission was unwilling to produce a comprehensive list of them. No such attempt will be made here either. But in this chapter a brief account will be given of the more important ones, arranged in a scheme that attempts to classify them.

8.2 *Confessions: PACE 1984* Confessions are a long-standing exception to the hearsay rule, the main elements of which are now governed by PACE 1984, sections 76 and 77, between which section 128 of the CJA 2003 has now inserted a new section 76A. Confessions are separately dealt with in Chapter 10.

8.3 *Provisions dispensing certain witnesses from the need to give oral evidence at trial* A number of statutory provisions allow a written statement from the witness to be read in place of his oral evidence where both sides are content with this. Foremost among these is CJA 1967, section 9, which potentially covers any type of evidence, and there are other provisions which are limited to particular types of evidence. These provisions were examined in Chapter 4.

8.4 In similar vein, but distinct, are other statutory provisions which allow a statement written or dictated by a witness to be read in place of his oral evidence, whether the other side is content with this or not. These include a number of old provisions about depositions where, instead of giving evidence formally at trial, the witness will have been examined formally ahead of trial before a magistrate; these were discussed in Chapter 2.[1] They also include CJA 1988, section 30, under which, where the court gives leave, the oral testimony of an expert may be replaced by his written report, which then 'shall be evidence of any fact or opinion of which the person making it could have given oral evidence'. They also include CJA 1948, section 41(1), according to which:

[1] See § 2.53 *et seq* above.

> In any criminal proceedings, a certificate purporting to be signed by a constable, or by a person having the prescribed qualifications, and certifying that a plan or drawing exhibited thereto is a plan or drawing made by him of the place or object specified in the certificate, and that the plan or drawing is correctly drawn to a scale so specified, shall be evidence of the relative position of the things shown on the plan or drawing.

8.5 The effect of this provision is that, if police officer X attended an accident and drew a sketch plan of the scene, his plan is admissible as evidence to help the court decide what happened; and this is so whether or not police officer X gives evidence to the court in person.

8.6 Related again, but rather different, are statutory provisions providing for a videotape of an earlier interview with a witness to be used in substitution for his evidence-in-chief, although subject to his availability for cross-examination live at trial. One such provision is Youth Justice and Criminal Evidence Act 1999, section 27, which permits the use of this procedure by witnesses who are vulnerable. A further and more general provision is added by CJA 2003, sections 137 and 138. The use of videotape evidence is discussed in Chapter 13 below.

8.7 *Provisions about specific types of record* Bankers' Books Evidence Act 1879, section 3, provides that:

> Subject to the provisions of this Act, a copy of any entry in a bankers' book shall in all legal proceedings be received as prima facie evidence of such entry, and of the matters, transactions and accounts therein mentioned.

8.8 The application of this Act presupposes a 'banker' and a 'book'. Both terms are defined in section 9. This interpretation section has been amended since the Act was originally passed. The terms 'banker' and 'bank' now include deposit-takers and the National Savings Bank, and the term 'bankers' books' now includes:

> ledgers, day books, cash books, account books and other records used in the ordinary business of the bank, whether those records are in written form or are kept on microfilm, magnetic tape or any other form of mechanical or electronic data retrieval system.

8.9 This definition, though wide, does not cover everything. Thus it has been held that it does not extend to notes or minutes of meetings between employees and customers[2] or, more surprisingly, paid cheques and credit slips, which the bank in question stored in unsorted bundles.[3]

[2] *Re Howglen Ltd* [2001] 1 All ER 376, [2001] 2 BCLC 695.

[3] *Williams v Williams* [1988] QB 161. This was because the Act refers throughout to 'a copy of an entry' in a book.

8.10 The ground covered by section 3 of this Act is now also covered, obviously, by CJA 2003, section 117. But the rest of the Act is still important because of other provisions which provide a legal mechanism for the compulsory inspection of bank records, and also provide that, where a copy of the bank records are admissible, the banker is not compellable either to produce the original or to come to court to testify orally.[4]

8.11 To rather similar effect is Merchant Shipping Act 1995, section 287, which makes various maritime records evidence of the matters they contain, in particular, a ship's log. This provision too, of course, is now duplicated by section 117.

8.12 Rather similar, but narrower, are a range of statutory provisions that allow certain specific facts to be established by producing written certificates from those whose role in life it is to make an official record of them. These include the Births and Deaths Registration Act 1953, section 34, which allows birth certificates and death certificates to be used to prove a person's birth or death.[5] They also include provisions of the Medical Act 1983[6] and the Dentists Act 1984,[7] which enable the fact that a person is (or is not) registered as a doctor or a dentist to be proved by certificate, and similar provisions in the Solicitors Act 1974 about proving that a solicitor holds (or has held) a practising certificate.[8] Similar in principle again is Video Recordings Act 1984, section 19, which in order to prove that a video has been officially approved by the British Board of Film Censors, allows a document from the authority to be put in evidence. There are many others.[9]

8.13 The provisions mentioned in the previous paragraph, and most of the others like them, merely say that the certificate or document is 'admissible in evidence'. Where that is so, the legal ground they cover is now covered by CJA 2003, section 117, which could equally well be used as the vehicle to put such evidence before the court. These specific provisions are, however, well known to practitioners, who no doubt find it comfortable to use what is familiar.

8.14 However, there are some other provisions of this sort which go further than section 117, and provide that the certificate in question is not merely admissible in evidence but also creates a rebuttable presumption that the facts stated in it are correct. One of these is Postal Services Act 2000, section 108, which provides that

[4] See s 6: '. . . unless by order of a judge made for special cause'.

[5] It is framed in strangely negative language: 'An entry or certificated copy of an entry of a birth or death in a register . . . shall not be evidence of the birth or death unless . . .'.

[6] See s 34(4).

[7] See s 14(6).

[8] See s 18.

[9] A number are listed in Law Commission, *Evidence in Criminal Proceedings and Related Matters* (Consultation Paper No 138, 1995) Appendix C.

the appropriate mark stamped on a postal package by a postal authority stating that the package was refused, rejected, unclaimed or undeliverable 'shall, unless the contrary is shown, be sufficient proof of that fact'. A few of these provisions go even further still, and provide that the certificate amounts to conclusive proof. One of these is Companies Act 2006, section 15, which deals with certificates of incorporation. This says that 'The certificate is conclusive evidence that the requirements of this Act as to registration have been complied with and that the company is duly registered under this Act'.

8.15 *Provisions relating to the proof of criminal convictions* At common law, it was possible to prove the fact of a person's criminal conviction by producing the original record of the court, a cumbersome procedure to which the Evidence Act 1854 added the more convenient alternative of an officially certified copy.[10] But (astonishingly) the fact that a person had been convicted of an offence was not in law admissible as evidence in subsequent proceedings that he had committed the office of which he had been convicted; and to establish that, it was necessary to produce the original witnesses to the crime to testify orally again. This rule, known as 'the rule in *Hollington v Hewthorn*' from the leading case in which it was affirmed,[11] was of course extremely inconvenient. For the purpose of the civil law it was abolished by the Civil Evidence Act 1968, and it was later also abolished as a rule of criminal evidence by PACE 1984, sections 74 and 75. The first of these two sections provides that, where a person has been convicted 'by or before any court in the United Kingdom or by a Service court outside the United Kingdom, he shall be taken to have committed that offence unless the contrary is proved'. The second provides for proof of the conviction by means of a certificate from the court; and also makes admissible as evidence of the details of the offence 'the contents of any document which is admissible as evidence of the conviction, and the contents of the information, complaint, indictment or charge-sheet on which the person in question was convicted'.[12]

8.16 PACE 1984, sections 74 and 75 only apply to convictions imposed by UK courts. Logically, it therefore appeared to follow that the rule in *Hollington v Hewthorn* still applied in relation to convictions imposed by foreign courts. However, in *Kordasinski* the Court of Appeal managed to avoid this inconvenient conclusion, holding that proof of the defendant's previous conviction for rape in Poland was admissible as evidence to establish, in later proceedings in England in which Kordasinski was charged with a further rape, that he had committed the

[10] See s 13.
[11] [1943] KB 587.
[12] PACE 1984, s 75(1).

earlier one.[13] But the effect of this decision was only to make evidence of the foreign conviction admissible; though prima facie evidence, the conviction does not (at least in theory) create a presumption that the convicted person committed the offence. As PACE 1984, section 74 does not apply to it, the foreign conviction, unlike a UK conviction, does not establish that he committed it 'unless the contrary is proved'.

8.17 *Other statutory exceptions: conclusion* This corner of the law contains nothing that is bad but much that appears to be unnecessary. Many or most of the specific provisions about records and certificates are in truth redundant now that there is an exception to the hearsay rule that applies to records in general. And if the law of criminal evidence were turned into a coherent code, there would presumably be one single broad provision for the taking of evidence on commission instead of the collection of antique and narrow provisions about depositions which currently exists.

[13] [2006] EWCA Crim 2984, [2007] 1 Cr App R 17 (238); for comment, see Spencer [2007] 2 *Archbold News* 6–9 and [2007] 7 *Archbold News* 4.

9

PRESERVED COMMON LAW EXCEPTIONS (CJA 2003, SECTION 118)

9.1 CJA 2003, section 118 does two things. First, by subsection (1) it preserves a list of eight existing common law exceptions to the hearsay rule. Secondly, in subsection (2) it provides that:

> With the exception of the rules preserved by this section, the common law rules governing the admissibility of hearsay evidence in criminal proceedings are abolished.

9.2 By section 118(2), obviously, all the remaining common law exceptions to the hearsay rule are abolished for the purpose of criminal proceedings. Less obviously, this provision also abolishes the original common law exclusionary rule as well, with the result, as we saw in Chapter 3, that the basic rule excluding hearsay is now the new statutory rule set out in the first sentence of CJA 2003, section 114(1).[1]

9.3 As will be seen when they are examined individually, most of the grounds these exceptions cover is also covered by a combination of sections 116 and 117, and where it is not, if the evidence were cogent, it could be admitted under the 'inclusionary discretion' conferred on the courts by section 114(1)(d). Despite this, the Law Commission recommended the retention of these exceptions on the ground that they had served a useful purpose in the past, and might possibly be of further use in the future.[2] Though not explicitly stated in this context, the Law Commission made it clear elsewhere in its Report that it was anxious that its proposed reform should not 'frighten the horses', in the shape of practitioners and

[1] See §§ 3.1–3.8 above; and *Singh* [2006] 1 WLR 1564 [**page 298 below**].

[2] 'We recommend that the following common law exceptions be retained, because they fulfil useful functions and we are not aware that they cause any difficulties': Law Commission, *Evidence in Criminal Proceedings: Hearsay and Related Topics* (Report No 245, Cm 3670, June 1997) (hereafter 'LC Report') § 8.132.

judges;[3] and another reason for retaining these old exceptions was probably to ensure practitioners of the continued comfort of the familiar.

9.4 The eight exceptions preserved by section 118(1) form a distinctly heterodox list. It includes some exceptions, like *res gestae*, which have traditionally played an important part in the workings of criminal evidence, and others, like the recondite rules about 'reputation or family tradition', which are of little or no practical significance in the criminal courts. Much of the content of the list derives from a similar list which appeared in Civil Evidence Act 1968, section 9,[4] a source which probably explains why it includes a number of exceptions which are of some importance in the civil law, but in criminal law are of virtually no relevance.

9.5 In the rest of this chapter the eight exceptions will be examined in turn.

Public information, etc

9.6 The first common law exception (in reality, a clutch of four distinct exceptions) is preserved under the heading 'Public information etc':

1 Any rule of law under which in criminal proceedings—
- (a) published works dealing with matters of a public nature (such as histories, scientific works, dictionaries and maps) are admissible as evidence of facts of a public nature stated in them,
- (b) public documents (such as public registers, and returns made under public authority with respect to matters of public interest) are admissible as evidence of facts stated in them,
- (c) records (such as the records of certain courts, treaties, Crown grants, pardons and commissions) are admissible as evidence of facts stated in them, or
- (d) evidence relating to a person's age or date or place of birth may be given by a person without personal knowledge of the matter.

9.7 Of this group, the first is occasionally important in civil disputes but of little likely relevance in criminal cases, and no more need be said about it here.[5]

[3] LC Report, n 2 above, para 6.31: 'By way of footnote, we would add that we are troubled by the change of attitude that [the proposed 'Option 3'] would require on the part of practitioners and judges. It would be necessary for them to change habits of a life-time and be re-educated. We do not underestimate this task'.

[4] Which was later modified by Civil Evidence Act 1995, s 7. A clause copying these provisions of the Civil Evidence Act was included in the Draft Bill attached to Criminal Law Revision Committee, *Eleventh Report (Evidence) General* (Cmnd 4991, London, HMSO, 1972) (hereafter 'CLRC Evidence Report')

[5] For further discussion, see *Cross and Tapper on Evidence* (11th edn, Oxford, OUP, 2007) 631.

9.8 The second, 'public documents', is potentially more relevant.[6] For a document to count as a public one, the following four conditions must be met. First, it must be part of a record made by someone who holds a public office which obliges him to enquire and control; thus although it covers the parish registers of the Established Church, it does not cover records of other sects or faiths or denominations.[7] Secondly, the information must be 'a public matter'.[8] Thirdly, the record must have been intended as something permanent, rather than transitory. And finally, the record must be available for public inspection: a requirement which excludes many documents kept by those who hold a public office, for example, regimental records.[9] Over the years, this rather narrow common law exception has been supplemented by a large number of highly specific statutes making particular documents, or certified copies of them, admissible in evidence, all of which remain in force. In practice, documents of a public nature are more likely to be put in evidence under one of these statutes or, failing that, by section 117.

9.9 The third member of the subgroup is self-explanatory and, like the first, is of little relevance in criminal cases.

9.10 The fourth and last preserves the common law rule that, although nobody can remember his own birth and a person only knows when and where it happened from what his parents or other people have told him, hearsay has traditionally been admissible as evidence on both matters. (If either matter is seriously disputed in a case today, it is much more likely, of course, that a birth certificate would be produced in evidence.)[10]

Reputation as to character

9.11 The second exception is entitled 'reputation as to character':

> 2 Any rule of law under which in criminal proceedings evidence of a person's reputation is admissible for the purpose of proving his good or bad character.
>
> *Note* The rule is preserved only so far as it allows the court to treat such evidence as proving the matter concerned.

[6] It was applied in *Halpin* [1975] QB 907 to justify the admission in evidence of extracts from the annual returns of a company filed at the Companies Registry.

[7] *Re Woodward, Kenway v Kidd* [1913] 1 Ch 392.

[8] See generally *Sturla v Freccia* (1880) 5 App Cas 623.

[9] *Lilley v Pettit* [1946] KB 401.

[10] See further, *Cross and Tapper on Evidence*, n 5 above, 768–9.

9.12 This exception derives from the nineteenth century case of *Rowton.*[11] In that case, it was said that where a defendant wishes to call evidence of good character, this must take the form of a good 'reputation' (that is, what people say about him) rather than specific good acts or the personal judgement of a particular person; and it was also said that, in order to rebut a claim of good character, similar principles applied, and this evidence must be of 'bad reputation', not specific bad acts or specific negative personal opinions. These remarks bear little relation to what actually happens in the criminal courts: witnesses to the good character of a defendant often give personal opinions and not infrequently describe good things that he has done; and evidence called to rebut a claim of good character will often consist of the fact that the defendant has a criminal record. However, what was said in *Rowton* still seems to be good law, to the limited extent that it is possible (if not obligatory) for evidence of good or bad character to consist of evidence of the person's reputation. As evidence of a person's reputation necessarily consists of what other people say about him, this of course is hearsay. To the extent that what was said in *Rowton* about evidence of reputation is good law, this exception enables it to continue.[12]

Reputation or family tradition

9.13 The third exception is entitled 'reputation or family tradition':

> 3 Any rule of law under which in criminal proceedings evidence of reputation or family tradition is admissible for the purpose of proving or disproving—
>
> (a) pedigree or the existence of a marriage,
> (b) the existence of any public or general right, or
> (c) the identity of any person or thing.
>
> *Note* The rule is preserved only so far as it allows the court to treat such evidence as proving or disproving the matter concerned.

9.14 *Pedigree or the existence of a marriage* At common law, 'pedigree' (ie descent or blood relationship) could be established by evidence of the statements of persons now deceased, provided they were made *ante litem motam*, before the dispute in question had arisen.[13] Classic examples would have included 'an entry in a family Bible, an examined copy of an inscription on a tombstone, a pedigree hung up

[11] (1865) Le & Ca 520, 169 ER 1497.
[12] See further Roderick Munday, *Evidence* (4th edn, Oxford, OUP, 2007) § 9.48.
[13] Cross, *Evidence* (3rd edn, 1967) 415–18; *Phipson on Evidence* (16th edn, London, Sweet and Maxwell, 2005) § 32.09.

in a family mansion, and the like'.[14] The rationale for making this exception to the hearsay rule was partly necessity, 'for those who would be most useful as witnesses are generally dead, and partly in the fact that there is some guarantee of trustworthiness as it is natural for people to talk of their family, and the evidence is of an unsuspicious kind—concerning, in most cases, remote times when there was no interest to be served or bias caused'.[15] The usual context, of course, was disputes about inheritance and family law matters in the civil courts. Whether such evidence would ever have been admissible to prove a blood relationship where this was necessary in a criminal case is uncertain,[16] and it seems likely that, in a prosecution for incest, for example, it would be regarded as insufficient evidence, even if it were admissible.[17]

9.15 In civil law, marriages could traditionally be established by evidence of 'cohabitation and repute'.[18] However, for the purposes of the criminal law (for example, prosecutions for bigamy) something more solid than this has always been required.[19] So the preservation of this exception by section 118 appears to serve no purpose.

9.16 *The existence of any public or general right* At common law, 'an oral, or written, declaration by a deceased person concerning the reputed existence of a public, or general right is admissible as evidence of the existence of such a right, provided the declaration was made before the dispute in which it is tendered had arisen, and, in the case of a statement concerning the reputed existence of a general right, provided the declarant had competent knowledge'.[20] In the past, this exception to the hearsay rule 'has produced decisions of breathtaking absurdity'.[21] In the light of that, it is fortunate that the existence or otherwise of public and general rights is principally a matter for the civil law, where for present purposes it is possible to leave them.

[14] Archbold, *Criminal Pleading, Evidence and Practice* (37th edn, 1969) § 1255, citing, inter alia, *Goodright v Moss* (1777) 2 Cowp 591 and the *Berkelely Peerage Case* (1811) 4 Camp 401.

[15] Cross, n 13 above, 416.

[16] Archbold, n 14 above, § 1255.

[17] Cf *Hemmings* (1939) 27 Cr App R 46, where in a prosecution for incest, the fact that the defendant was the woman's father was held not to have been sufficiently established by evidence that the defendant had been in the habit of referring to her as his daughter.

[18] Cross, n 13 above, 116–17.

[19] Hawkins, *Pleas of the Crown* (7th edn, Leach, London, 1795) para 42.9, citing *Morris v Miller* (1767) 4 Burr 2059.

[20] *Cross and Tapper on Evidence*, n 5 above, 637.

[21] *Ibid*, citing *Mercer v Denne* [1905] 2 Ch 538, where the issue was whether the fishermen of Walmer had a customary right of immemorial antiquity to dry their nets on a part of the foreshore, and the party opposing the right was not permitted to rebut the evidence by producing old maps which showed that, until relatively recently, the land in question had been permanently under the sea.

9.17 *The identity of any person or thing* Those writing wills, and other legal instruments, often make references to particular people or particular things: 'my friend John Smith', for example, or 'uncle Mott's pocket-watch'. Afterwards, disputes sometimes arise as to the identity or the person or object referred to and traditionally, hearsay evidence has then been admissible to clarify the issue.[22] Again, this is an exception to the hearsay rule which is of minimal practical importance in the criminal courts.

Res gestae

9.18 The fourth exception appears under the Latin rubric '*res gestae*'. This phrase means literally 'things done', and as used in the law of evidence it was originally shorthand for the proposition that, as an exception to the hearsay rule, it is possible to adduce evidence of things that were said at the time the offence was being committed. Such things are not usually assertive statements and where they are not, no question of hearsay arises: no hearsay issue arises, for example, about the fact that the robber said 'Your money or your life!' or that the victim shouted 'Help!'. But if the robber says 'I'm Jessie James: your money or your life!' or the victim replies 'Help! I'm being robbed!', assertive statements have been made, and traditionally, lawyers would have said that, though assertive, they were admissible as 'part of the *res gestae*'. Over the years, the scope of the phrase (and the exception to the hearsay rule it represented) expanded to cover certain other things as well, three of which are preserved by section 118, as follows:

> 4 Any rule of law under which in criminal proceedings a statement is admissible as evidence of any matter stated if—
>
> (a) the statement was made by a person so emotionally overpowered by an event that the possibility of concoction or distortion can be disregarded,
> (b) the statement accompanied an act which can be properly evaluated as evidence only if considered in conjunction with the statement, or
> (c) the statement relates to a physical sensation or a mental state (such as intention or emotion).

9.19 *A statement made by a person so emotionally overpowered by an event that the possibility of concoction or distortion can be disregarded* American lawyers call this exception 'excited utterances'. At first, it was strictly limited to what people said or shouted out as the offence was taking place; and so in the famous nineteenth century case of *Bedingfield*[23] it was held not to apply to what a woman had said when

[22] Cross, n 13 above, 51; *Cross and Tapper on Evidence*, n 5 above, 737; *Doe d v Gord v Needs* (1836) 2 M and W 129, 150 ER 698.

[23] (1879) 14 Cox CC 341.

she emerged from the adjoining room with her throat cut, which was 'Look what Harry [Bedingfield] has done to me!'. However, in *Ratten v The Queen*,[24] the Privy Council said that the test was not whether the words were uttered when the offence was actually taking place, but whether the person when he made the statement was so emotionally overpowered by the event that he is almost certain to have been telling the truth as he perceived it. This approach was adopted by the House of Lords in *Andrews*,[24a] where the *res gestae* exception was held to cover not only what the victim of an attack said at the time, but also what he told the police about it immediately afterwards. The primary test, said Lord Ackner, is 'can the possibility of concoction or distortion be disregarded?'. If this is so, the fact that the speaker might have been mistaken (for example, because he was drunk) goes to the weight of the statement, not to its admissibility.[25]

9.20 The more dramatic the event, and the closer in time to it that the words were spoken, the more likely it is that this exception will apply, and vice versa. Thus it was held to apply in *Nye and Loan*,[26] where following a collision between two cars, someone got out of one of the cars and punched the driver of the other, and when the police arrived shortly afterwards the victim of the assault pointed to the defendant and said 'That man hit me in the face'. But in *Tobi v Nicholas*[27] it was held not to apply to a remark made by one of the drivers 20 minutes after a not particularly dramatic traffic accident—in the aftermath of which nobody had punched anybody.

9.21 *The statement accompanied an act which can be properly evaluated as evidence only if considered in conjunction with the statement* Part of the evidence that a crime has been committed (or not committed) may be a physical act which, taken on its own, was equivocal. If a man is seen running away as a policeman approaches, for example, it makes a difference whether as he did so he was heard to say 'It's the Old Bill!' or 'I'm going to miss my train!'.[28] For this reason, explanatory statements of this sort are admissible. That evidence of what a person said could be given in order to explain his action was clearly established at common law,[29] and by this part of section 118 the exception to the hearsay rule that it represents has been retained.

9.22 *The statement relates to a physical sensation or a mental state (such as intention or emotion)* As a further exception to the hearsay rule, also traditionally listed

[24] [1972] AC 378.
[24a] [1987] 1 AC 281.
[25] See eg *Turnbull* (1984) 80 Cr App R 104 and *Edwards* [1992] Crim LR 576.
[26] (1977) 66 Cr App R 252.
[27] (1988) 86 Cr App R 323.
[28] *Andrews and Hirst on Criminal Evidence* (3rd edn, London, Sweet & Maxwell, 1997) § 20.016.
[29] *Howard v Malkin* (1878) 40 LT 196. For a fuller discussion, see earlier editions of *Cross on Evidence*, eg 3rd edn (1967), 461–4 or 6th edn (1985), 582–4.

under the heading '*res gestae*', it has always been possible to give evidence of what a person said in order to prove his physical sensations, for example, that he is in pain[30] or that he is hungry.[31] Such evidence may also be given to prove mental sensations, like disgust.[32] It has also been used to establish fear,[33] including (as we saw in Chapter 6) the fear of a person who for that reason is unavailable as a witness.[34] Similarly, a person's statements can also be adduced under this exception to disprove a particular state of mind, where its existence is asserted: as where a man accused of murdering his wife produced suicide notes to support his defence that she had killed herself and, to counter this, the prosecution called witnesses to say that she had told them that her husband had persuaded her to write imaginary suicide notes, claiming he needed them for a 'suicide course' on which he was allegedly engaged at work.[35]

9.23 It is usually said that this exception permits evidence of what a person said his feelings were, but not their cause. 'If a man says to his surgeon, "I have a pain in my head . . ." that is evidence; but, if he says to his surgeon, "I have a wound", and was to add "I met John Thomas, who had a sword, and he ran me through the body with it", that would be no evidence against John Thomas'.[36] However, the cases are not easy to reconcile. In *Edwards*[37] a neighbour was allowed to give evidence that a week before she died the murder victim deposited with her a carving knife and axe, saying 'my husband always threatens me with these and when they're out of the way I feel safer': which looks like evidence of fear, coupled with the reason for it.

9.24 This exception also allows a person's intention to be proved by evidence of what they earlier said they intended to do. The law here is complicated, however, because in the cases the question of hearsay is entangled with the separate question of relevance: whether, in law, it is permissible to lead evidence that a person intended to do something to support the allegation that he did it, when doubt exists as to whether he did it or not. Common sense suggests that the answer should be 'yes'. If the question is who broke X's window, the fact that Y has been heard to say that he intends to break it does not conclusively prove that it was him, but it is reasonable grounds for suspecting him and is surely something which

[30] *Aveson v Kinnair* (1805) 6 East 188.

[31] *Conde* (1868) 10 Cox CC 547.

[32] As in the blasphemy case of *Gott* (1922) 16 Cr App R 87, where evidence was given of a member of the public who saw Gott's pamphlets, said 'Disgusting!', and walked away.

[33] As in *Vincent* (1840) 9 C & P 275.

[34] See § 6.24 above; and see *Neill v North Antrim Magistrates' Court* [1992] 1 WLR 1221.

[35] *Gilfoyle* [1996] 1 Cr App R 302.

[36] *Nicholas* (1846) 2 Car & Kir 246, 248 per Pollock CB, 175 ER 102.

[37] (1872) 12 Cox CC 230.

could fairly be considered together with the other evidence. But the case law is conflicting.[38]

9.25 Where these '*res gestae*' exceptions have been used, the original maker of the statement has usually been unavailable, commonly because he or she is dead; but the unavailability of the maker is not a precondition for its admissibility under this exception. However, in *Attorney General's Reference (No 1 of 2003)*[39] the Court of Appeal deprecated its use to put contentious evidence before the court in a case where the witness was available to give oral evidence. Where this is so, and it is prosecution evidence, the Court of Appeal thought the trial court should consider excluding it under PACE 1984, section 78. If it was the defence that sought to make use of the exception in such circumstances, and it seemed that this was done in order to avoid the evidence being tested in cross-examination, it is at least arguable that the court should now exclude it under CJA 2003, section 126.[40]

9.26 In the light of this, it is difficult to see what useful purpose was served by retaining this group of exceptions to the hearsay rule, because they add little if anything to what is already provided by section 116.[41] They could, perhaps, be used to admit the statement of a witness who is unidentified, or not mentally competent, or who is unavailable for a reason that is not listed in section 116(2); but if it was cogent, and important, the court would probably admit it under the 'inclusionary discretion' in section 114(1)(d). The exceptions could also be used, perhaps, to admit the previous statement of a witness who does give evidence, like the assaulted driver's statement in *Nye and Loan* identifying the defendant as the person who had hit him. But in that case, and probably most others like it, it would now be admissible under one of the revised exceptions to the 'rule against narrative' set out in section 120.

Confessions, etc

9.27 The fifth 'rule of law' preserved by section 118 is said to be 'Any rule of law relating to the admissibility of confessions or mixed statements in criminal

[38] *Buckley* (1873) 13 Cox CC 293; *Wainwright* (1875) 13 Cox CC 171; *Thomson* [1912] 3 KB 19; Moghal (1977) 65 Cr App R 56; *Callender* [1998] Crim LR 337; for a discussion, see *Blackstone's Criminal Practice* (2008) § F16.37. And see Roderick Munday, 'Legislation that Would "Preserve" the Common Law: the Case of the Declaration of Intention', (2008) 124 *Law Quarterly Review* 46.

[39] [2003] EWCA Crim 1286, [2003] 2 Cr App R 29 (453).

[40] CJA 2003, s 126 is primarily directed against evidence that is likely to waste the time of the court, because of its low relevance or poor quality: see §§ 5.40–5.45 above.

[41] See David Ormerod, 'Redundant res gestae?' [1998] Crim LR 301; and Colin Tapper in *Cross and*

proceedings'. As the admissibility of confessions is essentially regulated under the 'confession' provisions of PACE 1984, and section 118 is concerned with common law exceptions to the hearsay rule, what is being preserved here is not immediately obvious—it appears to be preserving the grin of a Cheshire cat, the body of which has removed itself to another garden. Confessions are treated in the Chapter 10 and the question will be investigated there.

Admissions by agents, etc

9.28 The sixth preserved exception is stated in section 118 as follows:

> 6 Any rule of law under which in criminal proceedings—
> (a) an admission made by an agent of a defendant is admissible against the defendant as evidence of any matter stated, or
> (b) a statement made by a person to whom a defendant refers a person for information is admissible against the defendant as evidence of any matter stated.

9.29 As a general proposition, where a defendant makes a statement that incriminates him, the fact that he has done so is admissible as evidence to prove this. This was the basis on which 'admissions and confessions' were admissible at common law. In 1984, most aspects of the matter were regulated by statute under PACE, sections 76 and 77. But the wider principle of which confessions are an example has survived and (as we have just seen) has been expressly preserved as the fifth common law exception to the hearsay rule listed in CJA 2003, section 118(1). An aspect of the common law rule was that the prosecution could use against a defendant not only the admissions that he made himself but also any that were made by 'an agent' on his behalf; which means, in practice, his defending lawyer. It is this rule that is preserved by paragraph (a) of the sixth exception listed in section 118(1).

9.30 In criminal proceedings, a defendant is only bound by the admissions made on his behalf by his lawyer to the extent that he has actually instructed his lawyer to make them. So if a solicitor, without instructions, or exceeding them, writes a letter on behalf of his client making an admission or other damaging statement, this is not admissible against the client. Thus in *Downer*,[42] where a woman was prosecuted for attempting to defraud a railway company by making a false claim that it had lost a package she had deposited at a station, the prosecution were not allowed to establish the fact that she had made the claim by putting in evidence a

[42] *Downer* (1880) 43 LT 445.

letter that her solicitor had written to the company, in the absence of any evidence that the solicitor had been instructed to write it. In *Turner*, by contrast, it was held that if in court a barrister makes an admission damaging to his client, and the client is present in court and does not object, the client will be bound by it. 'Wherever a barrister comes into court in robes and in the presence of his client tells the judge that he appears for the client, the court is entitled to assume, and does assume, that he has his client's authority to conduct the case and to say on his client's behalf whatever in his professional discretion he thinks is in his client's interest to say'.[43]

9.31 Paragraph (b) refers to a related common law rule, according to which '[S]tatements made by someone to whom a party has referred others for information may be proved against him as admissions concerning the subject-matter of the reference'.[44] In such a case, the person who passed the enquirer on to the 'referee' is bound by the admissions that are made on his behalf: whether he wished the 'referee' to let this particular cat out of the bag, or not. The old cases on which the rule depends are civil ones,[45] and it is not clear to what extent it is properly applicable in criminal law. It was applied in the nineteenth-century case of *Mallory*,[45a] where the police asked a shopkeeper about some stolen goods that he had allegedly bought, and he 'referred' them to his wife, who later produced a list; but as she gave it to the police in his presence, and he did not dispute it, the case could have been decided on the basis that she had actual authority to make the statement, rather than that she had exceeded it but he was bound by what she had done. To the extent (if any) to which the rule applied in criminal law before CJA 2003 came into force, section 118 has clearly preserved it.

9.32 Clearly, the rules referred to in this part of section 118(1) are some way removed from the central core of the hearsay rule, and it seems unlikely that, without section 118(1), the courts would have assumed that any other part of the CJA 2003 had abolished them. But these rules were mentioned in the equivalent provision of the Civil Evidence Act 1968 and this probably explains why they were included here.[46]

43 (1975) 61 Cr App R 67, 82.
44 Cross, n 13 above, 441.
45 *Williams v Innes* (1808) 1 Camp 364; *Daniel v Pitt* (1806) 1 Camp 369; *Harrison v Vallance* (1822) 1 Bing 45.
45a (1884) 13 QBD 33.
46 See § 9.4 above.

Common enterprise

9.33 The seventh common law exception to the hearsay rule preserved by section 118 is stated thus:

> 7 Any rule of law under which in criminal proceedings a statement made by a party to a common enterprise is admissible against another party to the enterprise as evidence of any matter stated.

The general rule at common law is that the incriminating statements a person makes are admissible in evidence against himself, but not other people whom he mentions in it. Thus, for example, where D is arrested by the police and questioned, and admits committing a criminal offence in company with E, this confession is admissible at trial against D but not against E.[47] To this rule, an important exception exists for cases where it can be shown that the other person or persons he incriminates were acting in concert with him. A simple factual example is *Owen*,[48] which was discussed in Chapter 2. Owen, a prisoner, was accused of conspiracy with another prisoner and two people outside, one called Chick and the other (appropriately enough) Roach, to bring a supply of cannabis into Bridgend prison on his return from day release. There was evidence that, in the course of his day out of prison, Owen had telephoned Chick and had also tried to meet Roach, an appointment that fell through when Roach was arrested, 'pot' in hand, at the place they were supposed to meet, shortly before Owen arrived there. This being so, the prosecution could also use as evidence against Owen the telephone conversations overheard between the other three, in which they discussed the plan and the part that was to be played in it by Owen. The reason for the rule is usually said to be that, when two or more persons agree to commit a crime, each impliedly authorises the other to speak on his behalf.[49]

9.34 The 'common enterprise' exception is limited, naturally, to statements made by someone else who was himself involved in it, though it need not have been made *to* such a person and it is potentially applicable to statements that conspirators made to others who were not part of it.[50] It is also limited to statements made while the plan was being formulated and then carried out, so it does not cover statements made after the venture was over. Thus in *Blake*, it did not render admissible against D the counterfoil, in E's possession, of the cheque E had allegedly written to D in payment of D's share of the spoils after the crime had been carried out[51] (nor, a fortiori, would it cover what E said to police about D when E

[47] As to whether the CJA 2003 has made any difference to this, see Chapter 10.
[48] [2001] EWCA Crim 1018.
[49] See Dixon J in *Tripodi* (1961) CLR 1, 6–7; cited with approval in *Gray*, n 56 below.
[50] *Platten* [2006] EWCA Crim 140, [2006] Crim LR 920 at [45].
[51] (1844) 6 QB 126, 115 ER 49.

was later caught and confessed). It has also been held not to cover statements made by A and B before D was involved, for example, 'Let's see if we can get D to join us'.[52]

9.35 It is also limited to statements that are 'conspiratorial', meaning ones that are related to the plan. At one time, it was thought that, to be admissible under this exception, the statement must actually be *in furtherance* of the plan, for example, 'Jack, we want someone to drive the getaway car for D tomorrow. Are you free?'. But the more recent case law suggests that it is enough if it was made *in the course of the conspiracy*: 'Jack has come out of prison, and he's said he'll drive the getaway car for D'. In *Jones, Williams and Barham* the Court of Appeal said that the statements must represent 'the enterprise in operation'.[53] Whether the statement is sufficiently 'conspiratorial' to fall within the common enterprise exception is a matter of law, decided in a jury trial by the judge.[54]

9.36 It is sometimes suggested that the 'common purpose' rule only applies in conspiracy trials,[55] but this is certainly not the case: it applies wherever it is alleged that there was a joint enterprise to commit a crime, or indeed more than one single crime. However, in the situation where D1 is accused of one offence and D2 of another, D1's out-of-court statements incriminating D2 are only admissible against D2 under the 'common enterprise' exception if there was a connection between the two offences.[56] Thus, 'the common enterprise exception cannot apply in situations where defendants are charged with isolated offences, rather than with conspiring to commit a joint offence, nor where the common enterprise is neither clearly defined nor proven'.[57]

9.37 The final (and obviously necessary) condition for the 'common enterprise' exception is the existence of evidence, independent of the statement it is sought to admit, that D and E were involved in the offence together.[58] This causes a practical problem, obviously, where the evidence of E's statement incriminating D is given first, and then the independent evidence of D's involvement with E fails to materialise or is 'blown out of the water'. Where this happens at a jury trial, the judge will have to direct the jury to disregard E's statement in relation to D, and if the evidence was too damning to forget, stop the case and order a retrial.[59]

[52] *Platten*, n 50 above.

[53] [1997] 2 Cr App R 119, 130; accepted and approved in *Platten*, n 50 above.

[54] *Smart and Beard* [2002] EWCA Crim 772, [2002] Crim LR 684; *Platten*, n 50 above.

[55] *Dawson* [1960] 1 WLR 163, 170.

[56] *Gray, Liggins and others* [1995] 2 Cr App R 100; *Murray, Morgan and Sheridan* [1997] 2 Cr App R 136.

[57] Munday, n 12 above, § 9.70.

[58] *Donat* (1985) 82 Cr App R 173; *Smart and Beard*, n 54 above; *Jenkins* [2003] Crim LR 107.

[59] *Blackstone*, n 38 above, § F16.43.

9.38 The Law Commission made no serious attempt to justify the 'common enterprise' exception to the hearsay rule, much less to explain what its rationale is.[60] This is surprising, because some commentators have criticised it severely as potentially unfair.[61] However, if one takes as a starting-point the proposition that everything is in principle relevant if it tends to show the existence or non-existence of a disputed fact, then there does seem to be an acceptable rationale for the 'common enterprise' exception. It is that if A, B and C are involved with one another in doing something, each is likely to know what the others are up to, and what they say to one another about this, or say to other people, is more likely to be true than not. At this point in the story they are not accusing one another, or trying to shift the blame, as they may well do once they have been arrested and are being interrogated by the police. It was probably this consideration that led the Court of Appeal in *Owen* to rule that the admission of hearsay under this exception did not contravene the defendant's right to question the witnesses under ECHR, Article 6(3)(d).[62]

Expert evidence

9.39 The eighth common law exception concerns expert evidence. By section 118(1), there is preserved:

> 8 Any rule of law under which in criminal proceedings an expert witness may draw on the body of expertise relevant to his field.

9.40 Where an expert gives evidence, he or she is permitted to refer to experiments conducted by others which are part of his or her professional knowledge. Thus in *Abadom*[63] it was held that an expert who had measured the refractive index of certain fragments of glass and compared it with that of the broken glass found at the scene of the crime could properly refer to statistics collated by the Home Office Central Research Establishment, in order to demonstrate that the refractive index found in both samples was uncommon, thus suggesting that the defendant was there when the window was broken. It did not prevent him from using these statistics, the Court of Appeal added, that they had never

[60] LC Report, n 2 above, para 8.131: 'The exception can be justified as a pragmatic one, as it might be hard to prove a conspiracy without it, and we would not seek to change the law about how a conspiracy may be proved; and so it is our view that the exception should be retained'.

[61] A Arlidge and J Parry, *Fraud* (Waterlow, London, 1985) § 13.05 *et seq*. Tapper writes: 'It remains to be seen whether it will pass the scrutiny of the European Court of Human Rights should the matter there be considered': 623.

[62] See § 2.38 above.

[63] (1983) 76 Cr App R 48.

appeared in a textbook or similar publication. It is the common law exception that applied in that case which section 118 has preserved.

9.41 When it came to the tests on the samples themselves, however, the Court of Appeal stressed that these could not be proved by the expert referring to the work that other people in the laboratory had done: it was necessary to call as a witness the worker who had actually done them. As is explained in Chapter 14,[64] CJA 2003, section 127 now makes it possible, at least in some cases, for the expert to report in his evidence on tests which his co-workers have carried out.

[64] See §§ 14.5–14.6 below.

10

CONFESSIONS (AND OTHER EXTRA-JUDICIAL STATEMENTS BY DEFENDANTS)

Introduction

10.1 The defendant's extra-judicial confession to an offence is an exception to the hearsay rule that is very ancient. It is, indeed, as old as the exclusionary rule itself. From Tudor times, a routine step in a prosecution was the interrogation of the suspect before a justice of the peace, which 'being sworn by the justice or his clerk to be truly taken, may be given in evidence against the offender'.[1] It was against the background of the routine admission of the products of these official interrogations that the courts were prepared to accept evidence of the defendant's less official confessions made to the prosecutor, and to other people too.[2] At the time the rule excluding hearsay evidence grew up, all this was so much a matter of routine that it never occurred to anyone to argue that statements of this sort should fall within the scope of the exclusion, and so they emerged as a major exception to the rule.

10.2 From an early point, the attitude of the common law towards confessions as evidence was deeply schizophrenic. On the one hand, a confession was widely said to be 'the highest conviction that can be'.[3] On the other hand, confessions were also identified—correctly—as a form of evidence that is deeply problematical. That they are so is the result of two inherent weaknesses. First, confessions, like

[1] Hale, *History of the Pleas of the Crown* (c 1670) (Sollom Emlyn (ed), Nutt and Gosling, London, 1736) 585: 'The examination of the person accused, which ought not to be on upon oath, and these examinations ought to be put in writing, and returned or certified to the next gaol-delivery or sessions of the peace, as the case shall require by the Statute of 2 & 3 P. & M. cap 10, and being sworn by the justice or his clerk to be truly taken may be given in evidence against the offender'.

[2] For examples from the early eighteenth century, see John Langbein, *The Origins of the Adversary Criminal Trial* (Oxford, OUP, 2003) 218 *et seq.*

[3] Hawkins, *Pleas of the Crown* (7th edn,, Leach (ed), 1795) vol IV, 239.

other forms of hearsay, involve a risk of misreporting: the defendant may not have spoken the words attributed to him. Secondly, even if correctly reported, the defendant's words may not represent the truth: most obviously, because the confession may have been extracted from him under pressure.[4] With this in mind, during the eighteenth century a set of rules were developed by the judges, according to which confessions that might have been the result of pressure were excluded.[5]

10.3 The common law rules governing the admissibility of confessions were revised and cast into statutory form in Part VIII of PACE 1984.[6] These provisions, unlike the provisions of the CJA 2003 which rewrote the rules on hearsay and bad character, did not explicitly abolish the common law; and in consequence the common law survived, to the extent that it was compatible with the new statutory rules. The reform of the hearsay rule in 2003 was carried out on the basis that the law relating to confessions would be left essentially[7] alone. With that in mind, the hearsay provisions of the CJA 2003 preserve both the statutory rules about confessions contained in PACE 1984[8] and, as we saw in Chapter 9,[9] the residual common law.

10.4 The law relating to confessions is largely settled. In this book, which is mainly about the changes in the hearsay rule made by the CJA 2003, the detail of the law on confessions will be left to the standard textbooks and practitioners' works.[10] What follows in this chapter is an outline account of the law relating to confessions, with some general reflections on it; and then a more detailed account of the aspects of the law on confessions which have been (or may have been) modified by the CJA 2003.

[4] For a brief account of some notorious cases, see Roderick Munday, *Evidence* (4th edn, Oxford, OUP, 2007) § 10.2.

[5] For the history, see John Langbein, *The Origins of Adversary Criminal Trial* (Oxford, Clarendon Press, 2003) ch 4.

[6] The central provision, which is PACE 1984, s 76, derives from Criminal Law Revision Committee, *Eleventh Report (Evidence) General* (Cmnd 4991, London, HMSO, 1972) (hereafter 'CLRC Evidence Report'). For the background to the reform, see M Zander, *The Police and Criminal Evidence Act 1984* (5th edn, London, Sweet & Maxwell, 2005) § 8.19 onwards. One of the aims of the reform was to simplify the rules at common law, which were widely thought to be excessively complicated. As long ago as 1883 they were described as 'extremely detailed and elaborate': JF Stephen, *History of the Criminal Law of England* (1883) vol I, 446–7.

[7] Subject to the modification which is discussed at §10.47–§10.49 below.

[8] By virtue of CJA 2003, s 114(1)(a), which provides that hearsay evidence is admissible if 'any provision of this Chapter *or any other statutory provision* makes it admissible' (emphasis added); see Chapter 8 above.

[9] See § 9.27 above.

[10] Archbold, *Criminal Pleading, Evidence and Practice* (2008) ch 15; *Blackstone's Criminal Practice* (2008) § F17; Munday, n 4 above, ch 10; *Cross and Tapper on Evidence* (11th edn, Oxford, OUP, 2007) 666–80; IH Dennis, *The Law of Evidence* (3rd edn, London, Sweet & Maxwell, 2007) ch 6.

Defendant's extra-judicial confession as evidence for the prosecution

10.5 *Admissibility of confessions* PACE 1984, section 76 provides that:

> (1) In any proceedings a confession made by an accused person may be given in evidence against him in so far as it is relevant to any matter in issue in the proceedings and is not excluded by the court in pursuance of this section.

By PACE 1984, section 82(1):

> 'confession', includes any statement wholly or partly adverse to the person who made it, whether made to a person in authority or not and whether made in words or otherwise.

10.6 An initial question that arises from this definition is the meaning of a 'statement . . . adverse to the person who made it'. The phrase obviously covers statements which are damning to the defendant at the time he made them, such as 'Yes, I admit that I shot my wife last night'. But what about a statement which is exculpatory on the face of it, but becomes damning in the light of other information? For example, a murder suspect might say to the police: 'I didn't shoot my wife. I wasn't even there: I spent the whole night with my girl-friend', which though a denial, becomes 'adverse', ie potentially damning, once it becomes clear that his alibi is false and he was lying. In *Z (alias Hasan),*[11] the Court of Appeal took the line that a statement of this sort also counted as a confession. But the House of Lords took the narrower view and held that 'adverse' means overtly adverse to the defendant at the time that it was made.[12]

10.7 In this sort of case, the defendant's lying denial is admissible in evidence against him without any reference to the hearsay rule, because the purpose of putting it in evidence is not to show the truth of the matters contained in it.[13] And the result of the decision in *Hasan* is that, since the statement is not a 'confession', its admissibility is not limited by the restrictions imposed on confessions by section 76(2), which will be examined below. In so far as section 76(2) precludes the use in evidence of statements that were forced out of the defendant by using strong-arm methods, this is perhaps regrettable: when exposed to improper pressure, a person who is innocent might as easily be driven to tell a stupid lie as to make a false confession. However, in this situation the court would presumably exclude the suspect's lie by using its powers under PACE, section 78, which potentially applies to all forms of evidence. So fortunately, the suspect who lies when subjected to improper pressure is not left completely unprotected.

[11] [2003] EWCA Crim 191, [2003] 1 WLR 1489.

[12] [2005] UKHL 22, [2005] 2 AC 467; approving *Sat-Bhambra* (1988) 88 Cr App R 55.

[13] See § 3.13 above.

10.8 The first and main effect of PACE 1984, section 76, is, of course, to make admissible in evidence confessions made by the defendant in the course of formal interviews carried out by the police, or other agents of the state. But the definition of 'confession' set out in section 82 is a wide one, with the result that section 76 makes potentially admissible as prosecution evidence any confession made by the defendant, whether formal or informal, and whether made in the context of an official enquiry or privately. Thus, as well as admissions made in the course of formal interviews, the term 'confession' covers admissions of guilt made to the police informally, like the stereotypical 'It's a fair cop, gov' that criminals supposedly utter as they feel the policeman's hand upon their collar, and admissions made in discussions that were 'off the record'. When made to the police, 'verbals' and 'off the record' statements, though potentially admissible as confessions, are likely to be excluded under section 78, because (as is explained at § 10.23 below) some part of the rules governing the questioning of suspects by the police will usually have been broken. But this does not arise where an informal confession is made to someone who is not in authority, for example, to a fellow prisoner with whom the suspect shared a cell. In consequence, 'cell confessions' by defendants are in principle freely admissible in evidence.

10.9 If the 'cell confession' came about because the authorities deliberately planted an informer in the cell in the hope of getting information out of a suspect who in formal questioning had exercised his right to silence, the Court of Appeal has held that its use in evidence infringes the defendant's right of silence, and it must for that reason be excluded.[14] But even subject to this limitation, 'cell confessions' are a particularly worrying form of evidence, because of the risk that that the defendant never really said the words attributed to him. The person who gives evidence of the confession is a criminal and hence of bad character by definition; and the hope of ingratiating himself with the authorities if he 'shops' a cell-mate who has refused to talk to the police may well provide an unscrupulous person with a powerful incentive to lie. Mindful of this risk, the appeal courts expect judges to warn juries that evidence of this sort is inherently dangerous.[15] But if cell confessions are to be allowed in evidence at all, it is surely questionable whether any conviction that is based upon one, and nothing else, can properly be considered 'safe'.[16]

[14] *Allan* [2004] EWCA Crim 2236, [2005] Crim LR 716, a decision reached after the case had been referred back to the Court of Appeal following the decision of the Strasbourg Court in *Allan v United Kingdom* (2002) 36 EHRR 143.

[15] *Beneddeto v R; Labrador v R* [2003] UKPC 27, [2003] 1 WLR 1545.

[16] See D Wolchover and A Heaton-Armstrong, 'Confessors of the Prison Cloth' [2005] 5 *Archbold News* 8–10. An experienced defence solicitor has warned that 'cell confessions' are sometimes used by the police to manufacture evidence against those whom they 'know' are guilty: Jane Hickman, 'Playing Games and Cheating: Fairness in the Criminal Justice System' in E Cape (ed), *Reconcilable Rights* (Legal Action Group, 2004) ch 5.

10.10 *Automatic exclusion* Section 76(2) and (3) provide that:

(2) If, in any proceedings where the prosecution proposes to give in evidence a confession made by an accused person, it is represented to the court that the confession was or may have been obtained—

(a) by oppression of the person who made it; or
(b) in consequence of anything said or done which was likely, in the circumstances existing at the time, to render unreliable any confession which might be made by him in consequence thereof,

the court shall not allow the confession to be given in evidence against him except in so far as the prosecution proves to the court beyond reasonable doubt that the confession (notwithstanding that it may be true) was not obtained as aforesaid.

(3) In any proceedings where the prosecution proposes to give in evidence a confession made by an accused person, the court may of its own motion require the prosecution, as a condition of allowing it to do so, to prove that the confession was not obtained as mentioned in subsection (2) above.

These provisions make confessions automatically inadmissible where there was or may have been (a) oppression or (b) some reason for making it inherently unreliable. Around both limbs of this double test a substantial body of case law has now grown up.

10.11 *Oppression* Section 76(8) provides that 'In this section "oppression" includes torture, inhuman or degrading treatment, and the use or threat of violence (whether or not amounting to torture)'. This clarifies the meaning of the term, but only to a limited extent. The question, of course, is what other forms of behaviour, if any, the term 'includes'. The leading case on this is *Fulling*,[17] in which the Court of Appeal concluded that 'oppression' in section 76(2)(a) should be given its 'ordinary dictionary meaning', which according to the *Oxford English Dictionary* is 'Exercise of authority or power in a burdensome, harsh or wrongful manner; unjust or cruel treatment of subjects, inferiors, etc; the imposition of unreasonable or unjust burdens'. Although some case law prior to 1984 had given a wider meaning to the concept, whereby it potentially covered any treatment which might sap the suspect's will, the Court in *Fulling* said that enactment of PACE 1984 had wiped the slate clean, and for the future 'oppression' implies 'some impropriety on the part of the interrogator'. What is 'improper' is to some extent 'fact-specific'. In *Emmerson*[18] it was held not to be 'oppression' when during an interview a police officer briefly lost his patience with the suspect, raised his voice and swore at him. But in *Paris*,[19] by contrast, the Court of Appeal held there had been oppression where, during a lengthy interview in the course of which he

[17] [1987] QB 426.
[18] (1991) 92 Cr App R 284.
[19] (1993) 97 Cr App R 99.

had at first denied his guilt over 300 times, the suspect was 'bullied and hectored', and '[s]hort of physical violence, it is hard to conceive of a more hostile and intimidating approach by officers to a suspect'.

10.12 *Unreliability* Under this limb of the test, unlike the 'oppression' limb, improper behaviour by the authorities is not a necessary ingredient. If a suspect is dim, mad, ill, suggestible,[20] a compulsive mythomaniac[21] or in a state of shock, his condition may well be 'circumstances existing at the time' which, when taken in conjunction with police questioning that is entirely fair and proper, are likely to produce a false confession; and where this is so, the confession must be excluded. Although this is the line of reasoning that the courts normally adopt,[22] they have sometimes been unwilling to follow it when the suspect's vulnerable state is due to his having voluntarily taken drugs. In some of these cases they have taken the line that section 76(2)(b) requires the risk of a false confession to result from something 'said or done' to him by someone else; his voluntary consumption of drugs was something done to him by himself, and therefore section 76(2)(b) does not apply.[23] But this is to give a narrow and technical construction to the provision in disregard of its clear legislative purpose, which is to render inadmissible in evidence on policy grounds any confession that is tainted by a significant risk of falsity, whatever the underlying reason.

10.13 Although improper behaviour by the authorities is not a precondition for section 76(2)(b) to apply, many of the rules that regulate the conduct of police interviews are designed to minimise the risk of false confessions, and it follows that some breaches of these rules are likely to result in a confession being inadmissible as presumptively unreliable. In *DPP v Blake*,[24] for example, the Divisional Court held that a juvenile's confession had been properly excluded under section 76(2)(b) where it was given during an interview at which no 'appropriate adult' had been present, as required by Code C. As explained below, a confession obtained in circumstances where the rules regulating police interviews have been breached may also be excluded by the court under PACE 1984, section 78, as rendering the trial 'unfair'; and a 'grey area' exists on the borderline between mandatory exclusion under section 76(2)(b) and discretionary exclusion under section 78.

10.14 A recurrent situation is that a suspect initially confesses in circumstances that require the confession to be excluded under section 76(2)(b), and then

[20] *Raghip, The Times*, 9 December 1991.

[21] As in *Ward* (1993) 96 Cr App R 1. It is not necessary that the suspect's mental state should fall into any particular category of mental disorder: *Walker* [1998] Crim LR 211.

[22] See, inter alia, *Everett* [1988] Crim LR 826; *McGovern* (1991) 92 Cr App R 228; and *Walker*, n 21 above.

[23] *Goldenberg* (1988) 88 Cr App R 285; *Crampton* (1991) 92 Cr App R 372.

[24] [1989] 1 WLR 432.

repeats the confession at a later stage. Where this happens, the later confession is admissible (or not) according to whether the court believes that the second confession was also influenced by the circumstances that affected the first.[25] On this point, the burden of proof is on the prosecution, as indeed it is if an issue of 'oppression' or 'unreliability' is raised in respect of any confession, because, as we have seen, the final sentence of section 76(2) expressly says so.

10.15 Furthermore, in deciding whether or not to admit a confession which is challenged under section 76(2), the court is required to consider whether there was in fact oppression, or whether circumstances existed at the time which, when viewed in abstract terms, might have made the disputed confession unreliable. In the presence of either of these facts, section 76(2) requires the court to exclude the confession, 'notwithstanding that it may be true'. So if the court believes the confession to be true, it may not treat the circumstances leading up to the confession as what American lawyers call a 'harmless error' and admit it in evidence notwithstanding.[26]

10.16 If the confession that the prosecution wishes to use in evidence against the defendant stands to be excluded because of section 76(2)(a) or (b), can the prosecution circumvent the exclusion by invoking the court's general 'inclusionary discretion' in section 114(1)(d)? The answer to this question, unsurprisingly, is 'no'. This is made clear by CJA 2003, section 128(2) which, after adding the new section to PACE 1984 which is discussed below,[27] provides that:

> Subject to subsection (1) [which adds a new section 76A to PACE 1984], nothing in this Chapter makes a confession by a defendant admissible if it would not be admissible under section 76 of the Police and Criminal Evidence Act 1984 (c. 60).

10.17 *Mentally handicapped suspects: PACE 1984, section 77*[28] Where the suspect is mentally handicapped, PACE 1984, section 77 imposes what was intended as an extra safeguard. Where 'the case against the accused depends wholly or substantially on a confession by him' and was 'not made in the presence of an independent person',[29] the judge must warn the jury (and at summary trial the magistrates must exercise special caution) about the dangers of convicting on such evidence. In practice this section, for all its considerable length, adds little by way of extra protection. If the defendant's mental state creates a real risk that his confession may be false, it will be excluded under section 76(2)(a), as we have seen. And if,

[25] *McGovern* (1991) 92 Cr App R 228.
[26] *Ibid.*
[27] See § 10.47 below.
[28] For further details, see *Blackstone*, n 10 above, § F17.37.
[29] A term which PACE 1984, s 77(3) defines negatively as follows: '"independent person" does not include a police officer or a person employed for, or engaged on, police purposes'.

having passed the test that section 76(2)(b) lays down, the confession of a mentally handicapped person emerges as the only piece of evidence against him, the Court of Appeal has indicated that the judge should stop the case.[30]

10.18 *Discretionary exclusion under PACE 1984, section 78* PACE 1984, section 78(1) provides that:

> In any proceedings the court may refuse to allow evidence on which the prosecution proposes to rely to be given if it appears to the court that, having regard to all the circumstances, including the circumstances in which the evidence was obtained, the admission of the evidence would have such an adverse effect on the fairness of the proceedings that the court ought not to admit it.[31]

10.19 Section 78 is usually described as giving the court a 'discretion' to exclude such evidence. This is appropriate, to the extent that the section says the court '*may* refuse to allow evidence', not 'must'. But if it is useful shorthand, to say the court has 'a discretion to exclude evidence which it believes would make the trial unfair' is a bit misleading. No court, having once decided that the admission of a piece of evidence would make the trial unfair, would then seize upon the use of the word 'may' as justifying its decision to admit it. In reality, section 78 imposes on the court a *duty* to exclude evidence which it considers would make the trial unfair, but leaves it with a wide discretion to decide what evidence has that effect.

10.20 This provision supplements section 76 by giving the court the power to exclude a confession[32] which the prosecution wishes to use where the court considers that admitting it would make the trial unfair. It is widely invoked when in the course of obtaining the confession the police or other authorities have broken some part of the rules regulating the questioning of suspects,[33] but the infringement is not bad enough to trigger either limb of section 76.

10.21 The issue of when it makes a trial 'unfair' to allow the prosecution to use evidence obtained in breach of the rules has given rise to a large body of case law, the details of which are set out at length in practitioners' texts.[34] From this, the following four main points emerge. First, the courts regard as particularly serious the

[30] *MacKenzie* (1992) 96 Cr App R 98.

[31] Two further subsections are as follows: '(2) Nothing in this section shall prejudice any rule of law requiring a court to exclude evidence; (3) This section shall not apply in the case of proceedings before a magistrates' court inquiring into an offence as examining justices'.

[32] And, indeed, any other type of evidence which the prosecution proposes to use, including clues: see *AG's Reference (No 3 of 1999)* [2001] 2 AC 91; though earlier cases suggest otherwise: see *Khan* [1997] AC 558; *Chalkley and Jeffries* [1998] 2 Cr App R 79.

[33] That is, the major rules contained in PACE 1984 and the supplementary rules set out in Code C, issued by the Home Secretary under the authority conferred on him by PACE 1984, s 66.

[34] *Blackstone*, n 10 above, § F17.20; Archbold, n 10 above, § 15-452 *et seq.*

breach of any rule the purpose of which is to ensure that statements made by the suspect were properly recorded.[35] Secondly (despite dicta in some cases that suggest the contrary)[36] the good faith, or otherwise, of the police is an important factor; so the courts are more inclined to exclude evidence under section 78 where the rules were deliberately flouted rather than broken accidentally.[37] Thirdly (and obviously), major breaches of the rules are more likely to result in evidence being excluded than are minor ones. In the leading case, the Court of Appeal said that breaches of the rules were likely to result in exclusion under section 78 if they were 'significant and substantial',[38] a phrase which is now part of the everyday vocabulary of the courts.

10.22 As a fourth factor in deciding whether it makes the trial 'unfair' to admit evidence obtained in breach of the rules, the courts sometimes balance the gravity of the breach against the seriousness of the offence of which the defendant is accused. An illegal search committed in the course of gathering evidence for a minor regulatory offence (for example, a dairy company recycling another dairy's milk-bottles)[39] excites a sense of judicial outrage in a way that an irregular search when looking for evidence of a murder,[40] rape,[41] armed robbery[42] or large-scale drug-dealing does not.[43] (That said, however, the rules that were broken in the cases where the courts have condoned the breach because of the gravity of the offences were not ones which, when broken, undermine the credibility of the evidence. If the rule broken was designed to ensure the reliability of the evidence—for example, if the police failed to record the interview in the course of which the defendant allegedly confessed—it seems unlikely that they would condone the breach, however serious the offence.)

10.23 In concrete terms, any of the following irregularities are usually enough to persuade the courts to exclude a confession under PACE 1984, section 78. The first

[35] *Delaney* (1989) 88 Cr App R 338; *Christou* [1992] QB 979; and *Bryce* (1992) 95 Cr App R 320.

[36] *Delaney*, n 35 above: 'It is no part of the duty of the court to rule a statement inadmissible simply in order to punish the police for failure to observe the Code of Practice'.

[37] *Mason* [1988] 1 WLR 139, 86 Cr App R 349; *Canale* (1990) 91 Cr AppR 1: 'They were, one regrets to have to say, deliberate breaches and cynical breaches'.

[38] *Walsh* (1989) 91 Cr App R 161. In this case, the breach in question was a refusal to give the suspect access to legal advice, which ultimately resulted in the conviction being quashed, despite the rest of the evidence being strong.

[39] Cf the Scottish case of *Lawrie v Muir* 1950 JC 19.

[40] *Smurthwaite* (1994) 98 Cr App R 437 (incitement to murder).

[41] *Attorney General's Reference (No 3 of 1999)* [2001] 2 AC 91; see Lord Steyn at 118 C–F.

[42] *Bailey* (1993) 97 Cr App R 365 (armed robbers): see the comments of Simon Brown LJ at 375.

[43] *Khan* [1997] AC 558. In this case Lord Nolan, having decided the evidence was admissible, said (at 582 D-E): 'I confess that I have reached this conclusion not only quite firmly as a matter of law, but also with relief. It would be a strange reflection on our law if a man who has admitted his participation in the illegal importation of a large quantity of heroin should have his conviction set aside on the grounds that his privacy had been invaded'.

is failure by the police or other official investigators to observe the rules that require interviews with suspects to be recorded.[44] (Prior to PACE 1984, one of the recurrent causes of complaint against the practices of police was the 'verbal': implausible evidence from police officers that, at the time of arrest or afterwards, the suspect made a 'verbal admission of guilt'.[45] The provisions of PACE 1984 and Code C requiring proper records to be made of interviews with suspects, and of their comments, were intended to counter this and, entering into the spirit of the matter, the courts now tend to reject evidence of statements allegedly made by suspects to the police which were not properly recorded.) Secondly, improper refusal by the police to give the suspect access to a solicitor is usually enough to persuade the courts to invoke section 78.[46] Thirdly, failure to caution a suspect before questioning him usually has the same effect.[47]

10.24 A difficult issue that arises in this connection is when a suspect makes a confession 'off the record', usually as part of a deal (or attempted deal) in which he will help the police to catch other and more serious offenders. Whilst there is no rule, as such, that confessions made 'off the record' are inadmissible, the courts sometimes have taken the view that it is unfair for the prosecution to make use of them.[48]

10.25 The appeal courts are prepared to overturn the decision of first instance courts in relation to section 78 of PACE 1984 if they think that it was wildly unreasonable, or that the court took irrelevant matters into account, but otherwise they are reluctant to interfere. As Auld LJ said in *Jelen*,[49] 'The circumstances of each case are almost always different, and judges may well take different views in the proper exercise of their discretion even where the circumstances are similar. This is not an apt field for hard case law and well-founded distinctions between cases'.

10.26 At common law, the court had a discretionary power to exclude evidence which it considered to be 'more prejudicial than probative'.[50] Prior to the enactment of PACE 1984, section 78, this was sometimes used to suppress a confession. By PACE 1984, section 82(3), this pre-existing power is preserved,[51] though it is

[44] *Delaney*, n 35 above; *Canale*, n 37 above.

[45] See Lawton LJ's sarcastic remarks in *Pattinson* (1973) 58 Cr App R 417, 424.

[46] *Samuel* (1987) 87 Cr App R 232; *Absolom* (1988) 88 Cr App R 332.

[47] *Okafor* (1993) 99 Cr App R 97; *Weerdesteyn* [1995] 1 Cr App R 405; *Senior* [2003] 2 Cr App R 215, [2004] 2 Cr App R 215. Though (in contrast to the cases where the suspect was improperly denied legal advice) the Court of Appeal is often prepared in these cases to uphold the conviction as 'safe'.

[48] Eg in *Da Silva* [2002] EWCA Crim 2673, 2003 2 Cr App R 5 (74).

[49] (1989) 90 Cr App R 456.

[50] Originating from the decision in *Christie* [1914] AC 545.

[51] 'Nothing in this Part of this Act shall prejudice any power of a court to exclude evidence (whether by preventing questions being put or otherwise) at its discretion.'

questionable whether it really adds anything of substance to the statutory power that section 78 confers.[52]

10.27 *Facts found as a result of an inadmissible confession: 'the fruit of the poisonous tree'* English law, unlike the law in some other countries, has never taken the position that if a confession is inadmissible in evidence, so too are inadmissible any clues or facts discovered as a result of it. The traditional (and relaxed) position in English law is now codified in PACE 1984, section 76(4) to (6), which are as follows:

> (4) The fact that a confession is wholly or partly excluded in pursuance of this section shall not affect the admissibility in evidence—
>
> (a) of any facts discovered as a result of the confession; or
>
> (b) where the confession is relevant as showing that the accused speaks, writes or expresses himself in a particular way, of so much of the confession as is necessary to show that he does so.
>
> (5) Evidence that a fact to which this subsection applies was discovered as a result of a statement made by an accused person shall not be admissible unless evidence of how it was discovered is given by him or on his behalf.
>
> (6) Subsection (5) above applies—
>
> (a) to any fact discovered as a result of a confession which is wholly excluded in pursuance of this section; and
>
> (b) to any fact discovered as a result of a confession which is partly so excluded, if the fact is discovered as a result of the excluded part of the confession.

10.28 These subsections deal only with the position where the confession is excluded under section 76(2) and do not apply where it is excluded under section 78. What the position is when that situation arises is not wholly clear.[53] In principle, the evidence would be admissible, unless the court decided that the admission of the clue (as well as of the confession that led to its discovery) would make the trial 'unfair', and this would probably depend on the facts of the case.[54]

10.29 *Are 'confessions' ever admissible at common law in cases not covered by PACE 1984, section 76?* As we saw earlier, CJA 2003, section 118(1), which preserves eight common law exceptions to the hearsay rule, expressly preserves 'Any rule of law relating to the admissibility of confessions or mixed statements in criminal proceedings'. As we have seen, the admissibility of confessions in evidence is now

[52] In *Sat-Bhambra* (1988) 88 Cr App R 55, the Court of Appeal pointed out that PACE 1984, s 78, read literally, enables the court to forbid the prosecution to call evidence, but once it is admitted, does not empower the court to declare it inadmissible retrospectively; but the common law power would enable it to do this.

[53] *Blackstone*, n 10 above, § F17.40.

[54] The Privy Council decision in *Lam Chi-Ming v R* [1991] 2 AC 212 tends to suggest that the evidence so found should, in principle, be excluded.

mainly regulated by PACE 1984, and so what exactly are the remaining common law rules relating to the admissibility of confessions that are preserved by section 118? PACE 1984, section 76 regulates the admissibility of 'confessions' in evidence, and by section 82(1), these are defined as 'statements'. The common law recognised the possibility of a 'confession' which was not made in the form of a statement. At common law, it counted (and still counts) as a confession when, on being accused of an offence by a person with whom he was 'on equal terms' (which means, in essence, someone who is not a police officer), the suspect failed to deny the charge when someone who was innocent might have been expected to do so.[55] Silence of this sort can hardly be said to constitute a 'statement', and hence a 'confession' under section 76, but it is admissible at common law.

Defendant's extra-judicial 'non-confession' as evidence for the defence: 'mixed statements', etc

10.30 The traditional rule, well known to criminal lawyers, is that the defendant's extra-judicial confessions are admissible in evidence against him but his out-of-court denials are inadmissible as evidence in his favour. To this rule there is a partial exception, which is where in the course of admitting an offence the defendant adds some piece of information that is exculpatory: for example, 'Yes, I shot him, but I had to do it because he was threatening me'. In such a case, the whole of the 'mixed statement' is admissible as evidence of the matters contained in it, the unfavourable parts as evidence of guilt and the favourable parts as evidence of innocence.[56] But if the defendant's out-of-court statement contains no element of admission and is purely exculpatory, it falls foul of the rule against hearsay and as such it is inadmissible. If the defendant gives evidence in his defence at trial, his previous denials (like the previous statement of any other witness) will be excluded under the 'rule against narrative'; although, as with the previous statement of any other witness, it may be admissible under an exception to this rule.[57] The official value that English law puts upon the word of a suspect who denies his guilt emerges from the fact that, traditionally, such denials are unflatteringly called 'self-serving statements'.

[55] As in *Parkes* [1976] 1 WLR 1271, where the mother of a girl who had just been stabbed confronted the next-door neighbour, asking him why he had done it—and instead of answering, he tried to stab her too. Cf *Mitchell* (1872) 17 Cox 503; *Chandler* [1976] 1 WLR 585.

[56] *Sharp* [1988] 1 WLR 7; *Aziz* [1996] AC 41; for a full account, see *Blackstone*, n 10 above, § F17.61 *et seq*.

[57] See generally Chapter 12.

10.31 The theory that the defendant's 'self-serving statements' are inadmissible in evidence does not, of course, square with what happens every day in court, because in practice the prosecution always puts before the court what the defendant said to the police, whether it consisted of an admission or a denial. This universal practice has led to dicta from some judges to the effect that, though not legally admissible in evidence, the defendant's denial when accused of the offence by the police is a factor which the court may properly take into account in reaching its decision.[58] How the defendant's statement can be at once both inadmissible as evidence of his innocence and at the same time a matter which the court may take into account in deciding whether he is innocent or guilty is obviously something of a puzzle; but when the mystificatory language is stripped away, the legal reality beneath is relatively simple. The fact that the defendant has always denied the offence is, in general terms, admissible as evidence that he is innocent. But what he said to the police (or a fortiori to his lawyer) is not sufficient, as a matter of law, to discharge the evidential burden that lies on the defendant to raise any of a number of specific defences—for example, duress—in respect of which the courts expect the defendant, if he wishes the court to take the issue seriously, to go into the witness-box, give evidence on oath and subject himself to cross-examination.

10.32 If the rule about 'self-serving statements' is not unjust, at least as it is applied in practice, the theory underlying it is most unsatisfactory. The official rule, as we have seen, is that the defendant's extra-judicial confessions are admissible in evidence against him but his out-of-court denials are inadmissible as evidence in his favour. And the official reason for the official rule is said to be that 'if a person makes a statement against his own interests, it is likely to be true',[59] whereas, by implication, what he says in favour of them is likely to be false. In the context of criminal evidence this means, in effect, that the law officially presumes that suspects who confess their guilt are truthful and those who profess their innocence are liars: a rationale which is impossible to reconcile with the presumption of innocence.

10.33 In principle, the rule surely ought to be that every statement the defendant has made about the offence is in principle admissible as evidence of the matters contained in it, but that for certain legal purposes—in particular, discharging the evidential burden in respect of various defences—an extra-judicial statement by the defendant is not enough and the defendant who wishes the court to take the issue seriously must give evidence at the trial.

[58] *Pearce* (1979) 69 Cr App R 365. See *Blackstone*, n 10 above, § F6.22.

[59] CLRC Evidence Report, n 6 above, § 53. Other rationales are sometimes given: see JC Smith, 'Exculpatory Statements and Confessions' [1995] Crim LR 280.

10.34 In its Consultation Paper, the Law Commission initially floated the idea of reforming the common law rule, so that where the defendant gave evidence at trial, his out-of-court statements could in principle count as evidence, whether they were confessions or denials. Although this idea appears to have been well received, the Law Commission's courage eventually failed them and in their eventual Report the suggestion was withdrawn.[60] Thus the basic common law rule about the defendant's 'self-serving statements' remained and was not overtly changed by any of the new rules on hearsay evidence contained in the CJA 2003. However, the new 'inclusionary discretion' given to the court by section 114(1)(d) does give the court the power to treat a 'self-serving statement' as an item of admissible evidence, if it is satisfied that the interests of justice require this. In *S*[61] a defendant who had vainly sought to persuade the trial judge to do this appealed against his conviction, seeking to argue that the judge's refusal to invoke section 114(1)(d) had been wrong. His appeal failed—but because the Court of Appeal thought that the 'self-serving statement' which he wished to use added nothing of any substance (from the defence point of view) to the evidence he gave orally at trial, rather than because the section was inapplicable.

Extra-judicial statement of one co-defendant as evidence against another

10.35 It has long been 'black letter law' that, whereas what D1 says against D2 in the witness-box is admissible evidence against D2 on the basis of which the court is entitled to convict,[62] anything that D1 says against D2 outside the witness-box is not. This is so where D1 confesses to the offence in a way that implicates D2: 'Joe and I did it'.[63] This is so, a fortiori, where, instead of confessing, D1 makes a self-serving statement in which he puts all the blame on D2: 'It wasn't me, I'm innocent. It was Joe who did it'.

10.36 Where a person is convicted of an offence, PACE 1984, section 74 provides (unsurprisingly) that a person's conviction amounts in law to admissible evidence that he committed the offence charged and, as such, it may be used to establish his guilt of the offence where this is relevant in proceedings involving someone else.

[60] Law Commission, *Evidence in Criminal Proceedings: Hearsay and Related Topics* (Report No 245, Cm 3670, June 1997) (hereafter 'LC Report') § 8.92: 'Our proposal was supported by a large majority of those who commented . . . On further reflection, we experienced difficulties in devising an alternative scheme which works fairly and sensibly and covers both the case where the defendant testifies and the case where he or she does not'.

[61] [2006] EWCA Crim 2272.

[62] *Rudd* (1948) 32 Cr App R 80, where the Court of Criminal Appeal called the defendant's argument to the contrary 'astonishing'.

[63] *Gunewardene* (1951) 35 Cr App R 80; *Spinks* (1982) 74 Cr App R 263.

The case of *Hayter*[64] shows that this provision may sometimes impact on the rule stated in the previous paragraph. In this case, three defendants were jointly accused of murder. The prosecution case was that Angela Bristow had engaged her friend Hayter to find her a 'hit-man' to dispose of her unwanted husband, and that Hayter had obligingly found one in the person of Ryan, who duly murdered him. There was evidence aplenty against Bristow, and against Ryan too, in the form of Ryan's extra-judicial confession to his girl-friend, in the course of which he told her about Hayter's part in the story as well as admitting to his own. But against Hayter there was little evidence. The trial judge told the jury that, if they were convinced of Ryan's guilt sufficiently to convict Ryan, and did so, they could then treat the fact of Ryan's conviction as evidence against Hayter. This line of reasoning was eventually approved in the House of Lords.

10.37 The House of Lords decision was reached by a majority of three to two, and its reasoning has been criticised.[65] In the recent case of *Persad v Trinidad and Tobago*[66] the Privy Council was careful to state its limits. Here, burglars entered the house of a woman, V, and after taking her money, one raped her and another buggered her. As all three burglars wore masks she was unable to say who did what, and as the police had neglected to submit to DNA analysis the swabs they had taken from her bodily orifices, forensic evidence shed no light upon this issue. At a trial at which all three pled not guilty and denied everything, all three were convicted of the burglary, and in addition Wellington was convicted of the rape and Persad was convicted of the buggery. The only 'evidence' before the jury that suggested Persad as the culprit was (i) Wellington's extra-judicial confession that he (Wellington) had carried out the rape[67] and (ii) Kelly's 'mixed statement' in which he had admitted going to V's house with Wellington and Persad but claimed that he (Kelly) had remained outside; and the trial judge had directed the jury that if they accepted Wellington's confession to the rape, and also believed Kelly's statement that he had remained outside, it was open to them to conclude from this that Persad, by elimination, must have carried out the buggery. The Privy Council said that this was wrong. Wellington's and Kelly's extra-judicial statements were not admissible evidence against Persad and, unlike in *Hayter*, the jury's conviction of Wellington for the rape did not necessarily imply that Persad had committed the offence of which Persad had been accused.

10.38 In 1972, the Criminal Law Revision Committee, by a majority, proposed a change in the law to make one co-defendant's extra-judicial confession admissible against the other, as was already the case in civil proceedings. Its reasons were that:

64 [2005] UKHL 605, [2005] 1 WLR 605.

65 Munday, n 4 above, § 10.40 *et seq.*

66 [2007] UKPC 51, [2007] 1 WLR 2379 (23 July 2007).

67 In which, to add to the confusion, Wellington had said that the buggery was committed not by Persad but by Kelly.

> There are many cases where the interests of justice require that what any of the accused have said out of court about the part played by the others in the events in question should be before the court. For example, it often happens that, when A and B are charged jointly with an offence, A has made a statement implicating them both and B has made no statement; or again each may have made a statement seeking to throw the blame on the other. In the latter kind of case there may be much truth in both their statements, and their stories may be changed by the time of the trial. If there are discrepancies of this kind, it seems . . . particularly desirable that the out-of-court statements should be admissible in evidence in order that they may be compared with the makers' evidence at the trial.

Such a change, it said, was also desirable because it:

> gets rid of the absurd situation which occurs under the present law that, when A has made a statement implicating himself and B, it is necessary to direct the jury that the statement is admissible in evidence against A but not against B. This is a subtlety which must be confusing to juries, and in reality they will inevitably take this statement into account against both accused.[68]

10.39 This suggestion was opposed by a minority of the CLRC itself, and at the time provoked strong opposition.[69] It was not taken up by the Law Commission and does not feature among the express changes made to the law by the CJA 2003.

10.40 But have the previous rules about the use of co-defendants' statements as evidence for the prosecution now been *impliedly* modified by any of the general hearsay provisions in the CJA 2003? The answer to this question is 'yes', certainly where the statement was 'self-serving', and possibly also where it amounted to a confession.

10.41 First, the out-of-court statement of a co-defendant (D2) could, at least theoretically, be admissible as evidence for the Crown against the other (D1) under the 'inclusionary discretion' provided for by section 114(1)(d). D2's statement would only be admissible if the court gave leave,[70] and among the matters it would

[68] CLRC Evidence Report, n 6 above, para 251. The Commission gave a further reason in that, if D2 died or was otherwise unavailable, his statement would then become automatically admissible under its proposals for hearsay statements from witnesses who are 'unavailable'. But when the law was changed in 1988 to make the statements of 'unavailable' witnesses generally available, the provision (CJA 1988, s 23) expressly excluded 'a confession made by an accused person that would not be admissible under section 76 of PACE 1984'. The new 'unavailability' provision in CJA 2003, s 116 is limited in the same way, as a result of s 129(2) (see § 10.48 below, and for further discussion, §§ 12.37–12.39).

[69] The General Council of the Bar, in its Memorandum on the Eleventh Report (1973), wrote: 'We are totally opposed to the proposition . . . that the statement of an accused who either pleads guilty or does not give evidence can be used for—or more likely—against his co-accused. Without the maker of the statement being a witness in the case, we do not consider that a jury can ever be put in a position of properly assessing the truthfulness of that statement—either about the activities of the maker or about the activities of the person whom the maker implicates' (at 192).

[70] Hearsay statements from persons who do not testify through fear require judicial leave under CJA 2003, s 116(4) (see § 6.25 above); and to admit a statement under s 114(1)(d) the court is obliged to consider the factors set out in s 114(2) (see §§ 5.1 and 5.14 above).

have to consider would be the fact that D1, against whom the Crown sought to use it, would be placed in an awkward position through his inability to challenge its contents by cross-examination.

10.42 Secondly, if D2 gave evidence at trial that was favourable to D1, and his earlier out-of-court remarks implicating D1 were put to him in cross-examination as a previous inconsistent statement, his earlier statement would constitute admissible evidence of the matters contained in it, in consequence of the change in the status of previous inconsistent statements that has been effected by CJA 2003, section 119.[71] In at least two cases, *Read*[72] and *Ali*,[73] the Court of Appeal has dismissed, relying on these provisions, appeals brought by defendants at whose trials the judge had indicated to the jury that it could treat as evidence against them the incriminating statements their co-defendants had earlier made to the police.

10.43 If the co-defendant's statement was a confession rather than a self-serving statement, however, a possible complication arises because two other provisions of the CJA 2003 potentially come into play. One is section 128(2), which (as we saw at 10.16 above) provides that:

> Subject to subsection (1) [which adds the new section 76A to PACE 1984 making the confession of a co-defendant admissible for the defence], nothing in this Chapter [of the CJA 2003] makes a confession by a defendant admissible if it would not be admissible under section 76 of the Police and Criminal Evidence Act 1984 (c. 60).

The other is section 118(1), which lists among the common law rules which are preserved by the CJA 2003 'Any rule of law relating to the admissibility of confessions or mixed statements'.

10.44 How far (if at all) section 128(2) is an obstacle to the line of reasoning adopted in *Read* and in *Ali* is not entirely clear. In its most obvious reading, section 128(2) merely provides that none of the other hearsay provisions of the CJA 2003 will allow the Crown to use, *as evidence against the person who made it*, a confession that section 76(2) requires to be excluded if there is an attempt to admit it under section 76(1). On the other hand, it could be read more widely as saying (in effect): 'The only route by which the extra-judicial confessions of accused persons are admissible is PACE 1984, section 76. To that route, no bypass is created by any provisions of this Act, except for the new section 76A of PACE 1984, which now enables them to be used by co-defendants. Section 76 allows the Crown to use confessions against those who made them but not against others, and nothing in any other provision of the CJA 2003 alters that'. As the wider reading would produce the strange

[71] On which see § 12.33 below *et seq.*
[72] [2005] EWCA Crim 3292.
[73] [2006] EWCA Crim 3084.

result that the Crown could make use of D1's out-of-court statement against D2 if it was a 'self-serving statement' (eg 'I didn't do it, it was Joe') but not if it was confession ('I did it, and Joe helped me'), the narrower reading seems preferable.

10.45 Section 118(1) preserves 'any rule relating to the admissibility of confessions or mixed statements'. This provision is an impediment to the reasoning adopted in *Read* and in *Ali* if it is read as preserving not only any still-surviving common law rules as to when confessions or mixed statements are admissible, but also the common law rules about when such statements are *inadmissible*. However, section 118(1) was enacted with the aim of preserving existing exceptions to the hearsay rule, not imposing limits on the new exceptions created by other sections of the CJA 2003. In the light of this, it is suggested that it does not have the side-effect of putting beyond the reach of sections 116 or 114(1)(d) the common law rule that prohibited the Crown from using D1's confessions or mixed statements as evidence against D2. In *Y*,[73a] decided after this book went to press, the Court of Appeal interpreted section 118(2) in the manner suggested in the previous paragraph; but it was not asked to consider the argument based on section 128(2) that is discussed in § 10.44 above.

Extra-judicial statements of one co-defendant as evidence for another

10.46 *Confessions by third parties* In the well-known case of *Blastland*,[74] the House of Lords decided (in effect) that a defendant in a criminal case may not use as evidence in his defence the fact that someone else has made an extra-judicial confession to the crime with which he is charged; or, as on the facts of that case itself, that a third party has said things which, though not amounting to a confession, raise a strong suspicion that he was the person who was responsible for it. This decision was much criticised and it was partly in reaction to the criticism that the Law Commission proposed the 'inclusionary discretion', alias the 'safety-valve', which was created by CJA 2003, section 114(1)(d). The fact that a third party has extra-judicially confessed to the offence is now potentially admissible as evidence for the defence under this provision (and, of course, admissible under CJA 2003, section 116, if the person in question is 'unavailable' for the reasons listed in that section: see Chapter 6).[75]

[73a] [2008] EWCA Crim 10 (25 January 2008). (I am grateful to Hughes LJ for drawing this case to my attention).

[74] [1986] AC 41.

[75] In *Hare* [2006] EWCA Crim 2512, it should be noted, the Court of Appeal strongly discouraged the use of the 'inclusionary discretion' to admit at the instance of the defence hearsay evidence of confessions allegedly made by third parties whom the defence could have called to give live evidence, had they chosen so to do.

10.47 *Confessions by co-defendants* The rule preventing a defendant making evidential use of the fact that a third party had extra-judicially confessed to the offence with which he was charged seemed particularly harsh where the person in question was a co-defendant.[76] Eventually, the House of Lords in *Myers*[77] ruled that D1 could make evidential use of D2's confession if it was helpful to his (D1's) case; and furthermore, D1 could do so even if the prosecution had not adduced it as part of their case against D2. The reasoning behind the decision was criticised as rather obscure,[78] and in reaction to this the Law Commission proposed an amendment to the confession provisions of PACE 1984 to regulate this case.[79] The result of this was PACE 1984, section 76A, which was inserted into PACE 1984 by CJA 2003, section 128(1). Section 76A is as follows:

> 76A Confessions may be given in evidence for co-accused
>
> (1) In any proceedings a confession made by an accused person may be given in evidence for another person charged in the same proceedings (a co-accused) in so far as it is relevant to any matter in issue in the proceedings and is not excluded by the court in pursuance of this section.
>
> (2) If, in any proceedings where a co-accused proposes to give in evidence a confession made by an accused person, it is represented to the court that the confession was or may have been obtained—
>
> (a) by oppression of the person who made it; or
>
> (b) in consequence of anything said or done which was likely, in the circumstances existing at the time, to render unreliable any confession which might be made by him in consequence thereof,
>
> the court shall not allow the confession to be given in evidence for the co-accused except in so far as it is proved to the court on the balance of probabilities that the confession (notwithstanding that it may be true) was not so obtained.
>
> (3) Before allowing a confession made by an accused person to be given in evidence for a co-accused in any proceedings, the court may of its own motion require the fact that the confession was not obtained as mentioned in subsection (2) above to be proved in the proceedings on the balance of probabilities.
>
> (4) The fact that a confession is wholly or partly excluded in pursuance of this section shall not affect the admissibility in evidence—
>
> (a) of any facts discovered as a result of the confession; or
>
> (b) where the confession is relevant as showing that the accused speaks, writes or expresses himself in a particular way, of so much of the confession as is necessary to show that he does so.

[76] According to Glanville Williams, *The Proof of Guilt* (3rd edn, London, Stevens, 1963) 210, this was a rule which sympathetic trial judges would often bend in favour of defendants.

[77] [1998] AC 124.

[78] *Blackstone's Criminal Practice*, n 10 above, § F17.19.

[79] LC Report, above n 60, para 8.95.

(5) Evidence that a fact to which this subsection applies was discovered as a result of a statement made by an accused person shall not be admissible unless evidence of how it was discovered is given by him or on his behalf.

(6) Subsection (5) above applies—

(a) to any fact discovered as a result of a confession which is wholly excluded in pursuance of this section; and

(b) to any fact discovered as a result of a confession which is partly so excluded, if the fact is discovered as a result of the excluded part of the confession.

(7) In this section 'oppression' includes torture, inhuman or degrading treatment, and the use or threat of violence (whether or not amounting to torture).[80]

This provision is limited in a number of important respects.

10.48 The first is that it only operates to make admissible the statement of someone who is 'an accused person', who is 'charged in the same proceedings'. According to the Court of Appeal in *Finch*,[81] the facts of which are given in Chapter 5,[82] this means someone who at the trial is standing in the dock, shoulder to shoulder with the defendant, who wishes to use the statement in his defence. So it does not cover (as in that case) an accomplice who was originally charged together with the defendant and who has now dropped out of the picture by pleading guilty at an earlier stage. The reason behind this limitation is that, where this has happened, the remaining defendant can now call the alleged accomplice as a witness, and he is compellable.[83] By parity of reasoning, PACE 1984, section 76A does not make admissible the statement of an accomplice who is not currently in the dock for any other reason, for example, because the proceedings against him have been dropped or because he is to be tried separately. In these cases, too, the alleged accomplice is not only competent but also compellable as a witness, both for the prosecution and for the defence.[84] In such cases, it is open to the defendant to ask the court to admit the evidence of the accomplice's statement under the 'inclusionary discretion' in CJA 2003, section 114(1)(d), but the court is unlikely to grant the application. In *Finch* the Court of Appeal endorsed the refusal of the trial judge in that case to admit the statement via section 114(1)(d), saying that where the defendant calls the accomplice to give oral evidence, this is the course that he should take. The fact that the accomplice is reluctant to repeat on oath in

[80] PACE 1984, s 76A came into force on 4 April 2005 (except in relation to criminal proceedings which began before that date): see the Criminal Justice Act 2004, s 141 and SI 2005/950, art 2(1), Sch 1, para 6. Although drafted with confessions made to the police in mind, it potentially applies to confessions of any type, for example, a plea of guilty which the co-defendant later retracted: *Johnson* [2007] EWCA Crim 1651.

[81] [2007] EWCA Crim 36, [2007] 1 WLR 1645 [**page 308 below**].

[82] See § 5.28 above.

[83] *Boal* [1965] 1 QB 402; *Conti* (1973) 58 Cr App R 387.

[84] See *Blackstone*, n 10 above, § F4.16.

court what he told the police outside it is a good reason for refusing to admit his statement to the police as hearsay, rather than a good reason for admitting it: 'the reluctance only undermines the reliability of the evidence'.

10.49 The second limitation on section 76A is that, because of subection (2), the provision does not enable D1 to put before the court D2's confession if it was obtained from D2 by 'oppression' or in circumstances making it likely that it was unreliable. When viewed from the position of the D2 this is obviously satisfactory; but from D1's perspective it is potentially unfair. If after 12 hours of oppressive questioning Bill said to the police 'All right, I did it; it's all down to me, and Joe had nothing to do with it' there is every reason why the Crown should not be able to use this statement as evidence against Bill, but no clear reason why it should not be admissible in favour of Joe. The answer, one might have thought, was for the law to admit the statement as evidence in favour of Joe but subject to a warning to the magistrates or jury that they must not treat it as evidence against Bill. But that is not the solution that section 76A adopts: as far as that provision is concerned, the statement is simply inadmissible.[85] In such a case, it is arguable that the court could admit Bill's statement as evidence for Joe under section 114(1)(d), but this argument runs into the difficulty with CJA 2003, section 128(2) (which was discussed at § 10.43 above).

10.50 *'Non-confessions' by co-defendants* The third limitation on section 76A is that the only kind of extra-judicial statement by a co-defendant that it makes admissible is a 'confession'. This means a 'confession' in the sense given to it by PACE 1984, section 82(1) (see 10.5 above) and the case law interpreting it. So it would not allow D1 to use in his defence, if it were helpful to his case, the fact that D2 had said something to the police that was on the face of it exculpatory but was then shown to be a lie, suggesting D2 was really guilty, as in *Hasan*.[86] Similarly, it would not enable D1 to put in evidence the fact that D2 had made a statement that, without admitting to the crime himself, exonerated D1 from guilt: 'It wasn't me who did it, and it wasn't Joe either: the person who did it was Fred, I know, because I saw him'. In this case, section 114(1)(d) does potentially come to the rescue, as the Court of Appeal pointed out in *McLean*;[87] and here, because D2's statement is not a 'confession', the potential difficulty otherwise created by section 128(2) does not arise. (Furthermore, if D2 gave evidence at trial, retracting his earlier out-of-court statement exonerating D1, his out-of-court statement could then be admissible in favour of D1 by virtue of CJA 2003, section 119: see § 10.42 above.)

[85] Dr Munday suggests that s 76A is potentially in conflict with ECHR, Art 6, and the courts might therefore have to make a 'declaration of incompatibility' or else 'read it down' so that Bill's statement is admissible for Joe: Munday, n 4 above, § 10.49.

[86] See § 10.6 above.

[87] [2007] EWCA Crim 219, [2008] 1 CrAppR 11 (155).

Defendant's extra-judicial statements: conclusion

10.51 The provisions of the CJA 2003 may have removed some of the injustices in the area of the law covered in this chapter, but it has certainly not made it simpler. It seems a pity, in retrospect, that the Law Commission did not persevere with the suggestion that, in future, all the defendant's previous statements relating to the offence should be admissible in evidence (see §10.34 above).

11

MULTIPLE HEARSAY

11.1 The basic problem with hearsay is that it cannot usually[1] be subjected to the three tests which the law applies to test the sincerity and accuracy of disputed evidence: the oath, cross-examination and the ability of the court to observe the demeanour of the witness. In principle, this difficulty becomes worse when on its way to the courtroom the statement has been transmitted not just from A to B, but from A to B to C. The risks of 'transmission error', and of deliberate fabrication or exaggeration, are multiplied each time the statement changes hands. And the further away the original source of the statement is, the harder it usually is to discover any information about that person that would enable his credibility to be challenged. Hence it is generally recognised that 'multiple hearsay', or 'hearsay upon hearsay', is something which the tribunal of fact must handle with great care, if indeed it can be permitted to touch it at all.

11.2 But if multiple hearsay is typically even less trustworthy than first-hand hearsay is, this is not invariably so. As well as rumours starting from unknown sources and mutating in the course of dissemination, 'multiple hearsay' potentially includes some pieces of evidence which on the face of them are highly trustworthy. One obvious example was the key piece of evidence in *Maher v DPP*,[2] the case where W, a bystander, wrote down on a piece of paper the number of a car he had seen collide with V's car in a car-park and then drive off, and slipped it under the windscreen-wiper of V's car, where V later found it, and gave it to the police, who copied the information into their records, and then V lost the original note. Another hypothetical example would be the video-recorded statement that D's wife made to the police shortly before her death, in which she described how D had confessed to her a murder, and in the course of making her statement she was 'grilled' by a detective who was initially sceptical. Such a statement is not significantly less credible than her live evidence would have been at trial, and it is certainly more credible than the alleged 'cell confession' which X, a rogue with a

[1] Though some types of evidence which English law traditionally classes as 'hearsay' can be subjected to at least some of these tests: see Chapter 1 above.

[2] See *Maher v DPP* [2006] EWHC 1271 (Admin) [**page 302 below**]; see § 5.7 above.

string of convictions and a personality disorder, claims in oral evidence that he heard D make when they were locked up together.

11.3 For this reason, there are two theories as to how the law should deal with multiple hearsay. The first is that it should provide a formal rule excluding it, even where first-hand hearsay would be admissible. The second is that the issue is ultimately a question of weight, and if the fact that a given piece of evidence is multiple hearsay makes it correspondingly weaker, the tribunal of fact can be trusted to take account of this when deciding how much weight, if any, to give it. The second approach is the one which has now been adopted in the civil courts in all parts of the United Kingdom.[3] The Law Commission, true to its generally cautious approach, thought that if juries and magistrates have now become sufficiently intelligent to avoid being misled by certain types of first-hand hearsay, multiple hearsay must still be kept away from them, and in its Report proposed a formal rule to this effect.[4] Such a rule eventually found its way into the CJA 2003, where it is to be found in section 121.

11.4 This provision is slightly different from the one the Law Commission originally proposed. Under their scheme, there would have been a ban on using the 'unavailable witness' exception created by CJA 2003, section 116, twice over. So although W could testify that A (now dead) told him that he saw D shoot X, W would not be able to testify that A (now dead) told him that B (now also unavailable) told him that he saw D shoot X. There would also have been a similar ban on making cumulative use of any of the common law exceptions preserved by what is now section 118, and on using any of them together with section 116. But it would have been permissible to 'cumulate' the other exceptions to the rule; in particular, it would have been possible to use the 'inclusionary discretion'[5] (alias the 'safety-valve') together with other hearsay exceptions.

11.5 The Law Commission's draft clause appeared as clause 105 in the government's original Bill. Having passed the House of Commons without difficulty, this then ran into trouble in the House of Lords. The clause was said (with justice) to be opaquely drafted[6] and it was also criticised for being insufficiently restrictive.

[3] Civil Evidence Act 1995 (England and Wales); Civil Evidence (Scotland) Act 1988; Civil Evidence (Northern Ireland) Order 1997, SI 1997/2983 (NI 21).

[4] Law Commission, *Evidence in Criminal Proceedings: Hearsay and Related Topics* (Report No 245, Cm 3670, June 1997) § 8.23 and Recommendation 7.

[5] Which now appears in CJA 2003, s 114(1)(d).

[6] It was as follows: '*Multiple hearsay* (1) If there is a series of statements not made in oral evidence (such as "A said that B said that C shot the deceased") sections 98 [now s 114] and 100 [now s 116] apply as follows. (2) If a statement—(a) is relied on as evidence of a matter stated in it, and (b) is admissible for that purpose only under section 100 [now s 116] or as a rule preserved by section 102 [now s 118], the fact that the statement was made must be proved by evidence admissible otherwise than under section 110 [s 116]. (3) Otherwise—(a) sections 98 and 100 to 104 [ss 114 and 116–120] apply

As it stood, the clause would either have banned multiple hearsay completely or let it in; and where it let it in it would (in principle) have been admitted without restriction.[7] In these cases, the critics said, some further 'screening requirement' ought to be imposed. In the light of these criticisms the government produced a new provision at the Third Reading,[8] which was enacted without further argument to become CJA 2003, section 121. This is as follows:

> Additional requirement for admissibility of multiple hearsay
>
> (1) A hearsay statement is not admissible to prove the fact that an earlier hearsay statement was made unless—
>
> (a) either of the statements is admissible under section 117, 119 or 120,
> (b) all parties to the proceedings so agree, or
> (c) the court is satisfied that the value of the evidence in question, taking into account how reliable the statements appear to be, is so high that the interests of justice require the later statement to be admissible for that purpose.
>
> (2) In this section 'hearsay statement' means a statement, not made in oral evidence, that is relied on as evidence of a matter stated in it.

11.6 The effect of this provision is to create a general ban on multiple hearsay, which is subject to a list of exceptions, three which are automatic and the fourth of which is discretionary. In the paragraphs that follow, these exceptions will be examined, though not in quite the same order as they appear in the section.

11.7 *Multiple hearsay admissible by agreement* By section 121(1)(b), multiple hearsay is admissible where 'all the parties to the proceedings so agree'. This is in line, of course, with section 114(1)(c), which lays down the general rule that hearsay evidence not otherwise admissible can be admitted by agreement.[9]

11.8 *Multiple hearsay admissible when contained in a 'business or other document'* By section 121(1)(a), multiple hearsay is admissible where 'either of the statements is admissible under section 117', which is the provision creating a general exception for hearsay statements contained in what the marginal note to section 117 calls 'business and other documents'. Section 117 was examined in Chapter 7, and as we saw there, it is drafted in a way that makes it explicitly clear that it applies in principle not only where the person who made the document or record had first-hand knowledge of the fact that is noted in it, but also where the information reached the record having passed through several hands (or mouths) along the

to the admissibility of each statement, and (b) different statements may be admissible under different sections (or different provisions of the same section)'.

[7] Hansard, HL vol 654, cols 758–760 (4 November 2003).

[8] Hansard, HL vol 654, cols 1791–1794 (17 November 2003).

[9] See Chapter 4 above.

way. So if section 121 did not exempt evidence admissible under section 117 from the general ban on multiple hearsay that it imposes, there would be a conflict between the two sections.[10]

11.9 *Multiple hearsay admissible when it forms part of the previous statement of a witness who gives oral evidence* By section 121(1)(a) again, multiple hearsay is admissible where 'either of the statements is admissible under section . . . 119 or 120'. Sections 119 and 120 create exceptions to the branch of the hearsay rule traditionally known as the 'rule against narrative', the rule under which the previous out-of-court statements of a witness who gives oral evidence at trial are treated as 'hearsay' (as well as the out-of-court statements of those who do not give oral evidence at all).[11] Where the previous statement of a witness is admissible under sections 119 or 120, it counts for all legal purposes as evidence of the matters that are contained in it: a rule which marks a departure from the common law, the significance of which will be examined in the Chapter 12. So if W says to the police 'I saw D shoot V', and then when he fails to repeat this statement in his oral evidence at trial his statement to the police is admitted under section 119 or 120, this earlier statement counts as legally valid evidence that W saw D shoot V, though technically it is 'hearsay'.

11.10 Where W's oral evidence is that 'D confessed to me that he had shot V', this evidence is hearsay, admissible under the 'confessions' exception to the rule that was discussed in Chapter 10. And if W first says to the police 'D confessed to me that he had shot V', and then fails to repeat this statement at trial, and his original statement to the police is then put in evidence under section 119 or 120, the statement 'D confessed to me that he had shot V' counts (at least in theory) as 'multiple hearsay': 'multiple' because it consists of two hearsay elements, (i) D's confession, which is hearsay, and (ii) W's out-of-court statement to the police, in which D's confession is embedded, which also counts as 'hearsay' (in law, if not in common sense). When this type of situation arises, the effect of section 121(1)(a) is to make this piece of evidence admissible, despite its (technical) status as 'multiple hearsay'.[12]

11.11 *Multiple hearsay admissible 'in the interests of justice'* By section 121(1)(c) a piece of multiple hearsay is also admissible where:

[10] Statements in 'public records' have always been admissible at common law under an exception that is preserved by CJA 2003, s 118 (see § 9.8 above) and, rather oddly, the effect of s 121 seems to be to extend the general ban on 'multiple hearsay' to statements that are contained in those. But as anything that is admissible as part of a 'public record' is almost certain to be admissible under s 117 as well, this anomaly presumably does not matter.

[11] See Chapter 12 below.

[12] For an example of a case where multiple hearsay was admissible under this exception, see *Xhabri* [2006] 1 Cr App R 413 at [39]–[41] [**page 283 below**].

the court is satisfied that the value of the evidence in question, taking into account how reliable the statements appear to be, is so high that the interests of justice require the later statement to be admissible for that purpose.

11.12 In explaining this formula to the House of Lords, the Minister (Baroness Scotland) gave an example[13] of the sort of case in which she thought that 'the interests of justice' would justify a piece of multiple hearsay to be admitted by application of this provision. V, aged 80, is raped by an intruder in her house and shortly afterwards suffers a stroke which makes it impossible for her to tell the police what happened to her. However, before she was struck dumb she told the doctor what had happened and also told him that she could not identify her attacker. The doctor makes a written statement to the police in which he recounts what V had told him. By the time that D is tried for the offence, the doctor has gone abroad and cannot be produced as a live witness. On the key issue of identity, on which V's statement sheds no light, the prosecution have strong independent evidence but no medical evidence to show conclusively that V was raped (rather than had intercourse consensually). The doctor's statement to the police is multiple hearsay: V's '*res gestae*' statement to the doctor, incorporated in the doctor's written statement to the police, which is the evidence of an 'unavailable witness' admissible under section 116. But in these circumstances it is not unjust to D to admit this piece of multiple hearsay as evidence against him, and the interests of justice clearly require it.

11.13 In the course of its relatively short life, the 'interests of justice' exception created by section 121(1)(c) has already featured in a significant number of defence appeals[14] (in none of which, incidentally, the appeal has been successful). In holding that the 'multiple hearsay' evidence had been properly admitted under section 121(1)(c) (or would have been if the trial court had directed its mind to it) the appeal courts have made it clear that a key point to consider is whether the evidence was cogent. In *Maher v DPP*[15] (the facts of which were given at § 11.2 above) the Divisional Court said:

> The identification of the number of the offending vehicle appears, on its face, to be very reliable, as does its transmission via [the owner of the damaged car] to the police incident log. It would be extraordinary if there was an error of transmission, but the number of the vehicle recorded on the police log just happened to coincide precisely with the number and description of a vehicle that was in the car park at the time and seen by the witness.

[13] Based on the New Zealand case of *Hovell* [1986] 1 NZLR 500, [1987] 1 NZLR 610.

[14] *Maher v DPP* [2006] EWHC 1271, (2006) 170 JP 441; *Taylor* [2006] EWCA Crim 260, [2006] Cr App R 14; *Musone* [2007] EWCA Crim 1237 [2007] 1 WLR 2467; *Walker* [2007] EWCA Crim 1698; *Saleem* [2007] EWCA Crim 1923; *Cole* [2007] EWCA Crim 1924 [2007] 1 WLR 2716.

[15] *Maher v DPP*, n 14 above; see § 5.7, § 7.16 and § 11.2 above, and [**page 302 below**]; *Musone*, n 14 above.

And in *Musone*,[16] where a prisoner had been stabbed to death in his cell, the trial judge decided to admit via section 121(1)(c) the statement of another prisoner, who had refused to give evidence at trial, in which he repeated what the dying man had said to him; and when endorsing the judge's decision the Court of Appeal remarked that 'there is nothing novel in the proposition that a dying man's identification of the killer is of high value, as the judge observed'.

11.14 In a number of these cases, one component in the multiple hearsay has been a statement that was admitted under the 'inclusionary discretion' conferred on the court by section 114(1)(d). When deciding whether to admit a statement under this provision, the court is already required to ask itself whether this would be 'in the interests of justice', and section 114(2) sets out a list of no less than nine factors which the court is supposed to consider when answering this question.[17] In this situation, what is the relationship (if any) between this exercise and the further exercise that section 121(1)(c) requires the court to perform when deciding if it would be in 'the interests of justice' to admit a piece of multiple hearsay?

11.15 In *Maher v DPP* the Divisional Court said that, in principle, the 'interests of justice' test in section 121 should be considered 'cumulatively with the interests of justice criteria in section 114(2)' (at [24]). However, in *Walker*[18] the Court of Appeal pointed out that, once the court has decided that the 'interests of justice' test under section 114(2) is satisfied, it would be strange if it then decided that the 'interests of justice' test in section 121(1)(c) was not. In *Musone* the Court of Appeal said that the trial judge was right, when considering section 121(1)(c), to refer back to the matters he had already mentioned when discussing section 114(2). In *Taylor*,[19] where the trial judge had decided to admit the evidence under section 114(1)(d) and, later in the proceedings, when the defence pointed out that it was multiple hearsay, had refused to revisit the issue, the Court of Appeal endorsed his refusal.

11.16 In *Cole*[20] the defendant had been convicted on three counts of assaulting his girl-friend, causing her grievous bodily harm. She could not give evidence because, after the third alleged beating, she had hanged herself. The case against Cole largely depended on evidence from witnesses to whom she had complained about his beating her: hearsay evidence admissible by virtue of section 116, because the original maker was dead. At trial, one of these witnesses was herself unavailable because she was giving birth to a baby and the judge, applying

[16] See n 14 above.
[17] See generally Chapter 5 and 5.12 above *et seq* in particular.
[18] See n 14 above.
[19] See n 14 above, [**page 292 below**].
[20] See n 14 above, [**page 315 below**].

section § 11.16 again, admitted as evidence the statement she had earlier made to the police. To do so was, of course, to admit multiple hearsay. Although strictly speaking it was not applicable, the Court of Appeal looked at the 'interests of justice' factors listed in section 114(2) when evaluating the trial judge's decision to admit the evidence, which it approved.

11.17 If multiple hearsay is admitted, the judge at a jury trial is expected to give the jury 'a most careful direction' so that they 'may be in a position properly to evaluate the weight which they ought to give such hearsay evidence'.[21]

11.18 *Conclusion* When the CJA 2003 was first enacted, in connection with section 121 one commentator wrote the following: 'If the purpose of the new rules is to make the hearsay rule less complex, and easier to understand, and easier to apply, the result is likely to be a disappointment'.[22] The case law that it has generated suggests that section 121 achieves little, other than provide defendants with a usually unsuccessful ground of appeal in cases when, at trial, the 'multiple hearsay' issue was accidentally overlooked.

[21] Per Rose LJ, obiter, in *Joyce and Joyce* [2005] EWCA Crim 1785.
[22] Rudi Fortson, in his commentary to s 121 in *Current Law Statutes*.

12

THE RULE AGAINST NARRATIVE

Introduction

12.1 At common law a rule, closely related to the hearsay rule, provided that a witness giving evidence may not make use of his previous out-of-court statements either to supplement or to support his oral testimony; nor may evidence about them be given to this end by other people. This rule goes by at least three different names. In this book it is called 'the rule against narrative', but it is also known as 'the rule against previous consistent statements' and 'the rule against self-corroboration'.

12.2 Although at common law the previous consistent statement of a witness could not normally be used in support of what he says in court, sections 4 and 5 of the Criminal Procedure Act 1865 expressly provided (and still provide) that his previous inconsistent statements can be used to undermine his credibility. It might be thought that if the court can be told about a witness's previous inconsistent statement in an attempt to persuade it to disbelieve the witness, it could also be told about his previous consistent statements in order to redress the balance, particularly where, for example, the inconsistent statement was a retraction extracted under pressure. But as the law stands, the witness discredited by a previous inconsistent statement cannot be 'rehabilitated' by invoking previous consistent ones.[1]

12.3 The previous consistent statement of a witness was (and still is) admissible if any of the exceptions to hearsay apply to it. Most of the exceptions to the 'hearsay rule proper' presuppose the unavailability of the witness at the trial, and hence cannot apply to the previous statements of those who do. But some, however, could potentially apply: '*res gestae*', for example.[2]

[1] *Beattie* (1990) 89 Cr App R 303.

[2] See § 9.18 above.

12.4 In addition, before 2003 the rule against narrative was subject to a series of important exceptions, most created by the courts, but in one case, deriving from statute. The five main[3] exceptions were as follows:

(*a*) *refreshing memory*: at common law, a witness was allowed (within limits) to use his previous statement to 'refresh his memory' when giving evidence;
(*b*) *recent complaint*: at common law, where the defendant was charged with a sexual offence, the court could hear the terms in which the alleged victim originally complained, provided she or he did so spontaneously and at the first reasonable opportunity;
(*c*) *previous identification*: at common law, where an eye-witness to an offence gave evidence at trial, evidence could be given that he had previously identified the defendant at a confrontation or other identification procedure;[4]
(*d*) *to rebut 'recent fabrication'*: at common law, evidence of what a witness said at an early stage in the proceedings could be given to rebut a suggestion made that his or her story was a 'recent fabrication';[5]
(*e*) *videotapes of interviews with vulnerable witnesses*: by statute, a videotape of a previous interview with certain types of vulnerable witness could be put in evidence, potentially, in substitution for his or her live evidence-in-chief.[6]

12.5 Though commonly described as 'old',[7] the rule against narrative is not, as these things go, particularly ancient. The common law originally took the position that 'what a witness hath been heard to say at another time, may be given in evidence to invalidate *or confirm*[8] the testimony which he gives in court'.[9] Legal writers continued to state the law in these terms until long after the first cases[10] in which the rule against narrative was laid down by the courts,[11] and Stephen incorporated the earlier rule in the Indian Evidence Act as late as 1872.[12]

[3] There were some others. For further details, see RN Gooderson, 'Previous Consistent Statements' [1968] *Cambridge Law Journal* 64.
[4] *Christie* [1914] AC 545; in *Cook* [1987] QB 417 this exception was extended to the case where the victim composed a photofit that looked like him, or guided a police artist to draw his likeness in a sketch; on this, see § 3.23 above.
[5] See eg *Oyesiku* (1971) 56 Cr App R 240. (As cynics put it, evidence of the earlier statement could be given to show that the evidence was not a recent fabrication, but an ancient one . . .).
[6] Youth Justice and Criminal Evidence Act 1999, s 27, a provision which replaces similar but narrower provisions contained in the CJA 1988; see generally Chapter 13 below.
[7] Rupert Cross, *Evidence* (3rd edn, 1967) 193.
[8] Emphasis added.
[9] Hawkins, *Pleas of the* Crown (2nd edn, 1724) ch 46, § 14; cf Gilbert, *The Law of Evidence* (1760) 153.
[10] *Parker* (1783) 3 Douglas KB 242, 99 ER 634.
[11] Hawkins, *Pleas of the Crown* (7th edn, 1795) vol 4, 427.
[12] See s 157: 'In order to corroborate the testimony of a witness, any former statement made by such witness relating to the same fact, at or about the time when the fact took place, or before any authority legally competent to investigate the fact, may be proved'.

12.6 Old or not, the rule clearly does not accord with common sense. The orthodox reasons for refusing to listen to hearsay evidence are two: (i) How can we tell that he really said it? (ii) If he did, how can we be sure that he meant it? Both vanish when the person who originally made the statement is there in court and liable to cross-examination under oath. Furthermore, as mentioned earlier,[13] by making the court ignore every account he gave of the incident before he got there, and accept nothing except what he says in court, this rule requires us to accept the following two propositions of psychology as valid: (a) that memory improves with the passage of time, and (b) that stress improves the process of recall. As the Criminal Law Revision Committee said in 1972:

> assuming, as one must, that a person called as a witness in criminal proceedings is more likely than not to intend to try to tell the truth, it follows that what he said soon after the events in question is likely to be at least as reliable as his evidence given at the trial and will probably be more so.[14]

12.7 For civil proceedings in England, the rule against narrative has been completely abrogated by a series of changes culminating in the Civil Evidence Act 1995, section 6 of which, so far as relevant, is as follows:

> (1) Subject as follows, the provisions of this Act as to hearsay in civil proceedings [by which the rule is abolished] shall apply equally (but with any necessary modifications) in relation to a previous statement made by a person called as a witness in the proceedings.
> (2) A party who has called or intends to call a person as a witness in civil proceedings may not in those proceedings adduce evidence of a previous statement made by that person, except—
> (a) with the leave of the court, or
> (b) for the purpose of rebutting a suggestion that his evidence has been fabricated.
>
> This shall not be construed as preventing a witness statement (that is, a written statement of oral evidence which a party to the proceedings intends to lead) from being adopted by a witness in giving evidence or treated as his evidence.[15]

12.8 In Scotland, the rule against narrative has been largely abrogated for criminal proceedings too. North of the Border, the Criminal Procedure (Scotland) Act 1995 now makes the previous consistent statement of a witness freely admissible, provided it was made in written or other documentary form. Section 260 of this Act is as follows:

[13] See 1.34 above.
[14] Criminal Law Revision Committee, *Eleventh Report (Evidence) General* (Cmnd 4991, London, HMSO, 1972) (hereafter 'CLRC Evidence Report') para 239.
[15] CEA 1995, s 6(3), (4) and (5) omitted.

(1) Subject to the following provisions of this section, where a witness gives evidence in criminal proceedings, any prior statement made by the witness shall be admissible as evidence of any matter stated in it of which direct oral evidence by him would be admissible if given in the course of those proceedings.

(2) A prior statement shall not be admissible under this section unless—

(a) the statement is contained in a document;

(b) the witness, in the course of giving evidence, indicates that the statement was made by him and that he adopts it as his evidence; and

(c) at the time the statement was made, the person who made it would have been a competent witness in the proceedings.[16]

And some 20 years earlier, the Criminal Law Revision Committee had called for the abolition of the rule against narrative for England.[17]

12.9 In the light of all this, it was a surprise to many when in 1997 the Law Commission said in its Report that the rule against narrative ought to be retained. The Law Commission's argument (which it had rejected earlier in the Report when dealing with the hearsay rule proper) was that the exclusionary rule was needed here to prevent the court being overwhelmed by 'superfluous testimony' of little value.[18] In his Review,[19] Lord Justice Auld disagreed with this position and instead proposed a rule for England similar to the Scottish one.[20] In addition, Sir Robin recommended a change to the existing rules about when witnesses giving oral testimony could refresh their memory from notes, which he thought were needlessly restrictive.[21]

12.10 The scheme the government eventually adopted, and which eventually found its way into Part 11 of the CJA 2003, was a compromise adopting elements

[16] Some further qualifications are made by s 260(3) and (4), which I have not set out.

[17] Clause 31 of their Draft Bill would have provided: '(1) In any proceedings a statement made, whether orally or in a document or otherwise, by any person shall, subject to this and the next following section and to section 2 of this Act, be admissible as evidence of any fact stated therein of which direct oral evidence by him would be admissible if—(a) he has been or is to be called as a witness in the proceedings'.

[18] Law Commission, *Evidence in Criminal Proceedings: Hearsay and Related Topics* (Report No 245, Cm 3670, June 1997) (hereafter 'LC Report') § 10.12.

[19] *Review of the Criminal Courts of England and Wales: Report* (London, The Stationery Office, October 2001) ch 11, §86–92 (pages 551–4).

[20] 'I recommend consideration of amendment of the law as to admissibility of witness statements so that:—where a witness has made a prior statement, in written or recorded form, it should be admissible as evidence of any matter stated in it of which direct oral evidence in the proceedings would be admissible provided that he authenticates it as his statement;—an integral part of the new rule should be that a defendant's previous statement should in principle be admissible whether it supports or damages his case and the fact that it may appear to be self-serving should go only to weight; and—the witness should be permitted, where appropriate, to adopt the statement in the witness box as his evidence in chief.'

[21] Auld Review, n 19 above, ch 11, § 81–85 (pages 548–51).

of both the Law Commission's scheme and Auld LJ's proposals. In essence, the changes made by the CJA 2003 to this area of the law of evidence are these:

(a) the rule against narrative is retained; but
(b) the rules about 'memory refreshment' are significantly relaxed;[22] and
(c) the other common law exceptions to the rule are reformed and put into statutory form;[23] and
(d) where, exceptionally, the court now hears the previous statement of a witness (whether consistent or inconsistent), the legal standing of that statement has been raised; whereas in most cases the previous statement was, in theory, admissible only as a matter bearing on the credibility of the witness's oral evidence in court, the previous statement now counts, in law, as 'evidence of any matter stated in it'.[24]

These points will be examined in turn in the paragraphs that follow.

Rule against narrative is retained

12.11 The retention of the rule against narrative follows from the way in which CJA 2003, section 114(1), which sets out the basic rule excluding hearsay evidence, is drafted. As we saw in Chapter 3, this provides that 'In criminal proceedings a statement not made in oral evidence in the proceedings is admissible as evidence of any matter stated if, but only if' one of the exceptions set out in the rest of the section applies to it. The previous statement of a witness who testifies at trial is, of course, 'a statement not made in oral evidence in the proceedings', just as much as is a statement made by a non-witness who does not come to court.

12.12 From this it follows that the previous statement of a witness is only admissible in evidence if it is covered (i) by one of the exceptions to the hearsay rule set out in CJA 2003, section 1(1), which have been examined in the previous chapters, or (ii) by one of the further specific exceptions dealing explicitly with previous statements, set out in sections 119 and 120, which are examined in this chapter and the next.

12.13 The consequence of this is that any exception to the rule against narrative that may have existed at common law, and which has not been either codified by section 120 of the CJA 2003 or expressly preserved by section 118,[25] has now

[22] CJA 2003, s 139; see § 12.14 *et seq* below.
[23] *Ibid* s 120; see § 12.21 *et seq* below.
[24] *Ibid* ss 119 and 120 passim; see § 12.32 *et seq* below.
[25] See Chapter 9 above.

been abolished. This creates a possible difficulty in relation to the admissibility of the previous statement of the defendant who, on being accused of the offence by the police, denies it. As we saw in Chapter 10, such 'self-serving' statements have always been put before the court in the past, although their legal status is rather vague.[26] If (as has been suggested) the basis on which they were put before the court was a common law exception to the rule against narrative,[27] then it could be argued that, as a result of section 114(1) of the CJA 2003, the court should no longer hear them. The practice of the courts in this respect has not been modified in response to this provision, and such a change, it is suggested, would not be welcomed by judges, or practitioners—or, a fortiori, defendants. If section 114 were ever raised as an objection to the admissibility of these statements, the courts would presumably overcome it by arguing that these statements, though routinely put before the court, are not technically 'evidence'.

Rules about 'refreshment of memory' are relaxed

12.14 At common law, a witness was allowed, when giving oral evidence, to refresh his memory from a statement he had made (or dictated) provided this was done at a time when the matters were fresh in his mind.[28] At one time the courts took the view that, once in the witness-box, the witness could only prompt himself from a note that was 'contemporaneous' with the incident in question, and if the note was made significantly after the incident, the witness was denied access to it once his oral testimony had started; but as a result of case law in the 1990s, these requirements had been significantly relaxed.[29]

12.15 It was against this background that Auld LJ proposed 'making the only condition for a witness's use of a written statement for refreshing his memory that there is good reason to believe that he would have been significantly better able to recall the events in question when he made or verified it than at the time of giving evidence'.[30] It was in response to this that section 139 was included in the CJA 2003, which is as follows:

> Use of documents to refresh memory
>
> (1) A person giving oral evidence in criminal proceedings about any matter may, at any stage in the course of doing so, refresh his memory of it from a document made or verified by him at an earlier time if—

[26] See §§ 10.30–10.34 above.
[27] See Gooderson, n 3 above.
[28] *Attorney-General's Reference (No 3 of 1979)* (1979) 69 Cr App R 411.
[29] *Da Silva* (1990) 90 Cr App R 233; *R v South Ribble Justices, ex p Cochrane* [1996] 2 Cr App R 544.
[30] Auld Review, n 19 above, ch 11, § 85 (page 551).

(a) he states in his oral evidence that the document records his recollection of the matter at that earlier time, and
(b) his recollection of the matter is likely to have been significantly better at that time than it is at the time of his oral evidence.

(2) Where—

(a) a person giving oral evidence in criminal proceedings about any matter has previously given an oral account, of which a sound recording was made, and he states in that evidence that the account represented his recollection of the matter at that time,
(b) his recollection of the matter is likely to have been significantly better at the time of the previous account than it is at the time of his oral evidence, and
(c) a transcript has been made of the sound recording,

he may, at any stage in the course of giving his evidence, refresh his memory of the matter from that transcript.

12.16 This provision is clearly drafted and no further commentary is necessary to enable it to be understood. However, it should be noted that a precondition for the rest of the section to apply is that the witness must first be asked the two questions set out in subsection (1). These are not the same as the questions which counsel would traditionally have put to a witness when asking the court to allow him to use a note to refresh his memory, and a practical issue now is what the legal position is if, by oversight, the party calling the witness fails to put these questions to him. The answer, presumably, is that in such a case the witness may still properly use the note provided it complies with the stricter conditions required by the common law which section 139 was meant to supersede; but if this is right, a question then arises as to the evidential status of the note, which may or may not be determined by section 120(3) (which is discussed below). Clearly, advocates should avoid this pitfall by routinely asking the questions set out in section 139(1) when calling witnesses who will be refreshing their memories from notes.[31]

12.17 Section 139 is silent as to the method by which a witness may refresh his memory and, in particular, it does not say whether this is to be done by allowing the witness a brief adjournment to read the document, or by allowing him or her to have it with him in the witness-box to use as a prompt. Before section 139, the usual practice was to allow witnesses who had made contemporaneous notes to have them with them in the witness-box and it seems unlikely that, in enacting section 139, Parliament wished to change this. If the witness has a 'memory refreshing' document with him, then he may be 'reading it as a script'; but on the other hand, if the witness has to refresh his memory from the document outside the witness-box and then give evidence without it, the process of giving evidence becomes a test of his short-term memory. Of the two evils, the second is surely the greater of the two.

[31] I am grateful to the judges at Snaresbrook Crown Court for pointing this problem out to me.

12.18 *Evidential status of the memory-refreshing document* At common law, a document that a witness was allowed to use to refresh his memory when giving evidence did not thereby acquire the status of a piece of evidence; and this was so, in principle, even where the document was 'made an exhibit'. This is something that happens where a witness is cross-examined on the document, and in his attempt to undermine the witness's evidence the cross-examiner strays beyond the parts of the document which the witness had been using as a prompt. Where this occurs, the party calling the witness could (and still can) require the whole of the document to be given to the tribunal of fact, to make up its own mind as to whether, viewed as a whole, it really does undermine the testimony of the witness (as the cross-examination had suggested). Where the document was 'made an exhibit' under this procedure, it then did acquire the legal status of a piece of evidence, but only to a limited extent. Although 'evidence', it was not, in law, evidence of the matters stated in it and (in theory if not in practice) was only evidence bearing upon the credibility of the oral evidence the witness had given directly to the court.[32]

12.19 The Law Commission thought this was unsatisfactory and, with unusual daring, proposed that where the memory-refreshing document acquired the status of a piece of evidence in this way, it should in future become evidence for all purposes. A clause to this effect appeared in the Draft Bill annexed to its Report, the terms of which are now reproduced as CJA 2003, section 120(3). This provides that:

> A statement made by the witness in a document—
>
> (a) which is used by him to refresh his memory while giving evidence,
> (b) on which he is cross-examined, and
> (c) which as a consequence is received in evidence in the proceedings,
>
> is admissible as evidence of any matter stated of which oral evidence by him would be admissible.

The Law Commission intended this provision to alter the legal status of the memory-refreshing document if it became 'evidence' by reason of the common law rules about a document 'becoming an exhibit' described at § 12.18 above, but not to change those rules, abstruse as they may appear to be. In *Pashmfouroush*[33] the Court of Appeal, quoting with approval a statement from the 2006 edition of Arcbhold,[34] held that its effect is indeed limited to this.

[32] *Britton* (1987) 85 Cr App R 14; *Sekhon* (1987) 85 Cr App R 19; though there was said to be an exception where the document 'provides, because of its nature, material by which its authenticity can be judged', when 'in respect of that material and only for the purpose of assessing its authenticity it can amount to evidence in the case'.

[33] [2007] EWCA Crim 2330.

[34] At § 8.86.

12.20 Where the 'memory-refreshing' document does not acquire the status of a piece of evidence by virtue of section 120(3), it could still become evidence by virtue of section 120(6), which creates an exception to the hearsay rule in favour of statements 'made by the witness when the matters stated were fresh in his memory but he does not remember them, and cannot reasonably be expected to remember them'. This provision is discussed at § 12.27 below.

Other common law exceptions to the rule are reformed and put into statutory form

12.21 This is done by section 120 of the CJA 2003, a lengthy and tortuous provision, which exactly reproduces clause 8 of the Law Commission's Draft Bill. It is as follows:

> Other previous statements of witnesses
>
> (1) This section applies where a person (the witness) is called to give evidence in criminal proceedings.
>
> (2) If a previous statement by the witness is admitted as evidence to rebut a suggestion that his oral evidence has been fabricated, that statement is admissible as evidence of any matter stated of which oral evidence by the witness would be admissible.
>
> (3) A statement made by the witness in a document—
>
> (a) which is used by him to refresh his memory while giving evidence,
> (b) on which he is cross-examined, and
> (c) which as a consequence is received in evidence in the proceedings,
>
> is admissible as evidence of any matter stated of which oral evidence by him would be admissible.
>
> (4) A previous statement by the witness is admissible as evidence of any matter stated of which oral evidence by him would be admissible, if—
>
> (a) any of the following three conditions is satisfied, and
> (b) while giving evidence the witness indicates that to the best of his belief he made the statement, and that to the best of his belief it states the truth.
>
> (5) The first condition is that the statement identifies or describes a person, object or place.
>
> (6) The second condition is that the statement was made by the witness when the matters stated were fresh in his memory but he does not remember them, and cannot reasonably be expected to remember them, well enough to give oral evidence of them in the proceedings.
>
> (7) The third condition is that—
>
> (a) the witness claims to be a person against whom an offence has been committed,
> (b) the offence is one to which the proceedings relate,

(c) the statement consists of a complaint made by the witness (whether to a person in authority or not) about conduct which would, if proved, constitute the offence or part of the offence,
(d) the complaint was made as soon as could reasonably be expected after the alleged conduct,
(e) the complaint was not made as a result of a threat or a promise, and
(f) before the statement is adduced the witness gives oral evidence in connection with its subject matter.

(8) For the purposes of subsection (7) the fact that the complaint was elicited (for example, by a leading question) is irrelevant unless a threat or a promise was involved.

12.22 This section now gives statutory form to five exceptions to the rule against narrative, four of which previously existed under common law. The exceptions covered in section 120 are: (i) previous statements adduced to rebut suggestions that the witness's courtroom testimony was a 'recent fabrication'; (ii) memory-refreshing documents which have been 'made exhibits' under the rules previously described; (iii) 'inability to remember': previous statements containing details which the witness can no longer recall, an exception which, unlike the others, is a new creation; (iv) 'previous identification'; and (v) 'recent complaint'. In the paragraphs that follow, each of these will be examined (apart from (ii), which was examined earlier at § 12.18 above).

12.23 Although four of these five exceptions cover much the same ground as the common law rules on which they are based, there is one difference of great importance: whereas at common law the previous consistent statement of a witness, where admissible, was only evidence supporting the credibility of the witness's oral evidence in court, and not (at least in theory) independent evidence of the facts stated in them, section 120 now makes all of them 'admissible as evidence of any matter stated of which oral evidence by the witness would be admissible'. (This point is further explained at § 12.31 *et seq* below.)

12.24 It should also be noted that all of these exceptions, except for the one relating to 'memory-refreshing documents', apply whether the previous statement was made orally or in writing or some other durable form.

12.25 *Rebuttal of 'recent fabrication'* Section 120(2) puts into statutory form the rule that the previous consistent statement of a witness (or defendant) can be adduced as evidence to rebut a suggestion that his courtroom evidence was a recent invention. It exactly reproduces the common law,[35] except for the important

[35] As derived from cases like *Benjamin* (1913) 8 Cr App R 146 and *Oyesiku* (1971) 56 Cr App R 240. In LC Report, n 18 above, § 10.45, the Law Commission 'concluded that the circumstances in which this minor exception can be used are best left alone'. For this exception to apply, it is not a precondition that the previous statement should have been made soon after the incident in question: *Kirk and Kirk* [2008] EWCA Crim 434.

modification about the evidential status of the statement that was explained at § 12.23 above.

12.26 *Memory-refreshing documents 'treated as exhibits'* This is covered by section 120(3). The exception was explained earlier (at § 12.14 to § 12.19 above).

12.27 Section 120 groups the other three exceptions to the rule against narrative together, prefacing them in subsection (4) with a general precondition that 'while giving evidence the witness indicates that to the best of his belief he made the statement, and that to the best of his belief it states the truth'.

12.28 *Previous identification* Provided the witness fulfils the condition mentioned in subsection (4), subsection (5) makes his previous statement admissible where 'the statement identifies or describes a person, object or place'. This preserves, and also extends, an exception to the rule against narrative that existed at common law. At common law, the exception applied where a witness had previously identified a person[36] (usually the defendant, at a 'line-up' or other identification procedure) or had produced a likeness of the defendant by using Photofit or something similar.[37] The Law Commission approved of this exception and thought that, in principle, it could and should be extended to cover previous descriptions as well as previous identifications, and that it should apply to identifications or descriptions of objects and places as well as people.[38]

12.29 *Inability to remember* Sceptics often pointed out that where a witness gave oral evidence prompted by a note (for example, where a policeman gave evidence prompted by his notebook) the theory that his 'memory was refreshed' by the note often failed to correspond with reality: in truth, the witness would often be reading a note recording details which had entirely slipped his mind.[39] Furthermore, the 'business documents' exception to the hearsay rule created by CJA 1998, section 24 sometimes rendered admissible a statement made by a someone who never testified in court at all, where 'the person who made the statement cannot reasonably be expected . . . to have any recollection of the matters dealt with in the statement'.[40] Putting these two elements together, the Law Commission thought it would be sensible to make a new exception to the rule against narrative covering the case 'where the statement was made by the witness when the matters stated were fresh in his memory but he does not remember them, and cannot reasonably be expected to remember them, well enough to give oral evidence of them in the

[36] *Christie* [1914] AC 545; *Osborne and Virtue* [1973] QB 678.

[37] *Cook* [1987] QB 417.

[38] LC Report, n 18 above, §§ 10.46–10.52.

[39] Cross, n 7 above, 191–2 (quoting Hayes J in *Lord Talbot de Malahide v Cussack* (1864) 17 ICLR 313, 220, and also referring to Lord Goddard in *Bryant and Dickson* (1946) 31 Cr App R 146).

[40] CJA 1998, s 24(4)(iii); see now CJA 2003, s 117(5)(b), at § 7.20 above.

proceedings'; and that is what section 120(6) of the CJA 2003 now provides. As with the exceptions described in § 12.28 above and § 12.30 below, a precondition (set by subsection (4)) is that the witness 'indicates to the best of his belief that he made the statement, and that to the best of his belief it states the truth'.

12.30 *Recent complaint* A common law exception to the rule against narrative was 'recent complaint in sex cases'. Where the complainant testified in a sex case, evidence could be given of what she (or he) said about the incident when first making a complaint, provided this was done at 'the first reasonable opportunity' and the statement was made spontaneously.[41] The origins of this exception were obscure and it was widely said to be irrational. First, the requirement that the complaint be made 'at the first reasonable opportunity' overlooked the point that many victims of sex offences are too traumatised, scared or embarrassed to report the incident immediately. Secondly, if it was important to know the terms in which the complaint was made in a sex case, it was hard to see why it was any less important to know this where the accusation was of a non-sexual assault, or indeed of any other offence.[42] The Law Commission thought this second point was valid and accordingly recommended that the 'recent complaint' exception be retained and extended to complaints of other offences. But it thought that, in principle, the exception should continue to be limited to complaints made at 'the first reasonable opportunity' and that the courts could be trusted to adapt this condition to growing knowledge about the psychology of victims.[43] The draft they produced to achieve this result eventually became CJA 2003, section 120(7) and (8), which to remind us, are as follows:

(7) The third condition [for the admissibility of a prior statement] is that—
   (a) the witness claims to be a person against whom an offence has been committed,
   (b) the offence is one to which the proceedings relate,
   (c) the statement consists of a complaint made by the witness (whether to a person in authority or not) about conduct which would, if proved, constitute the offence or part of the offence,
   (d) the complaint was made as soon as could reasonably be expected after the alleged conduct,
   (e) the complaint was not made as a result of a threat or a promise, and
   (f) before the statement is adduced the witness gives oral evidence in connection with its subject matter.

(8) For the purposes of subsection (7) the fact that the complaint was elicited (for example, by a leading question) is irrelevant unless a threat or a promise was involved.

[41] *Osbourne* [1905] 1 KB 551; *Camelleri* [1922] 2 KB 122.

[42] As had long been the case in Scotland: WG Dickson, *A Treatise on the Law of Evidence in Scotland* (2nd edn, Skelton (ed), Edinburgh, Bell and Bradfute, 1865) § 95.

[43] As they were already beginning to do: *Valentine* [1996] 2 Cr App R 213; cf *S* [2004] EWCA Crim 1320, [2004] 1 WLR 2940.

As with the 'previous identification' and 'inability to remember' exceptions, a precondition for this exception, imposed by section 120(4), is that 'while giving evidence the witness indicates that to the best of his belief he made the statement, and that to the best of his belief it states the truth'.

12.31 These provisions looks as if they were drafted with the aim of extending the common law exception about 'recent complaint' to a wider range of offences, but otherwise reproducing them faithfully. In *O*,[44] however, the Court of Appeal declined to read them in this spirit and took the view instead that they had wiped the slate clean, and the earlier case law was therefore no longer pertinent. The case involved a man who had been sentenced to 11 years' imprisonment for systematically abusing his step-daughter over a period of eight years, from when she was nine until she was 17. When she was 17 she had left home after an argument and gone to stay with friends, and when some three days later they tried to persuade her to go back home she told them about the abuse; some four months after that she also told her elder brother. The prosecution sought to admit evidence of these two complaints under section 120(7). This the defence resisted, arguing that the requirement in section 120(7)(d) that 'the complaint was made as soon as could reasonably be expected after the alleged conduct' was intended to reflect the common law requirement that it be made at 'the first reasonable opportunity', and the case law interpreting that requirement clearly suggested that these complaints would have failed this test. At trial, Judge Swift rejected this argument, gave the words what he considered to be their normal meaning, and on that basis held that the new statutory test was satisfied. The Court of Appeal endorsed his approach:

> The appellant sought to argue that the new hearsay provision as to complaints merely codify the old law of recent complaint and should be regarded as importing the restrictions inherent in some regards to that law. Again we disagree. The statutory provisions are freestanding and provide their own criteria.

Where the previous statement of a witness is admissible, it is now 'evidence of any matter stated in it'

12.32 *Previous consistent statements* As already mentioned (see § 12.18 to § 12.19 and § 12.23 above), where the previous consistent statement of a witness is admissible under one of the exceptions to the rule against narrative set out in section 120, it is now 'evidence of any matter stated in it'—and not, as was usually the case

[44] [2006] EWCA Crim 556, [2006] 2 Cr App R 27.

before, just evidence suggesting that the oral evidence the witness gave in court was truthful. In the law of civil evidence this change had been made in 1968, and in 1972 the Criminal Law Revision Committee (CLRC) had recommended that the same change be made in criminal evidence as well.[45] Unlike most of the CLRC's other proposals on hearsay, this one was adopted by the Law Commission in its Report. Its reason for doing so was as follows:

> the distinction between treating a statement as evidence on the issues and evidence as to credibility is one which is likely to cause confusion, particularly with juries, and it should for that reason be dispensed with. We do not believe that fact-finders (especially juries) can distinguish between using previous statements to show consistency and as evidence of their truth.[46]

12.33 This change is important because the previous consistent statement may be more complete and detailed than the witness's courtroom testimony. For example, it may contain a positive identification of a person or a vehicle at a given place at a particular time, which establishes the prosecution case against the defendant (or in the case of defence witness, provides the defendant with an alibi).

12.34 *Previous inconsistent statements* The CJA 2003 changed the law in the same way with respect to the evidential status of a witness's previous *in*consistent statements.

12.35 The previous inconsistent statement of a witness often comes before the court when at trial he tells a different tale from the one he told at an earlier stage. If this happens, the side against which he is giving evidence (or the side calling him if the court allows them to treat him as a hostile witness)[47] may confront him with his previous statement, under a procedure set out in Criminal Procedure Act 1865, sections 3, 4 and 5. Traditionally, a previous inconsistent statement so proved did not count as admissible evidence of the matters contained in it and in law its only function was to undermine the credibility of the evidence the witness had given orally in court. If the witness, under cross-examination, 'turned' and admitted that his previous statement was the truth, he had then 'adopted' it as part of his courtroom testimony and the court could act upon its contents; but if under cross-examination the witness would not adopt his previous statement, the tribunal of fact could not treat it as evidence of the matters it contained. If the court believed the previous statement was true, this was evidence in the light of which the court might decide to disbelieve the courtroom testimony, but it could not accept the previous statement as the truth and proceed to act on that instead. So if the witness told the police 'the answer is a lemon', but later told the court 'the answer is

45 CLRC Evidence Report, n 14 above, § 236.
46 LC Report, n 18 above, § 10.39.
47 ie a witness who is being deliberately obstructive, as against tiresomely forgetful.

an orange', there would be no legally admissible evidence before the court that the answer was a lemon, but there would be evidence that the answer was an orange, plus a good reason for disbelieving it.

12.36 If hindersome to law students, who found this rule difficult to learn and understand, it was very helpful to those defendants who (or whose muscular friends) were able to persuade the prosecution witnesses to retract the statements they had earlier given to the police. By CJA 2003, section 119, this position is reversed and the previous inconsistent statement, even if 'unadopted', is evidence of the matters it contains:[48]

> Inconsistent statements
>
> (1) If in criminal proceedings a person gives oral evidence and—
>
> (a) he admits making a previous inconsistent statement, or
>
> (b) a previous inconsistent statement made by him is proved by virtue of section 3, 4 or 5 of the Criminal Procedure Act 1865 (c. 18),
>
> the statement is admissible as evidence of any matter stated of which oral evidence by him would be admissible.
>
> (2) If in criminal proceedings evidence of an inconsistent statement by any person is given under section 124(2)(c), the statement is admissible as evidence of any matter stated in it of which oral evidence by that person would be admissible.

12.37 The significance of this change is illustrated by the case of *Joyce and Joyce*.[49] Following a shoot-out in broad daylight in the streets of Liverpool, three witnesses gave statements to the police identifying the defendants as the persons responsible; and then at trial, each in turn disavowed his previous statement and claimed that he could not say who did it. The judge, relying on section 119, directed the jury that, if they thought the witnesses had told the police the truth and were lying to the court, they could convict on the basis of the earlier statements, and they did so. The Court of Appeal upheld the convictions, saying:

> In the light of the new statutory provisions in relation to hearsay, in our judgment it would have been an affront to the administration of justice, on a trial for offences based on this terrifying conduct, if the jury had not been permitted by the judge to evaluate, separately and together, the quality of the three witnesses' oral evidence and to rely, if they thought fit, on the terms of their original statements.

It also rejected a defence submission that, because the prosecution evidence consisted essentially of witness statements that had been retracted at trial, the judge ought to have stopped the case, invoking the new duty imposed by CJA

[48] As a result of the CEA 1968.

[49] [2005] EWCA Crim 1785, [**page 278 below**]; comment, [2006] *Cambridge Law Journal* 518.

2003, section 125, to direct an acquittal (or discharge the jury) where the case against the defendant consists wholly or mainly of hearsay evidence that is unconvincing.[50]

12.38 Difficult problems potentially arise where the witness gives not one but a serious of different accounts of the incident before his or her eventual oral evidence at trial. In *Coates*,[51] the complainant in a rape case tried at a court-martial had given no less than four previous accounts of what had happened. These ranged in gravity from her first account, which was equivocal, and could have been interpreted as an account of intercourse consented to under the influence of drink, through to her fourth account, which described an unquestionable rape, carried out with the use of force. At trial, she gave evidence in accordance with her fourth account, whereupon the defence put her first account to her in cross-examination. The court-martial then convicted the defendant on the basis that they believed the complainant's first account and interpreted it as a rape. The Court of Appeal, unsurprisingly, quashed the conviction. One reason it gave for doing this was that the court-martial had convicted the defendant on a different basis from the one on which the prosecution had put the case before the court. A second and rather more problematic reason was that, notwithstanding CJA 2003, section 119, the court-martial should not in this case have treated the complainant's first statement as evidence of the matters of fact contained in it. The court-martial should, said the Court of Appeal, have invoked its power under section 78 of PACE 1984 to suppress the evidence as tending to make the trial unfair. The difficulty with this, however (as Professor Ormerod points out)[52] is that section 78 applies to evidence tendered by the prosecution but not evidence tendered by the defence. As an extra ground it would have been better, surely, to have said that, given the balance of evidence in the case, a conviction based solely on the complainant's first statement could not properly be seen as 'safe'.

12.39 Clearly, where previous statements (whether consistent or inconsistent) are part of the evidence, judges at jury trials will sometimes need to be careful as to how they direct juries on the weight to give them.[53]

12.40 The change also has potentially important implications in relation to the evidential status of confessions. In Chapter 10, we saw that D1's out-of-court confession is in principle admissible as evidence against himself but not against a

[50] See further 15.34 *et seq* below.

[51] [2007] EWCA Crim 1471, [2007] Crim LR 887.

[52] In his commentary in the *Criminal Law Review*, see n 52 above; here Prof Ormerod also discusses whether the statement might have been suppressed in reliance on CJA 2003, s 126, but as he says, this would require 'a wide and strained reading' of the section. For s 126, see Chapter 5 above.

[53] On this, see further § 15.31 below.

co-defendant, D2, whom he implicates in it.[54] Where D1 confesses the crime to the police, implicating D2 in the offence, and then at trial gives evidence denying the offence, he may be confronted with his confession; and if so, the effect of section 119 appears to be that D1's confession, if the tribunal of fact believes it, is then evidence on which it can find not only that D1 committed the offence but that D2 helped him. The Court of Appeal has indeed already held that this is the result in two decided cases: on the first occasion with hesitation[55] and on the second occasion, with apparent certainty.[56]

12.41 There is an argument against this position, however, which was not considered by the court in either case. CJA 2003, section 118, as we have seen, expressly preserves certain parts of the common law rules on hearsay, including 'any rule of law relating to the admissibility of confessions or mixed statements in criminal proceedings', and section 128, subsection (1) of which makes the confession of one co-defendant admissible in favour of the other, goes on in subsection (2) to say that '[s]ubject to subsection (1), nothing in this Chapter makes a confession by a defendant admissible if it would not be admissible under section 76 of the Police and Criminal Evidence Act 1984'. It could be argued that, between them, these two provisions prevent section 119 operating in the way that was described in the previous paragraph.[57]

A practical point: a previous statement, if in documentary form, must not normally be given to the jury when they retire

12.42 CJA 2003, section 122 is as follows:

Documents produced as exhibits

(1) This section applies if on a trial before a judge and jury for an offence—
   (a) a statement made in a document is admitted in evidence under section 119 or 120, and
   (b) the document or a copy of it is produced as an exhibit.

(2) The exhibit must not accompany the jury when they retire to consider their verdict unless—
   (a) the court considers it appropriate, or
   (b) all the parties to the proceedings agree that it should accompany the jury.

[54] See § 10.35 *et seq* below.
[55] *Read* [2005] EWCA Crim 3292.
[56] *Ali* [2006] EWCA Crim 3084.
[57] See further § 10.40 *et seq* above.

12.43 As the Court of Appeal pointed out in *Hulme*, the idea behind this provision is that, if the jury took the earlier written statement with them into the jury room, they might 'place disproportionate weight on the contents of the document, as compared with the oral evidence'.[58] Subsection 122(1)(a) permits the judge to allow the jury to take a copy of the statement with them where 'the court considers it appropriate'. Reading between the lines of the judgment in this case, it would be 'appropriate' if the jury could not make sense of the document without looking at it, but not otherwise.

12.44 In a case where the judge does decide to allow the jury to take the document with them, the Court of Appeal in *Hulme* said that he must give them 'robust directions', impressing on them 'the reason why they were being given the document and the importance of not attaching disproportionate weight to it simply because they had it before them' (at [26]).

[58] [2006] EWCA Crim 2899, [2007] 1 Cr App R 26 (334) at [19].

13

VIDEOTAPED EVIDENCE-IN-CHIEF

Introduction

13.1 As we saw in the last chapter (at § 12.4 above), at the time the CJA 2003 was enacted an important statutory exception to the 'rule against narrative' already existed in respect of videotaped interviews. This was Youth Justice and Criminal Evidence Act (YJCEA) 1999, section 27, which allows a previous video-interview to be played to the court when a 'vulnerable' witness is called to give evidence at trial. To this provision, the CJA 2003 adds (in principle at least) a new and more general exception, which if it ever comes into force will enable the videotape of a previous video-interview with *any* witness, whether vulnerable or not, to be used as a vehicle to communicate his story to the court at trials for serious criminal offences. This new exception is contained in sections 137 and 138. (At the time of writing these sections have not been brought into force, and no date for this has been announced.)

Background

13.2 In 1989 a Home Office advisory committee chaired by Judge Thomas Pigot QC proposed a radical new system under which children under 14 (or 17 in sex cases) would be examined in advance of trial and a videotape of the examination would be shown to the court in place of a live appearance by the child.[1] Under the Pigot scheme, the main examination of the child would have been conducted by a trained examiner and videotaped. The defence, having seen the tape, would then have had a chance to cross-examine the child, in chambers before a judge, this session also being videotaped. At trial, the tape of the first interview would have

[1] *Report of the Advisory Group on Video Evidence* (Chairman Judge Thomas Pigot, QC, London, Home Office, 1990). For the background, see JR Spencer and R Flin, *The Evidence of Children* (2nd edn, London, Blackstone Press, 1993) ch 7.

replaced the child's live examination-in-chief, and the tape of the second interview would have replaced the child's live cross-examination. Although the Pigot proposals attracted widespread support they attracted opposition too, and in the end the government introduced a half-measure, under which the first part of the scheme was carried out, but not the second. Under provisions enacted in 1991[2] (and which took the confusing legislative form of inserting a new section 32A into the CJA 1988) it was made possible for the initial interview to replace the child's evidence in-chief; but on condition that the child attended the trial to undergo a live cross-examination. This new procedure obviously represented a major exception to the rule against narrative which, but for this provision, would have made the previous interview of a child who testified at trial inadmissible.

13.3 By section 27 of the Youth Justice and Criminal Evidence Act (YJCEA) 1999, this 'semi-Pigot' arrangement was then extended for the benefit of vulnerable witnesses in general. This provision, which replaced section 32A of the CJA 1988,[3] borrowed some of the detail of earlier provision. Section 27 of the YJCEA is still in force[4]—and seems likely to remain so if sections 137 and 138 of the CJA 2003 are ever brought into operation. The text of section 27 is set out as an Appendix to this chapter. It will not be discussed further here, and for further details readers are referred to the practitioners' texts.[5] (But to complete the story about vulnerable witnesses, it should also be mentioned here that section 28 of the YJCEA, with a further gesture towards the Pigot proposals, attempts to provide for the videotaped cross-examination of a vulnerable witness to be carried out ahead of trial as well; but this section has never been implemented, and it now seems most unlikely that it ever will be.)[6]

13.4 *Achieving Best Evidence* These legislative changes allowing videotaped interviews in evidence were introduced as part of a reform package from the government which included official guidance to interviewers when conducting interviews which might later be used in evidence. The first, which appeared in 1992, dealt only with interviewing children.[7] With the advent of the YJCEA 1999 this was replaced by a more comprehensive document, *Achieving Best Evidence*, a

[2] Criminal Justice Act 1991, s 54.

[3] CJA 1988, s 23A was repealed by YJCEA 1999, s 67, Sch 6.

[4] But not fully operational: see the note at the end of the Annex to this chapter.

[5] *Blackstone's Criminal Practice* (2008) § F16.45 *et seq*; Archbold, *Criminal Pleading, Evidence and Practice* (2008) § 8.55k *et seq.*

[6] See the note at the end of the Annex to this chapter. At the time of writing, the government is consulting on whether s 28 should be implemented: see Office of Criminal Justice Reform, *Improving the Criminal Trial Process for Young Witnesses: a Consultation Paper* (June 2007).

[7] *Memorandum of Good Practice on Video Recorded Interviews with Child Witnesses for Criminal Proceedings* (London, HMSO, 1992).

co-operative venture between several government departments, in which a group of expert consultants was involved.[8]

13.5 *Proposal in the Auld Review* Writing extra-judicially in 1999, a senior judge[9] condemned the way in which videotaped evidence-in-chief had first been introduced for children and then extended to other classes of vulnerable witness as an example of the 'sticking-plaster culture' of law reform. With this remark Auld LJ agreed, and in his Review argued that the use of video-recorded interviews as evidence-in-chief should in principle apply to all witnesses, at any rate in serious cases. This change, he thought, should be introduced together with a system of safeguards governing police practices when questioning witnesses, similar to those provided by PACE 1984 and its Codes for police interviews with suspects. With that in mind, he recommended 'consideration in the long term of extending the present provisions for the use of video-recorded evidence to the evidence of all critical witnesses in cases of serious crime, coupled with provision where required of a record and/or transcripts or summaries of such evidence and also of that in cross-examination and re-examination'.[10]

13.6 *CJA 2003, sections 137 and 138* It was this proposal which gave rise to CJA 2003, sections 137 and 138. These are as follows:

137 Evidence by video recording

(1) This section applies where—

(a) a person is called as a witness in proceedings for an offence triable only on indictment, or for a prescribed offence triable either way,

(b) the person claims to have witnessed (whether visually or in any other way)—

(i) events alleged by the prosecution to include conduct constituting the offence or part of the offence, or

(ii) events closely connected with such events,

(c) he has previously given an account of the events in question (whether in response to questions asked or otherwise),

(d) the account was given at a time when those events were fresh in the person's memory (or would have been, assuming the truth of the claim mentioned in paragraph (b)),

(e) a video recording was made of the account,

[8] First published by the Home Office Communication Directorate as *Achieving Best Evidence in Criminal Proceedings: Guidance for Vulnerable or Intimidated Witnesses, including Children* in 2002. A revised version was published towards the end of 2007. This can be found online on the Crown Prosecution Service website at http://www.cps.gov.uk/publications/docs/achieving_best_evidence_final.pdf.

[9] Sir Anthony Hooper, 'The Investigation and Trial of Criminal Offences in the New Century: the Need for Radical Change' (1999) 21 *Liverpool Law Review* 131, 136–8.

[10] *Review of the Criminal Courts of England and Wales: Report* (London, The Stationery Office, October 2001) ch 11, at § 91 (pages 555–6).

(f) the court has made a direction that the recording should be admitted as evidence in chief of the witness, and the direction has not been rescinded, and
(g) the recording is played in the proceedings in accordance with the direction.

(2) If, or to the extent that, the witness in his oral evidence in the proceedings asserts the truth of the statements made by him in the recorded account, they shall be treated as if made by him in that evidence.
(3) A direction under subsection (1)(f)—

(a) may not be made in relation to a recorded account given by the defendant;
(b) may be made only if it appears to the court that—

(i) the witness's recollection of the events in question is likely to have been significantly better when he gave the recorded account than it will be when he gives oral evidence in the proceedings, and
(ii) it is in the interests of justice for the recording to be admitted, having regard in particular to the matters mentioned in subsection (4).

(4) Those matters are—

(a) the interval between the time of the events in question and the time when the recorded account was made;
(b) any other factors that might affect the reliability of what the witness said in that account;
(c) the quality of the recording;
(d) any views of the witness as to whether his evidence in chief should be given orally or by means of the recording.

(5) For the purposes of subsection (2) it does not matter if the statements in the recorded account were not made on oath.
(6) In this section 'prescribed' means of a description specified in an order made by the Secretary of State.

138 Video evidence: further provisions

(1) Where a video recording is admitted under section 137, the witness may not give evidence in chief otherwise than by means of the recording as to any matter which, in the opinion of the court, has been dealt with adequately in the recorded account.
(2) The reference in subsection (1)(f) of section 137 to the admission of a recording includes a reference to the admission of part of the recording; and references in that section and this one to the video recording or to the witness's recorded account shall, where appropriate, be read accordingly.
(3) In considering whether any part of a recording should be not admitted under section 137, the court must consider—
(a) whether admitting that part would carry a risk of prejudice to the defendant, and
(b) if so, whether the interests of justice nevertheless require it to be admitted in view of the desirability of showing the whole, or substantially the whole, of the recorded interview.

(4) A court may not make a direction under section 137(1)(f) in relation to any proceedings unless—

(a) the Secretary of State has notified the court that arrangements can be made, in the area in which it appears to the court that the proceedings will take place, for implementing directions under that section, and

(b) the notice has not been withdrawn.

(5) Nothing in section 137 affects the admissibility of any video recording which would be admissible apart from that section.

13.7 The fact that these provisions are not in force yet, and that there is no sign at present that they ever will be, makes the task of minutely dissecting their contents a rather pointless one. However, some general comments should be made.

13.8 First, the scope of the provisions is limited. First, they only apply at the trial of offences purely indictable, or either-way offences in respect of which the Secretary of State has made an order; and at the time of writing, no such order has, of course, been made. Secondly they only apply to the evidence of what are called, in police terminology,[11] 'significant witnesses': those who claim to have seen with their own eyes the actus reus of the offence take place, or some other event closely connected with it. Thirdly, like YJCEA 1999, section 27,[12] they do not extend to defendants. Fourthly, like section 27 again, the new provisions can only be used where the court gives leave. Fifthly, unlike section 27, they may only be used where the witness made the statement soon after the event, because section 137(1)(d) imposes a condition that 'the account was given at a time when those events were fresh in the person's memory'.

13.9 Furthermore, borrowing from section 27, the new provisions create a procedure that is, in principle, 'all or nothing'; by section 138(1), 'the witness may not give evidence in chief otherwise than by means of the recording as to any matter which, in the opinion of the court, has been dealt with adequately in the recorded account'. Thus, the party calling the witness may use the videotape as a substitute for his live evidence-in-chief but not, in principle, to supplement it.

13.10 If and when sections 137 and 138 come into force, it seems likely that the courts will follow some of the case law decided under YJCEA 1999, section 27 when deciding how to operate it.[13] A touchy point under section 27 has been the question whether it is proper for a videotape, once played at trial, to be played again. One of the advantages of a videotape as evidence is that, unlike testimony given orally in court, there can be an 'action replay', in which the evidence can be scrutinised more carefully than when it was heard initially. But with this advantage goes the risk (or perceived risk) that it then has a greater impact than it should,

[11] See the CPS document, *Video Recorded Evidence*, available on the CPS website at http://www.cps.gov.uk/legal/section13/chapter_r.html.

[12] Defendants are explicitly excluded from all the special measures provided by the YJCEA 1999 by virtue of ss 16(1) and 17(1); although Police and Justice Act 2006, s 47, has now added a new s 33A to the YJCEA 1999, making it possible for a vulnerable defendant to give evidence via a live video-link.

[13] See generally *Blackstone*, n 5 above, § F16.49.

simply because the tribunal of fact has seen and heard it twice. In *Rawlings and Broadbent*[14] the Court of Appeal held that, at a jury trial, the judge had a discretion to allow the videotape to be replayed if the jury requested this. But it said the judge should allow this only where the issue was *how* the witness said his words, and not what he said, a matter which could usually be resolved by the judge reminding them from his own notes. If a replay was allowed, the judge should warn the jury against giving the evidence extra weight just because they had seen it twice, and should also remind them of what had then transpired during the witness's cross-examination and re-examination. In *M*[15] the Court of Appeal discouraged judges from allowing 'action replays' except where juries asked for them.

13.11 *Why have CJA 2003, sections 137 and 138 not been brought into force?* Videotaped evidence is perceived to raise a series of thorny practical issues. The first is the need to provide the necessary equipment, both in police stations, to record the interviews, and in courtrooms, to show them. Another and related 'resource issue' is the cost of transcribing the tapes, and the understandable unwillingness of each part of the criminal justice system to be the one that has to pay for it. A further 'resource issue' involves the expenditure of extra time. If videotaped evidence is to be used, then those involved in preparing the case will often have to view the tape, a process which, of course, takes considerably longer than reading a written proof of evidence. Related to this, there is the likely need for 'editing', a process which also takes up precious time. The people who conduct these interviews are usually policemen who, unlike judges, solicitors and barristers, do not have an encyclopaedic knowledge of the rules of criminal evidence, and whose questioning, in consequence, may elicit material that has to be 'edited out' before the videotape is heard at trial. This problem is related to the more general problem, discussed in Chapter 15, that the questioning of witnesses by the police (as against the questioning of suspects) is not regulated by a Code of Practice. (Indeed, as we have seen, when Auld LJ made the proposal which gave rise to these provisions of the CJA 2003, he also underlined the need for such a Code.) Furthermore, section 27 of the YJCEA 1999, though theoretically in force, is not in practice fully operational. As is further explained in the note at the end of the Annex to this chapter, the provision can only be used in courts which the Secretary of State has authorised to use video-recording and (for want of equipment, it seems) it is available only in certain courts. While this remains the case, it is not surprising that sections 137 and 138 are still no more than 'virtual law'.

13.12 If this state of affairs is unsurprising, it is depressing nonetheless. At present, some police forces already make a practice of video-recording interviews with certain crucial witnesses, including in many cases where the recording could be played at trial if sections 137 and 138 were in force. Even if videotaped evidence-

[14] [1995] 1 WLR 178. But also see Mullen [2004] EWCA Crim 602, [2004] 2 Cr App R 18 (290).
[15] [1996] 2 Cr App R 56.

in-chief is not the 'magic bullet' by which all the problems of forgetful, frightened, tongue-tied or reluctant witnesses could be solved, it would surely be helpful in many cases. It seems stupid that, where a videotape exists, it still cannot be used in evidence, even though in 2003 Parliament, incited by the government, enacted legislation that permits its use.

Annex: Youth Justice and Criminal Evidence Act 1999, Section 27

Video recorded evidence in chief

(1) A special measures direction may provide for a video recording of an interview of the witness to be admitted as evidence in chief of the witness.

(2) A special measures direction may, however, not provide for a video recording, or a part of such a recording, to be admitted under this section if the court is of the opinion, having regard to all the circumstances of the case, that in the interests of justice the recording, or that part of it, should not be so admitted.

(3) In considering for the purposes of subsection (2) whether any part of a recording should not be admitted under this section, the court must consider whether any prejudice to the accused which might result from that part being so admitted is outweighed by the desirability of showing the whole, or substantially the whole, of the recorded interview.

(4) Where a special measures direction provides for a recording to be admitted under this section, the court may nevertheless subsequently direct that it is not to be so admitted if—

  (a) it appears to the court that—

    (i) the witness will not be available for cross-examination (whether conducted in the ordinary way or in accordance with any such direction), and

    (ii) the parties to the proceedings have not agreed that there is no need for the witness to be so available; or

  (b) any [Criminal Procedure Rules] requiring disclosure of the circumstances in which the recording was made have not been complied with to the satisfaction of the court.

(5) Where a recording is admitted under this section—

  (a) the witness must be called by the party tendering it in evidence, unless—

    (i) a special measures direction provides for the witness's evidence on cross-examination to be given otherwise than by testimony in court, or

    (ii) the parties to the proceedings have agreed as mentioned in subsection (4)(a)(ii); and

  (b) the witness may not give evidence in chief otherwise than by means of the recording—

    (i) as to any matter which, in the opinion of the court, has been dealt with adequately in the witness's recorded testimony, or

(ii) without the permission of the court, as to any other matter which, in the opinion of the court, is dealt with in that testimony.

(6) Where in accordance with subsection (2) a special measures direction provides for part only of a recording to be admitted under this section, references in subsections (4) and (5) to the recording or to the witness's recorded testimony are references to the part of the recording or testimony which is to be so admitted.

(7) The court may give permission for the purposes of subsection (5)(b)(ii) if it appears to the court to be in the interests of justice to do so, and may do so either—

(a) on an application by a party to the proceedings, if there has been a material change of circumstances since the relevant time, or

(b) of its own motion.

(8) In subsection (7) 'the relevant time' means—

(a) the time when the direction was given, or

(b) if a previous application has been made under that subsection, the time when the application (or last application) was made.

(9) The court may, in giving permission for the purposes of subsection (5)(b)(ii), direct that the evidence in question is to be given by the witness by means of a live link; and, if the court so directs, subsections (5) to (7) of section 24 shall apply in relation to that evidence as they apply in relation to evidence which is to be given in accordance with a special measures direction.

(10) *Repealed*

(11) Nothing in this section affects the admissibility of any video recording which would be admissible apart from this section.

Note: Though in force in principle, this section must be read subject to YJCEA 1999, section 18(2), which provides that 'special measures' (including this one) are not available unless the court has been 'notified' by the Secretary of State that 'relevant arrangements' have been made for implementing the measure. These notices are given in letters, sent to courts or groups of courts by the Minister and often not publicly available, which tell the courts to which they are directed not only whether they can use the special measures, but also for what types of case. The practical result of this opaque micro-management from Whitehall is that, at present, section 27 is not fully operative: either in the Crown Court or in the magistrates' courts. In the Crown Court, until recently the position was that section 27 could be used to help witnesses who were 'vulnerable' because of youth or mental incapacity, but not those who were 'vulnerable' through fear; but by virtue of a Circular emanating from the Better Trials Unit in the Office of Criminal Justice Reform in June 2007 (Ministry of Justice Circular 25/06/07), section 27 may now be used for all witnesses in sex cases who are likely to suffer from fear or distress, provided 'the investigations of the offence began on or after 1 September 2007'. For the complicated details of which magistrates' courts can use section 27, and for what purpose, readers should see *Stones' Justices' Manual* (2007 edn) fn1 to § 2.143. In *Rochester* [2008] EWCA Crim 678, decided on 4 April, the Court of Appeal criticised these labyrinthine arrangements, and rejected an appeal brought on the ground that the court had used section 27 when it was not yet authorised under them to do so.

14

OTHER MATTERS: EXPERTS (CJA 2003, SECTION 127) AND PROOF OF DOCUMENTS (SECTION 133)

14.1 Towards the end of Part 11 Chapter 2 of the CJA 2003 there are sections dealing with a number of incidental issues. This brief chapter treats two of them which, unlike the others, do not fall conveniently within any of the other chapters of this book.

Expert evidence: preparatory work

14.2 In its classic form, the hearsay rule created a number of practical difficulties in relation to experts. The most basic one was that the expert was invariably required to come to court to give his or her evidence orally, which, in cases where the evidence was non-contentious, was a waste of time for both the expert and the court. Under CJA 1967, section 9, a written report could replace the expert's oral evidence if the other side agreed; something it would refuse to do, obviously, if it wished to challenge the evidence, and something which it might also refuse to do, less obviously, if it just wanted to make difficulties for the other side. In answer to this, CJA 1988, section 30 (discussed in Chapter 8 above) empowers the court to admit the expert's written statement in place of his or her oral evidence even where there are objections to this: a course the court is unlikely to take, of course, if the objecting side genuinely wishes to challenge his or her conclusions.

14.3 Other problems arose from the fact that the opinion of an expert is almost invariably based, at least in part, on information that has come from others, and hence is open to objections on the ground that it is hearsay.

14.4 One was that experts will usually base their opinion on general scientific knowledge in their area of work which derives from experiments and studies carried out by others. In *Abadom* the Court of Appeal held that when experts refer to these, the information they supply is admissible under an exception to the hearsay rule: 'Once the primary facts on which their opinion is based have been proved by admissible evidence, they are entitled to draw on the work of others as part of the process of arriving at their conclusion'.[1] As we saw in Chapter 9,[2] this is one of the common law exceptions to the hearsay rule which has been expressly preserved by CJA 2003, section 118.

14.5 A different but related problem is that laboratory work is often carried out in teams, so that (for example) A and B, who are lab assistants, run routine tests on the material, the results of which are then evaluated by W, the head of the team, who on the basis of the tests produces a report. This situation was not covered by the common law exception in *Abadom*, with the consequence that if W in his evidence (whether oral or written) referred to what A and B had told him, his references infringed the hearsay rule. Nor was the problem covered by section 30 of the CJA 1988, if it was W who had written relevant parts of the report, rather than A and B themselves. The resulting need for A and B to testify (or to produce their own written reports) was justified if the other side had genuine reasons for doubting the quality of their work, but if not, it could be an expensive and time-consuming obstacle to justice.[3] As a solution to this problem, the Law Commission proposed a new, conditional exception to the hearsay rule. Where W relies on the work of collaborators A and B in preparing his report, W should state this in his report; and provided he does so, and the report is served on the other side in time for them to digest it before the hearing, W may then refer to the work of his collaborators in the course of his opinion, unless, in advance of trial, the other side has entered an objection. If an objection is entered, the court will require A and B to give evidence themselves, if it is satisfied that the interests of justice so require; but if not, it will overrule the objection, and allow W to speak for his collaborators.

14.6 A long and detailed provision to give effect to this scheme was included in the Law Commission' Draft Bill. In due course this found its way into the CJA 2003, where it appears as section 127, which is as follows:

> Expert evidence: preparatory work
>
> (1) This section applies if—
>
> > (a) a statement has been prepared for the purposes of criminal proceedings,
> > (b) the person who prepared the statement had or may reasonably be supposed to have had personal knowledge of the matters stated,

[1] [1983] 1 WLR 126 at 131F.
[2] See § 9.39–§ 9.41 above.
[3] For an example, see *Jackson* [1996] 2 Cr App R 420.

(c) notice is given under the appropriate rules that another person (the expert) will in evidence given in the proceedings orally or under section 9 of the Criminal Justice Act 1967 (c. 80) base an opinion or inference on the statement, and
(d) the notice gives the name of the person who prepared the statement and the nature of the matters stated.

(2) In evidence given in the proceedings the expert may base an opinion or inference on the statement.
(3) If evidence based on the statement is given under subsection (2) the statement is to be treated as evidence of what it states.
(4) This section does not apply if the court, on an application by a party to the proceedings, orders that it is not in the interests of justice that it should apply.
(5) The matters to be considered by the court in deciding whether to make an order under subsection (4) include—

(a) the expense of calling as a witness the person who prepared the statement;
(b) whether relevant evidence could be given by that person which could not be given by the expert;
(c) whether that person can reasonably be expected to remember the matters stated well enough to give oral evidence of them.

(6) Subsections (1) to (5) apply to a statement prepared for the purposes of a criminal investigation as they apply to a statement prepared for the purposes of criminal proceedings, and in such a case references to the proceedings are to criminal proceedings arising from the investigation.
(7) The appropriate rules are Criminal Procedure Rules made by virtue of—

(a) section 81 of the Police and Criminal Evidence Act 1984 (advance notice of expert evidence in Crown Court), or
(b) section 20(3) of the Criminal Procedure and Investigations Act 1996 (c. 25) (advance notice of expert evidence in magistrates'courts).[4]

Documents: evidential status of a copy

14.7 Once upon a time, a person who wished to rely on a document as evidence was required, at least in principle, to produce in court the original, and copies of documents could be used as evidence only where the person wishing to make use of them did not have the original 'available in his hands':[5] a rule which was usually said to be a remnant of the 'best evidence rule', a general rule (or supposed rule) which forbade a party to produce an inferior form of evidence where a superior

[4] As amended by Courts Act 2003 (Consequential Amendments) Order 2004, SI 2004/2035 para 47.

[5] 'if an original document is available in one's hands, one must produce it; . . . one cannot give secondary evidence by producing a copy': *Kajala v Noble* (1982) 75 Cr App R 149 per Ackner LJ at 152, a case in which the Court of Appeal construed the rule restrictively and refused to apply it to a videotape.

form of evidence was available to him.[6] In the days when multiple copies could only be made by printing, business and legal documents were hand-written, and the only way of reproducing them was to copy them by hand, the ban on using copies of documents as evidence obviously made sense. But with the invention of first copying ink and then carbon-paper, and ultimately photocopying, the rule became an inconvenient anachronism. In 1986 the Roskill Committee on Fraud Trials recommended that judges should have a general discretion to allow copies of documents to be produced, but two years later Parliament, at the instance of the Home Office, went much further. CJA 1988, section 27 made copies of documents generally admissible, to the same extent as the original was or would have been.[7]

14.8 Together with the other hearsay provisions of the CJA 1988, section 27 was repealed and replaced by the CJA 2003. The replacement provision in this case is section 133, which is as follows:

> Proof of statements in documents
>
> Where a statement in a document is admissible as evidence in criminal proceedings, the statement may be proved by producing either—
>
> (a) the document, or
> (b) (whether or not the document exists) a copy of the document or of the material part of it,
>
> authenticated in whatever way the court may approve.

14.9 This provision exactly reproduces the wording of CJA 1988, section 27 except in one respect. To make it plain that the provision made admissible not only copies, but copies of copies, section 27(b) concluded with a final sentence which said 'and it is immaterial for the purposes of this subsection how many removes there are between a copy and the original'. This sentence does not appear in the new provision, an omission which is possibly significant, because it could be taken as indicating Parliament's intention that the new provision, unlike the earlier one, makes only 'first copies' of documents admissible, with the result that 'a copy of a copy', though formerly admissible under section 27, is now admissible no longer.

14.10 That this was really the intention of Parliament, or of those who drafted the provision, seems unlikely. CJA 2003, section 133 ultimately derives from the Draft

[6] See *ex p Osman*, n 7 below. For a statement of the 'best evidence rule', see Rupert Cross, *Evidence* (3rd edn, 1967) 11. In *Springsteen v Masquerade Music Ltd* [2001] EWCA Civ 563, the Civil Division of the Court of Appeal expressed the view that the 'best evidence rule' was dead: see n 9 below.

[7] A provision which the government then neglected to bring into force, doing so only after the common law rule had been strongly criticised by the Court of Appeal in *R v Governor of Pentonville Prison, ex p Osman* [1990] 1 WLR 277. See Victor Smith, 'Lost, Altered or Destroyed Evidence' (2007) 171 *Justice of the Peace Newspaper*, 556.

Bill annexed to the Law Commission's final Report, in which there was no indication anywhere of any desire to change the rule that section 27 had introduced; nor is there any indication of an intended change in the Explanatory Notes to the CJA 2003, which say 'This section corresponds to the position under section 27 of the Criminal Justice Act 1988, whereby a statement in a document can be proved by producing either the original document or an authenticated copy. It is intended to cover all forms of copying including the use of imaging technology'.[8]

14.11 So it seems likely that the phrase was omitted from the new provision merely because the draftsman thought that it was no longer necessary; the point it made was obvious and if it had been prudent to make it *ex abundanti cautela* in 1988, there was no need to make it now. As the courts today are ever less receptive towards technical objections to the admissibility of cogent evidence, an argument that 'copies of copies' now fall outside the scope of section 133 seems unlikely to succeed. What their attitude would be can be predicted from this passage from the Court of Appeal's judgment in a civil case in which one of the points at issue was the use of secondary evidence to prove the contents of a document (at [85]):

> the time has now come when it can be said with confidence that the best evidence rule, long on its deathbed, has finally expired. In every case where a party seeks to adduce secondary evidence of the contents of a document, it is a matter for the court to decide, in the light of all the circumstances of the case, what (if any) weight to attach to that evidence. Where the party seeking to adduce the secondary evidence could readily produce the document, it may be expected that (absent some special circumstances) the court will decline to admit the secondary evidence on the ground that it is worthless. At the other extreme, where the party seeking to adduce the secondary evidence genuinely cannot produce the document, it may be expected that (absent some special circumstances) the court will admit the secondary evidence and attach such weight to it as it considers appropriate in all the circumstances. In cases falling between those two extremes, it is for the court to make a judgment as to whether in all the circumstances any weight should be attached to the secondary evidence. Thus, the 'admissibility' of secondary evidence of the contents of documents is, in my judgment, entirely dependent upon whether or not any weight is to be attached to that evidence. And whether or not any weight is to be attached to such secondary evidence is a matter for the court to decide, taking into account all the circumstances of the particular case.[9]

14.12 Three final points about this section should be made. First, section 133, like its predecessor CJA 1988, section 27, is permissive but not mandatory. It provides one method, other than the production of the original, by which the terms of a document may be proved, but in so doing, it does not exclude others. Thus the contents of a missing document could be proved not only by producing a copy, if

[8] At § 436.
[9] *Springsteen v Masquerade Music Ltd* [2001] EWCA Civ 563.

there is one, but also from oral evidence.[10] Secondly, a potentially difficult point arises as to the relationship between section 133 and statutory provisions (of which there are many) which lay down specific rules about the production and admissibility of copies of certain types of document, for example, the Bankers' Books Evidence Act 1879,[11] which makes copies of entries in the records of banks admissible, provided they are authenticated in the manner provided for by section 5 of that Act. On this issue two views are possible. One is that, in such a case, the special statutory procedure must be followed and section 133 cannot be used.[12] The other and perhaps more plausible view is that section 133 could be used as an alternative, but the failure to follow the special statutory procedure could affect its weight; and in particular, where the particular statute creates a presumption that statements contained in a document proved in the manner stated are correct, this presumption would not then arise. Thirdly and lastly, section 133 is concerned with the way in which the contents of a document, if admissible in evidence, can be put before the court, not with what statements, when contained in documents, are admissible. A statement that is inadmissible because of the hearsay rule, or a fortiori because it is irrelevant, does not become admissible by virtue of section 133 just because it is contained in a document, whether the document is an original or a copy.

[10] See *Nazeer* [1998] Crim LR 750; and *Blackstone's Criminal Practice* (2008) § F8.3.
[11] See generally § 8.7 above.
[12] As is suggested in *Blackstone,* n 10 above, § F8.3.

15

PRACTICAL ISSUES

Taking, recording and preservation of statements, and the rules on access to them

15.1 *Taking statements* PACE) 1984, and Codes C and E made under it, create a comprehensive system for regulating police interviews with suspects. This scheme consists of detailed rules about the way in which interviews are to be conducted, and detailed rules as to how they are to be recorded. In particular, they require interviewers to take contemporaneous notes, which are read over to the suspect at the end of the interview, when he is invited to sign them to certify that they contain an accurate record of what took place. And they require interviews of those who are suspected of any indictable offence (including 'either-way offences') to be tape-recorded, using audio equipment. The details of these rules are beyond the scope of this book.[1] But here it can and should be said that the scheme introduced in 1984 has been extremely beneficial. Previously there was no tape-recording and when interviewing suspects the police did not take contemporaneous notes. Instead, they wrote notes of the interview afterwards, which the suspect was not even asked to sign. Predictably, 'the result was that trials were disfigured by endless arguments over what was or was not said in interview, the accused complaining that he had been "verballed" by the police'.[2] Nowadays, happily, this no longer happens. If there is any doubt as to what the suspect said in interview, or what was said or done to him to make him say it, the prosecutor, the defence lawyer and court can all verify what happened by listening to the tape.[3]

15.2 By contrast, there is, broadly speaking, no equivalent set of rules to regulate the taking of statements from ordinary witnesses.

15.3 Where the witness is a child, or vulnerable for other reasons, an official Code of Practice for conducting and recording interviews was issued by the government

[1] For the details, see M Zander, *The Police and Criminal Evidence Act 1984* (London, Sweet & Maxwell) (5th edn, London, Sweet & Maxwell 2005); *Blackstone's Criminal Practice* (2008) § D.1.

[2] John Sprack, *A Practical Approach to Criminal Procedure* (10th edn, Oxford, OUP, 2004) § 2.71.

[3] For a striking example of this procedure revealing improper conduct by the police at interview, see *Paris* (1993) 97 Cr App R 99; see § 10.11 above.

in 2002 and revised in 2007,[4] entitled *Achieving Best Evidence: Guidance for Vulnerable or Intimidated Witnesses.* This was drawn up by a team of respected experts, led by a well-known psychologist, who based their work on an earlier official document containing guidance on interviewing children.[5] Although not formally promulgated under statutory powers, like the Codes made under PACE, *Achieving Best Evidence* was issued under the joint names of the Home Office, the Lord Chancellor's Department (as it then was), the Crown Prosecution Service, the Department of Health and the Welsh Assembly, and the police regard themselves as bound by it. It contains extensive and detailed guidance about the way in which interviews with vulnerable witnesses should be conducted and operates on the basis that all such interviews should be video-recorded.

15.4 But in other cases, the police are basically left to their own devices. For interviews with ordinary witnesses there is no national official guidance, comparable to *Achieving Best Evidence*, to regulate the way in which the questions are put. Some efforts have been made in this direction. In 1992, the Home Office issued a circular on the principles of investigative interviewing,[6] which was published together with some booklets for training purposes.[7] One of the main aims of this circular, and its accompanying documents, was to inculcate in police investigators the need to question witnesses with an open mind, rather than to ask questions designed to confirm the hypothesis that the investigator had already formed. The style of interviewing that was recommended later became known as the PEACE model: P for 'planning and preparation', E for 'engage and explain', A for 'account, clarification and challenge', C for 'closure' and E for 'evaluation'. Following a Home Office funded evaluation of the training programme for the PEACE method,[8] in 2001 the Association of Chief Police Officers (ACPO) issued a document[9] encouraging its wider use, together with a policy of ensuring that, for investigations into the most serious crimes, the best-trained and most experienced interviewers are used. But all this falls far short of the national standard-setting achieved by PACE 1984 in respect of interviews with suspects, and by *Achieving Best Evidence* for interviews with witnesses who are vulnerable. The documents in which the policy and principles are set out are obscure and not readily available outside the police

[4] The text of the Code can be found on the CPS website at http://www.cps.gov.uk/publications/docs/achieving_best_evidence_final.pdf.

[5] Home Office and Department of Health, *Memorandum of Good Practice on Video Recorded Interviews with Child Witnesses for Criminal Proceedings* (HMSO, 1992).

[6] Home Office Circular 22/1992.

[7] Home Office Central Planning Unit, *A Guide to Interviewing, The Interviewer's Rule-Book* and *The Interview Workbook* (1992).

[8] Colin Clarke and Rebecca Milne, *National Evaluation of PEACE Investigative Interviewing Course.*

[9] *ACPO Investigative Interviewing Strategy* (2001). In reacting to this, some forces have made their policy publicly available, eg Gloucestershire, whose policy is available at www.gloucestershire.police.uk/sei/s/931/f87.pdf

service,[10] and in the words of ACPO, 'certain forces have invested heavily within the interviewing arena, where others have not recognised the role it has to play in improving performance and narrowing the justice gap'.[11]

15.5 When it comes to recording interviews with 'normal' witnesses, the usual practice is still for the investigating officer to ask the witness questions, and to write down his answers, long-hand, on an official form, which the witness is invited to read and sign when the interview is concluded. After he has been given the chance to amend it before he does so, the witness is usually required to sign a statutory declaration recording that:

> This statement is true to the best of my knowledge and belief and I make it knowing that, if it is tendered in evidence, I shall be liable to prosecution if I have wilfully stated in it anything which I know to be false or do not believe to be true.[12]

15.6 As compared with video-recording, or even audio-recording, this method is obviously both primitive and deficient. The written statement, unlike a tape-recording, typically contains the answers that the witness gave but omits the questions that provoked them, so making it impossible to tell whether the answer was given freely or in response to pressure or to suggestion or to leading questions. As the interviewer usually writes down the answers in his own words, there are obvious risks of omission, error and distortion.

15.7 That this can lead to miscarriages of justice should be obvious. The most usual sort are acquittals of the guilty, because truthful prosecution witnesses are discredited when this is not deserved. Prosecution witnesses whose statements were inaccurately recorded by the police, and who then give accurate oral evidence at trial, are 'crucified' in cross-examination by defence lawyers, who (naturally) accuse them of having changed their story and exploit to the full the fact that, having made the statement, they signed the formal declaration promising that it was true. But there is a risk of wrongful convictions too. Witnesses whose statements were inaccurately recorded may forget what really happened, and then when they read their statements before giving evidence, fill their minds with an inaccurate account, which they then regurgitate, in good faith and convincingly, in the witness-box. Where the witness is unavailable, and his statement to the police is used at trial in substitution for his oral evidence, the damage that inaccurate recording can do is all the greater. As the earlier chapters have shown, the general effect of

[10] The current document is the *Practical Guide to Investigative Interviewing* (4th edn, 2004), a DVD published by the National Specialist Law Enforcement Centre, which is part of the National Police Improvement Agency.

[11] ACPO, n 9 above, § 4.

[12] A declaration of this sort is required in order for the statement to be eligible for use as a 'section 9 statement': on which see Chapter 4, in particular § 4.4 above.

the hearsay provisions of the CJA 2003 is to make such statements more widely admissible in evidence than they were, and hence to expand the area of risk.

15.8 Following *Achieving Best Evidence*, interviews with vulnerable witnesses are routinely video-taped, and sometimes the police also record interviews with other 'significant witnesses' too, even though the tape will not (as the law currently stands) be admissible in evidence at trial.[13] The case for moving from this position to a general system under which all police interviews with witnesses are conducted according to an official national protocol and, at least in serious cases, tape-recorded, is unanswerable.[14] As we saw in Chapter 12, it convinced Auld LJ and his recommendation led to sections 137 and 138 of the CJA 2003. It is depressing that, four years later, these provisions have still not been brought into force.

15.9 *Retaining statements* Sections 21 to 26 of the Criminal Procedure and Investigations Act (CPIA) 1996 require the Secretary of State to promulgate an official code to regulate how the police and other official investigators store evidence collected in the course of their inquiries. Paragraphs 5(4) and 5(5) of the current Code, which was made in 2005,[15] requires investigators to retain, inter alia:

—crime reports (including crime report forms, relevant parts of incident report books

—records which are derived from tapes of telephone messages (for example, 999 calls) containing descriptions of an alleged offence or offender;

—final versions of witness statements (and draft versions where their content differs from the final version), including any exhibits mentioned (unless these have been returned to their owner on the understanding that they will be produced in court if required);

—interview records (written records, or audio or videotapes, of interviews with actual or potential witnesses or suspects);

—records of the first description of a suspect by each potential witness who purports to identify or describe the suspect, whether or not the description differs from that of subsequent descriptions by that or other witnesses;

[13] See Chapter 12 above; and see the CPS guide on video-recorded evidence, available at www.cps.gov.uk/ legal/section13/chapter_r.html

[14] It was put, with great cogency, by Anthony Heaton-Armstrong and David Wolchover, 'Recording Witness Statements' in A Heaton-Armstrong, Shepherd and D Wolchover (eds), *Analysing Witness Testimony* (London, Blackstone, 1999) ch 15; and again by A Heaton-Armstrong, D Wolchover and Annabel Maxwell-Scott, 'Obtaining, Recording and Admissibility of Out-of-court Statements' in A Heaton-Armstrong, Shepherd, Gudjonsson and D Wolchover (eds), *Witness Testimony* (Oxford, OUP, 2006) ch 10.

[15] Criminal Procedure and Investigations Act 1996 (Code of Practice) Order 2005, SI 2005/985. This Order does not contain the text of the Code, which is available at the Home Office website at http://police.homeoffice.gov.uk/news-and-publications/publication/operational-policing/Disclosure_code_of_practice.pdf?view=Binary (or in Appendix A of the supplement to the current edition of Archbold, *Criminal Pleading, Evidence and Practice* (2008)).

—any material casting doubt on the reliability of a witness;
—any material casting doubt on the reliability of a confession.[16]

15.10 This Code also lays down minimum periods for which material of this type must be kept. By paragraphs 5.7 to 5.10, nothing must be got rid of until a decision has been taken about starting criminal proceedings; where they are started, nothing must be got rid of unless the case is dropped or the defendant is acquitted; and where they end in a conviction, until six months after the conviction or, if the defendant receives a prison sentence or a hospital order, until after his release.

15.11 These rules only apply, of course, to the police. If defendants or their friends (or lawyers) deliberately destroy relevant evidence they commit the common law offence of perverting the course of justice,[17] but they are under no particular legal obligation to actively preserve it.

15.12 *Access to statements* Where the prosecution hold a copy of a statement from a witness that is relevant to the proceedings, when (if ever) are they required to disclose its contents to the defence?

15.13 Traditionally, their duty to do so was extremely limited. Prosecutors were, broadly speaking, expected to give the defence advance notice of what their witnesses were expected to say at trial, and hence would usually have to give the defence access to statements prosecution witnesses had made to the police in which their expected evidence at trial was indicated,[18] and if their intended witnesses had previously made statements inconsistent with what they were expected to say in evidence, they were required to give the defence access to those too.[19] But that was the limit of their obligation and they could, and often did, refuse to give the defence access to other potentially important statements that witnesses had made, in particular, the initial complaint.[20] With the important Court of Appeal decision in *Ward*,[21] and then the CPIA 1996, the position changed radically.

[16] The list given relates only to materials that consist of statements, or matters casting doubt on the truth of statements. For a full list, readers should see para 5 of the Code.

[17] Archbold, n 15 above, § 28.14.

[18] At any rate, in proceedings on indictment. For many years, prosecutors were not obliged to give the defence advance notice of what their witnesses were expected to say in summary proceedings. This deficiency was cured by a combination of the Magistrates' Courts (Advance Information) Rules 1985 (now codified in CPR Rule 21) and the Attorney-General's Guidelines on Disclosure (November 2000) § 43 of which provides that 'The prosecutor should . . . provide to the defence all evidence upon which the Crown proposes to rely in a summary trial'.

[19] *Berry v R* [1992] 2 AC 364; *R v Liverpool Crown Court, ex p Roberts* [1986] Crim LR 622.

[20] Anthony Heaton-Armstrong and David Wolchover, 'Recording Witness Statements' [1992] Crim LR 160; *Analysing Witness Testimony*, n 13 above, 231.

[21] (1993) 96 Cr App R 1.

Prosecutors are now, in principle, required to share with the defence any 'unused material' they have collected which 'might reasonably be considered capable of undermining the case for the prosecution against the accused or of assisting the accused'.[22]

15.14 At common law the defence was obliged to disclose neither the way it proposed to defend the case, nor the evidence it proposed to call. Various pieces of legislation later required the defence, in cases tried on indictment, to give details in advance of alibis and expert evidence, and in serious fraud cases to give advance notice of the broad lines of the defence. The CPIA 1996 imposed on the defence, in cases tried on indictment, a further general obligation to reveal the broad lines upon which it proposes to fight the case. At first, this obligation was to disclose the general nature of the defence and not to give details of the evidence to be used in support of it. In principle, the CJA 2003 expands the duty so that the defence is henceforth under a general duty to give the prosecution notice of the witnesses it proposes to call;[23] but at the time of writing, this part of the Act has not been brought into force. But the defence is not obliged to disclose 'unused material', if it has any; nor is it required, when calling a witness, to disclose any previous inconsistent statement he has made.

Evidence on commission

15.15 As previously mentioned, there is still no general provision in English criminal procedure under which a witness who is thought likely to be unavailable to give oral evidence at the trial can be judicially examined on commission. There are, however, various narrowly-drawn provisions which allow this to be done in particular circumstances, and provide that the deposition so obtained is then to be admissible in criminal proceedings.[24] In addition to these, Chapter 2 of the Crime (International Co-operation) Act 2003 creates a mechanism under which courts in the United Kingdom, plus 'designated prosecutors',[25] can make mutual legal assistance requests to courts and certain other legal authorities abroad in order to have

[22] CPIA 1996, s 3 (as amended by CJA 2003, s 32).

[23] CJA 2003, s 34, adding new CPIA 1996, s 6C; and CJA 2003, s 35, adding new CPIA 1996, s 6D.

[24] Children (Children and Young Persons Act 1933, ss 42 and 43); merchant seamen (Merchant Shipping Act 1995, s 286); overseas witnesses whose evidence is needed for prosecutions for crimes committed on board aircraft (Civil Aviation Act 1982, s 95); and in Northern Ireland, witnesses who are extremely ill (Magistrates' Courts (Northern Ireland) Order 1981, SI 1981/1675 (NI 26)). For further details, see Archbold, n 14 above, para 10.41 *et seq*, and §§ 2.48–2.58 above.

[25] Those listed by the Crime (International Co-operation) Act 2003 (Designation of Prosecuting Authorities) Order 2004, SI 2004/1032, as amended by the Crime (International Co-operation) Act 2003 (Designation of Prosecuting Authorities) (Amendment) Order 2004, SI 2004/1747.

witnesses examined in other countries; but, astonishingly, that Act fails to provide that statements so obtained are then admissible in the United Kingdom, which means that, in England and Wales, they are potentially excluded by the hearsay rule and only admissible under the exceptions described in earlier chapters of this book.[26]

15.16 This is in stark contrast with the position in most other countries, including Scotland, where the criminal courts have a general power to order evidence to be taken on commission.[27]

15.17 In some cases where witnesses are unavailable to give live evidence at court, sections 51 to 56 of the CJA 2003 now provide a solution by enabling the witness to testify from a distance by using a live video-link. After languishing unimplemented for four years, these sections were brought into force, very suddenly, and for the purpose of prosecutions for certain offences only, with effect from 7 December 2007.[27a] Obviously, they do only solve the problem insofar as the witness is still alive and willing to give evidence.[28]

Requirement to give notice of hearsay evidence: criminal procedure rules

15.18 CJA 2003, section 132, creates a power to make rules as 'necessary or expedient for the purposes of this Chapter', and sketches out a list of matters that could be covered by them, at the head of which are 'the procedure to be followed' by those wishing to adduce hearsay evidence, and provisions about giving notice. Rules have been made under this section, which are to be found in Part 34 of the consolidated Criminal Procedure Rules. For the details, readers should consult the Rules, Part 34 of which is set out in Appendix II.

15.19 In broad terms, they require a party wishing to adduce hearsay evidence to give notice to the court and all other parties within 14 days of various 'trigger' events, which differ according to whether the case is to be heard in the Crown Court or the magistrates' court. A party who wishes to oppose the application has

[26] Though if the route by which they are admitted is CJA 2003, s 117, the path to admission is smoothed by s 117(4).

[27] Criminal Procedure (Scotland) Act 1995, s 272.

[27a] Criminal Justice Act 2003 (Commencement No 19 and Transitional Provisions) Order 2007 SI 2007/3451. Though in theory issued before the commencement date the Order was not in fact published until after it had passed; and for good measure, it originally appeared with the wrong number attached to it—blunders which moved the editor of *Criminal Law Week* to say 'the drafting of statutory instruments plumbs new depths' ([2008], issue 1, § 29).

[28] CJA 1988, s 32 already enables witnesses to give evidence by live link when they are outside the United Kingdom; and under YJCEA 1999, s 24, evidence by live link is one of the possible 'special measures' for helping vulnerable witnesses to give their evidence.

14 days from receipt of the notice in which to do so.[29] The form in which these notices are to be given, and the information they must contain, are set out in a Practice Direction, which is also reproduced in Appendix II.

15.20 Strict compliance with the notice requirements in the Rules is not mandatory. Rule 34.7 provides that the court may allow a party to call hearsay evidence without notice, or on notice the formalities of which differ from those the Rules lay down, and Rule 34.8 allows the party entitled to notice to waive his right to receive it. However, where a party seeks to adduce hearsay evidence without complying with the Rules, CJA 2003, section 132(5)–(7) imposes limits and a potential penalty. These subsections are as follows:

> (5) If a party proposing to tender evidence fails to comply with a prescribed requirement applicable to it—
>
> (a) the evidence is not admissible except with the court's leave;
> (b) where leave is given the court or jury may draw such inferences from the failure as appear proper;
> (c) the failure may be taken into account by the court in considering the exercise of its powers with respect to costs.
>
> (6) In considering whether or how to exercise any of its powers under subsection (5) the court shall have regard to whether there is any justification for the failure to comply with the requirement.
> (7) A person shall not be convicted of an offence solely on an inference drawn under subsection (5)(b).

15.21 In practice, courts will be reluctant to admit hearsay evidence tendered without notice where its arrival unannounced makes it difficult for the other side to check whether it is credible: and a fortiori if there is any suggestion of an ambush. In *Musone*,[30] A, B and C were jointly tried for a murder. On the ninth day of the trial, A sought to adduce without notice letters allegedly written by B, containing statements exonerating A and placing the blame on C. Both B and C objected and the judge refused the application, mentioning (inter alia) that the late appearance of the letters meant that C was unable to instruct an expert to check whether they were forgeries. The judge's refusal to admit the letters late was one of the grounds on which A later appealed, but the Court of Appeal rejected the appeal. In doing so, it said 'There is no basis for saying that the judge's conclusion exceeded the bounds of a reasonable decision': a form of words reflecting the fact that the Court of Appeal is in principle reluctant to criticise procedural decisions of this sort, and does so only where it thinks they were grossly unreasonable. Where, by contrast, the failure to give notice in due time does not cause the other

[29] CJA 2003, s 132(4) empowers the Criminal Procedure Rule Committee to make a rule to the effect that, if a counter-notice is not given, the hearsay is automatically admissible, but this possibility has not been taken up in the current Rules; see § 4.11 above.

[30] [2007] EWCA Crim 1237, [2007] 1 WLR 2467.

side any real prejudice, a late application should usually be allowed; the court should not deprive itself of evidence that is relevant and cogent, merely in order to punish one of the parties for his inefficiency and failure to respect the rules.[31]

15.22 Where an application to admit hearsay evidence is made out of time, the court is obliged at least to consider it. In *R (CPS) v Uxbridge Magistrates' Court*[32] a key witness failed to appear at trial, because she had been temporarily committed to a mental hospital. The magistrates first refused the prosecution's request for an adjournment, and then refused to consider their out-of-time application to admit her statements to the police as hearsay, on the ground that this was an attempt to reopen their refusal to adjourn, and so acquitted the defendant for want of evidence. The Divisional Court said that their refusal to consider the application was 'plainly wrong', quashed the acquittal and returned the case to the bench for further consideration.

Deciding applications to admit hearsay evidence and applications for hearsay to be excluded

15.23 This subject has been covered in detail in earlier chapters. But to recapitulate, the principle in criminal proceedings is still that hearsay evidence (including the previous out-of-court statements of witnesses who testify at trial) are in principle inadmissible in evidence; and such evidence is only admissible where one of the exceptions listed in CJA 2003, Part 11, Chapter 2 applies.

15.24 Of these, one of the most important in practice is that the parties all agree to its admission.[33] Where this is so there is, in principle, no contested issue for the court to decide. But in this situation it will often make sense for the court to consider with counsel the purpose (or purposes) for which the evidence is to be adduced, because the parties may have different purposes in mind; and in a jury trial, the judge may need to consider the purpose for which it is adduced when formulating his or her direction.

15.25 The other exceptions raise issues which the court, potentially, must rule upon. To remind us, the other exceptions are as follows:

—the 'general inclusionary discretion' (alias the 'safety-valve'): CJA 2003, section 114(1)(d), discussed in Chapter 5;

—where the witness in question is unavailable: CJA 2003, section 116, discussed in Chapter 6;

[31] *Cole* [2007] EWCA Crim 1924, [2007] 1 WLR 2716 at [68].

[32] [2007] EWHC 205 (Admin), 171 JP 279.

[33] See generally Chapter 4 .

—documentary records: CJA 2003, section 117, discussed in Chapter 7;
—a myriad of specific statutory exceptions: CJA 2003, section 114(1)(a), a number of which were discussed in Chapter 8;
—the eight common law exceptions preserved by CJA 2003, section 118, discussed in Chapter 9;
—confessions: PACE 1984, sections 76 and 76A, discussed in outline in Chapter 10;
—where the 'hearsay' is the previous statement of a witness who testifies at trial, the group of extra exceptions contained in CJA 2003, section 120, discussed in Chapter 12;
—videotapes of interviews with vulnerable witnesses: YJCEA 1999, section 27 and (potentially) CJA 2003, sections 137 and 138, discussed in Chapter 13;
—information from collaborators, incorporated by an expert in his or her report: CJA 2003, section 127, discussed in Chapter 14.

15.26 Where some of these exceptions apply, the hearsay evidence is admissible (at least in principle) automatically. But in many of them the court is required to exercise its discretion, in the sense that it has to consider two issues: (i) whether a particular condition or set of conditions are met and, if so, (ii) whether admitting the evidence is 'in the interests of justice'. This 'double-barrelled' approach is required in the following cases:

—where it is sought to admit the evidence under the general inclusionary discretion (section 114(1)(d) and (2));
—where it is sought to admit the evidence under section 116, the reason for the absence of the witness being that he is in fear (section 116(4));[34]
—where the evidence is multiple hearsay (section 121).[35]

In addition, even in the cases where the exception to the hearsay rule operates in principle automatically, the court will be obliged to consider whether it is 'in the interests of justice' to admit the evidence if it is asked to exclude the evidence under section 126, which empowers the court to exclude hearsay evidence of little value, or, where it is prosecution evidence, under PACE 1984, section 78.

15.27 Section 126 was examined in Chapter 5, and no more will be said about it here. PACE 1984, section 78 was discussed in Chapter 10, in the context of confessions, but as the provision potentially applies to other types of evidence (including other forms of hearsay) some further comments are in order. To remind us, PACE 1984, section 78(1) is as follows:

> (1) In any proceedings the court may refuse to allow evidence on which the prosecution proposes to rely to be given if it appears to the court that, having regard to all the circumstances, including the circumstances in which the evidence was obtained, the

[34] See § 6.25 above.
[35] See Chapter 11.

admission of the evidence would have such an adverse effect on the fairness of the proceedings that the court ought not to admit it.

In principle, there is of course a degree of potential overlap between this provision and the various sections of the CJA 2003 which empower the court to exclude otherwise admissible hearsay because it is not 'in the interests of justice' to admit it. However, the scope of section 78(1) is potentially wider. The factors listed as matters for the court to consider under the various sections of the CJA 2003 which require the court to exclude hearsay 'in the interests of justice' are centred primarily on the credibility (or otherwise) of the evidence, and the difficulty (or otherwise) for the other side in challenging it. But section 78(1), as interpreted by the courts, is potentially triggered by wider considerations, including whether or not the evidence was lawfully obtained. And when rejecting attempts to exclude evidence under section 78(1), the courts also look at the broader picture. Thus in *Loveridge*,[35a] for example, the defendant sought to invoke section 78 to persuade the court to exclude the hearsay statement of an 88-year-old man whom he had allegedly robbed, arguing that to admit it would make the trial 'unfair'. At the time of the trial, the defendant had absconded and the court proceeded in his absence. In upholding the trial judge's decision to admit the statement, the Court of Appeal took his wilful absence from the trial into account. It did not lie in the defendant's mouth to say that his inability to cross-examine the complainant had made the proceedings against him 'unfair', given that he had deliberately thrown away the chance of challenging the old man's statement by giving sworn evidence that it was false.

Time and place for deciding on the application

15.28 The decision on an application to admit (or reject) hearsay evidence will sometimes be made at a pre-trial hearing. In the Crown Court, this may be at the plea and case management hearing (PCMH), but the decision is more likely to be made, in accordance with a direction made at the PCMH, at a later pre-trial hearing nearer to the trial. This is partly because, at PCMH hearings, there is unlikely to be enough time to examine the question properly; and it also because it is generally felt that the judge who makes the decision should be the one who will have to try the case, and this will commonly be a different judge from the one who deals with the PCMH. But the law does not require the decision to be made ahead of trial, and in practice such decisions are quite often made either immediately before the trial or even after it has started. Where the issue arises at a late stage, or where the procedure laid down by the Criminal Procedure Rules has not been followed, decisions will inevitably have

[35a] [2007] EWCA Crim 1041.

to be made by the court of trial. In the Crown Court, the judge will naturally make the decision in the absence of the jury. At the trial stage in the magistrates' courts, where the bench are the deciders of both law and fact, the court is obviously unable to rule on the admissibility of the evidence while the fact-finders are absent. The magistrates may be willing to deal with the admissibility point as a preliminary issue at the start of the trial, but are not obliged to do so, and may properly either rule on it at the point where it is to be heard or even leave the decision until the end of the case.[36] At whatever stage they deal with the point, the situation is bound to arise occasionally in which the bench rejects a piece of hearsay evidence as inadmissible, but continues to deal with the case on the basis of other evidence. Where this happens, the legal system has to trust to the bench to be professional enough to leave the excluded evidence out of consideration when it is considering its verdict.

Giving reasons for the decision

15.29 Where courts make rulings in relation to evidence of bad character, CJA 2003, section 110 explicitly requires them to give reasons. The Act contains no equivalent provision in relation to rulings on the admissibility of hearsay, but notwithstanding this, courts deciding hearsay applications are expected to give reasons, and in doing so, they are expected to explain why they preferred the arguments of one side to those of the other. In *Boulton*,[37] where a trial judge had given minimal reasons for allowing the prosecution to produce hearsay evidence under section 116 of the CJA 2003 the Court of Appeal said (at [8]):

> It is unfortunate that the judge did not set out the reasons for reaching his conclusion other than by what appears to be an acceptance of (or at least some of) the submissions made by the respondent. This kind of decision is a particularly difficult one and may well lead to an appeal. The fuller the reasons which a trial judge can give for reaching the conclusions, the easier it is for this court to re-examine the issue both at the leave stage and at any full hearing.

15.30 In *Musone*,[38] the Court of Appeal said that it was in order for the judge, confronted with the need to make a ruling 'on the hoof', to make it then and there and give his reasons later. They said (at [30]):

> The judge sensibly, if we may say so, gave his reasons for his conclusions in admitting the evidence the day following the argument. It is important that the judge should give him-

[36] *F v Chief Constable of Kent* [1982] Crim LR 682; *Vel v Chief Constable of North Wales* (1987) 151 JP 510; *Halawa v. Federation Against Copyright Theft* [1995] 1 Cr App R 21. See generally, *Blackstone*, n 1 above, § F1.35. Where the disputed evidence is a confession the magistrates are required to hold a 'trial within the trial': *R v Liverpool Juvenile Court, ex p R* [1988] QB 1.

[37] [2007] EWCA Crim 942.

[38] [2007] EWCA Crim 1237, [2007] 1 WLR 2467.

self the opportunity clearly to identify the reasons by which he reached his conclusion as to admissibility. Maintaining the impetus of a trial will often prevent those reasons being given until after a decision is announced. So long as it is plain that the reasoning drove the judge to a particular conclusion and not vice versa, we commend that approach.

Enhanced status of a witness's previous statements

15.31 As was explained in Chapter 12, the CJA 2003 has made a number of important changes in the law relating to the previous statements of a witness who gives evidence at trial. Section 139 expands the range of cases where a witness may refresh his memory from 'a document made or verified by him at an earlier time'. Section 120 reformulates, in more expansive terms, the exceptions to the 'rule against narrative'.[39] Thirdly, sections 119 and 120 have radically changed the evidential status of the previous statements (including memory-refreshing documents) of witnesses who testify at trial; insofar as a witness's previous statements are admissible, they are all now, in law, evidence of the facts contained in them, and not just something which potentially affects the weight the tribunal of fact will put upon the witness's oral testimony.

15.32 From these new rules, a number of practical issues arise for advocates. First, if a the party calling a witness wishes to take advantage of the new and more relaxed rule about using memory-refreshing documents, he must remember to ask him, as required by section 139(1), whether 'the document records his recollection of the matter at [the time that it was written]', and whether 'his recollection of the matter is likely to have been significantly better at that time than it is at the time of his oral evidence'.[40] Secondly, if the party calling a witness wishes to take advantage of any of the exceptions to the 'rule against narrative' set out in section 120(4), he must remember to ask the witness whether he made the statement and, if so, whether 'to the best of his belief it states the truth'. Thirdly, if the party calling a witness wishes to invoke the exception to the rule against narrative set out in section 120(6), 'that the statement was made by the witness when the matters stated were fresh in his memory but he does not remember them, and cannot reasonably be expected to remember them, well enough to give oral evidence of them in the proceedings', he must remember to question the witness so as to establish these conditions.

15.33 The new rules also have practical implications for judges (and, to some extent, for magistrates and their legal advisers too). Judges, when directing juries,

[39] See § 12.20 *et seq* above.
[40] See § 12.16 above.

should remind them where necessary that the previous statement of a witness is evidence on which they are entitled to act, even in preference to the witness's oral evidence, if they are convinced that it is the earlier statement that contains the truth; and at summary trial, magistrates need to bear this point in mind as well. Where a prosecution witness has retracted his earlier evidence at the trial, the prosecution will be the potential beneficiaries of this new rule.[41] But where a defence witness has changed his tune, or failed to come up to proof, the defence are entitled to the benefit of it as well.[42] If judges at jury trials are tempted to give the jury a copy of the previous statement of a witness to read when they retire to consider their verdict, they must remember to look at section 122 before they do so.[43]

Stopping the case where the evidence is unconvincing

15.34 In jury trials, the basic rule is that the credibility or otherwise of the evidence is a matter for the jury, not the judge. The judge may rule a piece of evidence inadmissible on legal grounds but not because he or she does not believe it. Similarly, the judge may stop a case where the prosecution has failed to produce any admissible evidence to prove a key element of the offence; but if it has, the judge may not stop the case because he thinks the evidence is unconvincing.[44]

15.35 To this judge-made rule there are two judge-made exceptions: one in respect of eye-witness identification evidence on which the judge believes it would not be safe to convict,[45] and another in respect of confessions made by persons suffering from mental handicap.[46] If the case against the defendant consists entirely (or almost entirely) of evidence of one or other of these types, the judge at a jury trial is expected to stop the case.

15.36 In the Law Commission's view, one of the flaws with the common law approach to hearsay was that, where hearsay was (exceptionally) admitted, there were no formal limits to the weight the tribunal of fact could give to it. As hearsay is another form of evidence which can be very weak, they recommended that a further case should be added to the judge-made list of situations where the judge can stop the trial: where all or most of the evidence against the defendant consists of hearsay which the trial judge considers to be unconvincing.[47] To this end, a long

[41] As in *Joyce and Joyce* [2005] EWCA Crim 1785 [**page 278 below**]; see 12.37 above.

[42] As in *Croft* [2007] EWCA Crim 30.

[43] See §§ 12.42–12.44 above.

[44] *Galbraith* [1981] 1 WLR 1039.

[45] *Turnbull* [1977] QB 224.

[46] *MacKenzie* (1992) 96 Cr App R 98.

[47] Law Commission, *Evidence in Criminal Proceedings: Hearsay and Related Topics* (Report No 245, Cm 3670, June 1997) §§ 11.26–11.32.

and complex clause was included in the Draft Bill appended to their Report, which eventually found its way into the CJA 2003 as section 125. This is as follows:

(1) If on a defendant's trial before a judge and jury for an offence the court is satisfied at any time after the close of the case for the prosecution that—

(a) the case against the defendant is based wholly or partly on a statement not made in oral evidence in the proceedings, and
(b) the evidence provided by the statement is so unconvincing that, considering its importance to the case against the defendant, his conviction of the offence would be unsafe,

the court must either direct the jury to acquit the defendant of the offence or, if it considers that there ought to be a retrial, discharge the jury.

(2) Where—

(a) a jury is directed under subsection (1) to acquit a defendant of an offence, and
(b) the circumstances are such that, apart from this subsection, the defendant could if acquitted of that offence be found guilty of another offence,

the defendant may not be found guilty of that other offence if the court is satisfied as mentioned in subsection (1) in respect of it.

(3) If—

(a) a jury is required to determine under section 4A(2) of the Criminal Procedure (Insanity) Act 1964 (c. 84) whether a person charged on an indictment with an offence did the act or made the omission charged, and
(b) the court is satisfied as mentioned in subsection (1) above at any time after the close of the case for the prosecution that—

(i) the case against the defendant is based wholly or partly on a statement not made in oral evidence in the proceedings, and
(ii) the evidence provided by the statement is so unconvincing that, considering its importance to the case against the person, a finding that he did the act or made the omission would be unsafe,

the court must either direct the jury to acquit the defendant of the offence or, if it considers that there ought to be a rehearing, discharge the jury.

(4) This section does not prejudice any other power a court may have to direct a jury to acquit a person of an offence or to discharge a jury.

15.37 This new statutory rule is narrower than the judge-made rules it imitates, in that it is limited to proceedings in the Crown Court and jury trials. The judge-made duty to stop a case that turns on weak and uncorroborated identification evidence is equally applicable to summary trials conducted in the magistrates' courts, and so too, presumably, is the equivalent rule in relation to uncorroborated confessions by persons who are mentally handicapped. But magistrates confronted with a case where the entire prosecution evidence consisted of unconvincing hearsay would, one hopes, have the common sense and experience not to be convinced by it.

15.38 In *Joyce and Joyce*[48] the defence argued that, where the prosecution case consisted entirely of witness statements which the prosecution witnesses had then retracted at the trial, the judge should have invoked CJA 2003, section 125 to stop the case. But the Court of Appeal was not prepared to accept this. Where (as in that case) the witness statements were clear and had a ring of truth about them, there was no reason why the jury should not be invited to convict on them, even though at trial the witnesses now disavowed their contents.

Directing juries

15.39 Following the CJA 2003, the Judicial Studies Board issued a new specimen direction (No 35) for the help of judges who have to direct juries on how to approach hearsay evidence. Unsurprisingly, it encourages judges to remind the jury that evidence at criminal trials is normally given orally, and to advise the jury that, when deciding on the weight to give the hearsay evidence, they should remember that they have not seen and heard the witness in the flesh, the statement was not made on oath, and the evidence was not tested in cross-examination. And it tells them to consider hearsay in the light of the rest of the evidence (including the discrepancies between the hearsay and the oral evidence, if there are any).

15.40 The Judicial Studies Board also issued new specimen directions to guide judges when directing juries about the previous inconsistent statements of hostile witnesses (No 28), witnesses who have not been treated as hostile (No 29) and about previous consistent statements (No 31). In line with the change in the evidential status of previous statements brought about by CJA 2003, sections 119 and 120, all these specimen directions encourage judges to tell juries that the previous statement is, in principle, something which 'you may take into account when considering your verdict'.

15.41 In *AA*[49] the Court of Appeal added that, when directing a jury about how to treat a witness's previous consistent statement, the judge should also tell them that 'In deciding what weight the statement should bear, you should have in mind that it comes from the same person who now makes the complaint in the witness box and not from some independent source'.

15.42 The Judicial Studies Board Specimen Directions are reproduced in Appendix III.

[48] [2005] EWCA Crim 1785; see § 12.37 above and [**page 278 below**].
[49] [2007] EWCA Crim 1779.

Appendix I

Criminal Justice Act 2003, Sections 114–141

The Criminal Justice (Evidence) (Northern Ireland) Order 2004, SI 2004/1501 (NI 10) contains provisions which are virtually identical. For the benefit of Northern Ireland users, the numbers of the equivalent articles of the Order are set out in italics after the section numbers of the CJA 2003 which they reproduce.

Chapter 2 Hearsay Evidence

114 *(NI art 18)* Admissibility of hearsay evidence

(1) In criminal proceedings a statement not made in oral evidence in the proceedings is admissible as evidence of any matter stated if, but only if—

(a) any provision of this Chapter or any other statutory provision makes it admissible,
(b) any rule of law preserved by section 118 makes it admissible,
(c) all parties to the proceedings agree to it being admissible, or
(d) the court is satisfied that it is in the interests of justice for it to be admissible.

(2) In deciding whether a statement not made in oral evidence should be admitted under subsection (1)(d), the court must have regard to the following factors (and to any others it considers relevant)—

(a) how much probative value the statement has (assuming it to be true) in relation to a matter in issue in the proceedings, or how valuable it is for the understanding of other evidence in the case;
(b) what other evidence has been, or can be, given on the matter or evidence mentioned in paragraph (a);
(c) how important the matter or evidence mentioned in paragraph (a) is in the context of the case as a whole;
(d) the circumstances in which the statement was made;
(e) how reliable the maker of the statement appears to be;
(f) how reliable the evidence of the making of the statement appears to be;

(g) whether oral evidence of the matter stated can be given and, if not, why it cannot;
(h) the amount of difficulty involved in challenging the statement;
(i) the extent to which that difficulty would be likely to prejudice the party facing it.

(3) Nothing in this Chapter affects the exclusion of evidence of a statement on grounds other than the fact that it is a statement not made in oral evidence in the proceedings.

115 *(NI art 19)* **Statements and matters stated**

(1) In this Chapter references to a statement or to a matter stated are to be read as follows.

(2) A statement is any representation of fact or opinion made by a person by whatever means; and it includes a representation made in a sketch, photofit or other pictorial form.

(3) A matter stated is one to which this Chapter applies if (and only if) the purpose, or one of the purposes, of the person making the statement appears to the court to have been—

(a) to cause another person to believe the matter, or
(b) to cause another person to act or a machine to operate on the basis that the matter is as stated.

116 *(NI art 20)* **Cases where a witness is unavailable**

(1) In criminal proceedings a statement not made in oral evidence in the proceedings is admissible as evidence of any matter stated if—

(a) oral evidence given in the proceedings by the person who made the statement would be admissible as evidence of that matter,
(b) the person who made the statement (the relevant person) is identified to the court's satisfaction, and
(c) any of the five conditions mentioned in subsection (2) is satisfied.

(2) The conditions are—

(a) that the relevant person is dead;
(b) that the relevant person is unfit to be a witness because of his bodily or mental condition;
(c) that the relevant person is outside the United Kingdom and it is not reasonably practicable to secure his attendance;
(d) that the relevant person cannot be found although such steps as it is reasonably practicable to take to find him have been taken;
(e) that through fear the relevant person does not give (or does not continue to give) oral evidence in the proceedings, either at all or in connection with the

subject matter of the statement, and the court gives leave for the statement to be given in evidence.

(3) For the purposes of subsection (2)(e) 'fear' is to be widely construed and (for example) includes fear of the death or injury of another person or of financial loss.

(4) Leave may be given under subsection (2)(e) only if the court considers that the statement ought to be admitted in the interests of justice, having regard—

(a) to the statement's contents,
(b) to any risk that its admission or exclusion will result in unfairness to any party to the proceedings (and in particular to how difficult it will be to challenge the statement if the relevant person does not give oral evidence),
(c) in appropriate cases, to the fact that a direction under section 19 of the Youth Justice and Criminal Evidence Act 1999 (c. 23) (special measures for the giving of evidence by fearful witnesses etc) could be made in relation to the relevant person, and
(d) to any other relevant circumstances.

(5) A condition set out in any paragraph of subsection (2) which is in fact satisfied is to be treated as not satisfied if it is shown that the circumstances described in that paragraph are caused—

(a) by the person in support of whose case it is sought to give the statement in evidence, or
(b) by a person acting on his behalf,

in order to prevent the relevant person giving oral evidence in the proceedings (whether at all or in connection with the subject matter of the statement).

117 *(NI art 21)* Business and other documents

(1) In criminal proceedings a statement contained in a document is admissible as evidence of any matter stated if—

(a) oral evidence given in the proceedings would be admissible as evidence of that matter,
(b) the requirements of subsection (2) are satisfied, and
(c) the requirements of subsection (5) are satisfied, in a case where subsection (4) requires them to be.

(2) The requirements of this subsection are satisfied if—

(a) the document or the part containing the statement was created or received by a person in the course of a trade, business, profession or other occupation, or as the holder of a paid or unpaid office,

(b) the person who supplied the information contained in the statement (the relevant person) had or may reasonably be supposed to have had personal knowledge of the matters dealt with, and
(c) each person (if any) through whom the information was supplied from the relevant person to the person mentioned in paragraph (a) received the information in the course of a trade, business, profession or other occupation, or as the holder of a paid or unpaid office.

(3) The persons mentioned in paragraphs (a) and (b) of subsection (2) may be the same person.

(4) The additional requirements of subsection (5) must be satisfied if the statement—

(a) was prepared for the purposes of pending or contemplated criminal proceedings, or for a criminal investigation, but
(b) was not obtained pursuant to a request under section 7 of the Crime (International Co-operation) Act 2003 (c. 32) or an order under paragraph 6 of Schedule 13 to the Criminal Justice Act 1988 (c. 33) (which relate to overseas evidence).

(5) The requirements of this subsection are satisfied if—

(a) any of the five conditions mentioned in section 116(2) is satisfied (absence of relevant person etc), or
(b) the relevant person cannot reasonably be expected to have any recollection of the matters dealt with in the statement (having regard to the length of time since he supplied the information and all other circumstances).

(6) A statement is not admissible under this section if the court makes a direction to that effect under subsection (7).

(7) The court may make a direction under this subsection if satisfied that the statement's reliability as evidence for the purpose for which it is tendered is doubtful in view of—

(a) its contents,
(b) the source of the information contained in it,
(c) the way in which or the circumstances in which the information was supplied or received, or
(d) the way in which or the circumstances in which the document concerned was created or received.

118 *(NI art 22)* Preservation of certain common law categories of admissibility

(1) The following rules of law are preserved.

Public information etc 1 Any rule of law under which in criminal proceedings—

(a) published works dealing with matters of a public nature (such as histories, scientific works, dictionaries and maps) are admissible as evidence of facts of a public nature stated in them,
(b) public documents (such as public registers, and returns made under public authority with respect to matters of public interest) are admissible as evidence of facts stated in them,
(c) records (such as the records of certain courts, treaties, Crown grants, pardons and commissions) are admissible as evidence of facts stated in them, or
(d) evidence relating to a person's age or date or place of birth may be given by a person without personal knowledge of the matter.

Reputation as to character 2 Any rule of law under which in criminal proceedings evidence of a person's reputation is admissible for the purpose of proving his good or bad character.

Note The rule is preserved only so far as it allows the court to treat such evidence as proving the matter concerned.

Reputation or family tradition 3 Any rule of law under which in criminal proceedings evidence of reputation or family tradition is admissible for the purpose of proving or disproving—

(a) pedigree or the existence of a marriage,
(b) the existence of any public or general right, or
(c) the identity of any person or thing.

Note The rule is preserved only so far as it allows the court to treat such evidence as proving or disproving the matter concerned.

Res gestae 4 Any rule of law under which in criminal proceedings a statement is admissible as evidence of any matter stated if—

(a) the statement was made by a person so emotionally overpowered by an event that the possibility of concoction or distortion can be disregarded,
(b) the statement accompanied an act which can be properly evaluated as evidence only if considered in conjunction with the statement, or
(c) the statement relates to a physical sensation or a mental state (such as intention or emotion).

Confessions etc 5 Any rule of law relating to the admissibility of confessions or mixed statements in criminal proceedings.

Admissions by agents etc 6 Any rule of law under which in criminal proceeding.

(a) an admission made by an agent of a defendant is admissible against the defendant as evidence of any matter stated, or

(b) a statement made by a person to whom a defendant refers a person for information is admissible against the defendant as evidence of any matter stated.

Common enterprise 7 Any rule of law under which in criminal proceedings a statement made by a party to a common enterprise is admissible against another party to the enterprise as evidence of any matter stated.

Expert evidence 8 Any rule of law under which in criminal proceedings an expert witness may draw on the body of expertise relevant to his field.

(2) With the exception of the rules preserved by this section, the common law rules governing the admissibility of hearsay evidence in criminal proceedings are abolished.

119 *(NI art 23)* **Inconsistent statements**

(1) If in criminal proceedings a person gives oral evidence and—

(a) he admits making a previous inconsistent statement, or
(b) a previous inconsistent statement made by him is proved by virtue of section 3, 4 or 5 of the Criminal Procedure Act 1865 (c. 18),

the statement is admissible as evidence of any matter stated of which oral evidence by him would be admissible.

(2) If in criminal proceedings evidence of an inconsistent statement by any person is given under section 124(2)(c), the statement is admissible as evidence of any matter stated in it of which oral evidence by that person would be admissible.

120 *(NI arte 24)* **Other previous statements of witnesses**

(1) This section applies where a person (the witness) is called to give evidence in criminal proceedings.

(2) If a previous statement by the witness is admitted as evidence to rebut a suggestion that his oral evidence has been fabricated, that statement is admissible as evidence of any matter stated of which oral evidence by the witness would be admissible.

(3) A statement made by the witness in a document—

(a) which is used by him to refresh his memory while giving evidence,
(b) on which he is cross-examined, and
(c) which as a consequence is received in evidence in the proceedings,

is admissible as evidence of any matter stated of which oral evidence by him would be admissible.

(4) A previous statement by the witness is admissible as evidence of any matter stated of which oral evidence by him would be admissible, if—

(a) any of the following three conditions is satisfied, and
(b) while giving evidence the witness indicates that to the best of his belief he made the statement, and that to the best of his belief it states the truth.

(5) The first condition is that the statement identifies or describes a person, object or place.

(6) The second condition is that the statement was made by the witness when the matters stated were fresh in his memory but he does not remember them, and cannot reasonably be expected to remember them, well enough to give oral evidence of them in the proceedings.

(7) The third condition is that—

(a) the witness claims to be a person against whom an offence has been committed,
(b) the offence is one to which the proceedings relate,
(c) the statement consists of a complaint made by the witness (whether to a person in authority or not) about conduct which would, if proved, constitute the offence or part of the offence,
(d) the complaint was made as soon as could reasonably be expected after the alleged conduct,
(e) the complaint was not made as a result of a threat or a promise, and
(f) before the statement is adduced the witness gives oral evidence in connection with its subject matter.

(8) For the purposes of subsection (7) the fact that the complaint was elicited (for example, by a leading question) is irrelevant unless a threat or a promise was involved.

121 *(NI art 25)* Additional requirement for admissibility of multiple hearsay

(1) A hearsay statement is not admissible to prove the fact that an earlier hearsay statement was made unless—

(a) either of the statements is admissible under section 117, 119 or 120,
(b) all parties to the proceedings so agree, or
(c) the court is satisfied that the value of the evidence in question, taking into account how reliable the statements appear to be, is so high that the interests of justice require the later statement to be admissible for that purpose.

(2) In this section 'hearsay statement' means a statement, not made in oral evidence, that is relied on as evidence of a matter stated in it.

122 *(NI arti 26)* **Documents produced as exhibits**

(1) This section applies if on a trial before a judge and jury for an offence—

(a) a statement made in a document is admitted in evidence under section 119 or 120, and
(b) the document or a copy of it is produced as an exhibit.

(2) The exhibit must not accompany the jury when they retire to consider their verdict unless—

(a) the court considers it appropriate, or
(b) all the parties to the proceedings agree that it should accompany the jury.

123 *(NI art 27)* **Capability to make statement**

(1) Nothing in section 116, 119 or 120 makes a statement admissible as evidence if it was made by a person who did not have the required capability at the time when he made the statement.

(2) Nothing in section 117 makes a statement admissible as evidence if any person who, in order for the requirements of section 117(2) to be satisfied, must at any time have supplied or received the information concerned or created or received the document or part concerned—

(a) did not have the required capability at that time, or
(b) cannot be identified but cannot reasonably be assumed to have had the required capability at that time.

(3) For the purposes of this section a person has the required capability if he is capable of—

(a) understanding questions put to him about the matters stated, and
(b) giving answers to such questions which can be understood.

(4) Where by reason of this section there is an issue as to whether a person had the required capability when he made a statement—

(a) proceedings held for the determination of the issue must take place in the absence of the jury (if there is one);
(b) in determining the issue the court may receive expert evidence and evidence from any person to whom the statement in question was made;
(c) the burden of proof on the issue lies on the party seeking to adduce the statement, and the standard of proof is the balance of probabilities.

124 *(NI art 28)* Credibility

(1) This section applies if in criminal proceedings—

(a) a statement not made in oral evidence in the proceedings is admitted as evidence of a matter stated, and
(b) the maker of the statement does not give oral evidence in connection with the subject matter of the statement.

(2) In such a case—

(a) any evidence which (if he had given such evidence) would have been admissible as relevant to his credibility as a witness is so admissible in the proceedings;
(b) evidence may with the court's leave be given of any matter which (if he had given such evidence) could have been put to him in cross-examination as relevant to his credibility as a witness but of which evidence could not have been adduced by the cross-examining party;
(c) evidence tending to prove that he made (at whatever time) any other statement inconsistent with the statement admitted as evidence is admissible for the purpose of showing that he contradicted himself.

(3) If as a result of evidence admitted under this section an allegation is made against the maker of a statement, the court may permit a party to lead additional evidence of such description as the court may specify for the purposes of denying or answering the allegation.

(4) In the case of a statement in a document which is admitted as evidence under section 117 each person who, in order for the statement to be admissible, must have supplied or received the information concerned or created or received the document or part concerned is to be treated as the maker of the statement for the purposes of subsections (1) to (3) above.

125 *(NI art 29)* Stopping the case where evidence is unconvincing

(1) If on a defendant's trial before a judge and jury for an offence the court is satisfied at any time after the close of the case for the prosecution that—

(a) the case against the defendant is based wholly or partly on a statement not made in oral evidence in the proceedings, and
(b) the evidence provided by the statement is so unconvincing that, considering its importance to the case against the defendant, his conviction of the offence would be unsafe,

the court must either direct the jury to acquit the defendant of the offence or, if it considers that there ought to be a retrial, discharge the jury.

(2) Where—

(a) a jury is directed under subsection (1) to acquit a defendant of an offence, and
(b) the circumstances are such that, apart from this subsection, the defendant could if acquitted of that offence be found guilty of another offence,

the defendant may not be found guilty of that other offence if the court is satisfied as mentioned in subsection (1) in respect of it.

(3) If—

(a) a jury is required to determine under section 4A(2) of the Criminal Procedure (Insanity) Act 1964 (c. 84) whether a person charged on an indictment with an offence did the act or made the omission charged, and
(b) the court is satisfied as mentioned in subsection (1) above at any time after the close of the case for the prosecution that—
   (i) the case against the defendant is based wholly or partly on a statement not made in oral evidence in the proceedings, and
   (ii) the evidence provided by the statement is so unconvincing that, considering its importance to the case against the person, a finding that he did the act or made the omission would be unsafe,

the court must either direct the jury to acquit the defendant of the offence or, if it considers that there ought to be a rehearing, discharge the jury.

(4) This section does not prejudice any other power a court may have to direct a jury to acquit a person of an offence or to discharge a jury.

126 *(NI art 30)* Court's general discretion to exclude evidence

(1) In criminal proceedings the court may refuse to admit a statement as evidence of a matter stated if—

(a) the statement was made otherwise than in oral evidence in the proceedings, and
(b) the court is satisfied that the case for excluding the statement, taking account of the danger that to admit it would result in undue waste of time, substantially outweighs the case for admitting it, taking account of the value of the evidence.

(2) Nothing in this Chapter prejudices—

(a) any power of a court to exclude evidence under section 78 of the Police and Criminal Evidence Act 1984 (c. 60) (exclusion of unfair evidence), or
(b) any other power of a court to exclude evidence at its discretion (whether by preventing questions from being put or otherwise).

127 *(NI art 31)* Expert evidence: preparatory work

(1) This section applies if—

(a) a statement has been prepared for the purposes of criminal proceedings,
(b) the person who prepared the statement had or may reasonably be supposed to have had personal knowledge of the matters stated,
(c) notice is given under the appropriate rules that another person (the expert) will in evidence given in the proceedings orally or under section 9 of the Criminal Justice Act 1967 (c. 80) base an opinion or inference on the statement, and
(d) the notice gives the name of the person who prepared the statement and the nature of the matters stated.

(2) In evidence given in the proceedings the expert may base an opinion or inference on the statement.

(3) If evidence based on the statement is given under subsection (2) the statement is to be treated as evidence of what it states.

(4) This section does not apply if the court, on an application by a party to the proceedings, orders that it is not in the interests of justice that it should apply.

(5) The matters to be considered by the court in deciding whether to make an order under subsection (4) include—

(a) the expense of calling as a witness the person who prepared the statement;
(b) whether relevant evidence could be given by that person which could not be given by the expert;
(c) whether that person can reasonably be expected to remember the matters stated well enough to give oral evidence of them.

(6) Subsections (1) to (5) apply to a statement prepared for the purposes of a criminal investigation as they apply to a statement prepared for the purposes of criminal proceedings, and in such a case references to the proceedings are to criminal proceedings arising from the investigation.

(7) The appropriate rules are rules made—

(a) under section 81 of the Police and Criminal Evidence Act 1984 (advance notice of expert evidence in Crown Court), or
(b) under section 144 of the Magistrates' Courts Act 1980 (c. 43) by virtue of section 20(3) of the Criminal Procedure and Investigations Act 1996 (c. 25) (advance notice of expert evidence in magistrates' courts).

128 *(NI art 32)* Confessions

(1) In the Police and Criminal Evidence Act 1984 (c. 60) the following section is inserted after section 76—*(Police and Criminal Evidence (Northern Ireland) Order 1989, SI 1989/1341 (NI 12) section 74)*

'76A *(74A)* Confessions may be given in evidence for co-accused

(1) In any proceedings a confession made by an accused person may be given in evidence for another person charged in the same proceedings (a co-accused) in so far as it is relevant to any matter in issue in the proceedings and is not excluded by the court in pursuance of this section.

(2) If, in any proceedings where a co-accused proposes to give in evidence a confession made by an accused person, it is represented to the court that the confession was or may have been obtained—

(a) by oppression of the person who made it; or
(b) in consequence of anything said or done which was likely, in the circumstances existing at the time, to render unreliable any confession which might be made by him in consequence thereof,

the court shall not allow the confession to be given in evidence for the co-accused except in so far as it is proved to the court on the balance of probabilities that the confession (notwithstanding that it may be true) was not so obtained.

(3) Before allowing a confession made by an accused person to be given in evidence for a co-accused in any proceedings, the court may of its own motion require the fact that the confession was not obtained as mentioned in subsection (2) above to be proved in the proceedings on the balance of probabilities.

(4) The fact that a confession is wholly or partly excluded in pursuance of this section shall not affect the admissibility in evidence—

(a) of any facts discovered as a result of the confession; or
(b) where the confession is relevant as showing that the accused speaks, writes or expresses himself in a particular way, of so much of the confession as is necessary to show that he does so.

(5) Evidence that a fact to which this subsection applies was discovered as a result of a statement made by an accused person shall not be admissible unless evidence of how it was discovered is given by him or on his behalf

(6) Subsection (5) above applies—

(a) to any fact discovered as a result of a confession which is wholly excluded in pursuance of this section; and
(b) to any fact discovered as a result of a confession which is partly so excluded, if the fact is discovered as a result of the excluded part of the confession.

(7) In this section 'oppression' includes torture, inhuman or degrading treatment, and the use or threat of violence (whether or not amounting to torture).'

(2) Subject to subsection (1), nothing in this Chapter makes a confession by a defendant admissible if it would not be admissible under section 76 of the Police and Criminal Evidence Act 1984 (c. 60).

(3) In subsection (2) 'confession' has the meaning given by section 82 of that Act.

129 *(NI art 33)* Representations other than by a person

(1) Where a representation of any fact—

(a) is made otherwise than by a person, but
(b) depends for its accuracy on information supplied (directly or indirectly) by a person,

the representation is not admissible in criminal proceedings as evidence of the fact unless it is proved that the information was accurate.

(2) Subsection (1) does not affect the operation of the presumption that a mechanical device has been properly set or calibrated.

130 Depositions

In Schedule 3 to the Crime and Disorder Act 1998 (c. 37), sub-paragraph (4) of paragraph 5 is omitted (power of the court to overrule an objection to a deposition being read as evidence by virtue of that paragraph).

131 *(NI art 34)* Evidence at retrial

For paragraphs 1 and 1A of Schedule 2 to the Criminal Appeal Act 1968 (c. 19) (oral evidence and use of transcripts etc at retrials under that Act) there is substituted—

'1 Evidence

(1) Evidence given at a retrial must be given orally if it was given orally at the original trial, unless—

(a) all the parties to the retrial agree otherwise;
(b) section 116 of the Criminal Justice Act 2003 applies (admissibility of hearsay evidence where a witness is unavailable); or
(c) the witness is unavailable to give evidence, otherwise than as mentioned in subsection (2) of that section, and section 114(1)(d) of that Act applies (admission of hearsay evidence under residual discretion).

(2) Paragraph 5 of Schedule 3 to the Crime and Disorder Act 1998 (use of depositions) does not apply at a retrial to a deposition read as evidence at the original trial.'

132 *(NI art 35)* Rules of court

(1) Rules of court may make such provision as appears to the appropriate authority to be necessary or expedient for the purposes of this Chapter; and the appropriate authority is the authority entitled to make the rules.

(2) The rules may make provision about the procedure to be followed and other conditions to be fulfilled by a party proposing to tender a statement in evidence under any provision of this Chapter.

(3) The rules may require a party proposing to tender the evidence to serve on each party to the proceedings such notice, and such particulars of or relating to the evidence, as may be prescribed.

(4) The rules may provide that the evidence is to be treated as admissible by agreement of the parties if—

(a) a notice has been served in accordance with provision made under subsection (3), and
(b) no counter-notice in the prescribed form objecting to the admission of the evidence has been served by a party.

(5) If a party proposing to tender evidence fails to comply with a prescribed requirement applicable to it—

(a) the evidence is not admissible except with the court's leave;
(b) where leave is given the court or jury may draw such inferences from the failure as appear proper;
(c) the failure may be taken into account by the court in considering the exercise of its powers with respect to costs.

(6) In considering whether or how to exercise any of its powers under subsection (5) the court shall have regard to whether there is any justification for the failure to comply with the requirement.

(7) A person shall not be convicted of an offence solely on an inference drawn under subsection (5)(b).

(8) Rules under this section may—

(a) limit the application of any provision of the rules to prescribed circumstances;
(b) subject any provision of the rules to prescribed exceptions;
(c) make different provision for different cases or circumstances.

(9) Nothing in this section prejudices the generality of any enactment conferring power to make rules of court; and no particular provision of this section prejudices any general provision of it.

(10) In this section 'prescribed' means prescribed by rules of court.

133 *(NI art 36)* Proof of statements in documents

Where a statement in a document is admissible as evidence in criminal proceedings, the statement may be proved by producing either—

(a) the document, or
(b) (whether or not the document exists) a copy of the document or of the material part of it,

authenticated in whatever way the court may approve.

134 *(NI art 37)* Interpretation of Chapter 2

(1) In this Chapter—

'copy', in relation to a document, means anything on to which information recorded in the document has been copied, by whatever means and whether directly or indirectly;

'criminal proceedings' means criminal proceedings in relation to which the strict rules of evidence apply;

'defendant', in relation to criminal proceedings, means a person charged with an offence in those proceedings;

'document' means anything in which information of any description is recorded;

'oral evidence' includes evidence which, by reason of any disability, disorder or other impairment, a person called as a witness gives in writing or by signs or by way of any device;

'statutory provision' means any provision contained in, or in an instrument made under, this or any other Act, including any Act passed after this Act.

(2) Section 115 (statements and matters stated) contains other general interpretative provisions.

(3) Where a defendant is charged with two or more offences in the same criminal proceedings, this Chapter has effect as if each offence were charged in separate proceedings.

135 Armed forces

Schedule 7 (hearsay evidence: armed forces) has effect.

136 Repeals etc

In the Criminal Justice Act 1988 (c. 33), the following provisions (which are to some extent superseded by provisions of this Chapter) are repealed—

(a) Part 2 and Schedule 2 (which relate to documentary evidence);
(b) in Schedule 13, paragraphs 2 to 5 (which relate to documentary evidence in service courts etc).

(NI art 38: In the Criminal Justice (Evidence, etc.) (Northern Ireland) Order 1988, SI 1988/1847 (NI 17) the following provisions (which relate to documentary evidence and are to some extent superseded by provisions of this Part) are repealed: (a) Part II; (b) Sch 1.)

Chapter 3 Miscellaneous and Supplemental

137 *(NI art 39)* Evidence by video recording

(1) This section applies where—

(a) a person is called as a witness in proceedings for an offence triable only on indictment, or for a prescribed offence triable either way,
(b) the person claims to have witnessed (whether visually or in any other way)—

  (i) events alleged by the prosecution to include conduct constituting the offence or part of the offence, or
  (ii) events closely connected with such events,

(c) he has previously given an account of the events in question (whether in response to questions asked or otherwise),
(d) the account was given at a time when those events were fresh in the person's memory (or would have been, assuming the truth of the claim mentioned in paragraph (b)),
(e) a video recording was made of the account,
(f) the court has made a direction that the recording should be admitted as evidence in chief of the witness, and the direction has not been rescinded, and
(g) the recording is played in the proceedings in accordance with the direction.

(2) If, or to the extent that, the witness in his oral evidence in the proceedings asserts the truth of the statements made by him in the recorded account, they shall be treated as if made by him in that evidence.

(3) A direction under subsection (1)(f)—

(a) may not be made in relation to a recorded account given by the defendant;
(b) may be made only if it appears to the court that—

  (i) the witness's recollection of the events in question is likely to have been significantly better when he gave the recorded account than it will be when he gives oral evidence in the proceedings, and
  (ii) it is in the interests of justice for the recording to be admitted, having regard in particular to the matters mentioned in subsection (4).

(4) Those matters are—

(a) the interval between the time of the events in question and the time when the recorded account was made;
(b) any other factors that might affect the reliability of what the witness said in that account;
(c) the quality of the recording;
(d) any views of the witness as to whether his evidence in chief should be given orally or by means of the recording.

(5) For the purposes of subsection (2) it does not matter if the statements in the recorded account were not made on oath.

(6) In this section 'prescribed' means of a description specified in an order made by the Secretary of State.

138 *(NI art 40)* Video evidence: further provisions

(1) Where a video recording is admitted under section 137, the witness may not give evidence in chief otherwise than by means of the recording as to any matter which, in the opinion of the court, has been dealt with adequately in the recorded account.

(2) The reference in subsection (1)(f) of section 137 to the admission of a recording includes a reference to the admission of part of the recording; and references in that section and this one to the video recording or to the witness's recorded account shall, where appropriate, be read accordingly.

(3) In considering whether any part of a recording should be not admitted under section 137, the court must consider—

(a) whether admitting that part would carry a risk of prejudice to the defendant, and
(b) if so, whether the interests of justice nevertheless require it to be admitted in view of the desirability of showing the whole, or substantially the whole, of the recorded interview.

(4) A court may not make a direction under section 137(1)(f) in relation to any proceedings unless—

(a) the Secretary of State has notified the court that arrangements can be made, in the area in which it appears to the court that the proceedings will take place, for implementing directions under that section, and
(b) the notice has not been withdrawn.

(5) Nothing in section 137 affects the admissibility of any video recording which would be admissible apart from that section.

139 *(NI art 41)* Use of documents to refresh memory

(1) A person giving oral evidence in criminal proceedings about any matter may, at any stage in the course of doing so, refresh his memory of it from a document made or verified by him at an earlier time if—

(a) he states in his oral evidence that the document records his recollection of the matter at that earlier time, and
(b) his recollection of the matter is likely to have been significantly better at that time than it is at the time of his oral evidence.

(2) Where—

(a) a person giving oral evidence in criminal proceedings about any matter has previously given an oral account, of which a sound recording was made, and he states in that evidence that the account represented his recollection of the matter at that time,
(b) his recollection of the matter is likely to have been significantly better at the time of the previous account than it is at the time of his oral evidence, and
(c) a transcript has been made of the sound recording,

he may, at any stage in the course of giving his evidence, refresh his memory of the matter from that transcript.

140 ***(NI art 42)*** **Interpretation of Chapter 3**

In this Chapter—

'criminal proceedings' means criminal proceedings in relation to which the strict rules of evidence apply;

'defendant', in relation to criminal proceedings, means a person charged with an offence in those proceedings;

'document' means anything in which information of any description is recorded, but not including any recording of sounds or moving images;

'oral evidence' includes evidence which, by reason of any disability, disorder or other impairment, a person called as a witness gives in writing or by signs or by way of any device;

'video recording' means any recording, on any medium, from which a moving image may by any means be produced, and includes the accompanying sound-track.

141 ***(NI art 43)*** **Saving**

No provision of this Part has effect in relation to criminal proceedings begun before the commencement of that provision.

Appendix II

Criminal Procedure Rules, Part 34

Hearsay evidence

Contents of this part

34.1 When this applies

This Part applies in a magistrates' court and in the Crown Court where a party wants to introduce evidence on one or more of the grounds set out in section 114(1)(d), section 116, section 117 and section 121 of the Criminal Justice Act 2003, and in this Part that evidence is called 'hearsay evidence'.

Section 114 of the 2003 Act provides that a statement not made in oral evidence in criminal proceedings is admissible as evidence of any matter stated only on certain conditions. This Part applies only to evidence that is admissible on one or more of the following grounds set out in the 2003 Act, namely where (a) it is in the interests of justice for it to be admissible (see section 114(1)(d)), (b) the witness is unavailable to attend (see section 116), (c) the evidence is contained in a business, or other, document (see section 117) or (d) the evidence is multiple hearsay (see section 121). The meaning of 'statements' and 'matter stated' is explained in section 115 of the 2003 Act. 'Oral evidence' is defined in section 134(1) of that Act. For the introduction of hearsay evidence in the Court of Appeal, see rule 68.20.

34.2 Notice of hearsay evidence

The party who wants to introduce hearsay evidence must give notice in the form set out in the Practice Direction to the court officer and all other parties.

34.3 When the prosecutor must give notice of hearsay evidence

The prosecutor must give notice of hearsay evidence—

(a) in a magistrates' court, at the same time as he complies or purports to comply with section 3 of the Criminal Procedure and Investigations Act 1996 (disclosure by prosecutor); or
(b) in the Crown Court, not more than 14 days after—

  (i) the committal of the defendant, or
  (ii) the consent to the preferment of a bill of indictment in relation to the case, or
  (iii) the service of a notice of transfer under section 4 of the Criminal Justice Act 1987 (serious fraud cases) or under section 53 of the Criminal Justice Act 1991 (certain cases involving children), or
  (iv) where a person is sent for trial under section 51 of the Crime and Disorder Act 1998 (indictable-only offences sent for trial), the service of copies of the documents containing the evidence on which the charge or charges are based under paragraph 1 of Schedule 3 to the 1998 Act.

34.4 When a defendant must give notice of hearsay evidence

A defendant must give notice of hearsay evidence not more than 14 days after the prosecutor has complied with or purported to comply with section 3 of the Criminal Procedure and Investigations Act 1996 (disclosure by prosecutor).

34.5 Opposing the introduction of hearsay evidence

A party who receives a notice of hearsay evidence may oppose it by giving notice within 14 days in the form set out in the Practice Direction to the court officer and all other parties.

34.6 *Revoked*

34.7 Court's power to vary requirements under this Part

The court may—

(a) dispense with the requirement to give notice of hearsay evidence;
(b) allow notice to be given in a different form, or orally; or
(c) shorten a time limit or extend it (even after it has expired).

34.8 Waiving the requirement to give a notice of hearsay evidence

A party entitled to receive a notice of hearsay evidence may waive his entitlement by so informing the court and the party who would have given the notice.

NOTICE OF INTENTION TO INTRODUCE HEARSAY EVIDENCE

Notice of intention to introduce hearsay evidence under s.114, Criminal Justice Act 2003 *(Criminal Procedure Rules, rr 34.2, 68.20(1))*	
This form must be used to give notice of intention to introduce hearsay evidence on one or more of the grounds set out in s. 114(1)(d), s. 116, s. 117 and s. 121, Criminal Justice Act 2003.	
Details of party giving notice Surname: Forename(s): Address:	State the name and address of the party giving notice of hearsay evidence. (If in custody give address where detained.)
Case Details The Court at Case Reference Number Name of Judge: Date the trial or proceedings is due to start/started: Name of prosecuting agency (if relevant): Name of defendant(s): **Charges:**	Enter the name of the Court and the case no. Give brief details of the charges to which this notice applies.
To the named recipient(s) of this notice: I give you notice of my intention to introduce hearsay evidence, details of which are set out below, in these proceedings.	

Grounds for introducing the hearsay evidence

On which of the following grounds do you intend to introduce the hearsay evidence?

(a) ☐ It is in the interests of justice for it to be admissible.

(b) ☐ The witness is unavailable to attend.

(c) ☐ The evidence is contained in a business etc. document.

(d) ☐ The evidence is multiple hearsay.

Tick as appropriate to show which of ss.114(1)(d), 116, 117 or 121 of the CJA 2003 you rely on to introduce the evidence.

Where box (a) is ticked you must specify below which of the factors set out in s. 114(2), CJA 2003 are relevant and explain how they are relevant.

Further details of grounds:

Details of hearsay evidence

The details of the hearsay evidence are as follows:

Give brief details of the evidence that you want to introduce as hearsay evidence.

A complete copy of that evidence must be attached to this notice, if it has not already been served on the other parties.

Extension of time

Are you applying for an extension of time within which to give this notice? Yes/No

If yes, state your reasons:

Signed:
Dated:

Notice of opposition to the introduction of hearsay evidence under s. 114 Criminal Justice Act 2003
(Criminal Procedure Rules, rr 34.3, 34.5, 68.20(1))

This form shall be used to give notice of opposition to the introduction of hearsay evidence, as specified in a notice of hearsay evidence given under rule 34(2).

Details of party opposing the introduction of hearsay evidence

Surname Forenames Address Date that you were given notice that hearsay evidence will be introduced in these proceedings:	State the name and address of the party giving notice of their opposition to the introduction of hearsay evidence. (If in custody give address where detained.)

Case Details

The .. .. Court at.. .. .. Case Reference Number..	Enter the name of the Court and the case no.
Name of judge:	
Date the trial or proceedings is due to start/or started:	
Name of prosecuting agency (if relevant) Name of defendant(s):	
Charges:	Give brief details of the charges to which this notice applies.

- page 1 -

Details of the hearsay evidence that you want to exclude	Give a brief description of the hearsay evidence that you want to exclude from the proceedings. Specify whether you object to all or part of that evidence.
Grounds for excluding the evidence	Set out the grounds for excluding the hearsay evidence that you object to. Any relevant skeleton argument or case law that might bear on the issue may be attached to this notice.
Extension of time Are you applying for an extension of time within which to give this notice? *YES/NO If yes, state your reasons:	*delete as appropriate
Signed: **Dated:**	

- page 2 -

Appendix III

Judicial Studies Board Specimen Directions

28. Hostile Witness

1. X was called by the [prosecution/defence] but gave evidence which did not support the [prosecution's/defence's] case. The [prosecution/defence] was therefore allowed to treat him as a 'hostile' witness—a witness who had in effect 'changed sides'—and to cross-examine him to show that he had given an account on a previous occasion which was inconsistent with the account which he gave in court. [*Identify the inconsistency.*]

2. You may take into account any inconsistency [and X's explanation for it] when considering X's reliability as a witness. It is for you to judge the extent and importance of any inconsistency. If you conclude that there is a serious conflict between the account he gave in court and his previous account, you may think that you should reject his evidence altogether and not rely on anything said by him either on the previous occasion or when giving evidence.

3. However if, after careful consideration, you are sure that you can rely on [all or part of] what he said on the previous occasion or when giving evidence, you may take it into consideration in reaching your verdict[s].

Notes

1. Under section 119 of the Criminal Justice Act 2003, the previous inconsistent statement becomes evidence of the truth of its contents. If it was made in a document which becomes an exhibit, it must not accompany the jury when they retire to consider their verdict, unless the court considers it appropriate or all the parties agree that it should: see section 122.

2. The provisions of sections 121 (additional requirement for admissibility of multiple hearsay) and 123 (capability to make statement) may also have to be considered on the facts of an individual case.

29. Statement, Previous Inconsistent: Witness Not Having Been Treated as Hostile

1. [X has admitted that he] [You may be satisfied that X] made a previous statement which was inconsistent with the evidence he gave in court. [*Identify the inconsistency.*]

2. You may take into account any inconsistency [and X's explanation for it] when considering X's reliability as a witness. It is for you to judge the extent and importance of any inconsistency. (*If appropriate:*) If you conclude that he has been inconsistent on an important matter, you should treat both his accounts with considerable care.

3. If, however, you are sure that one of X's accounts is true [in whole or in part], then it is evidence you may consider when deciding upon your verdict[s].

Notes

1. This direction is based on section 119 of the Criminal Justice Act 2003, under which the previous inconsistent statement becomes evidence of the truth of its contents. If it was made in a document which becomes an exhibit, it must not accompany the jury when they retire to consider their verdict unless the court considers it appropriate or all the parties agree that it should: see section 122.

2. The provisions of sections 121 (additional requirement for admissibility of multiple hearsay) and 123 (capability to make statement) may also have to be considered on the facts of an individual case.

31. Previous consistent statement

1. In this case you have heard both evidence from X, and a statement [said to have been] made by X on a previous occasion.

2.

(*Only when section 120(2) applies:*)

The law permitted this because it had been suggested to X that his evidence in court had been made up. The previous statement is evidence you may take into account, if you think fit, when considering X's reliability as a witness, and when considering your verdict[s].

(*Only when section 120(3) applies:*)

The law permitted this because X had used the previous statement to refresh his memory when giving evidence, and had then been asked questions about it in cross-examination. The previous statement is evidence you may take into account, if you think fit, when considering your verdict[s].

(*Only when section 120(4) and (5) apply:*)

The law permitted this because X said he believed that [he made] the previous statement [and that it] was true, and because it [identified/described] a [person/object/place]. If you accept X's evidence that he believed this, the previous statement is evidence you may take into account, if you think fit, when considering your verdict[s].

(Only when section 120 (4) and (6) apply:)

The law permitted this because X said he believed that [he made] the previous statement [and that it] was true, and was made when matters which he did not now remember were fresh in his memory. If you accept X's evidence in this regard, the previous statement is evidence you may take into account, if you think fit, when considering your verdict[s]. (*If the issue arises:*) When deciding whether or not to take it into account, consider whether or not X could reasonably be expected to remember now the matters referred to in his previous statement.

(Only when section 120(4) and (7) apply:)

The law permitted this because X said he believed that [he made] the previous statement [and that it] was true, and because it consisted of a complaint of [part of] the offence now being tried, made by X [to Y] shortly afterwards. If you accept the evidence of X [and Y] about the complaint, the complaint itself is evidence you may take into account, if you think fit, when considering X's reliability as a witness and when considering your verdict[s]. (*If the issue(s) arise(s)*:) When deciding whether or not to take the complaint into account, consider whether or not it was [made as soon as could reasonably be expected] [made as a result of a threat or promise] [drawn from X rather than being volunteered by him].

Notes

1. This direction, which is based on section 120 of the Criminal Justice Act 2003, supercedes the previous direction which dealt only with recent complaints of sexual offences. Under section 120 a written or oral complaint of *any* offence is now admissible as evidence of the matters complained of if the conditions set out in section 120(4) and (7) are met, this being a decision of law for the judge. Moreover, other kinds of previous consistent statements are also available as evidence of the truth of their contents if any of the conditions set out in section 120(2), (3), (4) (5) or (6) are met.

2. If the previous statement was made in a document which becomes an exhibit it must not accompany the jury when they retire to consider their verdict unless the court considers it appropriate or all the parties agree that it should: see section 122.

35. Hearsay Evidence under the Criminal Justice Act 2003

1. *Of the different categories of hearsay evidence referred to in sections 114 to 118 of the 2003 Act, the following direction does not relate to the following:*

- *Trade, business or professional documents, unless they fall within section 117(4) and (5).*
- *Public documents.*
- *Evidence of reputation and family tradition.*
- *Confessions (as to which see Direction 25).*
- *Admissions by agents.*

- *Common enterprise (as to which see Direction 11.2).*
- *Expert evidence.*

2. *Section 119 of the Act is dealt with in Directions 28 and 29, and section 120 in Direction 31.*

3. *The following direction will need to be suitably adapted in a case involving multiple hearsay.*

1. The general rule in the courts is that evidence is given orally from the witness box, or by the reading of agreed statements or admissions. However, the law allows evidence to be given in other ways. In this case you have heard evidence from X [by reading of X's statement] [by Y's telling you what X said to him] even though X did not come to court and his evidence is not agreed.
2. [*If the reasons for admitting the hearsay evidence are before the jury, summarise them briefly.*]
3. *(See Note 1.)*Although it is for you to decide what weight, if any, you attach to X's evidence, you should examine it with particular care, bearing well in mind that it does have certain limitations, which I must draw to your attention:

   (a) You have not had the opportunity of seeing and hearing X in the witness box and of assessing him as a witness. When you do see and hear a witness you may get a much clearer idea of whether his evidence is honest and accurate.
   (b) X's statement was not made or verified on oath.
   (c) His evidence has not been tested under cross-examination, and you have not had the opportunity of seeing how his evidence survived this form of challenge.
   (d) X's statement forms only a part of the evidence, and it must be considered in the light of all the other evidence in the case. You must reach your verdict having considered all the evidence. (*If there are discrepancies between the statement and the oral evidence of other witnesses, add:*) You should also have regard to the following discrepancies between X's statement and the oral evidence: [*here set out the discrepancies*].
   (e) [*Refer to any particular matters canvassed during the trial which might further affect the jury's view of X's evidence: for example, its probative value, its importance, the circumstances in which X made his statement, X's reliability and Y's reliability.*]

Notes

1. See *Grant v The State* [2006] 2 WLR 835.

Appendix IV

Leading Cases

R v Sellick (Carlo) and Sellick (Santino) **[2005] EWCA Crim 651, CA, 14 March 2005, Waller LJ, Owen and Fulford JJ**

Stephen Solley QC and Alexander Dos Santos for the Appellants
Timothy Raggatt QC and Jonathan Salmon for the Crown

Lord Justice Waller:

Introduction

1. On the 16th December 2002 in the Crown Court in Birmingham before Butterfield J and the jury, after a sixteen-day trial the appellants were convicted of murder and sentenced to life imprisonment. A co-accused, Marandola, was acquitted. On a second indictment, including counts alleging the intimidation of witnesses by the appellants, the counts were ordered to lie on the file on the usual terms. The appellants appealed by leave of the full court (Potter LJ, Gibbs J and Sir Michael Wright). In the judgment of the full court, given by Potter LJ, permission was granted on the basis that the appeal raised, in a more acute form than in *M(KJ)* [2003] EWCA Crim 357, [2003] 2 CrAppR 21 (322), issues as to the proper construction of s.23 and s.26 of the Criminal Justice Act 1988, in the light of the jurisprudence of the European Court of Human Rights.

2. Butterfield J exercising his discretion under ss.23 and 26 of the 1988 Act gave leave for four statements to be read. In relation to two of the statements he gave leave on the basis that he was sure the witnesses had been kept away through fear. In relation to two of the witnesses he gave leave on the basis that reasonable steps had been made to trace the witnesses. The submission on behalf of the appellants is that, by admitting the statements of

these witnesses their rights to a fair trial under Article 6 of the European Convention on Human Rights (the ECHR) has been infringed. In particular the submission is that the 'minimum rights' provided for by Article 6(3)(d) 'to examine or have examined witnesses against him and to obtain the attendance and examination of witnesses on his behalf under the same conditions as witnesses against him;' have been infringed.

3. Reliance is placed on a paragraph in *Lucà v Italy* (2003) 36 EHRR 46 at paragraph 40, where the court stated as follows:

> As the court has stated on a number of occasions . . . it may prove necessary in certain circumstances to refer to depositions made during the investigative stage (in particular where the witness refuses to repeat his deposition in public owing to fears for his safety, a not infrequent occurrence in trials concerning Mafia-type organisations). If the defendant has been given an adequate and proper opportunity to challenge the depositions, either when made or at a later stage, their admission in evidence will not in itself contravene Article 6.1 and 3(d). The corollary of that, however, is that where the conviction is both solely or to a decisive degree based on depositions that had been made by a person whom the accused has had no opportunity to examine or to have examined, whether during the investigation or at the trial, the rights of the defence are restricted to an extent that is incompatible with the guarantees provided by Article 6.

4. The submission is that the appellants in this case were given no adequate or proper opportunity to challenge the statements which were admitted in evidence at any stage of the proceedings. It is submitted that for that reason alone this is a case where the judge should not have allowed the statements to be read. In the alternative it is submitted that the statements were the decisive or sole evidence against the appellants and even if otherwise permission might have been given to read the statements, then in those circumstances permission should not have been granted.

5. The prosecution do not accept that the evidence was the sole or decisive evidence, but in any event submit that in particular where a witness is being kept away by fear by persons acting on behalf of a defendant, those are the very circumstances with which, even if the evidence is decisive, it should be admitted pursuant to sections 23 and 26, and that the Strasbourg jurisprudence does not preclude the English Court taking that view.

The facts

6. At about 7 pm on the 3 December 2001 the deceased, Paul Chambers (Moonie), was shot dead in the rear car park of the Talisman public house in Wolverhampton. The fatal wound passed through his shoulder-blade and torso and ruptured his descending aorta. He sustained one bullet wound to his hand. Two bullets were recovered: they were probably fired from the same weapon and bore marks which suggested that it was an old Webley revolver. The murder weapon was never found.

7. The prosecution alleged that the second appellant (Santino Sellick) was the gunman. They asserted that he shot the deceased because Moonie represented competition in drug dealing and because a few hours earlier he, Santino, had learned that Moonie had slept with his girlfriend, Tammy Pardoe (Tammy). It was further alleged that the first appellant (Carlo Sellick) was Santino's partner in drug dealing. It was asserted that Carlo drove Santino to the scene and provided the weapon, knowing what Santino intended to do. It was alleged

that the co-accused, Marandola, was present and both knew and assisted with what was going to happen.

8. The defence denied involvement in the murder at all. It was claimed that Santino was ill in bed at the time of the murder. Carlo asserted that he was not present and had no knowledge that it would take place. Marandola's case was that he was present at the shooting but had been unaware that it was to take place and he was not party to it.

Who's who?

9. Carlo and Santino are brothers. Their half brother is Lee Sellick ('Lee'), who is a friend of Moonie. Lee had resumed a relationship with Carla Wedge (Carla); Tammy was a girlfriend of Santino and she was the niece of Carla and lived at her address. Carina Jackson ('Carina') was Tammy's friend, and through her met both Carlo and Santino, and she began a sexual relationship with Carlo. Prior to the commencement of the trial on 27 November 2002 the judge gave the prosecution permission to read, as part of the evidence, the statements of Lee and Carla. The trial commenced and he gave leave to read the statements of Carina and another witness, Donna Mills, on the 2 December 2002. Tammy gave evidence on the 4 December 2002 behind a screen, and the judge gave the Crown leave to treat her as hostile.

The evidence itself

10. No witness actually saw the shooting. Madeline Bannister gave evidence. She was walking with a friend in the vicinity when she heard two gunshots, then after a gap another two. She could see two or three people standing around at the Talisman. Then she saw three people running from the Talisman to a car and driving away. Peter Thomas, her friend, also gave evidence orally. He heard a loud bang. He saw two people in the Talisman car park. He continued walking, then heard two bangs followed by three people running away to a car which was driven away at high speed. One of them wore a light coloured sports jacket. It was then that he noticed a body.

11. Stephen Perry and John Huntbatch also gave evidence. They served coffee from a van. Perry's evidence was that he was not paying much attention but noticed Moonie exit the pub with a group of others, who left in a Citroen. Moonie was then on his own. Then he heard a raised voice and looked up to see Moonie. Then he heard a bang and shortly after he saw Moonie fall over. The Citroen and occupants returned and one of them tried to resuscitate Moonie. Huntbatch said he had seen two men joined by a third, and from inside the van he heard some discussion which could have been about drug dealing. One had a Timberland jacket. They walked away from the car park and moments later he heard two loud bangs.

12. David Allen gave evidence. He went to Lee Sellick's flat, when paramedics arrived because he knew the person who had been with Moonie in the pub earlier had gone there with Lee about half an hour before. Lee, Carla and another woman returned to the car park with him.

13. In the period after the shooting there was mobile telephone traffic between Lee and Carlo. Later, after death had been certified, someone used a payphone at the hospital and attempted to call each of the mobile phones belonging to Carlo, Santino and Marandola,

but no connection was made. Cell site analysis indicated that the phone attributable to Carlo was in use in the area of the Talisman prior to the shooting and moved south and towards Porlock on the North Somerset coast after the shooting.

14. On 4th December the phones of Carlo and Marandola were used in the Porlock area and appeared to migrate back towards Wolverhampton.

The witnesses who were read

15. Carina stated that she had travelled in a red Golf with Santino and following phone calls they went to various locations where Santino sold crack and brown in £20 wraps. The three Sellick brothers and another man named Dickens used Carla's bedroom to cut and weigh drugs. It was her understanding that Carlo and Santino Sellick obtained their supplies from Moonie. Her relationship with Carlo ended before Moonie was killed. Some days after Moonie was killed she saw Tammy with a black eye. She also referred to an occasion in November 2001 when Carlo asked her to look after a balaclava and gun: she took the items from him and stored them overnight in a wardrobe. The gun was like a cowboy gun, silver barrel and cream handle. She gave the gun back to Carlo the next morning.

16. Lee stated that he had met Moonie when they were in prison. He said they were best mates and like brothers. Lee had an extensive criminal record, of which the jury were made aware. He was arrested for conspiracy to murder Moonie and at the conclusion of interview had made his witness statement. He stated that Carlo bought drugs from Moonie. The day after Moonie supplied one ounce of crack to Santino for Carlo he agreed to collect another ounce of crack from Moonie for Carlo. Lee stated he told Carlo that Moonie wanted paying the £2000 due the following day. That night Tammy and Santino had a row. He went to intervene and Santino said Tammy had just told him that she had slept with Moonie. On the 3 December he made phone calls to Carlo urging him to pay his debt. He spoke to Moonie about the money and learned he would be at the Talisman that evening. Lee said he told Carlo where to find Moonie that night. He phoned Carlo from the pub to say Moonie was there and waiting for his money. He confirmed he wore a beige Timberland jacket that evening. He stated that in the phone calls after the shooting he asked Carlo what was going on. Carlo told him to make sure no-one saw anything. When Lee asked how he could do that, Carlo told Lee to sort himself out or he would get the same. He would be next. Lee passed the phone to Michael Whitehouse and when he took the phone back Carlo asked him if Moonie was dead or alive.

17. Lee stated that on the evening of the 4 December he received a call from Santino via his father's mobile telling him to organise booking them into an hotel. He described how Carlo, Santino and Marandola arrived in the early hours. They all assembled in a bedroom. Santino said 'It was not supposed to happen like that'. Carlo also said of Marandola 'How do you think he feels? He only came along for the ride'.

18. Carla stated that before the shooting incident there had been a blazing row at her flat, during the course of which Tammy admitted sleeping with Moonie. Santino used considerable violence on Tammy. Her account of events at the hotel was on the same lines as Lee. She had agreed that if asked by police she would limit her account to events in the car park after finding Moonie collapsed. She stated she was scared, not just for herself but for Lee and for Tammy and for her children. She could not do anything else but agree.

19. Donna Mills stated that she was the former girlfriend of Santino. She simply dealt with the types of car that Santino drove.

The evidence of Tammy

20. After a sequence of questions and answers, which did not accord with the contents of her statement, the Crown applied for and were given leave to treat her as a hostile witness. She had said she could not remember what she saw at Carlo's flat. Then she said Lee brought cocaine to the flat. Then she agreed that in her statement to the police she had stated that Carlo and Santino brought drugs to the flat and she had taken bags to cars and collected money on three occasions. In evidence she said it was part-true, part-lie. She only took a bag to someone once and learned about the drugs from something said by Carla and not as a result of something she saw herself. She met Moonie in about October. She slept with him once after a night out pubbing. Santino learned about it when they had a row on the 2 December and he hit her.

21. The following night at the Talisman Santino was angry. He said she should not have slept with Moonie and he would kill him. She regarded that as the sort of thing people say when angry, without meaning it. She agreed that she had told the police he said it was her fault and Moonie was going to get done and that was the truth.

22. Initially she denied there was any conversation about the shooting at the hotel on the 4 December, but then said the content of her statement was the truth. Santino had told her no-one would know who pulled the trigger except him and Carlo. She told him it was him or Carlo. He said if anyone told they would get done. If she told she would have to get the same. If she cried for Moonie, the dirty rapist, she would be joining him. Next she spoke to Carlo and he told her to keep her mouth shut. She did sleep with Santino that night. She was frightened by what had been said to her. Carla and Lee told her what to say if she was questioned.

23. On New Year's Eve she asked Santino to tell her what had happened on the 3 December. Santino explained the way the conversation went, that he got the gun and how Moonie said if he was going to use the gun to use it. He fired off two shots which missed and shot again, which he thought hit Moonie in the leg. She thought he said that the last thing Moonie said was 'you have got me in the back you bastard'.

24. That night there was a fight in which Carlo was injured and bled. She visited Santino who was in prison for other reasons and he told her the police had 'nothing on us'. The only thing they could trace was a phone call. He told her to stick to the same story if the police questioned her. Tammy maintained that these accounts given to police after she was arrested for conspiracy were the truth. She had been frightened after arrest. The police told her she could go to jail for ten years. She disagreed with the assertion that Santino never said any of these things to her, which suggested he was involved in the killing of Moonie. She had loved him but disliked Carlo.

Other evidence for the prosecution

25. Whilst detained in their cells Santino and Carlo had certain conversations which were recorded covertly. They spoke in code—a form of back-slang. The conversations, so the Crown alleged, showed plotting and planning to subvert evidence against them. The defence admitted the conversations and what was said but asserted it was done to wind the police up. In particular, the reference to disposing of a jacket was in relation to the event on New Year's Eve.

26. Both Santino and Carlo made no comment to questions put to them by the police in their interviews on the advice of their solicitors.

Defence evidence

27. Santino and Carlo gave evidence but their co-accused, Marandola, did not. Santino denied killing Moonie. He said it was Lee who was dealing with crack and heroin. He said he was unaware that Tammy had been unfaithful to him with the victim and he had not assaulted her in the hours before the shooting. They had rowed but that was because it was he who had slept with Carina. It was nothing to do with Moonie. Tammy invented their conversation in the pub the night after. He went with the others to the hotel for the night because there was cannabis in the car to be dropped off for Lee. He understood Carla and Tammy had gone there because of the police activity outside their flats, and it was a chance to meet up with Tammy. She said she could not believe he slept with Carina and he told her to get over it. She said she would get back at him one day. The only reference to Moonie was in the context of having heard about it on the news. Tammy sent him affectionate letters and a birthday card in prison.

28. Carlo said he did not obtain drugs from or supply drugs to Moonie. He said he had no involvement in and was not present at Moonie's death. He used cannabis and ecstasy and began to use crack following the death of his father. He was a heavy user and all the crack found when his home was searched was for his personal use. He denied that the money found was the proceeds of dealing. He denied ever having had a gun and said Carina was malicious and tried to cause him trouble after their relationship ended. It was Lee who bought drugs from Moonie. He maintained that when Lee phoned him up on 3 December Lee was trying to borrow money. Carlo had planned to go to Porlock to take some cannabis to his uncle. He had seen Marandola and invited him along. He had not seen Santino all day. At some point on the journey he spoke to Santino, who was ill in bed. He did phone Lee, who sounded drugged or drunk, and he said that Moonie was dead. There was to-ing and fro-ing in the Taunton area because they got lost. It was not a case of looking around for somewhere to dispose of the gun. Lee called to request cannabis and said he was staying at the hotel. They collected Santino on the way back and there was no conversation or suggestion that Carlo was responsible for Moonie's death. He agreed he had written to Marandola and accepted he was afraid he would falsely implicate Carlo in the murder.

29. Marandola did not give evidence, but in his police interview he had stated that he was shocked as said he was at his girlfriend's at the time of the murder. But in a subsequent interview he said the appellants had picked him up in a red car and said they were going to meet someone. He had been told to stay in the car but he did not remain in the car, but could see the other two and a third man approach from the pub. He heard two shots and then the appellants returned to the car and they left. He did not see any gun.

The Judge's rulings on permission to read certain statements

30. The prosecution, prior to the commencement of the trial, submitted that it was their belief that attempts were being made to subvert the trial. Their initial application was for leave to read the statements of Lee and Carla on alternative grounds, either that they could not be found and all reasonable steps had been taken to find them, or that there was plain

evidence their absence was through fear. The judge heard evidence in chambers from Mrs Fox, who was the mother of Carla, and from certain police officers. There is no challenge to his findings of fact and it is thus unnecessary to go through the details of their evidence. The judge directed himself by reference to sections 23 and 26 of the 1988 Act, and it is important to have the provisions of those sections in mind. section 23 provides:

> 23.(1) Subject—
>
> (a) to subsection (4) below:
> (b) to paragraph 1A of Schedule 2 to the Criminal Appeal Act 1968 (evidence given orally at original trial to be given orally at retrial): and
> (c) to section 69 of the Police and Criminal Evidence Act 1984 (evidence from computer records).
>
> a statement made by a person in a document shall be admissible in criminal proceedings as evidence of any fact of which direct oral evidence by him would be admissible if—
>
> (i) the requirements of one of the paragraphs of subsection (2) below are satisfied; or
> (ii) the requirements of subsection (3) below are satisfied.
>
> (2) The requirements mentioned in subsection (1)(i) above are—
>
> (a) that the person who made the statement is dead or by reason of his bodily or mental condition unfit to attend as a witness;
> (b) that—
>
> (i) the person who made the statement is outside the United Kingdom; and
> (ii) it is not reasonably practicable to secure his attendance; or
>
> (c) that all reasonable steps have been taken to find the person who made the statement, but that he cannot be found.
>
> (3) The requirement mentioned in subsection (1)(ii) above are—
>
> (a) that the statement was made to a police officer or some other person charged with the duty of investigating offences or charging offenders; and
> (b) that the person who made it does not give oral evidence through fear or because he is kept out of the way.
>
> (4) Subsection (1) above does not render admissible a confession made by an accused person that would not be admissible under section 76 of the Police and Criminal Evidence Act 1984.

Section 26 provides:

> Where a statement which is admissible in criminal proceedings by virtue of section 23 or 24 above appears to the court to have been prepared, otherwise than in accordance with section 29 below or an order under paragraph 6 of Schedule 13 to this Act or under section 30 or 31 below, for the purposes—
>
> (a) of pending or contemplated criminal proceedings; or

(b) of a criminal investigation

the statement shall not be given in evidence in any criminal proceedings without the leave of the court, and the court shall not give leave unless it is of the opinion that the statement ought to be admitted in the interests of justice; and in considering whether its admission would be in the interests of justice, it shall be the duty of the court to have regard—

(i) to the contents of the statement;
(ii) to any risk, having regard in particular to whether it is likely to be possible to controvert the statement if the person making it does not attend to give oral evidence in the proceedings, that its admission or exclusion will result in unfairness to the accused or, if there is more than one, to any of them; and
(iii) to any other circumstances that appear to the court to be relevant.

31. It is also important to have in mind, as the judge did, section 28 and Schedule 2. Schedule 2(1) provides as follows:

1. Where a statement is admitted as evidence in criminal proceedings by virtue of Part II of this Act—

(a) any evidence which, if the person making the statement had been called as a witness, would have been admissible as relevant to his credibility as a witness shall be admissible for that purpose in those proceedings;
(b) evidence may, with the leave of the court, be given of any matter which, if that person had been called as a witness, could have been put to him in cross-examination as relevant to his credibility as a witness but of which evidence could not have been adduced by the cross-examining party; and
(c) evidence tending to prove that that person, whether before or after making the statement, made (whether orally or not) some other statement which is inconsistent with it shall be admissible for the purpose of showing that he has contradicted himself.

32. The essence of the judge's ruling was contained in the following passages of his ruling:

They were each arrested on suspicion that they were involved in the murder. Each was interviewed. Records of those interviews have been disclosed to the defence. Each made statements concerning the circumstances of and surrounding the murder. Those statements implicate to a greater or lesser extent the defendants Santino Sellick and Carlo Sellick. In the course of his statement, Lee Sellick said this: 'Since the shooting there has not been a day when Carla, my partner, and myself have not spoken about it. It has caused a lot of stress. I still feel scared, not only for me by my family and my girlfriend.' Later in that same statement, he said: 'I am frightened for my safety and any revenge they may take against me but I am willing to go to court.' Carla Wedge, in the course of her statement made on 23rd February, said this: 'What I said in my first statement is true but there is more to tell. I have not told you up to now because I am very frightened and I have my children to think about.'

Having heard and seen the witnesses called in this application, I am satisfied so that I am sure of the following facts:

(1) Following the arrest of the defendants in February 2002, both Carla Wedge and Lee Sellick were made subjects of a witness protection scheme;

(2) Both Carla Wedge and Lee Sellick voluntarily withdrew from that scheme in about April 2002 and returned to the Wolverhampton area where the murder had been committed. They were living together and continued to live together until November of this year;

(3) Carla Wedge and Lee Sellick were informed in writing of the date of this trial in August 2002 and September 2002 and were notified on those occasions that they were required to attend as witnesses;

(4) On 18 September 2002, Carla Wedge attended Billeston Street Police Station where she spoke to DC Hutton. In that conversation, she described an incident which had taken place outside her son's school when members of the Gamboni family, associates of the defendants, told her she should not be a grass;

(5) Carla Wedge told DC Hutton on 18 September that she felt intimidated by the approach made to her by the Gamboni family and that she anticipated that that intimidation would become more intensive as the trial date approached. DC Hutton believed, from what Carla said to him and her general demeanour, that the Gamboni connection was capable of intimidating her and that she was fearful for her own safety and that of her family;

(6) In November 2002, Carla Wedge and Lee Sellick both knew of the trial date, the place of trial and that they were required to attend to give evidence at trial;

(7) From 18 November 2002 onwards, police officers have made repeated attempts to find Carla Wedge and Lee. Police officers have visited all addresses in any way associated with either witness and have pursued all available avenues of enquiry. Despite all those efforts, neither witness has been found;

(8) The mother of Carla Wedge, Mrs Fox, has not seen her daughter for the past two weeks. Carla Wedge has left her home and her children, two boys aged nine and 15 months, and effectively disappeared. The children are being cared for by Mrs Fox. Mrs Fox has no knowledge of her daughter's whereabouts and does not know how to get in touch with her. Since Carla Wedge left, her younger child was admitted to hospital but even that event, of which Carla learned through telephone contact with her grandmother, did not prompt her to reappear;

(9) Mrs Fox told WDC Pearson that Carla was staying away from her children for two weeks until the trial was over to avoid getting killed and putting her children in danger;

(10) Mrs Fox told WDC Pearson that Lee was frightened and thought he would be killed whether he gave evidence or not. He had tried to commit suicide;

(11) Mrs Fox herself is a very frightened woman. She refused to make a written statement about the events surrounding the disappearance of her daughter. Her attendance at court had to be secured by a witness summons and a threat of arrest. The public gallery had to be cleared before she was prepared to give evidence.

Against those findings of fact, I turn to consider the application made by the Crown. In doing so, I take into account all the decisions of the Court of Appeal, Criminal Division, and the House of Lords, to which I have been referred, and all the submissions made on behalf of the crown and the defendants. I am satisfied so that I am sure that all reasonable steps have been taken by the police to find both Carla Wedge and Lee Sellick but neither witness can be found. I reject the suggestion that the police should have done more to keep in contact with the witnesses in the months leading up to the trial. I am satisfied that the steps taken by the police were appropriate and reasonable in the light of the information available to them. The Crown further submit that I should be satisfied that the witnesses are not prepared to give oral evidence through fear. On that issue, I remind myself that the evidence of fear must not be second-hand, as it would be from Mrs Fox. I accordingly ignore her evidence on that topic completely. Whether the witnesses' direct assertion of feeling fearful is hearsay or not is not the crucial issue. If it is not hearsay, it is admissible as original evidence and if it is hearsay, it is admissible by way of exception to the rule. See *Neill v North Antrim Magistrates Court* [1992] 1 WLR 1220. There is, in my judgment, clear admissible evidence that both witnesses were in fear at the time they made their witness statements to the police. There is further admissible evidence that Carla Wedge was fearful about giving evidence in September 2002. There is, however, no admissible evidence that Lee Sellick was in fear of giving oral evidence and whilst it would be possible for me to infer from all these circumstances that he was, I am not able, in his case, to exclude the reasonable possibility that other factors may have influenced his disappearance. It is highly probable that fear of the consequences of giving evidence against the defendants and that alone has prompted him to disappear but I cannot be sure of that conclusion. However, in the case of Carla Wedge, I am entirely satisfied that fear for her own safety and fear for the lives of her children have driven her to behave as she has, abandoning her own children even when one of them was admitted to hospital. I am further satisfied, in the case of both witnesses, that no adjournment will secure their attendance.

Thus the provisions of Section 23 of the 1988 Act are satisfied in respect of both witnesses. The statements which the Crown wish to adduce were prepared for the purpose of criminal proceedings. The provisions of Section 26, accordingly, apply. The court must not give leave unless it is of the opinion that the statements or either of them ought to be admitted in the interests of justice having regard to the particular matters identified in the section and to all the circumstances of the case. I have carefully considered the contents of the statements. Each of them contains a wealth of detail which is compelling and, in my judgment, wholly credible. The defendants are all in a position to controvert the contents of the statements if they dispute them. I accept, however, that there is a disadvantage to the defence if the statements are read and if they are admitted, the jury must receive clear directions emphasizing that disadvantage. Further, so far as Lee Sellick is concerned, the defence point to a number of features which they submit undermine his credibility. However, Section 28 of Schedule 2 of the 1988 Act provides a wholly sufficient remedy for that concern. Having taken into consideration all the submissions made and given full weight to the provisions of Section 26, I am of the clear view that the statements made by Lee Sellick and Carla Wedge ought to be admitted in the interests of justice. I so rule.

33. After the trial commenced on the 2 December 2002, the Crown also applied for leave to read the statements of Carina and Donna Mills. We have got a transcript of the judge's

ruling in their regard. He ruled that he was sure Carina was being kept away by fear, relying on section 23(3) of the 1988 Act. So far as Donna Mills was concerned he ruled that reasonable steps had been taken to find her, and applied section 23(2)(c). In both instances he also applied section 26 of the 1988 Act, holding that it was in the interests of justice to allow the statements to be read. He also bore in mind section 28 and Schedule 2 of the 1988 Act.

Strasbourg jurisprudence

34. It appears that the judge was not referred to any of the Strasbourg jurisprudence on Article 6. That may be because in the Court of Appeal *R v Gokal* [1997] 2 Cr App R some general observations were made by Lord Justice Ward, who gave the judgment of the court at a time prior to the coming into force of the Human Rights Act, that would indicate that there was no reason to think that Article 6 rights would be infringed if sections 23 and 26 were utilised by courts. In that case, it should be said, the main attack being made by the appellant was to the effect that he would only be able to controvert the written statements if he gave evidence, and it was submitted that that would infringe his right to silence. That involved an attack on previous decisions of the English Court of Appeal in, for example, *R v Cole* [1990] 1 WLR 866. There was cited to Ward LJ certain of the Strasbourg authorities to which we will refer hereafter, and it was in that context that he said:

> . . . there is nothing there to concern us and we remain confident that the conduct of the application before Buxton J and the procedures by which he would conduct the trial accord fully with our treaty obligations.

35. Mr Raggatt QC before us submitted that the only real question was whether the provisions of sections 23 and 26 of the 1988 Act had been complied with and that little assistance could be gained from the Strasbourg authorities. We cannot accept that submission. By Section 6 of the Human Rights Act 1998 it is unlawful for a public authority (including a court) to act in a way, which is incompatible with a Convention right. Obviously, when a court is exercising its discretion under s.26, it is doing so by reference to 'the interests of justice' and it would hopefully be unlikely that in so doing it would be infringing a defendant's Convention right. But there is a wide spectrum of circumstances to which sections 23 and 26 of the 1988 Act must be applied, and indeed a wide spectrum of circumstances to which section 23(3) of the 1988 Act (oral evidence not given through fear) may apply, which will become wider still under the Criminal Justice Act 2003, where under new provisions the court is enjoined to give a wide definition to fear (see section 116(3)). It is clearly of relevance to obtain guidance from the Strasbourg authorities as to the situations in which a defendant's Article 6 rights might have been infringed when considering how to exercise the discretion under these sections.

36. In approaching the Strasbourg jurisprudence, however, it must be borne in mind that it began its development by reference to cases which were being or had been tried under the inquisitorial processes common in many European countries and without regard to such safeguards as have been built into the English process. During the trial process of many countries there may be more than one moment in time when a witness may have been able to be questioned by or on behalf of the defendant. Under the common law process, the only moment for examination of a witness is at the trial itself. That has the consequence that there is just that one moment when, if the witness can be kept away by fear a defendant may

be able to escape conviction because the evidence is simply unavailable. Being aware of the difficulties for a defendant controverting evidence which may be read, under the 1988 Act the English court has the power provided by section 28 and Schedule 2 to allow in evidence not normally admissible. That counterbalance is important in considering whether a defendant's rights have been infringed under Article 6.

37. Furthermore, the fact that there is only one moment in time when the defendant may have an opportunity to cross-examine a witness gives rise to a point which so far as we can see has not received any attention in the Strasbourg authorities. If a defendant, through fear, keeps a witness away from an English trial, then it is, as it would seem to us, the defendant who is depriving himself or herself of the right and the only right that the defendant has to examine that witness. How, we ask rhetorically, can it be said to be an infringement of the defendant's Article 6 rights for him to deprive himself of that opportunity?

38. It is necessary to review certain of the Strasbourg authorities but it must be borne in mind that, as we see it, the question whether Article 6 has been infringed is very fact sensitive. Despite that fact-sensitivity, certain general principles have been stated from time to time. Care must however be taken not to construe such general principles as words of a statute, particularly having regard to the fact they are stated in cases where the facts are very distant from those in the present case. It is clear that the Strasbourg court is fully aware of the problem of intimidation of witnesses but has a reluctance to give way to expediency. There is, however, no case as far as we know where the Strasbourg court has actually had to deal with a key witness being kept away by fear by a defendant from a trial in the English jurisdiction.

39. We can take the authorities to which we were referred in chronological sequence. First there is *Unterpertinger v Austria* (1996) 13 EHHR 175. In that case a man was tried for violence against his wife and stepdaughter, but in the context of serious disputes as to whether had attacked them or they had attacked him. The wife and stepdaughter refused to give evidence, and the Court of Appeal refused to allow in evidence going to the credibility of the wife and stepdaughter. The court held that paragraph (3)(d) of Article 6 was an aspect of the general concept of a fair trial and that thus the court should view the matter from the angle of paragraph (1) of Article 6 taken together with the principles inherent in paragraph (3)(d). It further held that the reading out of statements, as occurred in that case, could not be regarded as inconsistent with Article 6 (1) and (3)(d), but it held 'the use made of them as evidence must nevertheless comply with the rights of the defence'. It found that there had been an infringement of Article 6 on the basis that the Court of Appeal founded its judgments 'mainly' on the statements and on the basis 'that the defendant was convicted on the basis of 'testimony' in respect of which his defence rights were appreciably restricted'.

40. There are then cases dealing with witnesses whose identity was not revealed to the defence. *Kostovski v Netherlands* (1990) 12 EHRR 343. K was convicted of armed robbery on the basis of statements of anonymous witnesses. He was unable to question those witnesses at any stage. Being unaware of the identity of the witnesses deprived K of the very particulars which would have enabled him to demonstrate the witnesses unreliability. The court again stated that the reading out of the statements would not necessarily be inconsistent with Article 6. But it held that, since the government accepted that the convictions were based to 'a decisive extent' on the anonymous evidence, there had been a breach of Article 6. It was in that case where the court stated:

> The right to a fair administration of justice holds so prominent a place in a democratic society that it cannot be sacrificed to expediency. The Convention does not preclude reliance at the investigation stage of criminal proceedings on sources such anonymous informants. However, the subsequent use of anonymous statements as sufficient evidence to found a conviction as in the present case is a different matter. It involved limitations on the right of the defence which were irreconcilable with the guarantees contained in Article 6.

41. *Windisch v Austria* (1990) 13 EHRR 281. W was convicted on the evidence of a mother and daughter, who gave statements on the basis that their identity would not be revealed. The police gave evidence of the statements made by the mother and daughter and the identities of the mother and daughter were not revealed. In its judgment the court recited various principles in the following terms at paragraph 26:

> All the evidence must in principle be produced in the presence of the accused at a public hearing with a view to adversarial argument. However, the use as evidence of statements obtained at the pre-trial stage is not always inconsistent with paragraph (3)d and (1) of Article 6, provided the right to the defence had been respected. As a rule, these rights require that the defendant be given an adequate and proper opportunity to challenge and question a witness against him, either when he was making a statement or at a later stage of the proceedings.

The court held, however, in this case, at paragraph 28:

> Being unaware of their identity, the defence was confronted with an almost insurmountable handicap: it was deprived of the necessary information permitting it to test the witnesses' reliability or cast doubt on their credibility.

42. The court recognised the interests of the two women and the interests and importance of the collaboration of the public in the police's struggle against crime, but again referred to the right to the fair administration of justice holding 'so prominent a place in a democratic society that it cannot be sacrificed'. The court stressed that the identification made by the two anonymous witnesses was 'the only evidence indicating the applicant's presence on the scene of the crime'. In the result the court held that the trial court relied 'to a large extent' on this evidence. It held there had been a breach of Article 6.

43. *Ludi v Switzerland* (1992) 15 EHRR 173. The conviction in that case was based on the evidence of an undercover agent not called at the trial. It was held that the witness could have been called in a way which could have preserved that witnesses' anonymity, and thus there had been a violation.

44. In *Saidi v France* (1993) 17 EHRR 251, S was convicted on the basis of the evidence of drug addicts and in the situation where there was no opportunity to confront the witness. In the judgment that court stated at paragraph 43:

> The court reiterates that the taking of evidence is governed primarily by the rules of domestic law, and that it is in principle for the national courts to assess the evidence before them. The court's task under the Convention is to ascertain whether the proceedings in their entirety, including the way in which evidence was taken, were fair. All the evidence must normally be produced in the presence of the accused at a public

> hearing, with a view to adversarial argument. However, the use as evidence of statements obtained at the stage of the police enquiry and judicial investigation is not in itself inconsistent with Article 6(3)(d) and (1) provided that the right to the defence had been respected. As a rule these rights require that the defendant be given an adequate and proper opportunity to challenge and question the witness against him either when he was making a statement or at a later stage of the proceedings.

The court however held that there had been a breach of Article 6 since the testimony constituted 'the sole basis' for the applicant's conviction, and the lack of any confrontation had deprived the defendant in certain respects of 'a fair trial'. The court recognised the difficulties of the fight against drug trafficking, but 'such considerations cannot justify restricting to this extent the rights of the defence of everyone charged with a criminal offence'.

45. In 1996 we detect a slight shift in the attitude of the court in *Doorson v Netherlands* (1996) 22 EHRR 330. That case was concerned with evidence being given by anonymous witnesses and also with evidence being read as a result of a witness having appeared at the trial but then absconding. The case was concerned with a conviction for drug trafficking. As regards the anonymous witnesses, they were ultimately questioned at an appeal stage, in the presence of counsel, but not the defendant, and without the identity of the witnesses being revealed to counsel. The court stated at paragraph 74:

> While it would clearly have been preferable for the applicant to attend the questioning of the witnesses, the court considers on balance that the Amsterdam Court of Appeal was entitled to consider that the interests of the applicant were in this respect outweighed by the need to ensure the safety of the witnesses.

46. The court in *Doorson* seems to us to bring higher up in the scales than heretofore the interests of victims and witnesses. It stated, for example, at paragraphs 70–76:

> 70. It is true that Article 6 does not explicitly require the interests of witnesses in general, and those of victims called upon to testify in particular, to be taken into consideration. However, their life, liberty or security of person may be at stake as may interest coming generally within the ambit of Article 8 of the Convention. Such interests of witnesses and victims are in principle protected by other substantive provisions of the Convention, which imply the contracting state should organise their criminal proceedings in such a way that those interests are not unjustifiably in peril. Against this background principles of fair trial also require that in appropriate cases the interests of the defence are balanced against those of witnesses or victims called upon to testify.
>
> 71. As the Amsterdam Court of Appeal made clear, its decision not to disclose the identity of Y15 and Y16 to the defence was inspired by the need, as assessed by it, to obtain evidence from them while at the same time protecting them against the possibility of reprisals by the applicant. This is certainly a relevant reason to allow them anonymity. It remains to be seen whether it was sufficient. Although, as the applicant has stated, there has been no suggestion that Y15 and Y16 were ever threatened by the applicant himself, the decision to maintain their anonymity cannot be regarded as unreasonable *per se*. Regard must be had to the fact, as established by the domestic courts and not contested

by the applicant, that drug dealers frequently resorted to threats or actual violence against persons who gave evidence against them. Furthermore, the statements made by the witnesses concerned to the investigating judge show that one of them apparently on a previous occasion suffered violence at the hands of a drug dealer against whom he had testified while the other had been threatened. In sum there was sufficient reason for maintaining the anonymity of Y15 and Y16.

72. The maintenance of the anonymity of the witnesses Y15 and Y16 presented the defence with difficulties, which criminal proceedings should not normally involve. Nevertheless no violation of Article (6)(1) taken together with (6)(3)(d) of the Convention can be found if it is established that the handicaps under which the defence laboured were sufficiently counterbalanced by the procedures followed by the judicial authorities.

73. In the instant case the anonymous witnesses were questioned at the appeal stage in the presence of counsel by an investigating judge who was aware of their identity, even if the defence was not. She noted in the official record of her findings dated 19 November 1990 circumstances, on the basis of which the Court of Appeal was able to draw conclusions as the reliability of their evidence. In this respect the present case is to be distinguished from that of *Kostovski*. Counsel was not only present, but he was put in a position to ask the witnesses whatever questions he considered to be in the interest of the defence, except in so far as they might lead to the disclosure of their identity, and these questions were all answered. In this respect also the present case differs from that of *Kostovski*.

74. While it would clearly have been preferable for the applicant to have attended the questioning of the witnesses, the court considers on balance that the Amsterdam Court of Appeal was entitled to consider that the interests of the applicant were, in this respect, outweighed by the need to ensure the safety of the witnesses. More generally the Convention does not preclude identification—for the purpose of Article 6(3)(d)—of an accused.

75. In addition, although it is normally desirable that witnesses should identify a person suspected of serious crimes in person if there is any doubt about his identity, it should be noted in the present case that Y15 and Y16 identified the applicant from a photograph, which he himself acknowledged to be of himself, moreover both gave descriptions of his appearance and dress. It follows from the above considerations that in the circumstances of the counterbalancing procedure followed by the judicial authorities in obtaining the evidence of witnesses Y15 and Y16 must be considered sufficient, to have enabled the defence to challenge the evidence of the anonymous witnesses and attempt to cast doubt on the reliability of their statements, which it did in open court by amongst other things drawing attention to the fact that both were drug addicts.

76. Finally it should be recalled that even when counterbalancing procedures are found to compensate sufficiently the handicaps under which the defence labours, a conviction should not be based either solely or to a decisive extent on anonymous statements. That however is not the case here: it is sufficiently clear that the national court did not base its finding of guilt solely or to a decisive extent on the evidence of Y15 and Y16. Furthermore, evidence obtained from witnesses under conditions in which the rights of

> the defence cannot be secured to the extent normally required by the Convention should be treated with extreme care. The court is satisfied that this was done in the criminal proceedings leading the applicant's conviction, as is reflected in the express declaration by the Court of Appeal that it had treated the statements of Y15 and Y16 'with the necessary caution and circumspection.

47. It is also of some interest that the court dealt with another witness, R, at paragraphs 78–79:

> 79. Repeated but unsuccessful attempts were made to bring the main witness, R, before the regional court, following which the applicant withdrew his request to have him heard. In the appeal proceedings R was brought before the court by force, but absconded before he could be questioned. A subsequent attempt to have him brought before the Court of Appeal was likewise unsuccessful, after which no further attempt was made.
>
> 80. Despite the Court of Appeal's efforts it was impossible to secure R's attendance at the hearing. In the circumstances it was open to the Court of Appeal to have regard to the statement obtained by the police, especially since it could consider that statement to be corroborated by other evidence before it. Accordingly no unfairness can be found in this respect either.

48. *Van Mechelen v Netherlands* (1997) 25 EHRR. In this case the defendants were convicted of attempted manslaughter and robbery. The evidence identifying the defendant constituted statements made before their trial by anonymous police officers, none of whom gave evidence before either the regional court or the investigating judge. The Court of Appeal had referred the case back to the investigating judge. The investigating judge had arranged hearings in which he and the registrar and the anonymous witnesses were in one room and the applicants and their lawyers and the advocate general were in another. The two rooms were connected by a sound link. The court in this instance held that the balancing of interests of the defence in favour of maintaining the anonymity of witnesses raised special problems where the witnesses in question were members of the police force of the state. Although their interests and the interests of their families deserved protection under the Convention their position was different from that of disinterested witnesses or victims. For these reasons alone, their use as anonymous witnesses should only be resorted to in exceptional circumstances. The court held that it had not been adequately explained to the court why it was necessary to resort to the extreme limitations on the rights of the accused or why less far-reaching measures were not considered. The case was distinguished from *Doorson v The Netherlands.*

49. Finally we refer again to *Lucà v Italy* (2001) 36 EHRR 807. The case was not concerned with a witness being kept away by fear. The defendant had been arrested for possession of cocaine. N was questioned originally as a witness but then later as an accused, but separate proceedings were brought against N for possession. In the case against *Lucà*, N was called as a witness but he chose to remain silent as he was entitled to do and by Article 5(1)(3) of the Code of Criminal Procedure, N's statement could be read. It was in that context that the general statement made in paragraph 40, which we have already quoted at the outset, was made. The court held that the domestic courts convicted the defendant solely

on the basis of statements made by N before the trial, and that thus there had been an infringement of Article 6 of the Convention.

50. What appears from the above authorities are the following propositions:

i) The admissibility of evidence is primarily for the national law;
ii) Evidence must normally be produced at a public hearing and as a general rule Article 6(1) and (3)(d) require a defendant to be given a proper and adequate opportunity to challenge and question witnesses;
iii) It is not necessarily incompatible with Article 6(1) and (3)(d) for depositions to be read and that can be so even if there has been no opportunity to question the witness at any stage of the proceedings. Article 6(3)(d) is simply an illustration of matters to be taken into account in considering whether a fair trial has been held. The reasons for the court holding it necessary that statements should be read and the procedures to counterbalance any handicap to the defence will all be relevant to the issue, whether, where statements have been read, the trial was fair.
iv) The quality of the evidence and its inherent reliability, plus the degree of caution exercised in relation to reliance on it, will also be relevant to the question whether the trial was fair.

51. The question is whether there is a fifth proposition to the effect that where the circumstances justify the reading of the statement where the defendant has had no opportunity to question the witness at any stage of the trial process, the statement must not be allowed to be read if it is the sole or decisive evidence against the defendant. Certainly at first sight paragraph 40 of *Lucà v Italy* seems to suggest that in whatever circumstances and whatever counterbalancing factors are present if statements are read then there will be a breach of Article 6, if the statements are the sole or decisive evidence. Furthermore there is some support for that position in the previous authorities. But neither *Lucà v Italy* nor any of the other authorities were concerned with a case where a witness, whose identity was well-known to a defendant, was being kept away by fear, although we must accept that the reference to Mafia-type organisations and the trials thereof in paragraph 40 shows that the court had extreme circumstances in mind.

52. The question we have posed to ourselves is as follows. If the European court were faced with the case of an identified witness, well-known to a defendant, who was the sole witness of a murder, where the national court could be sure that that witness had been kept away by the defendant, or by persons acting for him, is it conceivable that it would hold that there were no 'counterbalancing' measures the court could take which would allow that statement to be read? If care had been taken to see that the quality of the evidence was compelling, if firm steps were taken to draw the jury's attention to aspects of that witnesses' credibility and if a clear direction was given to the jury to exercise caution, we cannot think that the European Court would nevertheless hold that a defendant's Article 6 rights had been infringed. In such a case, as it seems to us, it is the defendant who has denied himself the opportunity of examining the witnesses, so that he could not complain of an infringement of Article 6(3)(d), and the precautions would ensure compliance and fairness in compliance with Article 6(1). We for our part see no difficulty in such a clear case.

53. More difficulty arises in cases where it is not quite so clear cut, but the court believes, to a high degree of probability, that identified witnesses are being intimidated for and on

behalf of the defence, and where the court is sure to the criminal standard of proof that witnesses cannot be traced and brought before the court (Butterfield J's state of mind on Lee in the instant case). In our view, having regard to the rights of victims, their families, the safety of the public in general, it still cannot be right for there to be some absolute rule that, where compelling evidence is the sole or decisive evidence, an admission in evidence of a statement must then automatically lead to a defendant's Article 6 rights being infringed. That would lead to a situation in which the more successful the intimidation of the witnesses, the stronger the argument becomes that the statements cannot be read. If the decisive witnesses can be 'got at' the case must collapse. The more subtle and less easily established intimidation provides defendants with the opportunity of excluding the most material evidence against them. Such an absolute rule cannot have been intended by the European Court in Strasbourg.

54. As Potter LJ said, referring to paragraph 40 in *Lucà v Italy*, said in *M(K)* (*supra*), at [59]:

> The judge rejected the submission of the defence that the last sentence of that paragraph could admit a no-exception. Certainly, if it did, then sections 23 and 26 of the 1988 Act could never apply in a case such as the present, where the essential or only witness is kept away by fear. That would seem to us an intolerable result as a general proposition and could only lead to an encouragement of criminals to indulge in the very kind of intimidation which the sections are designed to defeat. Certainly, decisions of the court before the passage of the Human Rights Act 1998, as well as common sense, suggest that no invariable rule to that effect should be either propounded or followed, where a witness gives evidence on a *voire dire* that he is unwilling to give evidence as a result of a threat which has been made to him, and the judge draws that the inference that the threat was made, if not at the instigation of the defendant, at least with his approval. This should normally be conclusive as to how the discretion under s.26 should be exercised: see *R v Harvey* [1998] *Archbold News* (Issue 10) 2. So too, as made clear in a case concerning a witness too ill to attend, who gave clear identification evidence in his witness statement, this court observed: 'The fact that there is no ability to cross-examine, that the witness who is absent is the only evidence against the accused, and that his evidence is identification evidence, is not sufficient to render the admission of written evidence from that witness, contrary to the interests of justice or unfair to the defendant *per se.* What matters in our judgment, is the content of the statement and the circumstances of the particular case bearing in mind the considerations which section 26 require the judge to have in mind: per Lord Taylor CJ in *R v Dragic* [1996] 2 Cr App R 232 at 237.

55. The above dictum was cited again in *R v Arnold* [2004] EWCA (Crim) 1293. In that case, however, the court held that they were prepared to assume that the witness had not been kept away by fear, but ruled that the statement was admissible. The court, however, issued a note of warning in the following terms at paragraph 30:

> We cannot leave this case without sound a word of caution. The reference in *Lucà* to the not infrequent occurrence of the phenomenon of frightened witnesses being unwilling to give evidence in trials concerning Mafia-type organisations is echoed across a wider range of serious crime in this country. Counsel both confirmed that this problem was becoming commonplace and the experience of the members of this Court concerned

with the conduct of criminal trials is likewise. Inevitably, applications under section 23 will follow but this judgment should not be read as a licence for prosecutors. Very great care must be taken in each and every case to ensure that attention is paid to the letter and spirit of the Convention and judges should not easily be persuaded that it is in the interests of justice to permit evidence to be read. Where that witness provides the sole or determinative evidence against the accused, permitting it to be read may well, depending on the circumstances, jeopardise infringing the defendant's Article 6(3)(d) rights; even it is not the only evidence, care must be taken to ensure that the ultimate aim of each and every trial, namely, a fair hearing, is achieved.

56. We endorse entirely the view that attention must be paid to the letter and spirit of the Convention and the need for caution. We do, however, register one point. It seems to us that paragraph 30 does not take full account of the case in which the defendant is shown to have kept a witness away by fear, in which, as we have suggested, there should in reality be no question of his Article 6(3)(d) rights having been infringed, since he is the author of his inability to examine the witness.

57. Our view is that certainly care must be taken to see that sections 23 and 26 of the Criminal Justice Act 1988, and indeed the new provisions in the Criminal Justice Act 2003, are not abused. Where intimidation of witnesses is alleged the court must examine with care the circumstances. Are the witnesses truly being kept away by fear? Has that fear been generated by the defendant, or by persons acting with the defendant's authority? Have reasonable steps been taken to trace the witnesses and bring them into court? Can anything be done to enable the witnesses to be brought to court to give evidence and be there protected? It is obvious that the more 'decisive' the evidence in the statements, the greater the care will be needed to be sure why it is that a witness cannot come and give evidence. The court should be astute to examine the quality and reliability of the evidence in the statement and astute and sure that the defendant has every opportunity to apply the provisions of Schedule 2 to the 1988 Act. It will, as section 26 of the 1988 Act states, be looking at the interests of justice, which includes justice to the defendant and justice to the victims. The judge will give warnings to the jury stressing the disadvantage that the defendant is in, not being able to examine a witness.

58. The direction given to the jury we accept is a delicate one. In the defendant's own interests he or she will not wish stress to be placed on the fact that the reason why a witness has not come to give evidence orally is because a judge has formed the view that the witness has been kept away by fear. Mr Solley QC suggested that there was a difficulty in the summing up in this case by virtue of the fact that, when directing the jury quite properly, the interview of the co-accused was not evidence against the appellants, the judge gave as the reason because the appellants were not present when that interview was given. Yet, submitted Mr Solley, the jury were not given an explanation as to why statements were read and were evidence against the appellants, albeit the appellants were not present when those statements were taken. But he submitted it would have been wrong to tell the jury of the true reason.

59. That criticism seems to us to be misplaced. If Mr Solley were correct about it there would be no circumstances in which a statement could be read without giving a direction as to the finding of the judge that the witness had been kept away by fear. That is not a direction that the appellants would have welcomed, indeed, if he had so directed the jury it would have formed a ground of appeal.

60. There is in fact no illogicality in not admitting the statement of a co-accused as evidence, but admitting the evidence of a statement of a witness kept away by fear. The fact that one gives an explanation for the non-admission, which assists the appellant and gives no explanation where it does not, cannot form a legitimate basis for complaint.

Discussion and conclusion in relation to the facts in this case

61. This was a case in which the judge was sure that Carla was being kept away through fear by virtue of the conduct of the appellants or those acting on their behalf. So far as Lee was concerned, his view was that it was 'highly probable' but he could not exclude the reasonable possibility that other factors may have influenced his disappearance. What he was sure of was that Lee could not reasonably be found, and it was legitimate to make part of his reasoning the high probability.

62. The judge was further sure that Carina had been kept away through fear. He was simply sure so far as Donna Mills was concerned that she could not reasonably be found. So far a Donna Mills is concerned, her evidence was not of any great importance. Furthermore, so far as Carina was concerned, she supported the fact that the appellants were involved in drug dealing and she provided some evidence that Carlo had had in his possession at one time a gun which was broadly similar to that which expert evidence had been indicated for the killing. But in relation to that evidence the judge gave a clear warning to the jury about the limitations of that evidence over and above reminding the jury to bear in mind the criticisms made of Carina and her evidence.Thus the evidence of Carina could certainly not be described as decisive.

63. Lee and Carla certainly did give important evidence. It was however certainly not the sole evidence. Lee, for example, gave evidence of a conversation with Carlo immediately after the shooting in which Carlo told him 'to sort himself out, get control or he'd get the same', which the judge described as 'very important evidence in the case of Carlo'. Both Lee and Carla provided descriptions of the return of Santino, Carlo and Marandola to the Fox Hotel.

64. However, there was a great deal of circumstantial evidence, including the tracking of the mobile phones of the appellants and Marandola. But, in particular, there was the oral evidence of Tammy. True, Tammy was treated as a hostile witness. True, also, that Tammy's evidence was strongest against Santino, but it was powerful against Carlo too.

65. We have no doubt that the judge properly exercised his discretion in this case. So far as Carla and Carina are concerned, they were witnesses kept away by fear, a fear for which the appellants were responsible. It should not be forgotten that part of the evidence against the appellants related to covert telephone calls in which they were seeking to subvert the trial. The statements originally taken from Lee and Carla contained statements to the effect that they were fearful of what might happen to them. Mrs Fox, who gave evidence in chambers, was clearly a frightened woman. Tammy was clearly a frightened witness. This was a trial in which fear was being generated by the appellants or those acting for them in order to prevent evidence being given against them. Where the judge was sure of that it seems to us that the appellants cannot complain that their Article 6 rights were being infringed simply by references to those witnesses not being at the trial.

66. So far as Lee is concerned, the circumstances in which he could not reasonably be found included all the above circumstances and the high degree of probability as to his fear.

In his case it cannot be said that the defendants lose their right to complain of an infringement under Article 6, but even in his case, where the evidence was 'important' as against Carlo, even if that meant 'decisive', our view is that provided counter-balancing procedures were properly in place the judge was entitled to admit his statement.

67. Counter-balancing procedures clearly were in place in that the judge took account of section 28 and Schedule 2 to the 1988 Act. Lee was an identified witness and it was open to the appellants to attack the credibility of Lee; indeed they did so, suggesting that he was in fact himself responsible for the murder, that being the reason why he made the statement that he did. Furthermore, the judge warned the jury in relation to all the statements that were read in clear and unequivocal terms. He gave them a strong direction at the time the statements were read. And then he said :

> You will, I am sure, recall that I told you when the first of those statements was read how you should approach their evidence, but it is important that I remind you again of what I told you. Their statements are emphatically not agreed. The defendants would have wished that all of them should be called to give evidence before you. However, there are circumstances where I, as the judge, may permit the prosecution to read the statements of a witness even when the defence wish those witnesses to be called. That is a matter for my decision and you are not, please, to speculate on why I have reached that decision. You will of course immediately appreciate that the defence are disadvantaged by the course I have permitted to take place. You cannot see the demeanour and appearance of the witness when assessing the extent, if at all you are able to rely on the content of the statement. The defence cannot cross-examine, cannot test the accuracy and honesty of the evidence, cannot suggest to the witness a different account or explore with the witness other matters to which the witness does not speak in his or her statement. Thus, when you consider this evidence, bear those observations clearly in mind and give the disadvantage arising from the procedure the weight you think right in determining whether you can rely in any way on the witness statements read to you and if so to what extent. In this connection, bear in mind submissions of the defence on the accuracy and reliability of the statements of those witnesses. It is suggested that each of them may have a sinister motive for not wanting to give evidence and their protestations of fear in their statements are, submit the defence, (my words not theirs) simple weasel words designed to protect themselves, not from any of the defendants but from the consequences of their own involvement on what occurred on the night of the 3 December. You heard their submissions, you give them the weight you think right.

68. If we had formed the view that there was a breach of Article 6, that would have rendered the trial unfair and we could not have, in those circumstances, upheld the conviction as safe and a retrial would have had to have been ordered. We are quite clear that the appellants' rights under Article 6 were in no way infringed in this case. We are equally clear that the convictions of these appellants are safe and this appeal must be dismissed.

Appeals dismissed

R v Joyce (Richard James) and Joyce (James Paul) [2005] EWCA Crim 1785, CA, 27 June 2005; Rose LJ (Vice-President), Holland and Hughes JJ

A Menary and D Nolan for the applicants
J McDermott and T Vindis for the Crown

Vice President, Rose LJ:

1. On 27 April 2005, at Liverpool Crown Court, following a trial before His Honour Judge Gilmour QC, these two applicants were convicted of possessing a firearm with intent to cause fear of violence. A further count of possessing a firearm when prohibited was ordered to remain on the file, on the usual terms: that was count 2, in relation to Richard Joyce and count 3, in relation to James Joyce. So far as Richard Joyce is concerned, there was also an offence of driving whilst disqualified which was remitted to the magistrates' Court, for a plea of not guilty to be entered. Richard Joyce was sentenced to 7 years' imprisonment and James Joyce to 8 years' imprisonment. Prior to the trial, Richard Joyce had failed to answer bail on 28 February 2005. He was tried and sentenced in his absence. So far as this Court knows he is still at large.

2. Both applicants apply for an extension of time of eight days in which to seek leave to appeal against conviction and sentence. We grant the extension of time.

3. The applications have been referred to the Full Court by the Registrar, as this appears to be one of the first, if not the first, cases to come before this Court in relation to the new hearsay provisions of the Criminal Justice Act 2003, to which, in a moment, we shall come.

4. The facts were these. On 23 July 2004, in broad daylight, in Kirby, two undisguised men approached the home of the complainant, Darcy, in a black motorcar. One, holding a loaded shotgun, got out of the car and fired three or four times at the windows of the house before returning to the car. The men then drove away. It was the prosecution case that the applicant, James Joyce, fired the shots and the applicant, Richard Joyce, was the driver of the car. The allegation was that both had, in the car, been in possession of the shotgun with intent to cause fear of violence.

5. The prosecution relied on witness statements which had been made by Darcy, by a woman called Natalie Rogers and by Peter Wilson. In each of those statements, each of those three witnesses told the police that (in the case of Darcy and Wilson) the applicants were the two involved. In the case of Miss Rogers, she identified only James Joyce.

6. Subsequently, those statements were retracted by all three witnesses. Each gave evidence before the jury that their initial statement was wrong, and they were mistaken when identifying of the applicants. The judge, exercising his new powers under section 119 of the Criminal Justice Act 2003, admitted the witness statements made by each of the witnesses.

7. The prosecution also relied on a statement by Darcy and his evidence that both the applicants had been part of a gang of four who had come to his front door, two or three weeks before the offence with which the two applicants were charged and, on that occasion, James Joyce had punched him. The prosecution also relied, so far as James Joyce was concerned, on the 'no comment' interviews which he had given.

8. The case for Richard Joyce, in his absence, was to put the prosecution to proof. The defence for James Joyce was that he had been incorrectly identified by the three witnesses in their statements. He had been at home, on his own, on 23 July, and he relied on the evidence of the three witnesses that they were mistaken in their initial identifications. The issue was whether the retracted witness statements and other supporting evidence sufficed to prove the guilt of the applicants of this offence.

9. Darcy, who was treated as hostile, gave evidence that, some two weeks before, he had been assaulted by four men, including the two applicants. This was because James Joyce claimed that one of Darcy's sons, Mark, owed him money. In a statement made, it is to be noted, on the day of the incident, 23 July 2004, Darcy told the police he had been outside with his grandson. His son, Brian, was sitting in a motorcar nearby with another man. A black car arrived, with its windows down. Richard Joyce was sitting in the front passenger seat. Someone shouted: 'Do you want a straightener?' James Joyce got out, came into full view, carrying a shotgun and pointing it towards Darcy and Brian's car. The Darcy family all ran inside. There was a loud bang as the gun was discharged. The windows in the house were smashed. Darcy telephoned the police. Then, together with another son, Peter, they armed themselves with baseball bats and chased James Joyce, who dived headfirst into the black car through the window. James Joyce then reloaded the gun. Darcy and his son ran back into the house. Further shots were fired and glass smashed. James Joyce then smashed the car windows and bodywork of his son's car, using the butt of the shotgun. Darcy added that he had known James Joyce and his family for years.

10. In the witness-box, Darcy said he had tried to retract his statement of 23 July on 25 November, when he made a statement to solicitors that he had been mistaken as to his identification. He had, he said, seen the true perpetrators in a car in Bewley Drive, and had then realised the mistake he had made. In cross-examination, he relied on his statement of 25 November and claimed that he did not know how his son's car had come to be damaged or how his windows had come to be broken.

11. Natalie Rogers gave evidence that she had originally, in a statement likewise made on the day of the incident, 23 July, identified James Joyce as being the gunman and she had seen him damaging the car. She had not seen a second male. Some two or three weeks later, she saw another man in the area, who looked exactly like James Joyce. Knowing that James Joyce was in custody at that time, she went to Kirby police station and told the police she had made a mistake about the identification. She too knew the Joyce family: Richard Joyce was a friend of her brothers.

12. Peter Wilson, like Darcy, was treated as hostile. He gave evidence that, on the day in question, he had been working at the Darcys. He had known that family for more than 18 years. He was present and witnessed the shooting but, he claimed, he could not identify the gunman. He too had made a statement on 23 July, saying Richard Joyce had been driving the car and James Joyce, the passenger who got out, discharged the loaded shotgun into the front window of the house. He said in evidence that he was wrong to identify James Joyce as discharging gun. He had not seen the driver of the car, but he had heard other people shouting 'Richard Joyce'.

13. In interview, as we have said, James Joyce made no comment in response to all the questions he was asked. Therefore, it is apparent that he failed to mention the fact, as he was to claim in the course of his trial, that he had been at home all day on the occasion of the shooting.

14. A submission was made, at the close of the prosecution case, on behalf of James Joyce, that the identification evidence was so weak that there was no case to answer, in the light of *Turnbull* [1977] QB 224. Alternatively, it was submitted, on behalf of both defendants, the evidence provided by the retracted witness statements was unconvincing, to such an extent that, in accordance with his powers under section 125 of the Criminal Justice Act 2003, the judge ought to direct an acquittal. The judge ruled that the case should be left to the jury, as the identifications were made in broad daylight, by people who knew the applicant's. Those identifications did not become weak because they were subsequently retracted. The jury had to consider why the witnesses had changed their accounts and could come to the view that they were lying in court and that it was their original identification which was correct.

15. James Joyce gave evidence. He said that he had always lived in Kirby. Darcy was known to his family but he did not know Natalie Rogers or Peter Wilson and had never spoken to either them. He had been at home on his own at the time of the incident. He had not made any comment in interview because he thought that was the safest option.

16. The focus of this application for leave to appeal against conviction, is on the provisions in Part 11 Chapter 2 of the Criminal Justice Act 2003, in particular, sections 114, 119 and 125. By Chapter 2 Parliament modernised the hearsay rule. The reforms enshrined in that legislation are derived from the Law Commission's Report No 245, *Evidence in Criminal Proceedings, Hearsay and Related Topics* which was presented to Parliament as long ago as June 1997 and was followed by a government white paper, *Justice For All* in 2002.

17. The provisions relevant to this appeal are, first, section 114(1)(a) which is in these terms:

> In criminal proceedings a statement not made in oral evidence in the proceedings is admissible as evidence of any matter stated if, but only if—
>
> (a) any provision of this Chapter or any other statutory provision makes it admissible.

Section 119(1) is in these terms:

> If in criminal proceedings a person gives oral evidence and—
>
> (a) he admits making a previous inconsistent statement, or
> (b) a previous inconsistent statement made by him is proved by virtue of section 3, 4, or 5 of the Criminal Procedure Act 1865.
>
> the statement is admissible as evidence of any matter stated of which oral evidence by him would be admissible.

Section 125(1) is in these terms:

> If on the defendant's trial before a judge and jury for an offence the court is satisfied at any time after the close of the prosecution that—
>
> (a) the case against the defendant is based wholly or partly on a statement not made in oral evidence in the proceedings, and.
> (b) the evidence provided by the statement is so unconvincing that, considering its importance to the case against the defendant, his conviction of the offence would be unsafe,

the court must either direct the jury to acquit the defendant of the offence or, if it considers that there ought to be a retrial, discharge the jury.

18. On behalf of both applicants, Mr Menary QC, who did not appear at trial, submits, first, that the judge should have directed not guilty verdicts at the close of the prosecution case, either under section 125(1) or, in the light of *Turnbull*, or possibly under *Galbraith*, [1981] 1 WLR 1039, because the quality of the evidence was poor, unsupported and so tenuous that no jury could properly convict on the basis of it. He accepts that the judge was entitled to treat Darcy and Wilson as hostile, so as to permit proof of their previous inconsistent statements and he accepts that Miss Rogers admitted making her previous inconsistent statement. Accordingly, he concedes that the provisions of section 119, for admissibility, were fulfilled and, in consequence, the contents of the written statements were capable of supporting a conviction.

19. It is submitted, and we accept, that section 125 should not be regarded as requiring a higher standard than *Galbraith*. But it provides, in accordance with the Law Commission's recommendation in §11.31 and §11.32 of their report, an additional safety valve obliging a judge to direct an acquittal where the previous statements are particularly unpersuasive. It is emphasised in paragraph 9 of Mr Menary's skeleton written submissions and in his oral argument before us that this was an identification case, based solely on the challenged evidence of three eyewitnesses, who could only support each other if they were reliable.

20. He submits that they could not be regarded as reliable, in that they had each contradicted their earlier written statement, by their oral evidence. Furthermore, as he rightly points out, none of them claimed to have been intimidated by, or on behalf of, the defendants into changing their evidence.

21. Those matters, he submits and we accept, are relevant to the judge's consideration as to whether the evidence was 'so unconvincing' in the terms of section 125(1)(b). In his ruling, the judge expressly had regard to the surrounding circumstances and it seems to us that it is highly unlikely that he overlooked the specific matters to which Mr Menary drew attention.

22. It has to be borne in mind, as it seems to us, that the circumstances of this offence were terrifying. That is a matter which the judge was entitled to take into consideration, (as indeed in due course were the jury) when considering, whether the earlier statements were so unconvincing that an acquittal should be directed.

23. Mr Menary also points out, correctly, that the three witnesses were not wholly independent of each other. Darcy and Wilson were friends and Miss Rogers was a neighbour of Darcy's. Furthermore, there was no evidence as to the circumstances in which either the original accusatory statements, or the later retractions came to be made. So, Mr Menary submits, there is the possibility that all three witnesses may have been honestly confused or mistaken in their initial statements. Accordingly, Mr Menary submits that there was, absent any further investigation by anybody as to how the change of accounts came to be made, inadequate material for the judge to reach a conclusion as to whether the initial statements were unconvincing or not.

24. Mr Menary accepts that the initial written statements on their face provide strong, cogent, evidence against each of the applicants, but, he says, the judge had to have regard, not just to that, but also to all the surrounding circumstances. We take all these matters into account.

25. Having seen and heard the three witnesses, the judge was well placed (certainly better placed than the members of this Court) to assess the quality of the evidence which they gave before the jury and to decide whether their original statements merited consideration by the jury or were so unconvincing as to require a directed acquittal.

26. On the material before us, we would have been astonished if the judge had reached a different conclusion than he did. The shootings took place in broad daylight, at midday, in summer. The defendants were known to all three witnesses, who had unobstructed views of them, over a significant period of time, at least in the case of Darcy and Miss Rogers. In the circumstances, the suggestion that all three witnesses were initially confused or mistaken in the statements which they made on the day of these events strains credulity.

27. In the light of the new statutory provisions in relation to hearsay, in our judgment, it would have been an affront to the administration of justice, on a trial for offences based on this terrifying conduct, if the jury had not been permitted by the judge to evaluate, separately and together, the quality of the three witnesses' oral evidence and to be able to rely, if they thought fit, on the terms of their original statements. The jury would, no doubt, have been assisted in this regard, by, among other matters, Darcy's evidence that, although he was no longer sure of his identification, he did not know how his windows had come to be broken and his son's car damaged. Accordingly, Mr Menary's first submission seems to us to be unarguable.

28. His second submission is critical of the summing-up. It is said that the judge gave insufficiently clear and robust warnings, first, as to the challenged identification evidence. That complaint, as it seems to us, cannot survive the passage in the summing-up which, subject to one point, includes an impeccable direction in accordance with Turnbull. We accept Mr Menary's submission that it would have been better if the judge had referred to the possibility of mistakes being made by witnesses who purport to recognise rather than merely identify a particular person. But, in our judgment, the summing-up in the passage which we have identified, read as a whole, is a sufficient and proper direction as to the need for caution without significant flaw. Secondly, it is said that, in regard to the three witnesses two of whom were treated as hostile, because they were manifestly unreliable and self-contradictory, further directions were necessary as to the burden and standard of proof. In our judgment, the relevant passages in the summing-up, which it is unnecessary to rehearse save in relation to the last passage, from which, in a moment, we shall quote, were clear, comprehensive, fair and accurate directions as to the burden and standard of proof and as to how the jury should approach their decision as to which of the two versions of events they accepted.

29. We reject the further submission that another passage contained a misdirection. The direction which the judge there gave was as to the three options open to the jury, in the light of the prosecution case. First, they might accept the police statement by each of the witnesses, if sure that it was true and accurate. Secondly, they might accept what each witness said in his or her evidence, if sure that he or she was telling the truth.

30. The judge went on: 'The third possibility is, given the inconsistencies between the earlier statements and their evidence in court yesterday, you may take the view you cannot rely on any of that witness' evidence and you may choose to ignore completely what that witness has said.' It is said that that passage, in conjunction with a reference to Darcy and Wilson being treated as hostile witnesses: '. . . that is a witness who has in effect, changed

sides', gave rise to a misdirection. We do not agree. The use of the phrase 'changed sides', seems to us to be no more than a convenient shorthand for what had essentially happened in this particular case, so far as all three witnesses are concerned. In laying out, as he did, the options which the jury had when confronted by these differing accounts, the judge, as it seems to us, properly directed the jury on this aspect of the case. Because the circumstances of this case were so striking, it does not seem to us that it provides a good vehicle in which to give general guidance as to the form which a summing-up should take, when hearsay evidence is admitted under the new statutory provisions. Necessarily, judges must tailor their summing-up to the circumstances of the particular case. It will, for example, be essential, when the hearsay relied on is the product of multiple hearsay, to give a most careful direction that that is so in order that juries may be in a position properly to evaluate the weight which they ought to give to such hearsay evidence.

31. That, however, is not the situation which arises in the present case. It is apparent from what we have already said that the contents of the hearsay statements admitted in this case were the account solely of the maker of the statement. The judge's summing up was appropriate in the light of these considerations, as it seems to us, there is no arguable ground of appeal against the safety of these convictions and leave is accordingly refused.

[[32]–[35] The court considered the applications for leave to appeal against sentence.]

Applications for leave to appeal against conviction and sentence refused.

R v Xhabri [2005] EWCA Crim 3135, CA, 7 December 2005, Lord Phillips, CJ, Rafferty and Mackay JJ

R Offenbach for the appellant
J Livingston for the Crown

Lord Phillips, CJ:

1. On 24 May 2005 in the Crown Court at Snaresbrook, after a 12 day trial, the Appellant was convicted of the following offences: Count 1: false imprisonment; Counts 2 and 3: rape; Count 4: threats to kill; Count 5: control of prostitution for gain. On the first Count he was sentenced to 12 years imprisonment. On the 2nd and 3rd Counts he was sentenced to 12 years imprisonment concurrent. On each of the 4th and 5th Counts he was sentenced to 5 years imprisonment concurrent. His application for permission to appeal against conviction was referred to a full court by the Registrar. This case raises questions as to the application of the novel provisions in relation to hearsay introduced by the Criminal Justice Act 2003. For this reason, we gave permission to appeal at the beginning of the hearing.

The facts

2. The Complainant in this case is a young woman from Latvia. At the time to which this appeal relates she was 17 years old. There was little dispute as to what she did in the period covered by the charges. What was critically in issue was why she acted as she did.

3. In May 2004 Mr L, L's father, came to live in England. He found a flat in Newham, East London. On 25 July 2004, L came to England to live with him. Mrs L, L's mother,

remained in Latvia. L met and made friends with a young Lithuanian woman called Egla. Egla lived at a house in Walton Road, Ilford. Early in September L moved out of her father's flat and went to live in this house. The appellant lived in the same house. From the outset L shared a bedroom with him. On the second day that she was there L and the appellant had sexual intercourse. Thereafter they had sexual intercourse on frequent occasions.

4. While living at Walton Road, L worked as a prostitute in brothels described as saunas. Either the appellant or an associate of his would drive her to and collect her from the sauna.

5. On one occasion L left the sauna where she had been working at Kings Cross and took a train to York where she stayed with a Latvian friend for 5 days. She then returned to Ilford and continued working in saunas as before.

6. Early in November the appellant and L moved from Walton Road, Ilford to Strone Road, Forest Gate.

7. On the night of 11/12 November L was working in the sauna at Kings Cross. The appellant collected her by car in the morning and took her back to Strone Road. There they had sexual intercourse. He then left, locking her in the bedroom. The house was then raided by the police who broke down her bedroom door and took her away with them.

8. We now come to contentious areas of facts. Our summary of these is taken from the witness statements, for this was the material before the judge when he made the rulings which are the subject of this appeal. We do not believe that they differ significantly from the evidence subsequently given at the trial.

Duress or consent?

9. It was L's evidence that she acted in the manner we have described as a result of duress. The appellant is an Albanian. There were other Albanians living in the house at Walton Road. On the second night that she was there the appellant raped her. Equally when she and the appellant had sexual intercourse on subsequent occasions, this was because the appellant forced her to submit to him against her will. The appellant forced her to work as a prostitute by threats of physical violence against her and her father. Initially she was too frightened to run away. Another Latvian girl called Aija was brought to the house at Walton Rod and also made to work in the saunas and went to York. She made contact with L and arranged for L to run away to York to join her, which she did, having escaped from the sauna at Kings Cross. There was a foreigner called Iris living in the same house in York as Aija. He knew the appellant and must have informed the appellant of L's whereabouts, for after 5 days the appellant appeared in a car and took L by force back to London. Thereafter she was forced to continue working in the saunas as before.

10. The appellant made a defence case statement in which he denied that he had detained L against her will, raped her and forced her to act as a prostitute. It was his case that they began a consensual sexual relationship and that she then moved in with him at her instigation due to problems she was experiencing with her father. He knew that she was acting as a prostitute for some, if not all, of the time he knew her but that occupation was of her own choosing and not through any force or influence exerted by him.

The evidence under challenge

11. On 4 May 2005, before the trial began, the defence sought to exclude some of the evidence that the prosecution proposed to put before the jury. We shall refer to that

evidence in a little more detail in due course. Suffice it to say that, for the most part, it related to communications alleged to have been made by L, directly or indirectly, with her mother, her father, O, a friend who lived in the same building as her father, and the police. The defence did not seek to prevent L giving evidence of communications that she had made. They objected, however, to the recipients of those communications giving evidence of what they had been told. The prosecution submitted that this evidence was admissible under provisions of the 2003 Act. We shall now set out the relevant provisions.

Hearsay provisions of the Criminal Justice Act 2003

12. Section 118 abolishes the common law rules governing the admissibility of hearsay evidence in criminal proceedings, subject to certain exceptions which are not relevant in this case. Section 114 provides:

Admissibility of hearsay evidence

(1) In criminal proceedings a statement not made in oral evidence in the proceedings is admissible as evidence of any matter stated if, but only if—

... (d) the court is satisfied that it is in the interests of justice for it to be admissible.

(2) In deciding whether a statement not made in oral evidence should be admitted under subsection (1)(d), the court must have regard to the following factors (and to any others it considers relevant):

(a) how much probative value the statement has (assuming it to be true) in relation to a matter in issue in the proceedings, or how valuable it is for the understanding of other evidence in the case;
(b) what other evidence has been, or can be, given on the matter or evidence mentioned in paragraph (a);
(c) how important the matter or evidence mentioned in paragraph (a) is in the context of the case as a whole;
(d) the circumstances in which the statement was made;
(e) how reliable the maker of the statement appears to be;
(f) how reliable the evidence of the making of the statement appears to be;
(g) whether oral evidence of the matter stated can be given and, if not, why it cannot;
(h) the amount of difficulty involved in challenging the statement;
(i) the extent to which that difficulty would be likely to prejudice the party facing it.

13. Section 120 provides:

'Other previous statements of witnesses

(1) This section applies where a person (the witness) is called to give evidence in criminal proceedings.
(2) If a previous statement by the witness is admitted as evidence to rebut a suggestion that his oral evidence has been fabricated, that statement is admissible as evidence of any matter stated of which oral evidence by the witness would be admissible.

. . .

(4) A previous statement by the witness is admissible as evidence of any matter stated of which oral evidence by him would be admissible, if—

   (a) any of the following three conditions is satisfied, and
   (b) while giving evidence the witness indicates that to the best of his belief he made the statement, and that to the best of his belief it states the truth.

(5) The first condition is that the statement identifies or describes a person, object or place.
(6) The second condition is that the statement was made by the witness when the matters stated were fresh in his memory but he does not remember them, and cannot reasonably be expected to remember them, well enough to give oral evidence of them in the proceedings.
(7) The third condition is that—

   (a) the witness claims to be a person against whom an offence has been committed,
   (b) the offence is one to which the proceedings relate,
   (c) the statement consists of a complaint made by the witness (whether to a person in authority or not) about conduct which would, if proved, constitute the offence or part of the offence,
   (d) the complaint was made as soon as could reasonably be expected after the alleged conduct,
   (e) the complaint was not made as a result of a threat or a promise, and
   (f) before the statement is adduced the witness gives oral evidence in connection with its subject matter.

14. Section 121 provides:

Additional requirement for admissibility of multiple hearsay

(1) A hearsay statement is not admissible to prove the fact that an earlier hearsay statement was made unless—

   (a) either of the statements is admissible under section 117, 119 or 120,
   (b) all parties to the proceedings so agree, or
   (c) the court is satisfied that the value of the evidence in question, taking into account how reliable the statements appear to be, is so high that the interests of justice require the later statement to be admissible for that purpose.

(2) In this section 'hearsay statement' means a statement, not made in oral evidence, that is relied on as evidence of a matter stated in it.

15. Section 126 provides:

Court's general discretion to exclude evidence

(1) In criminal proceedings the court may refuse to admit a statement as evidence of a matter stated if—

(a) the statement was made otherwise than in oral evidence in the proceedings, and
(b) the court is satisfied that the case for excluding the statement, taking account of the danger that to admit it would result in undue waste of time, substantially outweighs the case for admitting it, taking account of the value of the evidence.

(2) Nothing in this Chapter prejudices—

(a) any power of a court to exclude evidence under section 78 of the Police and Criminal Evidence Act 1984 (c. 60) (exclusion of unfair evidence), or
(b) any other power of a court to exclude evidence at its discretion (whether by preventing questions from being put or otherwise).

L's evidence

16. L stated that initially the appellant dictated a reassuring letter for her to send to her father. She did not have access to a telephone but the appellant twice made her telephone her mother on his mobile phone in order to reassure her, stating that she was working as a cleaner.

17. After she had been working as a prostitute for about 3 weeks the appellant told her to go and see her father, tell him that she was all right and working in a restaurant and give him £400, which he handed to her. She was driven to her father's home by three associates of the appellant. She was told that if she did not come out after 15 minutes there would be trouble. The door was answered by O. She gave O a bag containing the money. She told O that she was being held by men who would not let her go; that she was scared and that they were watching for her outside. They were Albanians. She did not want to tell her father what was happening because she was frightened as to what might happen to all of them.

18. On a few occasions when working in the sauna at Kings Cross she managed to borrow a mobile phone and telephone her mother.

19. She told the security guard, Max, at the Kings Cross sauna about her circumstances. He said that he would go to the police and tell them what was happening. She gave him her father's name and address and the address at which she was being held in Walton Road. He told her that he had gone to the police with the sauna's receptionist, a short haired black woman.

20. Between 3 and 4 in the morning of 12 November L persuaded a Ukrainian woman who worked at the Kings Cross sauna to lend her her mobile. She telephoned her mother and gave her mother the number of this mobile telephone. Her mother said that she would pass this on to her father and that he would phone her. She had been unaware that her father had a mobile telephone. Her father then telephoned her. She gave her father the address in Strone Road where she was living and told her father that she would be at that address between 11am and 4pm on that day. Her father told her not to worry: they were going to release her.

The evidence to which objection was made

Mrs L's evidence

21. Mrs L stated that initially L telephoned her and explained that she had moved out from her father's flat because she wanted to live independently and she was earning well,

working in a private hotel. After that there was a long silence. On 18 October 2004 L phoned saying that she was in a lot of trouble, that she had been kidnapped by some Albanians, could not do anything without the help of the police and was being watched and guarded. After this she phoned a few more times. On 20 October her daughter dictated an address which she wrote down: 'King kross' 'Caledonian Road No1'.

22. Towards the evening of 2 November 2004 L phoned again and dictated an address, which she wrote down as 'IOFORT 'next to father'' 'VV' 'Alton Road 173' '7984590605'. She said that the telephone connection was unstable and she could only hear half of what was said. In a subsequent conversation she told L that she had phoned L's father who had gone to the police but the police could not find the address that had been given.

23. On 11 November 2004 during the night L phoned and gave her the number of a mobile phone which L had begged the guard to lend her. She immediately telephoned her husband's mobile phone and gave him that number. The next day, her husband phoned her and informed her that L was with him and everything was fine.

Mr L's Evidence

24. Mr L said that between the 4 and 7 October his neighbour called O, who rented the room opposite his, brought him a note from L saying that she was working a lot and studying and was passing on money for her mother. The note was accompanied by £400.

25. On 13 October, two young men came to his flat. They said that L had disappeared; that L lived with them and that on 12 October she had gone to work but had not come home. They said they were Albanians and asked him where L worked. He said that he did not know. On 17 October the 2 men came again. They asked if L had come back and he said no.

26. On 19/20 October his wife telephoned him and said L had phoned her saying that armed people were guarding her. If they found she was talking on the telephone they would kill her. They were Albanians. The name of the street was 1 Caledonian Road, Kings Cross. He must not contact the police because everything was very dangerous. Despite this he went to the police station at Romford Road on 23 October to report what he had been told. After that he spoke to his wife many times. She said that they had kidnapped L, would not let her sleep or get dressed and they were always threatening that they would kill her. His wife spoke of a subsequent phone call when L said that she was being kept by a gang of Albanians at 173 Alton Road, Ilford. At 5am on the morning of 12 November his wife called him and said that L had managed to pass on another address in Strone Road which she gave him. She also gave him a mobile number for L. He telephoned L on this number and she said that from 11am to 4pm she would be at the address in Strone Road. She was very scared and said that the Albanians were very cunning and if they saw people in police uniforms at this address they would kill her straightaway. He passed this information on to the police.

O's Evidence

27. O stated on the 2 or 3 October L came to their house. Her father was asleep. L told her that she was living with several Albanians in the house who would not let her go anywhere and accompanied her everywhere. One of them got her job in a massaging salon. They controlled all her telephone calls, beat her and always threatened her that if she didn't

listen to them they would kill her father. She stayed with them because she was scared for her father and her own life. She handed over a bag for her father.

The police evidence

28. PC Brandon was based at Islington Police Station. He stated that on 22 October a man and woman came in. The woman was black and the man was eastern European. They said they had information about the sex trafficking trade. In particular they gave L's name and an address in Walton Road. They said that she was kept in a house and prevented from leaving. They said that she was in fear of her life and had made attempts to leave and that she did not want to involve the police because she feared for her life. They gave the address of two saunas where she worked and the address where her father lived.

The Judge's ruling

29. The Prosecution sought to adduce the evidence of Mr and Mrs L and O pursuant to section 114 and 120 of the 2003 Act. They sought to adduce the evidence of PC Brandon under section 121. The Defence objected that is was unfair to admit this evidence, relying on the provisions of section 126.

30. The judge ruled that the evidence of the first three witnesses came 'four square within section 120 and that each of the conditions in subsections (5), (6) and (7) clearly applied to it'. Alternatively the evidence was admissible under section 114. It was highly probative. It was supported by the evidence of L herself. It was extremely important. The statements containing the hearsay evidence had been made in the normal way to police officers and, in the case of Mrs L, in accordance with normal protocol for statements taken abroad. There was no reason to doubt the reliability of those who had made the statements in question.

31. So far as the evidence of PC Brandon was concerned, this had caused the judge greater concerns. He had no doubt that the officer had recorded what he had been told contemporaneously. The two informants were not identified but they seemed to have given an accurate account of what they had been told. The evidence was admissible under either subsection (1)(a) or subsection (1)(c) to section 121 and should go before the jury.

Submissions made to us

32. Mr Offenbach, who appeared for the appellant, submitted that the evidence challenged did not fall within the provisions of section 120(4). He accepted though that it fell within the discretion afforded to the judge by section 114(1)(d) but submitted that its admission was not in the interests of justice and that it should have been excluded pursuant to section 126. So far as the evidence of the visit of the two the unnamed men to Mr L was concerned, these men had not been identified and were not available for cross-examination. The same was true of the two informants whose information formed the subject matter of PC Brandon's statement.

33. Mr Offenbach further submitted that the relevant provisions of the 2003 Act were incompatible with the Human Rights Act 1998. Alternatively he submitted that the judge's ruling was in breach of the requirements of that Act.

Our conclusions

34. As we observed earlier, the defence made no objection to L giving evidence of the various communications that she made to her mother, her father, O and to the security guard, Max, at the Kings Cross sauna. Prior to the 2003 Act there might have been some debate as to whether, and on what basis, such evidence could be admitted. Plainly it was in the interests of justice that such evidence should be admitted, not merely as evidence of how L was reacting but as evidence of the truth of the statements that she was making as to her predicament. The jury would obviously wish to know whether she had sought to communicate with the outside world and in what terms.

What of the evidence of those who received L's communications?

35. Mr L's evidence, Mrs L's evidence and O's evidence adduced in the form of hearsay the statements made to them by L during the time when she alleged she was effectively imprisoned by the appellant. The issue is whether these statements by L were properly admitted as evidence. Contrary to the view expressed by the judge, we do not consider that section 120(5) or (6) was applicable. We do, however, consider that the six requirements of section 120(7) were, or were likely to be, satisfied:

(a) L claimed to be a person against whom an offence had been committed.
(b) The offence was one to which the proceedings related.
(c) The complaint was about conduct which would, if proved, constitute part of the offence.
(d) The complaint was made as soon as could reasonably be expected after the alleged conduct. The complaints were, in fact, made while the alleged conduct was continuing.
(e) The complaint was not made as a result of a threat or promise.
(f) L was expected to give evidence before the material evidence relating to her previous statements was adduced.

36. Even if section 120 was not satisfied, the evidence in question plainly fell within the judge's discretion under section 114(1)(d), always provided that admission of the evidence was in the interests of justice. We can see no basis upon which it could be suggested that the admission of this evidence was not in the interests of justice. It was probably not clear at the time that the judge made his ruling whether the defence case would be that L never made the alleged statements or whether it would be that, when making them, she was lying. If the former, then there was every reason why the jury should hear evidence from those to whom L made the statements. If the latter, the introduction of the evidence could not unfairly prejudice the defendant.

37. As we understand it the only argument raised by Mr Offenbach against the admission of this evidence was that it was unreliable. We see no merit in this argument. Mrs L's evidence was supported by her husband, to whom she passed on what she had heard. No point was taken that this part of Mr L's evidence was double hearsay. Had such a point been taken, we think that the judge could properly have held this evidence admissible under section 121(1)(c). The evidence was of substantial value and, according as it did with the evidence of Mrs L and the evidence of L, apparently reliable. For these reasons we

reject the contention that this evidence should not have been admitted. We shall deal with the additional arguments advanced before us based on the Human Rights Act in due course.

38. We turn to the evidence given by Mr L of the two visits by the two Albanian men. In so far as this evidence was the effect that the two men were trying to ascertain the whereabouts of L, it was evidence of fact rather than hearsay. In so far, however, as it was evidence that the two men had stated that L had disappeared it was hearsay. This was a significant part of the story in that it fitted in with L's evidence of her escape to York. We consider that is was properly admitted under section 114.

The evidence of PC Brandon

39. This was double hearsay because, for the most part, the two witnesses who came to give information to PC Brandon were reporting what L had told them. Section 121 applied to this evidence. The earlier hearsay statement, that is the statement by L, was admissible under section 120(4) for the reasons that we have given when dealing with the other statements that she made. Thus the judge was correct to hold that section 121(1)(a) was satisfied. We think that the judge was also correct to rule that section 121(1)(c) was satisfied. This evidence was, as Mr Offenbach frankly accepted, very damaging to the appellant. The value of the evidence was, in our judgment, so high that the interests of justice required PC Brandon's statement to be admitted.

40. Mr Offenbach argued that admitting this evidence was unfair because the two witnesses who had conveyed the information to PC Brandon were not available for cross-examination. We see nothing in this point. We think that Mr Offenbach would have been in some difficulty in finding any question that it was safe to put to them. Furthermore all that they were doing was relaying information provided by L, who was available for cross-examination.

41. For these reasons we reject the contention that this evidence should not have been admitted.

The Human Rights Act

42. Mr Offenbach's arguments in relation to incompatibility, or non-compliance, with the Human Rights Convention were founded on the following provision of Article 6 of the Convention:

> 3. Everyone charged with a criminal offence has the following minimum rights:
>
> . . . (d) to examine or have examined witnesses against him . . .

Mr Offenbach submitted that because section 114 permitted the court to adduce in evidence a hearsay statement by a witness who was not available for cross-examination, that section was incompatible with Article 6 of the Convention. There is no merit in that argument. The discretion granted by section 114 is not restricted to the admission of a hearsay statement the maker of which is not available for cross-examination. To the extent that Article 6 would be infringed by admitting such evidence, the court has a power to exclude the evidence under section 126 and a duty so to do by virtue of the

Human Rights Act. There can thus be no question of section 114 being incompatible with the Convention.

43. As to the contention that the judge, by admitting the hearsay evidence, infringed Article 6, there is no merit in this either. Article 6(3)(d) is one of the provisions designed to secure 'equality of arms'. The hearsay provisions of the 2003 Act apply equally to prosecution and defence, so there is no inherent inequality of arms arising out of those provisions.

44. Article 6(3)(d) does not give a defendant an absolute right to examine every witness whose testimony is adduced against him. The touchstone is whether fairness of the trial requires this. In the present case almost all the hearsay evidence derived directly, or indirectly, from L. She was available for examination. This satisfied the requirements of Article 6(3)(d).

45. For all these reasons this appeal is dismissed.

Appeal dismissed

R v Taylor [2006] EWCA Crim 260, CA, 25 January 2006, Rose LJ (Vice President), Rafferty J and Sir Douglas Brown

P Sinclair for the applicant.
R Johnson for the Crown.

Vice President, Rose LJ:

1. On 15 September 2005 at Maidstone Crown Court, following a trial before His Honour Judge Patience QC, this applicant was convicted of causing grievous bodily harm with intent on count 1 in the indictment. On 16th September he was sentenced at the same court, by the same judge, to three-and-a-half years detention under section 91 of the Powers of Criminal Courts (Sentencing) Act 2000. A co-accused called Still was acquitted. The applicant applies for leave to appeal against his conviction, and the application has been referred to the Full Court by the registrar.

2. The facts were that, on the evening of 2 August 2004, a 16 year old called George Olliffe became involved in a fight with other youths in Paddock Wood, Kent. He fell to the ground and was repeatedly kicked in the head and face. He was taken to hospital with bruising of the head and face and a laceration to the right eyebrow. He was discharged but, two days later, readmitted and then underwent two operations to stem heavy bleeding from his nose which was, at that stage, found to have been fractured, with damage to a nasal artery. In consequence, he was in hospital for some 10 days and required a considerable blood transfusion.

3. It was the prosecution case that the group of youths had been spoiling for a fight following an earlier incident involving the victim's brother, John. That, according to the prosecution, involved the applicant and Still. It was the defence on behalf of this applicant that he was present at the fight, but his participation was limited to a brief intervention in order to break up the fight. He said he had pushed Still out of the way, after seeing him kick George Olliffe. He, the applicant, had picked Olliffe up and told him to go home. The applicant said he had not punched or kicked Olliffe and had certainly not intended him any

bodily injury. Still also denied kicking Olliffe and claimed that he had only intervened in order to stop the fight.

4. There was an application made in relation to the admissibility or otherwise of hearsay evidence under section 114 of the Criminal Justice Act 2003. That came about in this way.

5. In their video recorded interviews, which constituted their evidence-in-chief, the prosecution witnesses, John Olliffe and Nandi Jones, both named the applicant as a participant in the attack after they had been told his name by someone else. In the case of Nandi Jones, the information had come from her ex-boyfriend.

6. The defence applied to exclude these references from the recorded interviews, under section 114 of the Criminal Justice Act 2003, on the basis that the evidence amounted to inadmissible hearsay.

7. The Crown argued that the evidence should be admitted under section 114(1)(d) on the ground that it was in the interests of justice for it to be admitted.

8. Before turning to the judge's ruling, it is convenient to rehearse the relevant provisions of section 114. This provides in subsection (1):

> In criminal proceedings a statement not made in oral evidence in the proceedings is admissible as evidence of any matter stated if, but only if—
>
> (a) any provision of this Chapter or any other statutory provision makes it admissible,
> (b) any rule of law preserved by section 118 makes it admissible,
> (c) all parties to the proceedings agree to it being admissible, or.
> (d) the court is satisfied that it is in the interests of justice for it to be admissible.
>
> (2) In deciding whether a statement not made in oral evidence should be admitted under subsection (1)(d), the court must have regard to the following factors (and to any others it considers relevant)—
>
> (a) how much probative value the statement has (assuming it to be true) in relation to a matter in issue in the proceedings, or how valuable it is for the understanding of other evidence in the case;
> (b) what other evidence has been, or can be, given on the matter or evidence mentioned in paragraph (a);
> (c) how important the matter or evidence mentioned in paragraph (a) is in the context of the case as a whole;
> (d) the circumstances in which the statement was made;
> (e) how reliable the maker of the statement appears to be;
> (f) how reliable the evidence of the making of the statement appears to be;
> (g) whether oral evidence of the matter stated can be given and, if not, why it cannot;
> (h) the amount of difficulty involved in challenging the statement;
> (i) the extent to which that difficulty would be likely to prejudice the party facing it.

9. The judge ruled that he had considered the factors in section 114(2) and he had also considered section 8 of the police section 78 of the Police and Criminal Evidence Act 1984, in order to ensure that admission of the evidence would not impair the fairness of the

proceedings. He concluded that he was unable to form a clear view on some of the factors set out in section 114, as the circumstances in which each witness was informed of the applicant's name were not clear. He was also unable to form a view on the reliability of the informants, because he knew nothing about them. He had been told nothing more than the brief passages in the transcript of the video interviews. It was not known whether either person could be identified so as to attend court and give evidence of the circumstances in which they had named the applicant to the witnesses.

10. The judge said that, if the applicant decided to give evidence, it was clearly open to him to challenge the assertion that he participated in the fight as the kicker. There were some 11 eyewitnesses and, may be, nine others. It was clearly possible to use the evidence of the nine others to challenge and undermine the assertion that the applicant had participated as a kicker. As conceded by the defence, the evidence of two witnesses was probative of the issue of whether the applicant was shown to be the kicker.

11. It was, in his judgment, in the interests of justice for the video recorded interviews of the two witnesses to be played to the jury, without editing out their naming of the applicant. In consequence, he refused the defence application to exclude and the evidence was duly admitted before the jury.

12. At a somewhat later stage, in the course of cross-examination of John Olliffe, he said that Nandi Jones had told him the applicant's name. That is to say, that he had derived the name from double hearsay, because she, as we have already indicated, had derived the name from her boyfriend.

13. In consequence, Mr Sinclair, then as now appearing for the defence, invited the judge to reconsider his ruling on the basis that multiple hearsay was involved and that therefore there were additional requirements for admissibility by virtue of section 121 of the Act. The judge declined to reconsider his original ruling.

14. Mr Sinclair frankly admits to us that, if the judge had reconsidered his ruling, bearing in mind that the jury had already heard the evidence, he is not at all clear what his next step would have been. Frankly and realistically he said that he would probably have asked for discharge of the jury and that application would probably have been rejected.

15. It is necessary to say just a little more about the evidence in the case. John Olliffe, in his recorded interview, described an earlier incident when he had gone to Paddock Wood Railway Station with Nandi Jones and another youth. There was a group of boys and a girl sitting on a platform bench and the boys included, as the applicant himself admitted, the applicant and another boy called Maguire. Maguire had come up behind John Olliffe and pulled his trousers down and there had been an exchange of oral and physical abuse.

16. As to the material fight, on 2nd August John Olliffe described a mob of some 20 or 25 people approaching. He recognised the applicant among that group from the incident earlier at the railway station. But, he said, he had not been told his name until after the crucial fight.

17. He described the applicant as wearing a TN hat, a dark blue polo, a thick gold earring in his left ear and eyebrow piercing. He also described the applicant walking by him and saying 'Don't look at me I've got enough of your brother's blood on me already'.

18. In cross-examination, he described the person whom he was accusing of involvement in this matter as around 16 years old and of medium build and he said Nandi Jones had told him the applicant's name.

19. George Olliffe, in his video recorded interview, said that he believed that the applicant was there at the time that he was beaten up but he could not remember who had told him that that was so.

20. Nandi Jones described Scott Maguire asking George Olliffe if he wanted a fight and throwing a punch and George throwing one back. Then she said 'Two other boys jumped up, one was the applicant.' She described Scott Maguire as getting on to John Olliffe, and a couple of other boys getting him on the floor and punching and kicking him. She looked back at George and saw they had got him on the floor. She said 'Stuart [the applicant] and Clinton [the co-accused] were stamping on his head and kicking and stamping on his face.' She said that the applicant kept on kicking George and would not stop, and at the same time shouting that he did not care if they told the police as he was going to prison any way.

21. That last piece of evidence from Nandi Jones was of some importance, because, according to the applicant's evidence later, only the family knew at the time of these events that he was on bail for another matter. However, that is what Nandi Jones said the applicant said. According to her, he kicked George countless times and made contact with his nose. She asked him to stop. Eventually he did, but then kicked him again, before running off. When she was asked how she knew the applicant, she said that she had previously seen him round with an ex boyfriend, with whom she had broken up a long time before. She knew the applicant's name through him. She did not know where he lived. On the night he was wearing shorts, trainers, a TN hat and had a gold hooped earring. He had buck teeth, was well built and aged 15 to 16.

22. In cross-examination, she said that the applicant and his co-accused were the first two people to join in the fight; she denied that the co-accused had acted as peace-maker, trying to break the fight up.

23. A witness called Michael Bailey described the applicant as jumping into the fight and kicking George in the head and face. He described him as 'Still kicking George's head as blood started coming from him face. Full swing 90-degree kicks had gone on for about 20 seconds and made George's body move backwards. His whole face was covered in blood.' The applicant then stopped. He said, in cross-examination, that he had had an unobstructed view of the incident.

24. Clair Draper described the applicant as joining in the fight to help Scott and as punching George. She described the co-accused as Scott. She described George as being on the floor with the applicant, about a metre away. She said she had been mistaken in her statement when she had said that the applicant had been hitting George when he was on the floor. She had seen the co-accused kicking and stamping on George's head, while he was on the ground. At that stage, the applicant had shouted: 'Stop' and the co-accused had stopped. In cross-examination, she agreed that she was friends with the applicant. She said that he was the last person to have physical contact with George when he had picked him up off the ground.

25. Stephen Fogg described the co-accused kicking George in the face and stamping on his head. He said a male whom he knew as Stuart, had pulled him off. He had seen the co-accused kicking George and the applicant not being involved in any way. On the contrary, he, Fogg, and the applicant had acted as peace-makers. He denied that he was seeking to protect the applicant. He had no reason to do so.

26. Daniel Griffin saw a boy on the floor, trying protect his face, while a white man aged around 18 years, 6 feet tall, of chunky build and wearing a baseball cap and blue track suit

bottoms kick him several times in the head. He saw the applicant push that man away. He knew the applicant, by sight. In cross-examination he said the applicant was among a crowd but there was no physical contact between him and the victim of this incident.

27. Jodie Draper described the applicant joining in and punching George. She refreshed her memory from her statement, in which she said the applicant and the co-accused had punched the victim more than once, and the applicant had grabbed him by the scruff of the neck and warned him not to call the police or he would burn his house. She said that she could not now remember the contents of her statement. She repeated, however, that the applicant had punched George. She had not however seen him kick him.

28. Another witness described the applicant pulling George up off the ground and saying something about 'stop fighting'. There were other witnesses to whom it is unnecessary to refer in relation to the incident.

29. There was forensic evidence from Helen Haworth, who had examined blood found on the applicant's trainers and baseball cap. Following DNA analysis, she concluded that the chances of the blood on the trainers having come from someone unrelated to George Olliffe was one in one billion. The applicant's right trainer had between 20 to 30 blood spots on the inner aspect. She was uncertain whether they were contact stains or smeared spots. They were small in size and the smaller the size, this meant the shorter the distance the blood had travelled. She could not say how many impacts into wet blood had been caused. She found some 15 to 20 similar sized spots on the left trainer. Her conclusion was that the applicant had been near to a source of airborne blood from George Olliffe, while wearing the trainers.

30. So far as the baseball ball cap was concerned, nothing turns on what she described as a non-descript area of blood on that. She said in cross-examination that she would have expected to find more blood on the trainers if the applicant had been kicking directly into wet blood.

31. When he was interviewed, following his arrest in August, the applicant made no comment to the questions which were asked. He was re-interviewed in October, following the results of the forensic analysis and, at that stage, he advanced an account of events which he later maintained in his evidence before the jury. That evidence included an admission of presence at the earlier railway station incident. He knew the witness, Nandi, through her ex-boyfriend. So far as the incident was concerned, he had tried to pull someone away. He had pulled George away and he had gone to the ground. He had not punched or kicked George while on the floor or otherwise. He had seen the co-accused punch and kicking George, but could not see whether kicks landed. He had run over and pushed the co-accused out of the way. He said he was, on the night, wearing trainers, a TN hat and T-shirt. He had pulled George by the shoulder from behind and the spots of blood on his trainers, he said, must have come from dripping blood, blood dripping from George's nose.

32. In cross-examination, he agreed that, in interview, he had said that the co-accused had kicked and stamped on George about six times. He accepted that that account contrasted with his evidence before the jury that he had seen only one kick. His explanation was that he had been all mixed up at the time of interview. The co-accused gave evidence on his own behalf and there was evidence called of his good character.

33. The submission which is made, attractively and admirably succinctly by Mr Sinclair, on behalf of the applicant, is that the judge was wrong to admit this hearsay evidence in

relation to the naming of the applicant. He puts the matter in this way. The judge, as is apparent from the terms of the ruling which we have already rehearsed, was unable to reach any conclusion in relation to four of the nine factors to which, by virtue of section 114(2), he was obliged to have regard. Mr Sinclair points out that factor (g) in subsection (2), which refers to whether oral evidence can be given and, if not, why it cannot, implies some sort of investigation by the judge. (If that is so, it does not appear that an implicit investigation by the judge is suggested by any of the other eight factors set out in the statute).

34. Mr Sinclair poses the question: can it be right to admit hearsay of this kind when it is impossible for the judge to give sufficient, or appropriate, consideration to the factors statutorily listed?

35. The second submission which Mr Sinclair makes is that it would have been open to the judge to hear oral evidence from Nandi's former boyfriend, whom she would be able to identify and, if he were to give evidence before the judge, the judge would then be in a position to assess the quality of that evidence and hence the reliability of the source of the name, so far as Nandi was concerned. Mr Sinclair, thirdly, in his oral submissions, suggested that the evidence against the applicant was not as strong as that against the co-accused and, the co-accused having been acquitted, there was a demonstrable case to be made that the case against the applicant was not open and shut. Finally, Mr Sinclair drew attention to the multiple hearsay aspect of the matter and the judge's refusal to reconsider his ruling.

36. On behalf of the Crown, Mr Johnson drew attention to the judgment of this Court in *Xhabri* [2005] EWCA Crim 3135; [2006] 1 CrAppR 26 (413). In paragraph 37 of the judgment of the Court given by the Lord Chief Justice, Lord Phillips, the Court's blessing was given to the admission of hearsay evidence which was apparently reliable by reason of its confirmation from other sources than the witness who was giving the hearsay evidence.

37. Mr Johnson also drew attention to the considerable body of other evidence implicating the applicant, for example the eyewitness' account of what the applicant had done, given by the Michael Bailey and the forensic evidence to which we have already referred.

38. As it seems to us, the first and crucial issue raised by this appeal is as to what is meant in section 114(2) by the words 'the court must have regard to the following factors'. If Mr Sinclair is correct and those words denote an obligation on a trial judge to embark on an investigation, resulting in some cases in the hearing of evidence, in order that he may reach a conclusion established by reference to each of the nine factors, it is apparent that trials are likely to be considerably elongated. Proper investigation of each of those factors, if carried out in that way, may well be a very lengthy process.

39. But do the words in the section require that course to be followed? In our judgment, they do not. They do not impose an obligation on the judge to reach a conclusion. What is required of him is the exercise of judgment, in the light of the factors identified in the subsection. What is required of him is to give consideration to those factors. There is nothing in the wording of the statute to require him to reach a specific conclusion in relation to each or any of them. He must give consideration to those identified factors and any others which he considers relevant, (as expressed in section 114(2) before the nine factors are listed). It is then his task to assess the significance of those factors, both in relation to each other and having regard to such weight as, in his judgment, they bear individually and in relation to each other. Having approached the matter in that way, he will be able, as it seems to us, in accordance with the words of the statute, to reach a proper conclusion as to whether or not

the oral evidence should be admitted. That is a process which, as it seems to us, the trial judge followed in this case. He followed it in the exercise of his discretion, in a way which, in our judgment, cannot be effectively challenged.

40. So far as the multiple hearsay point is concerned, it was, as it seems to us, entirely open to the judge, in the exercise of his discretion, to decline to revisit his earlier ruling bearing in mind the jury had already heard the evidence. There was, as we have already sought briefly to indicate, a considerable body of evidence against this applicant, quite apart from the naming of him by the two witnesses to whom we have referred. There is no reason, in our judgment, for regarding this conviction as unsafe and, accordingly, despite Mr Sinclair's valiant efforts, this application is refused.

Application for leave to appeal refused.

R v Singh [2006] EWCA Crim 660, CA, 23 February 2006, Rose LJ (Vice President), Rafferty J and Sir Douglas Brown

S Csoka for the appellant
L Blackwell for the Crown

Vice President, Rose LJ:

1. Rafferty J is unable to be here today, but she agrees with the terms of the judgment which we are about to give. McCombe J is present in relation to any ancillary matters which may arise.

2. On 6th July 2005 at Preston Crown Court, following a trial before His Honour Judge Robert Brown which had started in June, the appellant was convicted of conspiracy to kidnap and sentenced to 8 years' imprisonment. He appeals against conviction by leave of the Single Judge.

3. The appellant had previously been jointly indicted with seven others: Kaushall, Lattlay-Fottfoy, Arfan Javed, Chadwick, Mason, Mohammed Imran and Singh-Landa. The appellant did not stand trial with the others because of an incident between him and Chadwick, who was represented by the same solicitors who withdrew from representing the appellant, leaving him unrepresented. Lattlay-Fottfoy was acquitted and the others convicted. Chadwick, Mason and Singh-Landa had applications before this Court which were dealt with on 14 February. In this second trial the appellant was jointly indicted with Kasir Nadim, who had been arrested too late to be joined in the first trial. He was acquitted.

4. The victim of the offence, Alex Cunningham, was the owner of a shop in Burnley and lived with Sheila Murtagh and their three children in Briercliffe. At 7.00 pm on 17 June 2003 he was outside his house when three vehicles drove up. He was kidnapped by six white and two Asian men and taken to premises at an unknown location. The kidnappers contacted his family and friends using his mobile telephone and demanded money and jewellery. Sheila Murtagh received a ransom demand for half a million pounds. Michael Connelly, who had borrowed £10,000 from Mr Cunningham previously, received a call from someone using Mr Cunningham's mobile and demanding repayment. He went to Mr Cunningham's shop and handed over the money to 2 men. Two friends of the victim were given instructions to empty the safe at his shop, and at a meeting point in Stretford, they

handed over £5,000 in cash and £80,000 worth of jewellery to men in a Volkswagen car. When Sheila Murtagh returned home she found that £4,000 of her money had been taken. Police were called and hostage experts became involved. Eventually Mr Cunningham was left at a telephone kiosk wearing nothing but shorts. He telephoned 999 and was found by the police. He had bruising to his head and chest, stab wounds, blisters on his legs and feet from scalding and abrasions from being dragged over a hard surface. Eight men were arrested. A crucial part of the evidence was mobile telephone analysis.

5. The prosecution case against the appellant was that he was the user, at the time of the kidnapping, of mobile telephones ending in numbers 718 and 548, which he used to make and receive many calls to and from his co-conspirators on and around the date of the kidnapping. The memories of the telephones of co-accused contained these mobile numbers and Chadwick's telephone also contained the appellant's land line number for his home address, 73 Astbury Street. Kaushall's mobile phone had in its memory 'Alex' against the 548 number and an envelope containing the same information was recovered from Kaushall's home. The appellant admitted that two other phones, 817 and 588, were his and it was the prosecution case that 718 and 548 were his also. There were repeated calls from all four of these telephones in June, October and November 2003 and January 2004 to Chadwick. The Crown said it was open to the jury to find that it was the same person calling Chadwick in January as had called him in June at the time of the kidnapping. There were also calls between 548 and 718 and phones belonging to Kaushall, Arfan Javed and Singh-Landa on 17 and 18 June. The spider plan before the jury showed that, between 5.00pm on 17 and 7am on 18 there were approximately 200 calls between, on the one hand, 718 and 548 and, on the other, the phones of the four conspirators we have referred to and phone number 998 which admittedly belonged to another conspirator. Furthermore, call mapping suggested that the person using 718 and 548 was in the area of Mr Cunningham's home at the time he was kidnapped. The prosecution also relied on a call made from the appellant's mother's address to phone 718 during the period of the kidnapping.

6. The appellant's defence was alibi. He said he was at his mother's home at the time of the kidnapping and not using either 718 or 548. The owner of 718 was a plasterer known to him as Alex who was helping Chadwick, a joiner, in renovating the appellant's house at 73 Astbury Road. The defence accepted that it was proper to infer that the same person, called Alex or Al, was using 718 and 548 during the relevant period and was a party to the kidnapping.

7. The issue for the jury was whether they were sure the appellant was using 718 and 548 during the kidnapping and was therefore a party to it.

8. During the trial the judge gave a number of rulings which are challenged on appeal to this Court. He ruled that the bad character provisions of the Criminal Justice Act 2003 applied to the appellant's trial, notwithstanding that the original trial took place prior to 15th December 2004 when those provisions came into force. The application of section 101 in relation to bad character would not be unfair because its possible application had been pointed out to the appellant's representatives at the first trial and they were now acting for him again following their earlier withdrawal. He ruled that, in order to show that the appellant was a party to the conspiracy, evidence was admissible of the entries in the memories of mobile phones belonging to other conspirators and of the envelope found in Kaushall's home. A similar entry in phone 998, which the Crown said belonged to Lattlay-Fottfoy

(who had been acquitted), but which the defence admitted belonged to a co-conspirator, was also admissible to show that the appellant was party to the conspiracy. In particular, the judge ruled that number 998 was properly included in the schedule of six common numbers relied on by the Crown to show that the appellant was the person using 718 and 548 during the conspiracy. 718 and 548 were never recovered. But, in October 2003 the other telephones which the appellant admitted were his had contact with 998. In addition to the evidence already referred to, a neighbour of the appellant, Joanna Yates, had given evidence that, although she could not remember the appellant's mobile number, there were calls between March and May 2003 between her telephone and phone number 718. In interview the appellant failed to answer questions relating to 718 and 548 and, neither in interview nor in his defence statement, did he suggest that there was another Alex apart from himself. The defence submitted, at the close of the prosecution case, that there was no case to answer. The judge rejected this submission. In evidence before the jury, the appellant claimed that 718 belonged to Alex, the plasterer, and the call made from his mother's home to 718 was made by him to Alex, the plasterer. Alex, the plasterer, did not give evidence.

9. On behalf of the appellant, Mr Csoka advanced five grounds of appeal. First, he submitted that, despite this Court's judgment in *Bradley* [2005] EWCA Crim 20, [2005] 1 CrAppR 397, the provisions of the Criminal Justice Act 2003, in relation to the admissibility of evidence of hearsay and bad character, did not apply to this re-trial which started in June 2005 because the initial trial began on 8th November 2004, ie before 15th December 2004. He sought to distinguish paragraph 33(iii) in *Bradley*, where reference is made to cases remitted for retrial, on the basis that the passage is obiter and that, in such a case, a new indictment has to be preferred whereas, in the instant case, the appellant was being re-tried on the original pre-December 2004 indictment.

10. We disagree. The reference in Bradley to a re-trial ordered by this Court was merely an example of a difficulty which could arise if the legislation were construed as the appellant there contended. The ratio of the decision was that 'criminal proceedings' in section 112(1) and 141 mean a trial where issues of fact are determined, rather than the whole process following charging. The ratio is not limited in the way in which Mr Csoka seeks to suggest. The principles of *Bradley* apply to all trials starting after December 2004, whatever the date of the indictment: see paragraph 34 of the judgment; see also *Benguit* [2005] EWCA Crim 1953, at [31], and *H* [2005] EWCA Crim 2083 at [7], which Mr Csoka accepted are persuasive against his submission.

11. Secondly, he submitted that, although it was undoubtedly Parliament's intention to reverse the decision of the House of Lords about hearsay in *Kearley* [1992] 2 AC 228, section 114 and 115 fail to achieve that object.

12. The sections provide as follows:

Admissibility of hearsay evidence

114. (1) In criminal proceedings a statement not made in oral evidence in the proceedings is admissible as evidence of any matter stated if, but only if—

(a) any provision of this Chapter or any other statutory provision makes it admissible,

(b) any rule of law preserved by section 118 makes it admissible,

(c) all parties to the proceedings agree to it being admissible, or
(d) the court is satisfied that it is in the interests of justice for it to be admissible.

Statements and matters stated

115. (1) In this chapter references to a statement or to a matter stated are to be read as follows.
(2) A statement is any representation of fact or opinion made by a person by whatever means; and it includes a representation made in a sketch, photofit or other pictorial form.
(3) A matter stated is one to which this Chapter applies if (and only if) the purpose, or one of the purposes, of the person making the statement appears to the court to have been

(a) to cause another person to believe the matter, or
(b) to cause another person to act or a machine to operate on the basis that the matter is as stated.

13. Mr Csoka's argument was based on the adoption of an article in Professor Stephen Uglow in [2005] *Archbold News*, Issue 5 (23 May). The argument is this. Section 114 does not abolish the common law rule against the admissibility of hearsay which, albeit amended, remains. Section 114 restates but does not replace the common law rule of exclusion. It does not say there cannot be a hearsay statement outside the statutory parameters: there can be out-of-court statements which are still hearsay. Under *Kearley* an unintentional implied assertion was excluded as hearsay. The object of section 115(3) is to draw a line between intentional implied assertions still caught by the hearsay rule and unintentional implied assertions no longer treated as hearsay. Accordingly, only hearsay statements within section 114 are admissible. Section 115(3) means that section 114 does not apply to statements unless the purpose of their maker was to cause belief in the hearer; an unintentional implied assertion remains hearsay, because this is what *Kearley* said, and is now always inadmissible. In the present case, the entries in the telephone memories and on the envelope were unintentional implied assertions outwith section 115(3) and therefore inadmissible.

14. The interrelationship between sections 114 and 115 is deeply obscure. But, in our judgment, as Miss Blackwell for the prosecution contends, the answer to Mr Csoka's submission is provided by the editor of *Archbold, Criminal Pleading, Evidence and Practice* (2006) §§11–14. Contrary to Professor Uglow's premise, the common law rule against the admissibility of hearsay is abolished by the clear express terms to that effect of section 118, to which Professor Uglow does not refer. When sections 114 and 118 are read together they, in our judgment, abolish the common law hearsay rules (save those which are expressly preserved) and create instead a new rule against hearsay which does not extend to implied assertions. What was said by the callers in *Kearley* would now be admissible as direct evidence of the fact that there was a ready market for the supply of drugs from the premises, from which could be inferred an intention by an occupier to supply drugs. The view of the majority in *Kearley*, in relation to hearsay, has been set aside by the Act.

15. So, in the present case, the telephone entries are not a matter stated within section 115. They are implied assertions which are admissible because they are no longer hearsay.

Furthermore they are also admissible under section 118(1(vii), as statements by an admitted co-conspirator against another party to the enterprise (see also *Cross and Tapper on Evidence* 10th ed p 612 note 295, approved in *Jones* [1997] 2 CrAppR 119, 129). A third possible route to admissibility is provided by section 114(2)(d).

16. It follows that the judge was right to admit this evidence against the appellant and ground 2 fails.

[The court considered, and dismissed, three further grounds of appeal.]

Appeal dismissed

The court certified the following point of public importance, but refused leave to appeal:

> 'Does Chapter 2 of Part 11 of the Criminal Justice Act 2003 (in particular sections 114, 115 and 118) have the effect of reversing the majority decision of the House of Lords in *Kearley* and thus render unintended implied assertions to be admissible non-hearsay evidence?'

Leave was then refused by the House of Lords: [2006] 1 WLR 2206.

Maher v Director of Public Prosecutions [2006] EWHC 1271, Divisional Court, 12 May 2006, Scott Baker LJ and Leveson J

D Graham for the claimant
C J Smith for the Director

Lord Justice Scott Baker:

1. The facts of this case are simplicity itself. The law is not quite so straightforward.

2. On 21st November 2004, the appellant had parked her BMW Mini which was light blue in colour, registration number YF51 SYR, in Sainsbury's car park in Monks Cross. Thomas Huddlestone had parked his Vauxhall Astra in the same car park nearby and was shopping with his girlfriend, Nichola McDonough, when Susan and David Dennis (Mr and Mrs Dennis) saw the appellant reverse her Mini into the Astra, get out and look at the damage, and then drive off.

3. Fortunately for Mr Huddlestone, the Dennises were public spirited enough to make a note of the appellant's registration number and their contact details and to leave it on the windscreen of the damaged Astra under the wiper. When Mr Huddlestone and Miss McDonough returned to their damaged Astra they found the note and telephoned the police, reciting the number of the offending vehicle. The police recorded the details in the police incident log.

4. A subsequent DVLA check of that registration number led to the appellant. She was spoken to three days later on 24th November 2004 by Police Constable Forth. In the course of interview under caution, she admitted to being the driver of a BMW Mini, registration number YF51 SYR. She further admitted to being in the car and in the car park at the material time and, whilst accepting that she had reversed out of a space in the car park, denied that she had been involved in a collision. She said that she had only found out that there had been a collision when she had been told earlier on that day by the police.

5. By the time of the trial, the note that had been left on the windscreen was no longer in existence, or, if it was, it could not be found. The magistrates admitted the police incident log in evidence, despite objection from those advising the appellant, and convicted the appellant of careless driving and failing to stop and report the accident. The issue is whether the log was rightly admitted. It is submitted that, as that was the only evidence that fully implicated the appellant, she should have been acquitted. Her submission is that the evidence was hearsay and should not have been admitted.

6. The admissibility of hearsay evidence is now governed by sections 114 to 136 of the Criminal Justice Act 2003. As the editors of the 2006 edition of Archbold say at § 11.1, the opening words of section 114(1), taken together with section 115, effectively define hearsay as 'any representation of fact or opinion made by a person otherwise than in oral evidence in the proceedings in question when tendered as evidence of any matter stated therein'. The general rule is that hearsay is inadmissible unless it can be brought within an exception defined in the legislation. There are additional requirements for multiple hearsay to be admitted (see section 121). In the present case, the evidence was not only hearsay but multiple hearsay.

7. Mrs Dennis identified the number of the offending vehicle and wrote it on a piece of paper, putting it under the wiper blade on the windscreen of Mr Huddlestone's car. When Mr Huddlestone and Miss McDonough returned to the car, Miss McDonough took the piece of paper, phoned the police and read the number to someone who recorded the number on the police log. The transmission of the material information (namely, the number of the car) is therefore Mrs Dennis to Miss McDonough via the note (since lost or destroyed) to the clerk in the police station who recorded it in the log.

8. It seems helpful to me to identify first-hand hearsay from the subsequent multiple hearsay which is what was ultimately sought to be admitted. Leaving aside the note on the windscreen, the first-hand hearsay is the owner of the car (which I take as, for present purposes, Miss McDonough) saying that Mrs Dennis said to her that the offending vehicle is the one with the number YF51 SYR.

9. The starting point for the admissibility of simple hearsay is section 114. Multiple hearsay comes in under section 121. Section 114 provides as follows:

Admissibility of hearsay evidence

(1) In criminal proceedings a statement not made in oral evidence in the proceedings is admissible as evidence of any manner stated if, but only if—

- (a) any provision of this chapter or any other statutory provision makes it admissible;
- (b) any rule of law preserved by section 118 makes it admissible;
- (c) all parties to the proceedings agree to it being admissible; or
- (d) the court is satisfied that it is in the interests of justice for it to be admissible.

Taking the first-hand hearsay for a moment and focussing on that, it is not, in my view, arguable that there is any route for that to be admitted in this case other than under 114(1)(d), the sweeping up interests of justice test. In that event, the court has to go on to consider a number of matters that have to be taken into consideration under section 114(2), but I shall return to that in due course.

10. It is important, in my judgment, to keep in mind that the thrust of the evidence sought to be admitted is that the vehicle that reversed into the Vauxhall Astra was YF51 SYR. Let us assume for present purposes that there would have been no difficulty in admitting the first-hand hearsay under section 114. I turn on to consider the real issue in this case which is the application of section 121, namely multiple hearsay. I am at this point focussing on the record in the police log which was what all the argument was about. Section 121 provides:

Additional requirement for admissibility of multiple hearsay

(1) A hearsay statement is not admissible to prove the fact that an earlier hearsay statement was made unless—

 (a) either of the statements is admissible under section 117, 119 or 120;
 (b) all parties to the proceedings so agree; or
 (c) the court is satisfied that the value of the evidence in question, taking into account how reliable the statements appear to be, is so high that the interests of justice require the later statement to be admitted for that purpose.

(2) In this section 'hearsay statement' means a statement not made in oral evidence that is relied on as evidence of a matter stated in it.

11. The magistrates admitted the evidence (namely, the contents of the police log) under section 117. What they said was this:

(a) The police incident log was a business document for the purposes of section 117 Criminal Justice Act 2003 and therefore admissible in evidence in that:

 (i) oral evidence of the matters stated in the log would have been admissible by oral testimony in court. Had Miss McDonough been called to give evidence she could have given oral evidence of what she found and subsequently did on returning to the damaged car.
 (ii) the said log was created by a person in the course of his or her occupation;
 (iii) Miss McDonough, who supplied the information to the police from the scene of the incident, had personal knowledge of the information contained in the note;
 (iv) since the information was relayed directly from a relevant person at the scene of the incident and not through any other person to the police, section 117(2)(c) was not applicable;
 (v) Miss McDonough could not reasonably be expected to have had any recollection of the actual registration number contained in the police incident log, having regard to the length of time since the information was supplied;
 (vi) the reliability of the information contained in the log was therefore not undermined in view of the circumstances which we accepted were applicable to this case.

12. I turn, therefore, to examine in a little detail section 117. It is headed 'Business and Other Documents'. Subsection (1) reads:

In criminal proceedings a statement contained in a document is admissible as evidence of any matter stated if—

(a) oral evidence given in the proceedings would be admissible as evidence of that matter;
(b) the requirements of subsection (2) are satisfied; and
(c) the requirements of subsection (5) are satisfied in a case where subsection (4) requires them to be.

There is no difficulty or issue about (a) or (c). The critical focus has been on (b), the requirements of subsection (2). Subsection (4) requires the requirements of subsection (5) to be satisfied because the police log was prepared for the purpose of a criminal investigation. Subsection (5) is satisfied, because under (5)(b):

> The relevant person cannot reasonably be expected to have any recollection of the matters dealt with in the statement having regard to the length of time since he supplied the information and all other circumstances.

I shall return to the relevant person in a moment. He/she is defined in subsection (2) as the person who supplied the information contained in the statement. For the reasons that I shall explain, that person was, in my judgment, in this case, Mrs Dennis.

13. Subsection (2) provides:

> The requirements of this subsection are satisfied if—
>
> (a) the document or the part containing the statement was created or received by a person in the course of a trade or business, profession or other occupation, or as the holder of a paid or unpaid office.

There is no dispute but that this criterion is met. (b) and (c) provide as follows:

> (b) the person who supplied the information contained in the statement (the relevant person) had, or may reasonably be supposed to have had, personal knowledge of the matters dealt with; and
> (c) each person, if any, through whom the information was supplied from the relevant person to the person mentioned in paragraph (a) received the information in the course of a trade, business, profession or other occupation, or as the holder of a paid or unpaid office.

It is here that the problems arise in this case. I have already read the conclusions of the magistrates in paragraph 6 of the case. In my judgment, their analysis of this section was in error.

14. Subsection (2)(b) directs the reader to the person who supplied the information contained in the statement. That is how the relevant person is defined. The statement is the registration number of the offending vehicle. The document in which it is contained is the police incident log. Who supplied the information about the registration number? Answer: in my judgment, Mrs Dennis. What happened thereafter was transmission of the supplied information via Miss McDonough and the police clerk to the police log. My view is fortified by subsection (2)(c) which clearly envisages the possibility of the information passing through several individuals from the supplier to its ultimate destination, in this case the police log.

15. Whilst the requirements of section 117(2)(b) are met, in that Mrs Dennis plainly had personal knowledge of the number of the offending vehicle when she recorded it, an

insuperable difficulty arises with section 117(2)(c) which provides that each individual in the line along which the information was transmitted must have received it in the course of a trade, business, et cetera. Miss McDonough did not. As Mr Smith for the respondent pointed out, the position would have been entirely different if the information had been given not to Miss McDonough but to the car park attendant. That, in my judgment, is an illustration that the sweeping up provisions with regard to the admissibility of hearsay should be applied with a measure of common sense and realism.

16. In my judgment, the magistrates were wrong to have admitted the evidence under section 117. Before leaving section 117, however, I do make mention of subsections (6) and (7). Subsection (6) provides:

> A statement is not admissible under this section if the court makes a direction to that effect under subsection (7).

Subsection (7) provides:

> The court may make a direction under this subsection if satisfied that the statement's reliability as evidence for the purpose for which it is tendered is doubtful in view of—
>
> (a) its contents;
> (b) the source of the information contained in it;
> (c) the way in which or the circumstances in which the information was supplied or received; or
> (d) the way in which or the circumstances in which the document concerned was created or received.

17. It is, it seems to me, a clear inference from the conclusion that the magistrates did admit the evidence under section 117 that they did not have any of the concerns to which they would have been directed under subsection (7) that might have caused concern about the reliability of the evidence.

18. I return, then, to section 121. Given that the gateway of section 117 was available, what about sections 119 or 120? In my judgment, neither of these sections even gets to first base. Section 119 is dealing with inconsistent statements, and section 120 with other previous statements of the witness. Mr Smith did seek briefly to suggest that the statement might be admissible under section 120, but I am quite unpersuaded by that argument and Mr Smith did not persist in it. It is unnecessary to go into any further detail.

19. Therefore, because there was no agreement about the admissibility of the evidence, neither the gateways in (a) and (b) of section 121 is a route that could be followed. The remaining provision is section 121(c):

> . . . the court is satisfied that the value of the evidence in question, taking into account how reliable the statements appear to be, is so high that the interests of justice require the later statement to be admissible for the purpose.

20. It is necessary to go back to the facts of the case. Bearing in mind that the appellant admitted that her car, YF51 SYR, was a blue BMW Mini and was parked in the Sainsbury's car park at the material time, and that she was the driver, and that Mr Huddlestone and Miss McDonough returned to find their car damaged, the only issue could be whether, for some inexplicable reason, Mrs Dennis wrote down the number of the appellant's car in

error for some other car, or there had been some misstatement of the number further down the line of communication to the police log.

21. In my judgment, both scenarios are unlikely in the extreme. Mrs Dennis could have been cross-examined about the possibility of an error on her part. The appellant would have been in a much stronger position had she not admitted to the police that she was indeed present and had reversed her car in the car park at the material time. The identification of the number of the offending vehicle appears, on its face, to be very reliable, as does its transmission via Miss McDonough to the police incident log. It would be extraordinary if there was an error in transmission, but the number of the vehicle recorded on the police log just happened to coincide precisely with the number and description of a vehicle that was in the car park at the time and seen by the witness.

22. In my judgment, the magistrates, having concluded that it was in the interests of justice to have admitted this evidence under section 117, would inevitably have come to the same conclusion had they applied their minds specifically to 114(2) or to 121(1)(c).

23. 114(2) is spelt out in somewhat greater detail than 121(1)(c). I shall read it:

> In deciding whether a statement not made in oral evidence should be admitted under subsection (1)(d), the court must have regard to the following factors (and any others it considers relevant)—
>
> (a) how much probative value the statement has (assuming it to be true) in relation to a matter and issue in the proceedings or how valuable it is for the understanding of other evidence in the case;
> (b) what other evidence has been or can be given on the matter or evidence mentioned in paragraph (a);
> (c) how important the matter or evidence mentioned in paragraph (a) is in the context of the case as a whole;
> (d) the circumstances in which the statement was made;
> (e) how reliable the maker of the statement appears to be;
> (f) how reliable the evidence of the making of the statement appears to be;
> (g) whether oral evidence of the matter stated can be given, and if not why it cannot;
> (h) the amount of difficulty involved in challenging the statement;
> (i) the extent to which that difficulty would be likely to prejudice the party facing it.
>
> Miss Graham, on behalf of the appellant, has emphasised particularly (d), (e), (f), (g), (h) and (i).

24. In my judgment the provisions about the interests of justice in section 121 should, in the circumstances of this case, have been considered cumulatively with the interests of justice criteria in section 114(2). But, as I have already mentioned, the possibility that there could have been any error in this case are so remote that there was an overwhelming case for evidence to be admitted. In fact, the magistrates admitted the evidence under section 117. The contrary criteria were matters that they no doubt had in mind under subsection (7). Had their attention been specifically drawn to the provisions to which I have adverted in sections 114(2) and 121(1), it is, in my judgment, inevitable that they would have reached the same conclusion on admissibility. In my judgment, the justices were right to admit the evidence but they did so for the wrong reasons.

25. I would answer the question posed in the stated case which is in these terms: 'Whether in the circumstances the police incident log was admissible as hearsay evidence under section 117' in the negative, but I would dismiss the appeal and allow the conviction to stand because, in my judgment, the evidence should have been admitted under the provisions to which I have referred.

Leveson J:

26. I agree. Although the purpose of the hearsay provisions set out in Chapter 2 of Part 2 of the Criminal Justice Act 2003 was undeniably to relax the previously strict rules against the admission of hearsay, it is important to underline that care must be taken to analyse the precise provisions of the legislation and ensure that any route of admissibility is correctly identified. In any case of multiple hearsay, that should be done in stages so that each link in the multiple chain can be tested.

27. In this case, as Scott Baker LJ has explained, the magistrates approached the issue of admissibility on an incorrect basis. Based on their reasons for admitting the evidence, however, it is abundantly clear that they would have exercised their discretion in an identical fashion had they been invited to deal with it through the correct statutory route.

28. In the circumstances, although I would also answer the question posed to this court in the negative, in my judgment, this evidence was admissible and would have been admitted under sections 114(1)(c) and 121(1)(c) of the Act. I would therefore also dismiss this appeal.

Appeal dismissed

R v Finch [2007] EWCA Crim 36, CA, 15 January 2007, Hughes LJ, Rafferty J and Sir Charles Mantell

P Radcliffe for the appellant
D Allen for the Crown

Lord Justice Hughes:

1. This appeal against conviction concerns the admissibility in evidence of the police interviews of a co-accused under two new statutory provisions. They are: (a) section 76A of the Police and Criminal Evidence Act 1984, and (b) section 114(1)(d) of the Criminal Justice Act 2003 .

2. Section 76A was inserted into the 1984 Act by section 128(1) of the Criminal Justice Act 2003. It provides as follows:

76A Confessions may be given in evidence for co-accused

(1) In any proceedings a confession made by an accused person may be given in evidence for another person charged in the same proceedings (a co-accused) in so far as it is relevant to any matter in issue in the proceedings and is not excluded by the court in pursuance of this section.

(2) If, in any proceedings where a co-accused proposes to give in evidence a confession made by an accused person, it is represented to the court that the confession was or may have been obtained—

(a) by oppression of the person who made it; or
(b) in consequence of anything said or done which was likely, in the circumstances existing at the time, to render unreliable any confession which might be made by him in consequence thereof,

The court shall not allow the confession to be given in evidence for the co-accused except in so far as it is proved to the court on the balance of probabilities that the confession (notwithstanding that it may be true) was not so obtained.

(3) Before allowing a confession made by an accused person to be given in evidence for a co-accused in any proceedings, the court may of its own motion require the fact that the confession was not obtained as mentioned in subsection (2) above to be proved in the proceedings on the balance of probabilities.

3. Section 114 of the Criminal Justice Act 2003 for its part provides as follows:

(1) In criminal proceedings a statement not made in oral evidence in the proceedings is admissible as evidence of any matter stated if, but only if—

(a) any provision of this Chapter or any other statutory provision makes it admissible,
(b) any rule of law preserved by section 118 makes it admissible,
(c) all parties to the proceedings agree to it being admissible, or
(d) the court is satisfied that it is in the interests of justice for it to be admissible.

(2) In deciding whether a statement not made in oral evidence should be admitted under subsection (1)(d), the court must have regard to the following factors (and to any others it considers relevant)—

(a) how much probative value the statement has (assuming it to be true) in relation to a matter in issue in the proceedings, or how valuable it is for the understanding of other evidence in the case;
(b) what other evidence has been, or can be, given on the matter or evidence mentioned in paragraph (a);
(c) how important the matter or evidence mentioned in paragraph (a) is in the context of the case as a whole;
(d) the circumstances in which the statement was made;
(e) how reliable the maker of the statement appears to be;
(f) how reliable the evidence of the making of the statement appears to be;
(g) whether oral evidence of the matter stated can be given and, if not, why it cannot;
(h) the amount of difficulty involved in challenging the statement;
(i) the extent to which that difficulty would be likely to prejudice the party facing it.

4. What a co-accused said to the police out of court is plainly hearsay. It is a statement made otherwise than in oral evidence in the proceedings and it is made with the purpose that it shall be believed by the policeman to whom it is said. Thus it is hearsay within the definition of section 115 of the 2003 Act.

5. The two new statutory provisions to which we have referred have both been enacted through the same Part of the 2003 Act, that is to say Part 11. They are part therefore of the same statutory process. There is, however, an important difference between the two provisions. Whereas section 76A of the Police and Criminal Evidence Act makes a confession of a co-accused admissible unless it is excluded on grounds of oppression or of equivalent unreliability, such a confession can only become admissible under section 114(1) if the court is satisfied that it is in the interests of justice for it to be admitted.

6. Both sections were brought into force, together with the other hearsay provisions of the 2003 Act, on 4th April 2005. By section 141 of the 2003 Act they do not apply to any criminal proceedings begun before that date. This trial took place in April 2006 and accordingly both new provisions applied to it.

7. In the present case, the indictment originally charged this appellant, together with a co-accused called Richer, with joint offences of possession of a prohibited firearm and of ammunition. Richer pleaded guilty. This appellant was thus tried alone. The appellant sought to put in evidence the police interviews with Richer. The judge ruled that the interviews were not admissible under section 76A because Richer was not being tried together with the appellant. He held that application could properly be made to admit them under the hearsay provisions of section 114(1)(d), subject to the rules contained in that section. Subsequently, however, on consideration of that application, he ruled against it on the ground that Richer was available to give evidence and it was thus not in the interests of justice for his hearsay statements to be admitted.

8. The appellant and Richer both live in Rugby. At about 9.30 on the evening of 6th December 2004 they were stopped in a Mercedes motorcar northbound on the M20 at Maidstone. They had just visited a service station where both of them had got out of the car. Richer was driving and Finch was in the front passenger seat. The front passenger seat in which Finch was sitting was fitted with a sliding drawer underneath it, which slid forwards into the footwell when you opened it. Inside the drawer wrapped in a plastic bag there was a 9mm self-loading pistol with a loaded magazine in place. Two of Richer's fingerprints and one of Finch's were found on the bag. Both defendants initially refused to say where they had come from or where they lived.

9. Finch when he was interviewed said that he had visited Richer the previous evening back in Rugby and had been asked by him to come for a ride to Maidstone where, he said, Richer had said he had got someone to meet. They had, according to Finch, set off more or less immediately after the invitation was given and accepted. Finch said that he had not at any stage asked why they were going or indeed where they were going, nor how long they might be and this despite the fact that it had seemed to him that Richer was 'a bit bothered'. Said Finch to the police, he had no idea there was a gun in the car, nor why they had gone all the way they had, nor even whose the car was, because it was not Richer's, as he knew. Finch said to the police that he had been groggy from a previous night's drinking. When he was told about the fingerprint on the plastic bag containing the gun, he said that he might easily have touched anything that had been in the footwell or under the passenger seat because at varying times they had had drinks, cigarettes, sandwiches and the like in the footwell and he had eaten some and passed others to the driver. He was, however, unable to explain how he could have touched the bag inside a closed drawer unless it was protruding from it. The evidence of the policeman who found the gun was that the drawer was fully closed with its

leading edge flush with the front of the seat and no part of the bag was visible. It remained, however, Finch's case at trial that he had had no idea that there was a gun in the car; he was simply accompanying his friend on the run out. That was the issue at the trial.

10. When Richer had been interviewed by the police, he had told them that he had been sent on an errand to deliver the gun by a man to whom he owed money and of whom he said he was very frightened. He said that he had been told to take the gun to a service station at Maidstone but that when he had got there whoever he had been meant to meet was not there. His account to the police was that he had then doubled back northwards and was thinking of jettisoning the gun when the police intervened. Richer told the police that Finch did not know that the gun was in the car.

Section 76A of the Police and Criminal Evidence Act 1984

11. We think that we should assume for the purpose of what follows that whatever part of Richer's police interviews Finch wished to adduce in evidence are properly described as 'confession' within the meaning of section 76A. The contrary has not been argued before us. We do observe that what Finch wanted to adduce was not confined to Richer's admission that he (Richer) was knowingly carrying the gun. Indeed that was not the principal matter which Finch wished to adduce. That Richer knew about the gun was neutral on the question of whether Finch also knew about it. This, in other words, was not a case such as were *Beckford and Daley* [1991] Crim LR 833, or *Myers* [1988] AC 124, in which the crime in question had been committed by either one defendant or the other. The issue in the present case was not either/or; it was one or both. What Finch really wanted to adduce was Richer's assertion that Finch was a mere innocent passenger. He also wanted some supplemental assertions of Richer which would have helped him to support that proposition, such as that he (Richer) was not acting in pursuit of any criminal enterprise beyond delivery of the gun and that they had bought food along the way.

12. We are conscious of the definition of 'confession' in section 82 of the 1984 Act, that is to say as including 'any statement wholly or partly adverse to the person making it'. However, to accept (as we do) that a statement may remain a confession whilst partially exculpatory and partly inculpatory, is not the same as to say that everything which is said at the same time as an admission falls within the definition 'confession'. We accept in the present case for the purpose of argument that the assertion that Finch was an innocent passenger was in effect part of Richer's admission that he was carrying out a gun delivery alone. But we think that we should leave for another day and for full argument the broader question of when the contents of a co-accused's police interviews, which go beyond admission of the offence but in some way serve the interests of somebody else, remain within the meaning of the word 'confession'.

13. That said, the issue in this case is whether Richer, having pleaded guilty and not being before the jury, was 'another person charged in the same proceedings (a co-accused)' so that his confession fell within section 76A. We are quite sure that he was not.

14. We agree with Miss Radcliffe that this question cannot necessarily be resolved by reference to the definition of 'criminal proceedings' as used in various sections of the 2003 Act—in particular sections 112, 134, 140 and 141. In all those provisions that expression is defined as 'criminal proceedings in relation to which the strict rules of evidence apply.'

Those last words of definition determined the issue in *Bradley* [2005] EWCA Crim 20; [2005] 1 CrAppR 24 (397) and also in *H* [2005] EWCA Crim 2083, [2006] 1 CrAppR 4 (50). In those cases the question related to the commencement of the bad character and hearsay provisions respectively of the 2003 Act. However, whilst it is true that the new section 76A was created by the 2003 Act, the statutory home into which it has been inserted is the Police and Criminal Evidence Act of 1984. That earlier Act of 1984 contains its own definition of 'proceedings' in section 82, that is to say 'proceedings means criminal proceedings . . .' (and it goes on to include those before courts martial). Accordingly, in the 1984 Act the words of qualification which appear in the various sections of the 2003 Act, which we have mentioned—'proceedings in relation to which the strict rules of evidence apply'—do not figure. Thus far, therefore, we are with Miss Radcliffe. Not however any further.

15. Irrespective of the use of the expression 'criminal proceedings' in those sections of the 2003 Act, it has been well established law for many years that a defendant who has pleaded guilty and who is not on trial before the jury is not a 'person charged with an offence' in the proceedings for the purpose of his status as a witness. Section 1 of the Criminal Evidence Act 1898, in this respect unaffected by the modification which was made of it in 1984 to deal with the position of spouses, has always provided that 'a person charged in criminal proceedings shall not be called as a witness in the proceedings except upon his own application.' A defendant who has pleaded guilty has long been held not to fall within that expression. Such a person is therefore a compellable witness for any remaining defendant who is on trial—see *Boal* [1965] 1 QB 402 and *Conti* (1973) 58 CrAppR 387. In enacting section 76A, Parliament must plainly be taken to have known and applied this well established proposition of law. Having pleaded guilty, Richer was no longer a person charged or accused in the proceedings which were afoot, namely the trial of Finch. For the same reason, Finch was not charged in the same proceedings as Richer. Therefore section 76A did not apply and what Richer said to the police was not admissible under that section.

16. We are fortified in that conclusion by consideration of what was the plain purpose of section 76A. It was enacted following the recommendations of the Law Commission in Consultation Paper No 245, and it was enacted to put the law onto a proper footing following the difficulties which had been exposed by *Beckford and Daly* (supra), *Campbell and Williams* [1993] CrimLR 448, and the decision of the House of Lords in *Myers* (supra). The plain purpose of the new section was twofold. First it was to put into statutory form the rule in Myers that defendant A in a joint trial could not only cross-examine defendant B on the latter's confession if B gave evidence, but could also adduce the confession even if B declined to go into the witness box. Secondly, it was to provide for B against A the same protection that he would have had against the Crown if the confession had been obtained by oppression or as a result of anything said or done which was likely to render it unreliable. The new rule, and for that matter the decision in *Myers*, were designed to meet the problem faced by defendant A who, if charged in the same trial as B, could not call B into the witness box because section 1 of the 1898 Act prevents B from being called except on his own application. That obstacle, however, does not exist except where A and B are tried together. It does not exist once B has pleaded guilty. A can then call B and B is compellable. Nor, now that section 114(1)(d) of the 2003 Act provides the court with an overriding power to admit hearsay evidence if the interests of justice require it, can it any longer be said that A needs to be able to rely on either *Myers* or section 76A to get relevant evidence before the jury even

if B is unavailable or for some other reason his evidence cannot be given orally. As we have already said, the creation of section 76A and the new provisions of section 114 are part of the same statutory process.

17. Miss Radcliffe urges on us that the confession, as she describes it, of Richer is the more cogent when Richer has pleaded guilty and, as she says, stood by it. It is no doubt true that he had pleaded guilty without resiling from his acceptance of responsibility and for that matter of sole responsibility. It may be that certainly in a case in which a criminal act must have been committed by either A or B, it could properly be said that the plea of guilty of B adds enormously to the weight of his previous confession. It is not quite the same, of course, where the case is not one of either A or B but of whether it is A plus B or A alone. In the latter case, of which this is an example, it is not in the least unlikely that one defendant may wish falsely to exonerate the other.

18. If section 76A had the meaning for which this appellant contends the jury would be presented with out-of-court assertions made by persons who had once been charged in circumstances where there may be every likelihood that they will not be reliable and would be deprived of any means of testing their veracity or reliability even though the maker was available to give evidence. That consequence would be highly undesirable. It is in no sense necessary, given the provisions of section 114, and we are quite satisfied that it is not what Parliament meant to achieve.

19. We should add, though it is not in those circumstances necessary for our decision, that if that were not the law there would be very considerable difficulties in deciding who was and who was not included within the expression 'person charged in the same proceedings'. Miss Radcliffe's initial submission to us was that anybody who had been charged with any offence arising out of the same investigation as the man on trial came within that expression. On reflection we understood her to accept that it might be necessary to curtail the ambit of that proposition to some unspecified extent and once that is accepted we see enormous difficulties in arriving at any sensible test of the expression. However, that does not arise because we are quite satisfied that the meaning is that which we have explained.

Section 114(1)(d) of the Criminal Justice Act 2003

20. The appellant made alternative application to adduce the contents of Richer's police interviews under this section. The Crown arranged for Richer to be produced at court and he was present. The judge was told that he was reluctant to give evidence. He may have had his solicitors present at court—he certainly had been represented. The judge was either shown or told about a letter which had been written by his solicitors some time beforehand and he was told that Richer declined to see Finch's representatives. The letter indicated that Richer had been advised not to give evidence because, as it was suggested, he did not wish to jeopardise his position so far as sentence was concerned and the letter said that he would refuse to answer questions on the grounds that they might incriminate him further, having already pleaded guilty. There was a reference in the letter to his having pleaded guilty on a basis. This was not a case in which any written basis for plea had been advanced, still less accepted, and had there been an assertion as to something falling short of the defence of duress but amounting to pressure to commit the offence, it is likely that there would have had to be some kind of fact-finding hearing in the case of Richer.

21. However that may be, the judge indicated that he was not satisfied with that bare assertion. After time for consideration, Miss Radcliffe declined to call Richer. The judge had plainly contemplated that Richer should be put into the witness box so that his reaction could be judged before any question arose of his out of court statements being admitted. He seems to have contemplated Richer being called for that purpose immediately before the jury. A possible alternative preliminary might have been to apply to call him into the witness box in the absence of the jury to explore his reaction and the legitimacy (if any) of his stance, but no application to do that was ever made. Instead, the appellant stood on the proposition that to call him when he was reluctant to give evidence, or (in the useful colloquial expression) blind, was something that could not be expected of him. Thus the judge had to resolve without hearing Richer the question whether the interests of justice required his out of court assertions to be adduced as hearsay.

22. The judge worked through the relevant factors set out in section 114(2). He accepted that the evidence was, if true, of substantial probative value. He was plainly well aware that the assertion went to the heart of the defence of Finch and that there was otherwise only the evidence of Finch himself, so that the assertion was of considerable importance to the case as a whole. He concluded, however, that oral evidence of what Richer said about Finch was available to be given. He was unable to see how Richer could damage his own position by giving evidence that Finch was an innocent passenger. He also considered, in reference to sub-paragraph (e) of section 114(2), the potential unreliability of Richer if he was not prepared to support in the witness box what he had said to the police. He correctly addressed the difficulty for the Crown of controverting or challenging Richer's assertion if Richer were not in the witness box to make it. His conclusion was that the interests of justice did not call for the interviews to be admitted as hearsay. Plainly in reaching that conclusion the principal factor was the fact that Richer was available to give oral evidence if compelled to do so, together with the various consequences which that entailed.

23. This was a situation calling for the exercise of the judgment of the trial judge. This court will interfere if, but only if, he has exercised it on wrong principles or reached a conclusion which was outside the band of legitimate decision available to him. We are unable to see that his decision can be criticised on either ground. We do accept that there are some difficulties for an appellant and his counsel in this situation when faced with a potential witness who is reluctant to give evidence. Richer would not of course have been called entirely blind. There may not have been a recent proof of evidence but there were the interviews with the police, properly recorded, available as an indication of what he could say. Had he in evidence not supported them it would have been open to Miss Radcliffe to seek to treat him as adverse and, had that been done and his previous inconsistent statements put to him, the latter would under the modern law have stood as evidence of any matter stated in them—see section 119 of the new Criminal Justice Act 2003. We understand, nevertheless, that an appellant might well decide, as this one did on advice, that calling such a witness was a risk that he was unprepared to take. It does not, however, follow that wherever that happens the interests of justice call for the admission in evidence of something which the reluctant witness has said out of court but is not prepared to support on oath. On the contrary, the reluctance only undermines the reliability of the evidence. We agree with the judge that in this case Richer's refusal to give evidence voluntarily plainly carried the suggestion that he was anxious that he would not be believed. Whether he was anxious that he would be

disbelieved about the role of Finch or about his own role or about both we cannot tell, and nor could the judge, but either way his credibility was put severely in question by his reluctance to enter the witness box. We should say that we reach that conclusion without examining in detail what are said to be several doubtful features of Richer's assertions which exonerate Finch. In the end, had his evidence been before the jury those criticisms of what he said would have been, we accept, for the jury.

24. Whatever might be the situation if an erstwhile co-accused were to be unavailable or had demonstrably good reason not to give evidence, it will, as it seems to us, often not be in the interests of justice for evidence which the giver is not prepared to have tested to be put untested before the jury. It is not in short the law that every reluctant witness's evidence automatically can be put before the jury under section 114. We are satisfied that in this case the judge was right on both issues and this appeal must in consequence be dismissed.

Appeal dismissed

The court certified the following point of public importance, but refused leave to appeal:

> 'Where two defendants (A and B) are jointly charged with an offence which it is alleged was committed by both of them together, and defendant A pleads guilty to it, do A and B remain 'charged in the same proceedings' for the purposes of section 76A of the Police and Criminal Evidence Act 1984, so that B may put in evidence the contents of A's confession to the police without calling him notwithstanding that he is a compellable witness?'

Leave was then refused by the House of Lords: [2007] 1 WLR 1613.

R v Cole; R v Keet [2007] EWCA Crim 1924, CA, 9 July 2007, Lord Phillips CJ, Elias and Griffith Williams JJ

M House and R Bryan for the appellants
T Adebayo and M Butt for the Crown

Lord Phillips, CJ:

1. The Registrar has referred to this Court two applications for permission to appeal against conviction to be heard together. In each case the trial judge acceded to applications by the Crown to adduce hearsay evidence pursuant to section 116 of the Criminal Justice Act 2003. In each case that evidence was critical in relation to at least one of the counts on which the defendant was convicted. The applications raise an issue of principle and we gave permission to appeal at the outset of the hearings. Before turning to the facts of the individual cases we propose to make some general observations.

2. Before 1988 it was a general rule, subject to some exceptions, that hearsay evidence was not admissible in a criminal trial. The following explanation for this rule was proffered by Lord Bridge in *Blastland* [1986] AC 41, 53–54:

> Hearsay evidence is not excluded because it has no logical probative value . . . The rationale of excluding it as inadmissible, rooted as it is in the system of trial by jury, is a

recognition of the great difficulty, even more acute for a juror than for a trained judicial mind, of assessing what, if any weight, can properly be given to a statement by a person whom the jury have not seen or heard and who has not been subject to any test of reliability by cross-examination . . . The danger against which this fundamental rule provides a safeguard is that untested hearsay evidence will be treated as having a probative force which it does not deserve.

3. This statement is relevant to a situation such as that before the court where the maker of the statement has not given evidence, but the rule against hearsay also excluded evidence of statements made by those who were called as witnesses. In neither situation was the rule satisfactory. It often excluded the most probative evidence. Significant inroads were made into the rule by sections 23 and 24 of the Criminal Justice Act 1988 . Chapter 2 of Part II of the Criminal Justice Act 2003 has reformed the law, making changes recommended by the Law Commission aimed at ensuring, subject to suitable safeguards, that relevant evidence is admitted when this is in the interests of justice. Subsection (1)(d) of section 114 gives the court a discretion to admit hearsay evidence when it is satisfied that 'it is in the interests of justice for it to be admissible'. Subsection (2) provides:

(2) In deciding whether a statement not made in oral evidence should be admitted under subsection (1)(d), the court must have regard to the following factors (and to any others it considers relevant)—

- (a) how much probative value the statement has (assuming it to be true) in relation to a matter in issue in the proceedings, or how valuable it is for the understanding of other evidence in the case;
- (b) what other evidence has been, or can be, given on the matter or evidence mentioned in paragraph (a);
- (c) how important the matter or evidence mentioned in paragraph (a) is in the context of the case as a whole;
- (d) the circumstances in which the statement was made;
- (e) how reliable the maker of the statement appears to be;
- (f) how reliable the evidence of the making of the statement appears to be;
- (g) whether oral evidence of the matter stated can be given and, if not, why it cannot;
- (h) the amount of difficulty involved in challenging the statement;
- (i) the extent to which that difficulty would be likely to prejudice the party facing it.

4. Section 116 deals with cases where a witness is unavailable. It provides:

(1) In criminal proceedings a statement not made in oral evidence in the proceedings is admissible as evidence of any matter stated if—

- (a) oral evidence given in the proceedings by the person who made the statement would be admissible as evidence of that matter,
- (b) the person who made the statement (the relevant person) is identified to the court's satisfaction, and
- (c) any of the five conditions mentioned in subsection (2) is satisfied.

(2) The conditions are—

(a) that the relevant person is dead;
(b) that the relevant person is unfit to be a witness because of his bodily or mental condition;
(c) that the relevant person is outside the United Kingdom and it is not reasonably practicable to secure his attendance;
(d) that the relevant person cannot be found although such steps as it is reasonably practicable to take to find him have been taken;
(e) that through fear the relevant person does not give (or does not continue to give) oral evidence in the proceedings, either at all or in connection with the subject matter of the statement and the court gives leave for the statement to be given in evidence.

In the case of (e), but not in the other cases, subsection (4) provides that the court can only admit the evidence if satisfied, having regard to specified criteria, that it is in the interests of justice to do so.

5. Section 121 deals with multiple hearsay. It provides:

(1) A hearsay statement is not admissible to prove the fact that an earlier hearsay statement was made unless—

(a) either of the statements is admissible under section 117, 119 or 120,
(b) all parties to the proceedings so agree, or
(c) the court is satisfied that the value of the evidence in question, taking into account how reliable the statements appear to be, is so high that the interests of justice require that later statement to be admissible for that purpose.

(2) In this section 'hearsay statement' means a statement, not made in oral evidence, that is relied on as evidence of a matter stated in it.

6. Section 126(2) preserves the power of the Court to exclude evidence under section 78 of the Police and Criminal Evidence Act 1978 ('PACE'). That section provides:

In any proceedings the court may refuse to allow evidence on which the prosecution proposes to rely to be given if it appears to the court that, having regard to all the circumstances, including the circumstances in which the evidence was obtained, the admission of the evidence would have such an adverse effect on the fairness of the proceedings that the court ought not to admit it.

7. It seems to us that this test is unlikely to produced a different result from that of 'the interests of justice' in section 114(1)(d). In either event the court can and must ensure that the requirements of a fair trial, as laid down by Article 6 of the European Convention of Human Rights ('ECHR'), are observed. Because the provisions of the 2003 Act leave the court free to comply with the requirements of Article 6 there is no question of the hearsay provisions of the Act being incompatible with the Convention—see *Xhabri* [2005] EWCA Crim 3135, [2006] 1 C rApp R 26 (413) at [42].

8. Article 6.1 of the ECHR provides that in the determination of any criminal charge against him, everyone is entitled to a fair hearing. Article 6.3 provides:

> Everyone charged with a criminal offence has the following minimum rights: . . .
>
> (d) to examine or have examined witnesses against him and to obtain the attendance and examination of witnesses on his behalf under the same conditions as witnesses against him.

9. Mr Robert Bryan, who has appeared for the appellant Keet, has argued that Article 6.3 was infringed by the admission of the hearsay evidence in his case, having particular regard to the fact, that in respect of three of the four counts that Keet faced, the prosecution's case was essentially founded on the hearsay evidence.

10. Mr Bryan relied on the decision of the Strasbourg Court in *Lucà v Italy* (2003) EHRR 46. The procedure in that case had been governed by the Italian Code of Criminal Procedure. That Code permitted the statements made by a person accused in connected proceedings to be adduced in evidence against the defendant although this witness exercised his right of silence and declined to give oral evidence. The Court held that Article 6.1 and 6.3 had been violated. It stated:

> The Court reiterates that the admissibility of evidence is primarily a matter for regulation by national law and as a general rule it is for the national courts to assess the evidence before them. The Court's task under the Convention is not to give a ruling as to whether statements of witnesses were properly admitted as evidence, but rather to ascertain whether the proceedings as a whole, including the way in which evidence was taken, were fair. The evidence must normally be produced at a public hearing, in the presence of the accused, with a view to adversarial argument. There are exceptions to this principle, but they must not infringe the rights of the defence. As a general rule, Art. 6(1) and (3)(d) require that the defendant be given an adequate and proper opportunity to challenge and question a witness against him, either when he makes his statement or at a later stage. As the Court has stated on a number of occasions, it may prove necessary in certain circumstances to refer to depositions made during the investigative stage (in particular, where a witness refuses to repeat his deposition in public owing to fears for his safety, a not infrequent occurrence in trials concerning Mafia-type organisations). If the defendant has been given an adequate and proper opportunity to challenge the depositions, either when made or at a later stage, their admission in evidence will not in itself contravene Art. 6(1) and (3)(d). The corollary of that, however, is that where a conviction is based soley or to a decisive degree on depositions that have been made by a person whom the accused has no opportunity to examine or to have examined, whether during the investigation or at the trial the rights of the defence are restricted to an extent that is incompatible with the guarantees provided by Art.6.

11. If this decision were treated as precluding the admission of hearsay evidence in any circumstance where the source of the evidence had died or was, for some other reason, no longer available to be cross-examined it would necessarily result in defendants avoiding conviction where their guilt was not in doubt. It does not seem to us that the requirements of a fair trial require this consequence. Nor does it follow from the decision in *Lucà*. In that case the witness was still available but, under the applicable code of procedure could not be cross-examined.

12. Looking at Article 6 without reference to authority, it is concerned with ensuring that there is a fair trial. Article 6.3 is premised on it being possible for witnesses to be called by the

prosecution or by the defendant. It does not deal with the position where, for one reason or another, this is simply not possible. Nor does *Lucà* hold that statements made by a witness who has since died, or whom it is otherwise impossible to call to give evidence, cannot be received.

13. Furthermore, *Lucà* was a case where the evidence in question was the main evidence against the accused. It cannot be treated as authority for the proposition that in all circumstances hearsay evidence cannot be adduced unless the defendant is able, or has had the opportunity, to examine the maker.

14. Is hearsay evidence of a witness who cannot be cross-examined precluded when it is the sole, or the decisive, evidence against a defendant? The wording of the Strasbourg Court in the passage from *Lucà* that we have cited above might suggest so. But Mr Bryan accepted that there was a line of domestic authority that establishes, so far as this court is concerned, that this is not the case.

15. In *KM* [2003] EWCA Crim 357, [2003] 2 Cr App R 357, after lengthy consideration of both domestic and Strasbourg authority, the court reached the following conclusion at [60]:

> . . . we would not subscribe to any formulation of the approach to be adopted which states without qualification that a conviction based solely or mainly on the impugned statement of an absent witness necessarily violates the right to a fair trial under Article 6.

On the facts of that case, however, the court held that the evidence in question should not have been admitted.

16. In *Sellick* [2005] EWCA Crim 651, [2005] 1 WLR 3257, four statements had been admitted in evidence at a murder trial pursuant to sections 23 and 26 of the Criminal Justice Act 1988. The judge held that he was satisfied that two of the witnesses had been kept away through fear and the other two could not be traced. The defendants appealed on the ground that their right to a fair trial under Article 6.1 and 6.3 had been violated. Once again this court considered the Strasbourg jurisprudence at length. It concluded that the authorities supported the following propositions:

> (i) The admissibility of evidence is primarily for the national law; (ii) Evidence must normally be produced at a public hearing and as a general rule Article 6(1) and (3)(d) require a defendant to be given a proper and adequate opportunity to challenge and question witnesses; (iii) It is not necessarily incompatible with Article 6(1) and (3)(d) for depositions to be read and that can be so even if there has been no opportunity to question the witness at any stage of the proceedings. Article 6(3)(d) is simply an illustration of matters to be taken into account in considering whether a fair trial has been held. The reasons for the court holding it necessary that statements should be read, and the procedures to counterbalance any handicap to the defence, will all be relevant to the issue, whether, where statements have been read, the trial was fair. (iv) The quality of the evidence and its inherent reliability, plus the degree of caution exercised in relation to reliance on it, will also be relevant to the question whether the trial was fair.

17. The court went on to consider, at [51], having particular regard to *Lucà*, whether there was a fifth proposition that

> where the defendant had had no opportunity to question the witness at any stage of the trial process, the statement must not be allowed to be read if it is the sole or decisive evidence against the defendant.

It reached the conclusion that, at least where witnesses were kept away through fear, such a proposition could not prevail:

> In our view having regard to the rights of victims, their families, the safety of the public in general, it still cannot be right for there to be some absolute rule that, where compelling evidence is the sole or decisive evidence, an admission in evidence of a statement must then automatically lead to a defendant's Article 6 rights being infringed. That would lead to a situation in which the more successful the intimidation of the witnesses, the stronger the argument becomes that the statements cannot be read. If the decisive witnesses can be 'got at' the case must collapse. The more subtle and less easily established intimidation provides defendants with the opportunity of excluding the most material evidence against them. Such an absolute rule cannot have been intended by the European Court in Strasbourg.

18. *Al-Khawaja* [2005] EWCA Crim 2697, [2006] 1 WLR 1078 the appellant was charged with two counts of indecent assault. By the time of the trial one of the complainants had died. Her statement was admitted under section 23 of the 1988 Act. On appeal it was argued that this violated Article 6.3 (d) of the ECHR. Dismissing the appeal, this court said this at paragraph 26:

> Where a witness who is the sole witness of a crime has made a statement to be used in its prosecution and has since died, there may be a strong public interest in the admission of the statement in evidence so that the prosecution may proceed. That was the case here. That public interest must not be allowed to override the requirement that the defendant have a fair trial. Like the court in Sellick we do not consider that the case law of the European Court of Human Rights requires the conclusion that in such circumstances the trial will be unfair. The provisions in Art.6(3)(d) that a person charged shall be able to have the witnesses against him examined is one specific aspect of a fair trial: but if the opportunity is not provided, the question is 'whether the proceedings as a whole, including the way the evidence was taken, were fair. *Doorson v The Netherlands* (1996) 22 EHRR 330, at [67].

19. Finally the Privy Council has recently commented on Article 6 in the present context in an appeal from the Court of Appeal of Jamaica. In *Grant v The Queen* [2007] 1 AC 1 the issue was whether section 31D of the Evidence Act was compatible with section 20(6)(d) of the Constitution. Section 31D permitted the statement of a witness who was not called to give evidence to be read in specified circumstances. Section 20(6)(d) was in similar terms to Article 6.3(d). Giving the advice of the Committee, Lord Bingham of Cornhill at [17] referred to the relevant Strasbourg authority and commented:

> The Strasbourg court has been astute to avoid treating the specific rights set out in article 6 as laying down rules from which no derogation or deviation is possible in any circumstances. What matters is the fairness of the proceedings as a whole.

He continued:

> Just as section 13 of the Constitution recognises that individual rights cannot be enjoyed without regard to the rights of others, so the Strasbourg court has recognised the need for a fair balance between the general interest of the community and the personal rights

> of the individual, and has described the search for that balance as inherent in the whole Convention . . . Thus the rights of the individual must be safeguarded, but the interests of the community must also be respected.

After referring to the case of a witness kept away through fear, Lord Bingham commented:

> Where a witness is unavailable to give evidence in person because he is dead, or too ill to attend, or abroad, or cannot be traced, the argument for admitting hearsay evidence is less irresistible, but there may still be a compelling argument for admitting it, provided always that its admission does not place the defendant at an unfair disadvantage.

20. Once one moves away, as both the Strasbourg and our domestic jurisprudence clearly have, from the proposition that there is an absolute rule that evidence of a statement cannot be adduced in evidence unless the defendant has an opportunity to examine the maker, it seems to us that there can be only one governing criterion. Is the admission of the evidence compatible with a fair trial? It is that question alone with which Article 6 is concerned.

21. There are many reasons why it may be impossible to call a witness. Where the defendant is himself responsible for that fact, he is in no position to complain that he has been denied a fair trial if a statement from that witness is admitted. Where the witness is dead, or cannot be called for some other reason, the question of whether the admission of a statement from that witness will impair the fairness of the trial will be depend on the facts of the particular case. Factors that will be likely to be of concern to the court are identified in section 114(2) of the Act.[1]

22. In accordance with these conclusions, we shall proceed to consider the individual appeals on the basis that Article 6 imposes no absolute embargo on the admission of the hearsay evidence adduced by the prosecution in either case.

R v Keet

23. On 19 April 2007, in the Crown Court at Winchester before Mr Recorder Vaitilingham, the appellant was convicted of attempting to obtain property by deception, which was Count 3 and damaging property, which was Count 4. He was acquitted of Counts 1 and 2, each of which charged him with obtaining property by deception. The deception alleged in each case was that a sum charged was a reasonable price for the work to which it related when in fact it was excessive. The appellant was sentenced to perform 240 hours unpaid work in respect of Count 3 and 60 hours unpaid work, to be performed concurrently in respect of count 4. He pleaded guilty to failing to answer bail, in respect of which he was fined £500. He appeals against conviction in relation to Count 3 but not Count 4.

The prosecution case and the procedural history

24. The following part of the prosecution case was based upon Mrs Soper's witness statement. On 22 April 2002 Mrs Soper, who was 82 years old, lived with her husband, who was aged 85, at 7 Everley Close in Whitehill, Bordon. At about 10 am the appellant and another

[1] See n 2 on p 323 below.

man drove up in a red van. The appellant said that they worked for Angles Roofing Limited and offered to remove a coating of moss on the roof of Mr and Mrs Soper's house. They themselves had already been concerned about this moss and they agreed to the offer.

25. The men got ladders off the roof of the van and set about removing the moss. At the end of the first day they asked for £500 by way of payment. The Sopers kept substantial sums in cash in the house and Mrs Soper gave the men the £500 that they had requested. This payment was the subject matter of Count 1. The following day the men returned and completed the task of removing the moss. They asked for and were given a further £480 in cash. This payment was the subject matter of Count 2. They said that there was further work to be done in the form of ridge tiles that were loose and needed re-cementing.

26. The men returned the next day to attend to this work. They then said that the roof was leaking. They returned the following day with wooden battens. At one point one of the men put a plastic sheet on the roof in case it rained.

27. At the end of the week the men said that further work was required at the rear that would cost £6,000. This was the subject matter of Count 3. Mrs Soper said that she would have to get this from the bank. However she told her daughter of these events and her daughter got angry, saying that her mother had been conned. She drove her mother to the police station, where she reported what had occurred.

28. The police attended on Monday 29th April, when the appellant and another man arrived in the red van. The police arrested both of them. Subsequent inspection of the roof disclosed that a tile had been lifted and a piece of roofing felt cut out. This formed the subject matter of Count 4. It was the prosecution case that this was damage deliberately effected so as to justify the further work.

29. Corroboration of Mrs Soper's evidence was to be provided by an elderly neighbour called Mrs Rapley. In her witness statement she said that Mrs Soper had told her that one of the men had come down from the loft with a wet piece of wadding and said that water had got into the loft. Mrs Soper told her that the men were asking for £6,000.

30. The appellant was interviewed by the police on a number of occasions, the first being 29 April 2002. He accepted that he had been paid £500, but said that this had been payment for 4 days spent removing moss. He found a hole in the felt and said that he would return on Monday (29 April) to attend to this and to some cementing work. He quoted £60 for this work, not £6,000. He denied cutting the felt but said that his assistant might have trimmed it up.

31. The trial was fixed for 25 March 2003, but then adjourned to 28 May 2003 because Mrs Rapley was not well. The trial did not, however, take place on that day because the appellant had absconded. Had he not done so it is very doubtful whether the prosecution would have been able to proceed. Both Mrs Soper and Mrs Rapley had, on 27 May, made it plain that they felt too frail to give evidence. The prosecution intended to seek to adduce the evidence of each pursuant to section 23 of the Criminal Justice Act 1988, but it was neither likely that these applications would succeed nor that, if they did not succeed, it would have been possible to prevail on either of the ladies to change her mind.

32. The appellant was arrested on 28 October 2006. By this time Mrs Soper was suffering from dementia. It is accepted on behalf of the claimant both that she was no longer fit to give evidence and that, in April 2003, she had the capacity to make the statement that she did. Mrs Rapley was not fit to give evidence and no application was made to read her witness statement.

The trial

33. The prosecution was granted permission to adduce in evidence the witness statement of Mrs Soper. They called a roofer who had been retained by the police in 2002. He gave evidence of lifting a protruding tile and finding that a hole had been cut in the felt underneath. He denigrated the work alleged to have been done by the claimant and said that it should have cost about £100. The prosecution called two other experts who also denigrated the work alleged to have been done.

34. The defence called an expert on moss in support of the appellant's case that he had cleared off all the moss and applied fungicide. The defendant gave evidence himself. This accorded with the statements made to the police. He said that he had only been paid £500 and this was for 4 days work. He agreed that it would have been extortionate to extract a further £480. Mrs Soper must have misunderstood the additional sum that he had asked for—this was £60, not £6,000.

35. So far as the cut felt was concerned, the appellant had said in his defence case statement that a leak became apparent after the jet washing started. He gave evidence that he had gone into the loft to inspect, saw some dampness and felt that was perishing, worn and hanging down. He had described this to his assistant who must have lifted off the tiles and found the hole in the felt.

Grounds of appeal

36. There are two grounds of appeal:

(i) The evidence of Mrs Soper was wrongly admitted in evidence under section 116 of the Criminal Justice Act 2003, contrary to section 78 of PACE and Article 6.3 of the ECHR.

(ii) The conviction on Count 3 is inconsistent with the acquittals on Counts 1 and 2.

The admission of Mrs Soper's statement

37. In his skeleton argument Mr Bryan submitted, as he had before the judge, that to admit a statement of a witness who could not be called when that statement was the sole or decisive evidence on a count was contrary to Article 6.3, relying, in particular, on *Lucà*. The judge had rejected this argument, holding that 'everything turns on the facts of the particular case'. For the reasons that we have given, the judge was right to do so. In oral argument, Mr Bryan departed from this extreme case. He submitted, however, that on the facts of this case it was unfair to admit Mrs Soper's statement. It was, he observed, the only evidence in relation to the first three counts. It was unfair that the appellant should be denied the chance of cross-examining the only witness.

38. Whenever the statement of a prosecution witness who cannot be called is read, the defendant will be denied the chance of cross-examination. This, of itself, does not make the trial process unfair. The judge will direct the jury in relation to the weight to be accorded to a statement that has not been given orally or tested in cross-examination and, if the defendant calls or gives oral evidence, that evidence, if it withstands cross-examination, is likely to carry more weight than the statement relied on by the prosecution.

39. Section 114 lists factors relevant to the interests of justice that the court must consider when admitting evidence under that section.[2] It does not state expressly which way each individual factor is intended to cut. We consider the inference is that the more important and the more reliable the statement appears to be, the stronger the case for its admission. Taking each factor in turn in the context of the present case: (a) Assuming that the statement is true, it had critical probative value so far as the issues in the first three counts were concerned. (b) No other evidence could be given on behalf of the prosecution on these issues. (c) The evidence was critically important in the context of the case as a whole. (d) The circumstances in which the statement was made suggested that the maker believed in the truth of the statement. It was not suggested by the appellant that the evidence in question was untruthful; indeed he accepted that part of it was accurate. He merely contended that Mrs Soper must have been mistaken as to certain other parts. (e) There is, as Mr Bryan has pointed out, a degree of confusion in the statement about particular dates. Overall, however, the statement paints a coherent picture and it has been accepted that Mrs Soper, although elderly and subsequently affected by dementia, was rational when she made it. (f) The evidence of the making of the statement is entirely reliable. (g) Oral evidence could not be given because of the maker's current mental ill-health. (h) The statement could readily be challenged by the appellant. It is sometimes argued that it is unfair to put in a statement if the defendant will have to go into the witness box to rebut it. This may be the case where the evidence is not strong, but we can see no unfairness on the facts of the present case. It would, of course, have been open to the appellant to decline to give oral evidence, leaving his counsel to do his best with the statements made to the police. The reality is, however, that where issues are as stark as in the present case, whether oral or statement evidence is adduced by the prosecution, the jury will expect to hear from the defendant. (i) This does not arise.

40. It is thus our view that the relevant factors weighed strongly in favour of the admission of Mrs Soper's evidence in this case. There is one further, and cogent point that was made by the Recorder that we would endorse:

> Offences of this type, or offences of the type here alleged, are deliberately aimed at those who are elderly and vulnerable, and it is inevitable in some case at least that a witness will be unable to attend court . . . Section 116 and its predecessors . . . provide an important weapon in the prosecution armoury in just such cases.

41. For these reasons we have concluded that the judge was right to admit Mrs Soper's statement and, accordingly, we reject the first ground of appeal

[2] Author's note. This is not in fact correct. The factors are listed in section 114(2), which requires the court to consider them '[i]n deciding whether a statement not made in oral evidence should be *admitted under subsection 1(d)*'—ie under the 'general exclusionary discretion', alias the 'safety-valve'. Thus the Act does not require the court to consider them when deciding whether to admit a statement under subsections 1(a)—1(c); and hence the court is not required to consider them when deciding, as here, to admit the statement under section 116—which, when the conditions set out in that section are present, is supposed to operate automatically (see Chapter 6 above, and in particular § 6.23). However, in general terms these factors are no doubt relevant to the question whether the admission of a hearsay statement infringes the defendant's right to confrontation under ECHR Article 6(3)(d) (on which see Chapter 2 above).

[In paragraphs 42–49, the court considered and rejected the defendant's second ground of appeal against conviction.]

R v Konrad Cole

50. On 12 December 2006, in the Crown Court at Basildon before Her Honour Judge Taylor, the appellant was convicted of three counts of assault occasioning actual bodily harm. He was sentenced to 30 months imprisonment on each count, to run concurrently.

The prosecution case and the procedural history

51. In the early hours of 3 January 2004 the appellant's girlfriend, Katy Smith, committed suicide by hanging herself in the bathroom of his flat. Police and ambulance men were called. They noticed that the body of the deceased bore black eyes and other injuries. A post mortem examination demonstrated that these could not have been the result of her suicide. By the time that the appellant came to stand trial, nearly three years later, the case advanced against him by the prosecution was as follows.

52. In relation to count 1, the prosecution case was based on the evidence of a woman called Tara Whittred, a friend of the deceased who had lodged with her and who was to give evidence of witnessing the appellant assault her on three separate occasions.

53. In relation to count 2, there were no eye witnesses of the alleged assaults. The prosecution case depended largely on statements alleged to have been made by the deceased to her brother and to three friends about the treatment that she had received from the appellant. The brother was called Martin Smith. The friends were Tara Whittred, Kerrian Miller and Sharon Tracey. So far as Sharon Tracey was concerned she spoke of an occasion when she saw the deceased get out of a car of which the appellant was the driver, crying and upset. She then lifted her top to show Sharon Tracey bruises on her belly. She also had a black eye. This would be real, not hearsay, evidence if given orally by Sharon Tracey. It was, however, accompanied by hearsay evidence, for the deceased indicated to Sharon Tracey that the appellant had caused the injuries and, in answer to a question, said that the appellant had acted in a similar way before.

54. So far as count 3 was concerned, the prosecution case was based on the inferences to be drawn from the injuries found on the body of the deceased, on the fact that she had been in the company of the appellant in the period before she committed suicide, and on what was alleged to be suspicious behaviour on the part of the appellant when the police and the paramedics attended the scene of the suicide. It is obvious, however, that the case advanced by the prosecution in relation to the first two counts had a significant bearing on the inferences that the prosecution submitted should be drawn in relation to the third count.

55. The appellant was originally charged on 3 January 2004 with assault causing actual bodily harm. In May 2004, after a police investigation, he was charged with manslaughter. In June 2004 that charge was dropped and he was told that no further action would be taken. However in January 2005 a summons was issued charging the appellant with what were to become counts 1 and 3.

56. Committal papers were served on the appellant that included statements of the witnesses whom the prosecution intended to call. These made it plain that it was intended that the hearsay evidence to which we have referred would be given by the relevant witnesses.

The case was committed to the Crown Court on 10 June 2005. Under Part 34 of the Criminal Procedure Rules 2005 the prosecution were required to give notice of intention to adduce hearsay evidence not more than 14 days after the committal, although the court had power to vary this period.

57. There were then no less than eleven pre-trial hearings. The effective plea and case management hearing was held on 15 December 2005. The prosecution filled in the standard form questionnaire indicating that they intended to call the hearsay witnesses. They also ticked the appropriate box to indicate that it was their intention to adduce hearsay evidence. However it was not until 21 November 2006 that an application to adduce hearsay evidence was served. This listed seven witnesses that the prosecution wished to call to give hearsay evidence. These included Martin Smith, Kerrian Miller and Sharon Tracy. At the same time the prosecution applied to add the further charge that became Count 2.

58. The judge dealt with these applications on 5 December 2006, which was the first day of the trial. She admitted the hearsay evidence to be given by Martin Smith, Kerrian Miller and Sharon Tracey, albeit that the application was 17 months out of time. She gave permission to add Count 2. On the following day she acceded to an application, that was made without notice, to admit hearsay evidence to be given by Tara Whittred in relation to Count 2.

59. On 8 December a further application was made to read the evidence of Sharon Tracey (by then McNeil). She was on the point of giving birth and was suffering from complications. It was impossible for her to come to court. The judge granted this application. This had the effect of admitting in evidence multiple hearsay to the extent that her statement itself contained hearsay.

60. On 11 December 2006, at the close of the prosecution case, the judge rejected a submission that there was no case to answer on Counts 2 and 3.

The evidence

61. We will summarise the evidence given at the trial on the basis of the judge's summing up, which has not been criticised. This will give sufficient indication of the evidence in the various witness statements that were the subject of the hearsay applications.

62. Tara Whittred gave evidence that she first met the deceased when Tara was having a relationship with the deceased's brother, Martin Smith. They became friends. In April 2002, Tara moved into the deceased's two bedroom flat in Neville Shaw in Basildon. The deceased had one room, which she shared with her daughter, Ayesha, then aged 3, and Tara had the other bedroom. Tara lived there until September 2002, when she moved out. During all of that time Tara had also worked with the deceased at McDonalds from April to August 2002 and then at Basildon Hospital until March 2003.

63. While Tara lived at the flat the appellant lived elsewhere, but he would often stay at the flat overnight. Whist Tara was living with the deceased, she witnessed three occasions when the appellant was physically violent to the deceased. She was not able to remember the order in which they occurred.

64. On one occasion, she was in the living room, playing with Ayesha, when she heard, from the deceased's bedroom, the appellant's angry voice and the deceased saying: 'no, no'. She left Ayesha and went towards the bedroom to find the deceased cowering by the door and the appellant throwing ferocious and violent punches at the deceased's face, which the

deceased was blocking with her arms. The deceased was scared and screaming and the applicant had an angry look on his face. Tara pulled the appellant away from the deceased and tried to help her up but the appellant then pushed her away. Ayesha came into the room and the appellant took the child out of the flat.

65. On another occasion, Tara had been listening to music when she heard the appellant arguing with the deceased in the hallway. She went out and took Ayesha into the other room. As she was doing this, the appellant pushed the deceased hard into the doorframe. The deceased began to cry. The deceased asked the appellant to leave but he refused to do so. When he finally left, the deceased showed Tara red marks and bruising to the top of her thighs, which she said had occurred during the argument with the appellant.

66. On the third occasion, the deceased found a text on the appellant's mobile from another girl. An argument ensued between the appellant and the deceased. During the argument, the applicant punched the deceased in the stomach. The deceased doubled over and was upset and crying. The applicant then left.

The grounds of appeal

67. The following grounds of appeal are advanced on behalf of the appellant:

i) The judge erred in allowing the prosecution to adduce hearsay evidence when the application to do this was made 17 months out of time.
ii) The judge erred in allowing the prosecution to adduce the hearsay evidence. She should have excluded it pursuant to section 78 of the Police and Criminal Evidence Act .
iii) The judge erred in not ruling that there was no case to answer on Count 2.
iv) The judge erred in not ruling that there was no case to answer on Count 3.

While none of these grounds relates directly to Count 1, Mr House for the appellant submits that the jury are likely to have been influenced in reaching their verdict on Count 1 by hearsay evidence, that should not have been admitted, in relation to Count 2.

Hearsay application out of time

68. Mr House rightly submitted that the conduct of the prosecution in failing to make the hearsay application until it was 17 months out of time was lamentable. He contended that judge erred in permitting the application to be made so long out of time. When considering whether to exercise his discretion to extend time the judge said that she would have regard to the interests of justice, having particular regard to any prejudice caused to the appellant by the delay. As to this she found that there was none as the defence was served with the witness statements that contained the hearsay, and dealt with the hearsay in the defence case statement. She decided that, having regard to all the circumstances of the case, the interests of justice lay in allowing the application to be made out of time.

69. Before us Mr House did not challenge the judge's finding that the delay had caused no prejudice to the appellant. In these circumstances he faced an uphill task in seeking to persuade us that the judge had erred in principle in the exercise of her discretion. He argued that the only appropriate response where the prosecution's shortcomings were as serious as

in this case was to refuse to extend time. Were such an approach not adopted the prosecution would have no incentive to improve in the future.

70. The conduct of this prosecution has been lamentable, not merely in respect of the delay in serving notice of intention to adduce hearsay evidence. The number of pre-trial hearings suggests a serious failure to get a grip of this case. We do not consider, however, that this required the judge to shut out the hearsay evidence. This is no ordinary case of causing actual bodily harm. This is a case of persistent physical abuse that only ended when the miserable victim took her own life. There was a strong public interest in prosecuting the perpetrator of her injuries. The exercise of the judge's discretion was a proper one, and this ground of appeal is rejected.

The admission of the hearsay evidence

71. Mr House took no independent point on the admission of the double hearsay evidence in Sharon Tracey's statement. He accepted that the single hearsay was admissible under section 116 of the Act but submitted that it should have been excluded under section 78 of PACE in the interests of a fair trial. His principal point was that the only way that the appellant could controvert the hearsay evidence was by giving evidence, a task for which he was mentally ill-equipped. A similar submission was made to the judge.

72. The judge held that it did not follow that if the evidence was admitted the appellant would have to go into the witness box to rebut it because his case could be put by cross-examination. That was not a realistic finding. Those who gave evidence of what the deceased had told them could, of course, be cross-examined as to what she had said. This was not, however, likely to be a fruitful task for counsel who would be unlikely to have any material to assist in such cross-examination. The reality is that the only way that the appellant would be able to rebut the hearsay evidence itself was by giving evidence himself that it was untrue. If he did not do so, the jury would be likely to draw the conclusion that this was because he could not deny the truth of the evidence.

73. The facts of this case are very different from those of Keet. If each statement is considered in isolation it is both less cogent and less significant than the evidence of Mrs Soper. The statements are lacking in detail and in precision as to date. When the factors in section 114 are considered in respect of an individual statement, the case for admission is weaker than it is in Keet. But the correct approach is not to consider each statement on its own, but to consider it in its context. Each statement is part of a wider picture. That picture is coherent and compelling. It is of a relationship between the deceased and the appellant that was punctuated by physical violence on his part. Count 1 is supported by the direct evidence of Tara Whittred. Count 3 is founded on circumstantial evidence. Each of those counts lends support to the hearsay evidence on which Count 2 is based and that evidence lends support to Counts 1 and 3. It was in the interests of justice that the hearsay evidence should go before the jury so that they would have the full picture painted by the evidence, subject always to the ability of the appellant to testify in his own defence. He had had a close relationship with the deceased and, if he was not the author of her injuries, he could be expected to be in a position to give some explanation as to how they had been incurred, subject always to the question of his mental capacity.

74. As to that there was conflicting evidence, obtained in the context of a possible issue as to the appellant's fitness to plead. Those acting for the appellant put before the judge the

report of a Dr Robert Halsey, who is not a physician but a chartered consultant in clinical and forensic neuro-psychology. He expressed the view, after conducting intelligence tests, that the appellant's 'significantly low level of intellectual functioning and his extremely poor verbal comprehension abilities' raised 'concerns about the reliability of any evidence he might provide in his own defence and the overall desirability of him providing testimony in court.'

75. The appellant was also examined by Dr Abou-El-Hadi, on instructions from the prosecution. He is a Bachelor of Medicine and Surgery and a Fellow of the Royal College of Psychiatrists. He is a consultant psychiatrist approved under section 12 of the Mental Health Act 1983. He recorded:

> The defendant was able to articulate a reasonable well thought defensive argument about the allegations against him. Regardless of the correctness, truthfulness or otherwise of his argument it was rationally and logically considered, which indicates a reasonable degree of verbal comprehension and verbal ability to communicate his ideas and thoughts. For example he considered that the allegations against him were motivated by his ex-girlfriend's family's desire to deprive him of his custody of his daughter. He considered that the witnesses' statements were contradictory. Moreover he considered that the self-harm behaviour of the alleged victim was related to previous violent and unhappy relationships, which is a valid argument regardless of whether it is acceptable. He also argued that she had a skin condition which may in his opinion explain the bruises on her face; again this is a considered argument not withstanding the possible inaccuracy of it. I therefore found that this defendant was able to exercise rationally articulated argument in his own defence which can then be examined and judged accordingly.

76. Dr Abou-El-Fadi's conclusion was as follows:

> It is therefore my considered opinion that the defendant is fit to plead and fit to stand trial. He understands the charges against him, he would be able to instruct counsel and formulate his own rationally considered defensive argument. He would be able to follow evidence in court. He is actually contemplating his own court case regarding access to his daughter. He would be able to challenge a juror if that becomes necessary.

77. The judge considered this evidence and plainly concluded that the appellant would be able to give coherent evidence if he chose to do so. Having read Dr Abou-El-Hadi's account of his discussions with the appellant it seems to us that he was well aware of the issues that he faced and able to meet them coherently. In the event he chose not to give evidence.

78. Mr House has not satisfied us that the judge was wrong to consider that the admission of the hearsay evidence was in the interests of justice and consistent with a fair trial. Accordingly the second ground of appeal is rejected.

The submission of no case to answer on Count 2

79. Mr House submitted to the judge that Count 2 should not be permitted to go to the jury as it was based exclusively on hearsay evidence. The judge concluded that on a proper direction as to the approach to be taken when dealing with hearsay evidence, the jury could

properly convict in relation to Count 2. Mr House submitted to us that the judge was wrong. We agree with the judge. The hearsay evidence was supported by the evidence of Tara Whittred as to what she had seen and by the evidence that related to both Count 1 and Count 3. There was a case fit to go to the jury on Count 2.

The submission of no case to answer on Count 3

80. So far as Count 3 was concerned, Mr House submitted to the judge and to us that it was not safe to leave that count to the jury as the case against the appellant was purely circumstantial. The judge decided that the jury, after a proper direction, could properly infer that the injuries found on the deceased after her suicide, had been caused by the appellant. Here again, we agree with the judge. Having regard to the evidence relating to Counts 1 and 2 and to the fact that the deceased was in the appellant's flat with him in the period leading up to her suicide, there was a strong inference that he was responsible for her recent injuries, even if one disregards his strange behaviour after her death. Count 3 was properly left to the jury.

81. For these reasons Mr Cole's appeal against conviction is dismissed.

Both appeals against conviction dismissed

INDEX

References in bold are to page numbers of the Appendices. Otherwise references are to paragraph numbers in the commentary. Because the entire volume deals with 'hearsay' and 'admissibility', these two terms are not used as entry points. Information will be found under the appropriate detailed entries (e.g. 'multiple hearsay').

Index